Advanced VCE

Information and Communication Technology

Geoffrey Knott BA, AIB, Cert Ed
Nick Waites BSc, MSc, Cert Ed

Brancepeth Computer Publications

2000

©Geoffrey Knott and Nick Waites 2000

ISBN 0-9538848-0-5

Cover Design by Nick Waites
Graphical illustrations by Nick Waites and Geoffrey Knott
Production and Editing by Geoffrey Knott

Published in Great Britain by

Brancepeth Computer Publications Limited
Brancepeth Castle
Durham
DH7 8DF

Tel: 0191 378 3363
Fax: 0191 378 2972
E-mail: enquiries@bcpublications.co.uk
Web site: www.bcpublications.co.uk

British Cataloguing-in-Publications Data

A catalogue record for this book is available from the British Library

Printed in Great Britain by Athenaeum Press, Gateshead

To Anne and Carolyn with love

The Authors

Geoffrey Knott and Nick Waites have long experience in Computing and IT education and have been producing highly successful course text books for over a decade. They are authors of Computer Studies, AS/A2 Information and Communication Technology, GNVQ Advanced Information Technology, GNVQ Intermediate Information Technology, Information Processing, Computing, Small Business Computer Systems, Information Technology Skills - A Student Guide, GCSE Information Systems and co-authors of Business GNVQ Advanced and Core Skills for GNVQ.

Acknowledgements

We would like to thank our friend Jim Morton for his meticulous proofing of several of the more technical chapters in this book.

We also wish to thank QCA for permission to include the Assessment Evidence tables which precede each of the Units in this book.

Other publications by the same authors:

Published by Brancepeth Computer Publications Ltd (Tel 0191 3783363):

Books

- ❏ BTEC Nationals in Computing

Booklets (available by the end of 2000)

- ❏ Computer Hardware
- ❏ Data Analysis and Design
- ❏ Data Communications & Networks
- ❏ Network Design and Administration
- ❏ Programming Concepts and Practice
- ❏ Introduction to Programming in Pascal
- ❏ Introduction to Programming in C
- ❏ Introduction to Programming in Visual Basic
- ❏ Systems Analysis and Design
- ❏ System Specification & Justification
- ❏ Website Development and Management
- ❏ The Internet: Systems & Services

Internet

- ❏ ICT Resource Bank (A large database of detailed information on ICT available for an annual subscription)

For more information on all of these publications visit the BCP website at

www.bcpublications.co.uk

Published by Business Education Publishers Ltd (Tel 0191 5252400) :

Books

- ❏ GCE AS/A2 Information and Communications Technology
- ❏ GNVQ Advanced Information Technology
- ❏ Information Processing
- ❏ Computing (A level)
- ❏ Small Business Computer Systems
- ❏ Information Technology Skills - A Student Guide
- ❏ GCSE Information Systems
- ❏ Business GNVQ Advanced (co-authors)
- ❏ Core Skills for GNVQ (co-authors)

CD

- ❏ ICT 2000 (an electronic information resource for ICT)

Contents

Unit 1
Presenting information

Chapters

- 1. Readability, style and presentation
- 2. Designing and creating documents
- 3. Designing and creating slide presentations
- 4. Managing information
- 5. Standard ways of working

Assessment Evidence

You need to produce

- [ ] six original documents created by you for different purposes to show a range of writing and presentational styles. The documents may be in printed form or shown on-screen. They must include one
- [ ] designed to gather information from individuals and one major document of at least three A4 pages
- [ ] a report describing, comparing and evaluating two different standard documents used by each of three different organisations (total of six documents).

To achieve a grade E your work must show:

- [ ] new information that is clear, easy to understand, uses a suitable style and is at a level that suits the intended readers
- [ ] text styles, page layout, paragraph formatting and, where appropriate, common standards for layout that suit the purpose of each document
- [ ] combinations of text, graphics, tables, borders and shading used effectively
- [ ] location, use and adaptation of existing information to suit a presentation and a list of your information sources in an appropriate form
- [ ] a clear and accurate description of each of the six collected documents, which identifies the common elements of similar documents
- [ ] careful checking of the accuracy of the layout and content of your six original documents and your report, and that you have proof-read them to ensure that fewobvious errors remain.

To achieve a grade C your work must show:

- [ ] by presenting original draft copies with proof-reading corrections and annotations, how you achieved a coherent and consistent style, made good use of standard formats, placed information in appropriate positions and ensured correct and meaningful content
- [ ] detailed descriptions of the content, layout and purpose of the six collected documents, accurately evaluating good and bad points about the writing and presentation styles of similar items, commenting on their suitability for purpose and suggesting how they could be improved
- [ ] that you can work independently to produce your work to agreed deadlines.

To achieve a grade A your work must show:

- [ ] a good understanding of writing style, presentation techniques, standards for special documents and attention to detail by organising a variety of different types of information into a single coherent, imaginative, easy to read presentation of several pages
- [ ] effective skills in the appropriate use of software facilities to automate aspects of your document production, such as bullets and numbering, paragraph and heading styles, standardised layout, contents lists and indexes
- [ ] appropriate use of lines, borders, shading, tables, graphics and writing style to create a form that is easy to understand and easy to use to enter data and retrieve the information collected
- [ ] effective skills in the use of graphics to improve a presentation by making appropriate use of pictures, drawings, clip art, lines and borders, graphs or charts.

Chapter 1

Readability, style and presentation

When you are preparing a document, you need to keep in mind:

- ❏ its purpose. What is the document meant to communicate?
- ❏ the reader. Who is meant to read and understand its contents?

To ensure that the documents you produce are readable, you will need to:

- ❏ pay careful attention to spelling;
- ❏ ensure that your sentences convey the meanings you intend;
- ❏ use a language style which is appropriate to the subject and the reader;
- ❏ use document layouts which present the information clearly and effectively.

To produce an effective document, you must have a clear understanding of the information you are trying to communicate and be familiar with the requirements of your readers. For example, this text book would be unlikely to be useful to you if we, the authors, had little knowledge of our subject, or the contents of the Advanced VCE course.

Spelling, grammar and meaning

Careful attention to spelling and good use of grammar are also important for clear communication. For example, you can probably work out the intended meaning of "The hows is neer the toun horl", but you can't be absolutely sure.

The aim of grammar is to ensure that the words of a sentence are arranged to convey a single meaning. Apart from giving a very bad impression to the reader, poor use of grammar can obscure meaning or convey a completely different, and unintended, message. Consider the following note provided by a parent to explain his child's absence from school.

"Albert has to stay at home today because he has diarrhoea through some bad fish."

We know what he means, but the sentence construction gives a completely different and peculiar message. A clearer explanation might have been: "As a result of eating some bad fish, Albert has diarrhoea and is unable to attend school."

For a business, such careless use of language in communications with customers not only damages its image of professionalism, but may also result in serious financial loss or contractual misunderstanding. Consider the following statements made by the Sales Manager of Global Supplies Limited to a customer.

"The goods we sold to you were supplied by Acme Systems. We believe that the goods are a disgrace to the company and that you should be able to sue for damages."

The Sales Manager intends to say that the goods are a disgrace to Acme Systems and that the customer should be able to sue that company for damages. However, the statements could suggest an admission that the poor quality goods disgrace Global Supplies and that they are prepared to be sued.

Writing style

This book is written in a style which makes the content easier to read, that is, one with relatively short sentences and a friendly tone. We also avoid the unnecessary use of 'difficult' vocabulary and provide numerous examples to illustrate ideas. On the other hand, the book has a serious purpose and an over-friendly, perhaps 'jokey' style, would simply be patronising and sometimes less common vocabulary can be used to express ideas more briefly. For example, the words "intercede" or "mediate"can be used instead of the phrase "to plead in favour of". As a general rule don't use 'big' words simply to impress, especially if you are not sure what they mean. The Thesaurus tool (see later) in a word processor will suggest alternative vocabulary and you should use it with extreme care.

Some documents are not trying to communicate ideas or concepts and require simple statements of fact, without explanation. For example, the Table of Contents in this book simply lists chapter titles and main headings, together with the relevant page numbers. Similarly, you would expect notice of an important staff meeting to briefly identify basic information, such as the subject of the meeting, for example, 'New car parking arrangements', its location, date and time. However, a notice advertising a newly released film would include slogans such as, "A real weepy", or "You'll never sleep again.", to encourage people to go and see it.

Personal writing style

A memorandum example

Although writing is a skill and rules of grammar and spelling are vitally important, it is also a highly creative process and if practised sufficiently can be as clear a part of your personality as the way you speak. Those who need to use sign language can bring their own personalities to they way in which they use their hands and facial expressions to express simple or complex information, feelings and emotions.

Admittedly, some documents such as invoices do not call for personal style, but most do. Even a brief memorandum asking people to attend a meeting can aggravate, annoy, or cause resentment if it is badly phrased.

Consider the following contrasting examples and judge what your response might be to each.

Memorandum

To: All Accounts staff

From: Mrs. V. Uptight, Accounts Department Manager

Subject: Upgrade of accounting software   **Date:** 14 June 2000

There will be a meeting at 5.30 p.m. tomorrow and all Accounts staff must attend. There is a lot to discuss and the meeting will take around two hours. Come and see me if you feel that you have an excuse for not attending.

Memorandum

To: All Accounts staff

From: Iris Pectu, Accounts Department Manager

Subject: Meeting 5.30 p.m. 15 June - Upgrade of accounting software   **Date:** 14 June 2000

I realise that this meeting is being called at very short notice, but the delay in the delivery of the software means that we have even less time than planned to complete the change to the new system. To ensure that the changeover to the new accounting software runs smoothly and does not disrupt services to our customers (and the vitally important task of receiving their invoice payments!), we need to discuss a number of different operating procedures. I cannot over-emphasise the importance of this meeting, so if you think that you may be unable to attend, please talk to me today and we will try to get the information to you some other way.

Unfortunately, the meeting is likely to take around 2 hours so I have arranged for sandwiches and coffee to keep us going.

Neither memo is likely to be welcome, but the first is abrupt, inconsiderate and does not even explain why the meeting is so important. It suggests little 'team spirit' and the dictatorial style of the memo probably reflects the Head of Department's management style. The memo would almost certainly cause resentment and if its tone is typical will not ensure that the operational changes to the accounting system go smoothly. The second memo appeals to the loyalty of staff and makes a real effort to explain the reasons for the meeting and the short notice given. The last two sentences demonstrate a care for the staff as individuals and a willingness to treat them as colleagues. Although the memos say a great deal about contrasting management styles, which is not relevant here, personal writing style is difficult to force and will, as with other forms of communication, reflect your own personality. Mrs. V Uptight would probably have great difficulty in writing the second memo.

Of course, you need to apply your personal style appropriately, to a number of different document types and target readers. The following section provides examples of formal and informal styles for a range of document types.

Choosing a style and form of presentation

Although presentational techniques such as page layout and font styles are dealt with later in this chapter the following examples illustrate the use of style and presentation to meet different communication needs, such as attracting attention, writing to impress and gathering information through questionnaires.

Attracting attention in advertisements

Example 1: Hair care products

Study the two example advertisements in Figures 1.1 and 1.2. They are for similar types of product but each is aimed at a very different audience. To be effective, advertisements must capture your attention, but the methods used will depend largely on the age, lifestyle and personal values of their intended readers.

The advertisement for RIGID hair gel in Figure 1.1 is short and to the point, and uses a 'no-nonsense' writing style designed to emphasise the gel's ability to keep your hair in one place. The opening question "Used to being in control?" is not a complete sentence, but is perfectly acceptable in the context of a 'punchy' advertisement. This question form of headline is often used in advertisements because it is an effective way of grabbing your attention. Simple phrases are often used in newspaper headlines, such

"Used to being in control?"

Now you can control your hair with **RIGID**, the high-performance gel from the Macho hair care range.

Call 0845 11110000 for more information and a free 5ml sample

Figure 1.1

as "Man bites dog" - put in this way it could be open to misinterpretation. (Does the man bite the dog repeatedly?) The sentence "Yesterday, a man bit a dog." would be clearer but would lack the same impact. Further impact in the RIGID advertisement is achieved both with the graphic of the 'lantern-jawed' man, to highlight the 'strength' element and the bold and stark (*sans-serif*) font used for

the word 'RIGID'. A sans-serif font lacks the short strokes at the ends of individual letters; the Arial font is of this type. The body text in this book is Times New Roman, which is a *serif* font.

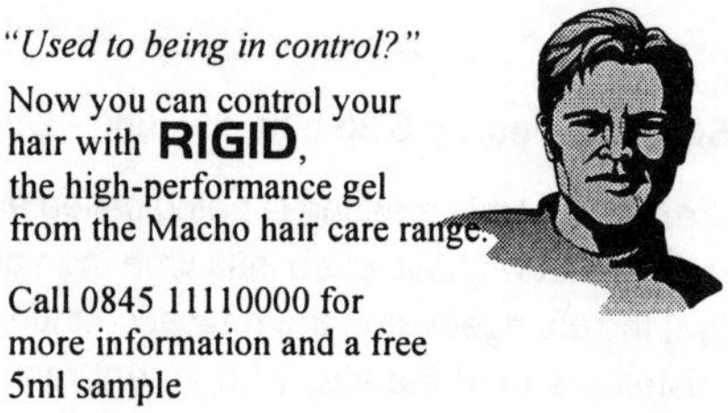

Natura Hair www.naturahair.co.uk

We understand that you care about your health and the environment, so we developed a shampoo that protects the environment and looks after your hair, NATURALLY.

INDULGENTE

The advertisement in Figure 1.2 for shampoo also uses a graphical image and capitalises the font to highlight the name of the product. However, the font is serif, in italics and is not in bold type, which is suited to the gentle tone of

only uses natural products which are not harmful to the environment. Indulgente is kind to your hair and washes without destroying the natural oils that give your hair vitality.

Call our hair consultancy team on **0345 888999** for more information on how you can look after your hair and care for our planet. 2% of our profits go to the Global Nature Foundation www.globalnature.org.

Figure 1.2

the message. Considerable detail is given about the product, and its highlighted (by under-scoring) benefits for the environment are obviously aimed at a particular category of reader. The advertisement uses well constructed and flowing sentences which assume the information is important to the reader in deciding whether or not to buy the shampoo. The reader's attention is probably drawn by the image and the word 'Natura' in the company's name. The Italian word 'Indulgente' hints at a slightly luxurious element in the product, despite its ecological soundness.

Neither of these advertisements require technical or other detail, but some products, such as computers and financial services cannot be sold by simple slogans. Before making a purchase, potential buyers will want to know, for example, the capabilities, features and quality of the product being advertised. The next examples illustrate this point.

Example 2: Advertisements for computers and financial services

The first advertisement in Figure 1.3 gives the precise technical information which is needed to make an informed choice.

Writing style is of minimal importance as the information comprises a simple list of technical features. To attract attention to what would otherwise be a fairly boring image of a computer system, it uses a jet aircraft which

Figure 1.3

helps to reinforce the impression of speed and perhaps, rather less credibly, the real-life quality of the graphics. The price is enclosed in an exploding star to indicate that the system is a real bargain. No time is spent on explanation, partly because it would require considerable space to do so for every technical feature and the seller is assuming that most readers of this particular advert will be familiar with the terminology.

Financial services legislation requires that certain information, such as the interest rate (using a standard method of calculation called the APR), must be included in advertisements for loan facilities. Advertisements for investments are also heavily controlled concerning the claims which can be made on the projected value of an investment, say, after 10 years. Figure 1.4 shows some typical features of an investment advertisement.

The style is more restrained, friendly but not over-familiar and emphasises security with a castle

Safe as Houses

How secure is your future?

If you are aged between 23 and 65 and have £2500 or more to invest for 5 years you could gain rich rewards with a Safe As Houses Investment Bond.

If you had invested £5,000 in 1995, it would now be worth

£9,365*

Contact us on 0800 11 00 22 for further information.

* Past performance is not a guarantee of future returns, as these depend on bonuses yet to be earned.

Figure 1.4

logo and a family picture. The amount of £9,365 in large, bold type is clearly designed to attract attention. The asterisk next to the amount is very important as it points to the fact that it relates to a past investment, which is no guarantee of what would be received in 5 years if the same amount were again invested. Apart from the statement, invariably in very small print, at the bottom of the advertisement, financial services legislation requires numerous other statements which qualify what is claimed in the main text.

Summarising information

Summarising refers to the process of preparing a shorter or condensed version of a body of information. To summarise information effectively, you must:

- ❑ thoroughly understand the information;

- ❑ select the main themes and major facts. You must not add to the content or alter any factual content;

- ❑ write the summary clearly and concisely (which is the whole point of a summary). The summary should 'flow' and read as a whole, not as a collection of disconnected sentences. A wide vocabulary will obviously help.

Minutes

Summarising is an important skill in many aspects of work. For example, the discussions at a formal meeting are recorded in the *minutes*, which then have to be agreed at the next meeting as a true record of what took place. Some minutes are referred to as Action Minutes and detail tasks to be completed and the names of the persons responsible for carrying them out, so it is important that minutes are accurately recorded and corrected if found to be in error. Consider the problems that may be caused if Mr. X was incorrectly quoted as admitting that he had failed to contact an important customer and lost valuable business as a result. The problem would be worse if he was not at the next meeting to put matters right. Minute taking is not an easy skill, especially if the meeting is not well managed and several people try to speak at the same time. The minutes secretary must be able to distinguish the important from the unimportant and learn to ignore flippant, indiscrete or irrelevant comments which are clearly not meant to be recorded. An example minutes document is given below (it relates to the Parish Council Agenda in the next section).

AMBRIDGE PARISH COUNCIL

MINUTES

OF THE MEETING of the PARISH COUNCIL held on MONDAY 19 JUNE 2000 at 7.30 p.m.

PRESENT	Councillors Smith, Brown, Ginelli, Jones (in the Chair), Patel and Kenelly.
	An apology for absence was received from Cllr Redman.
MINUTES	The Minutes of the meeting held on 19 May were agreed.

FINANCE	Agreed payment of fees to Cullen and Brown, solicitors of £1,654.50 for work done on Compulsory Purchase Order and £356 to Borchester County Council for installation of new lamp in Main Street.
PLANNING APPLICATIONS	Agreed no objection to extension at 13 Hayseed Cottages and that Cllr Patel look into the matter of the outhouse which has been constructed at the rear of Buttercup Way. It appears that planning permission has not been sought.
CORRESPONDENCE	Noted County Council report on government housing needs and the County Structure Plan. To be viewed by all members before next meeting.
TRAFFIC AND SAFETY	A365 - Cllr Ginelli had written to Inspector Plumridge concerning the increased traffic hazard and the danger to local residents. He will also write to the County Council arguing our case for a 30mph speed limit through Ambridge
AOB	None
NEXT MEETING	18 July 2000

At each meeting, the second item on the Agenda refers to the minutes of the previous meeting. Examples of other occasions when information needs to be summarised are given below.

❏ A member of staff attends a one-day conference on new VAT regulations and then has to pass on what he or she learned to the Financial Director.

❏ After numerous complaints to sales staff about the non-delivery of an order, a customer rings the Sales Manager, who then asks the Sales supervisor for a summary of the events since the first complaint was made.

Giving notice and details of meetings

Agendas

The quality and effectiveness of a meeting tends to be improved if the chairperson takes proper control and prevents members from speaking over one another. The meeting is also likely to be more productive if all members have proper notice of what is to be discussed and this is done through the agenda. If there are reports to be considered, these should be submitted for distribution to members before the meeting, rather than 'tabled'(presented at the meeting itself); this enables members to read them in advance and so, hopefully, be more able to make informed comment at the meeting. An example agenda follows.

AMBRIDGE PARISH COUNCIL

A MEETING of the **PARISH COUNCIL** will be held in the Village Hall, Ambridge on **MONDAY 26 JUNE 2000** at 7.30 p.m

<u>AGENDA</u>

1. Apologies for absence.

2. Minutes of the meeting held on 19 May 2000 (copy attached).

3. Matters arising.

4. Finance.

5. Planning applications.

6. Correspondence.

7. Traffic and safety reports.

8. Any other business.

9. Date of next meeting.

Albert Benbow, Clerk to the Parish Council,   18 June 2000

Item 2, 'Minutes of the last meeting ...', is the point at which members must agree that the minutes are an accurate record or what was discussed and agreed at the last meeting. If there are any corrections, these are made and the Chairperson signs them as a correct record. Item 3, 'Matters Arising' relates to the discussion of items in the meetings of the last meeting which may need further discussion.

Public meeting notices

The above agenda includes the notice details of the meeting, but for public meetings it is impractical to issue agendas and there is often only one topic. The format of such notices is largely up to the producer, but it must include all information that people need in order to attend, that is the location, date and time. For people travelling some distance, directions will also be valuable. Obviously, the subject of the event or meeting is crucial.

Writing to impress

When applying for a job or a place at university, for example, your letter of application and *curriculum vitae* (CV) are usually the only means by which the employers or admissions tutors can initially judge your suitability for selection. If you fail to impress at this stage, you may well not be asked to proceed to the next stage of application, which is normally an interview. If this happened, you might say to yourself, "If only they had had the chance to meet me and talk to me, they would have seen that I was perfect for the job/course." Letters of application and cv's, even interviews, are very imperfect tools for selecting people, but for most organisations they are often the only practical way of doing so. As with most things, practice will improve your letter writing skills.

Preparing a cv is a little more straightforward, as the contents and layout are fairly standard, but you will need to think very carefully about the content. It is likely that you will have to modify your cv, not only as your experience, achievements and qualifications increase, but also to suit the requirements of different applications. If you are applying for a post as a sports club trainer, you would emphasise your athletic achievements, whereas an application for a position as a computer technician would tend to place these achievements in the 'Outside interests/activities' section of the cv.

A curriculum vitae (CV)

A CV is a brief account of a person's career and personal development. It normally accompanies letters of job application, but the content may need to be incorporated in a special application form, if one is provided for the purpose. A CV is also useful in support of a general letter of enquiry about job availability in a particular organisation. A typical CV is likely to include the following:

1. personal details;
2. education;
3. qualifications;
4. work experience;
5. interests, hobbies;
6. supplementary information.

Here is an example of a CV.

Curriculum Vitae

Name: Shahin Hussain

Age: 19 Date of Birth:18.4.81
Marital Status: Single
Nationality: British
Home Address: 12 Neville View, Ambridge, BC1 4LS
Telephone Number: 0141 654321
E-mail: shahin@talk21.com

Education

1992 - 1997	Wood Lane Comprehensive School, Felpersham. Captain of school cricket team 1996-1997
1997 - 1999	Borchester College of Further Education, Felpersham. Secretary of Students Union Management Committee and member of Borchester College Soccer Team.

Qualifications

1997	GCSE Information Technology Grade A *
	GCSE English Grade B
	GCSE Mathematics Grade B
	GCSE History Grade C
	GCSE Art Grade C
	GCSE Geography Grade D
	(All with Welsh Joint Education Committee)
1998	Royal College of Music Piano Grade 7
1999	GNVQ Advanced Information Technology (Pass with Merit):

Information Technology Systems; Systems Analysis; Using
Information Technology; Software; Organisations and
Information Technology; Database Development;
Communications and Networking; Information Technology
Projects and Teamwork; Programming; Multimedia Systems.

Work Experience

1998	Work experience placement for 4 weeks as part of college course, with Kitchen Systems Ltd, Ambridge Road, Borchester, involved in IT support work in IT Services Department.
1999	Work experience placement for 5 weeks as part of college course, with National Farmers Union, Felpersham Road, Borchester, involved in database development work in Farming Services Department.
1999- to date	Assistant Network Engineer with Kitchen Systems Ltd, Ambridge Road, Borchester. (Present salary £9,800 p.a.)

Interests

I have a keen interest in all outdoor sports, particularly cricket. I am captain of
the Ambridge Cricket Club's first team which plays in the Borchester League.
I also play the piano for my own pleasure.

General Information

Career opportunities with my present employer are limited and I am seeking to
develop my career in network engineering. I am taking a 1 week course next
month (as part of my holiday entitlement) on a Novell Network Engineering
course on 4 July 2000.
I have to give 2 weeks notice to terminate my present job.

Referees

The following persons will act as referees:

Mr Roger Pearson, Human Resources Manager, National Farmers Union,
Felpersham Road, Borchester, Tel: 0141 364789

Mrs Anne McDonald, Course Leader, Advanced VCE in ICT, Borchester
College of Further Education, Felpersham, Tel: 0141 349821

Letters of application

Such letters are essentially formal, although as explained earlier, provided that your personal
writing style makes a positive contribution to the tone of the letter, then let it come through.
However, although e-mail communication is leading to greater informality in communication, it has to be assumed that the recipient of a job application expects to see a formal letter.

The first example, given below, is properly constructed, presented and written in an appropriate style. (The numbering is simply to cross reference with the comments which follow the letter.)

Shahin's letter contains the following points:

(i) The name, status and address of the recipient.

(ii) The company reference, to enable the recipient to identify the matter to which the letter relates.

(iii) The salutation. If the name of the recipient is not known, you would have to use 'Dear Sir/Madam and use the close 'Yours faithfully'. It is now usual to use the slightly less formal, 'Yours sincerely' when addressing people by name. There may be circumstances, however, when you judge it safer to use 'Yours faithfully'.

(iv) A formal application statement to identify the post and where he heard about it.

(v) Reference to any enclosures, in this case his CV.

(vi) A brief account of his educational qualifications and work experience, even though this information is provided in more detail in the CV. Although the CV is important, the letter will be read first and should make sufficient impact to encourage further consideration of your application. The statement of confidence, provided it is justified, will help to do this.

(vii) A closing paragraph which indicates a willingness to attend for interview and thereby a keen desire to be considered for the post..

---

12 Neville View
Ambridge
Borchester
BC1 4LS

28 June 2000

(i) Mrs. M. Marconi
Human Resources Manager
Ambridge Bathrooms Ltd
32-34 Downham Road
Felpersham
Borchester, BC2 3LD

(ii) Your ref: MM/NE1

(iii) Dear Mrs Marconi,

(iv) I wish to apply for the post of Assistant Network Administrator which was recently advertised in the Borchester Chronicle.

(v) I have enclosed my curriculum vitae in support of my application.

(vi)   My present post is Network Support Technician at Kitchen Systems Ltd in Felpersham, where I have worked since completing my GNVQ Advanced Information Technology course at Borchester College in June 1999. I believe that my experience and the further qualification I hope to gain next month as a Novell Accredited Network Administrator would enable me to take on the duties you require with confidence and skill. Your advertisement indicates that you use the Novell network operating system, which is also that used by Kitchen Systems Ltd.

(vii) I have to give two weeks notice to terminate my present job and can arrange to be available for interview at any time convenient to you.

Yours sincerely,

Shahin Hussain

Contrast the previous letter with following application for a Web Designer position.

---

12 Neville View
Ambridge
Borchester

Dear Madam,

I saw the advert of the job about Web Design in the Borchester Chronicle and I think that I would be good at it. I done a course on computers and the Internet at college and really liked it. I am 19 now and got 5 GCSE at school. I nearly passed the course at college. I would have passed but the tutor had it in for me. I don't really like working with peeple, so I thought the a computer job would be ideal. If you want to contact me you can get me on my mobile (0788 478590), but my top-up card might run out soon. Better still by e-mail at rodgerthedodger@supermail.com. If you want you can look at my personal website on www.rogerspalace.super.net, but I am still working on it and some of the links don't work.

Yours sincerley,

Roger Hutchinson

As you will notice, there are a number of major flaws in the letter:

❑   The name and address and reference of the recipient are missing and the letter is undated.

❑   The job is not clearly identified. The company may be advertising for several staff to work in the area of Internet and Web support.

❑   Roger refers to his GCSE's, but does not provide grades. The information about the course is obviously not helpful and the statements concerning his relationships with people and the course tutor suggest that he would not be able to work as part of a team.

❑ The contact information is not likely to inspire confidence and the use of silly names for his e-mail and web site address are clearly inappropriate as illustrations of his work.

❑ There are spelling mistakes and grammatical errors and the style is more appropriate for an e-mail to his friends.

Gathering information through questionnaires

A questionnaire is used to conduct a survey on an area of interest or research. It is a means of gathering information, and it consists of a number of questions that are to be answered by a single person. Sometimes the questions are of a personal nature, to do with people's opinions on various things such as the quality of television programmes, or the effectiveness of the government; at other times a questionnaire is used to gather factual information on such things as what banks people use, how often they visit their bank and for what main purposes, or what household products they generally purchase. Sometimes questionnaires will be posted to individuals (the *respondents*) who will complete and return them within a certain time span; on other occasions a questionnaire will be used by an interviewer to ask individuals questions directly.

Questionnaire design

There are a number of distinct stages in designing a questionnaire:

1. Identify the population.

   The *population* is the type of person to which the survey applies. It could be small, such as the members of a football team, or it could be all the students in a certain college. If the population is large, then it will generally be necessary to reduce the number of people involved. The usual method of doing this is to take a sample, that is, a proportion of the population selected according to some scheme. There are many methods of sampling, some designed to allow statistical analysis to be performed, others for convenience. In fact, one of the simplest methods, if the results of the survey are intended to give only a rough idea about something, is called convenience sampling, in which, as the name suggests, the interviewer uses the questionnaire on any suitable person who happens to be available. It is definitely not a reliable method, but it has the advantage of being quick and easy to use.

2. Design the layout of the questionnaire. Things to think about here are:

   (i) For interviewer administered questionnaires, using a front sheet to record the interviewer, the date and time, the length of the interview, and any other relevant information.

   (ii) A statement of the purpose of the survey.

   (iii) The number of questions. Too many will be both time consuming and tedious for the respondent as well as an interviewer.

(iv) The order of the questions. Generally start with broad, easy to answer, impersonal questions before going on to less interesting questions and then sensitive, personal and open-ended questions.

3.   Design the format for the answers. The following pages show some examples of different questions and answers.

Example 1

1.   **Please indicate your opinion of the importance of being able to use the college's computers for word processing assignments:**

CIRCLE ONE	
No opinion	1
Not desirable	2
Fairly desirable	3
Very desirable	4

This limits responses to defined categories and, by assigning a different number to each response, makes it easier to analyse the final survey results. It is best to limit the number of categories in this type of question to between three to seven, because people often find it difficult to discriminate between the categories when there are too many.

Example 2

The following method may be used to filter out people to whom a question does not apply, to reduce the number of questions to be answered.

2.   **Have you ever made use of the college's computers?**

RING	
Yes	1
No	2

If Yes: What types of software have you used?

Wordprocessor	3
Spreadsheet	4
Desktop publishing	5
Graphics	6
Other (specify).....................	7
....	

Example 3

An alternative is to indicate which question to answer next, depending on the answer to the current question:

3.   Have you ever made use of the college's computers?

RING ONE		
Yes	1	GO TO Q10
No	2	GO TO Q15

Example 4

Sometimes open-ended questions are appropriate:

4.   What do you most like about your course?

....

....

This type of question increases the amount of work required in the analysis phase of the survey because the answers must somehow be categorised and allocated a suitable code after the questionnaires have been administered. It is generally advisable to limit the number of this type of question and rely mainly on forced response questions like the other examples given earlier.

Example 5

Another possibility for responses is to provide a numeric scale to indicate how well or how badly something is rated:

5.   How relevant was the course you took to your current employment?

	Highly relevant				Irrelevant
CIRCLE ONE	1	2	3	4	5

The phrasing of the questions is very important. Here are a few things to avoid:

Double questions: Do you own a computer and do you use it just for playing games?

Vague questions: What do you think of the computer services section?

What sort of computers do you think the college should have?

Leading questions: Why did you enjoy your course so much?

Coding the questions

If a computer is to be used for analysing the completed questionnaires, it is important that each response to each question is given a unique code. This must be done at the design stage and incorporated into the questionnaire in order to reduce the amount of work required in the analysis stage of the survey. The code could simply be the question number followed by the response for a question. For instance, in Example 5, if the *Highly relevant box* (1) had been ringed, the code would simply be 51 representing question 5, response 1. Of course coding may not be necessary at all if the analysis of the questionnaires is to be done manually.

Questionnaire presentation

Apart from expressing questions clearly and unambiguously, the questionnaire needs to be clearly presented to encourage simple and accurate completion. Consider the medical questionnaire shown in Figure 1.5 and then compare it with the improved version in Figure 1.6. The layout in Figure 1.5 is cluttered and is likely to lead to mistakes in its completion, Notice particularly that the list at the bottom of the form leaves little room to circle individual items.

```
┌─────────────────────────────────────────────────────────┐
│                     MEDICAL HISTORY                        │
│                                                            │
│    ─────────────────────                                   │
│    Name                          Age ____                  │
│    ─────────────────────                                   │
│    Address                       Post code _____          │
│    Tel. no. _____                                 │
│                                                            │
│                                                            │
│         Do you smoke? _____                               │
│                                                            │
│    If YES, about how many do you smoke per day?  _____  │
│                                                            │
│    Is there any history of heart disease in your family? _____ │
│                                                            │
│    Is there any history of bronchial problems in your family? _____ │
│                                                            │
│    Is there any history of diabetes in your family? _____ │
│                                                            │
│                                                            │
│       Please  circle if you have had any of the following │
│                                                            │
│                        Measles                             │
│                        Mumps                               │
│                        Chicken Pox                         │
│                        Scarlet fever                       │
│                        Shingles                            │
│                        Black Plague                        │
│                                                            │
└─────────────────────────────────────────────────────────┘
```

Figure 1.5. *A poorly designed and presented questionnaire*

The form in Figure 1.6 is uncluttered, pleasing in appearance and the use of tick boxes should encourage accurate completion. Note also that some of the questions in Figure 1.5 are rather vague and have been re-phrased.

MEDICAL HISTORY

Please use BLOCK CAPITALS

SECTION 1 : Personal details

Mr/Mrs/Miss/Ms

First name(s)

Last name

Address

Date of Birth

/ /

Tel. no.

SECTION 2 : Current health

Do you smoke cigarettes?

Tick

NO

less than 10 per day

10-20 per day

more than 20 per day

Do any of your parents or grandparents have any of the following?

Tick

Heart problems

Bronchial problems

Diabetes

SECTION 3 : Past illnesses

Have you ever had any of the following?

Tick

Measles

Mumps

Chicken pox

Tick

Scarlet fever

Shingles

Black plague

Figure 1.6. *A well-designed and presented questionnaire*

Presenting facts

Tabular and graphical presentation

Facts and figures are often presented in table form which reflects the structure of the information and makes it easier to interpret. The example on the next page (Table 1.1) shows how Borsetshire County Council use a table presentation to set out details of their planned budget and inform council tax payers of how their money is to be spent.

The table presentation provides tax payers with detailed information, which is important for some people, but others may prefer to see be presented with, for example a pie chart (Figure 1.7) to show the distribution of spending or a bar chart (Figure 1.8) to compare the amounts of planned spending on the various services, with the spending figures for the previous year.

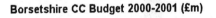

Borsetshire CC Budget 2000-2001 (£m)

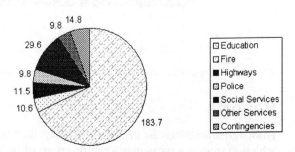

14.8
9.8
29.6
9.8
11.5
10.6
183.7

- Education
- Fire
- Highways
- Police
- Social Services
- Other Services
- Contingencies

Figure 1.7. *Pie chart showing distribution of budget*

Borsetshire County Council Budget				1999-2000
2000-2001				
	Gross Expenditure	Government Grant for Specific Services	Charges for Services	Net Expenditure	Net Expenditure
	£m	£m	£m	£m	£m
Education	210.1	10.2	16.2	183.7	145.2
Fire	12.3	1.2	0.5	10.6	8.1
Highways	22.3	5.6	5.2	11.5	9.5
Police	36.5	18.1	8.6	9.8	7.2
Social Services	42.1	8.1	4.4	29.6	22.3
Other Services	15.1	3.1	2.2	9.8	6.7
Contingencies	20.8	3.2	2.8	14.8	12.4
Total Expenditure	359.2	49.5	39.9	269.8	211.4
Less:		Government Block Grant		134.5	112.3
		Use of Balances		1.3	3.8
		To be raised from Council Tax		134.0	95.3

Table 1.1. *A budget set out in table form*

Borsetshire CC - Net Expenditure 2000-2001 and 1999-2000

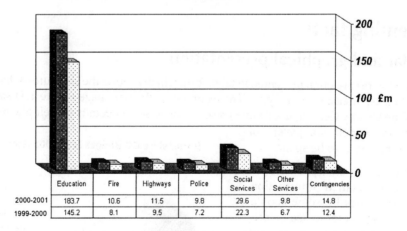

	Education	Fire	Highways	Police	Social Services	Other Services	Contingencies
2000-2001	183.7	10.6	11.5	9.8	29.6	9.8	14.8
1999-2000	145.2	8.1	9.5	7.2	22.3	6.7	12.4

Figure 1.8. *Bar chart comparing planned expenditure with that of previous year*

Reports

Although reports may be delivered verbally, they are usually written. A report is a document which examines a particular topic or group of topics to: communicate information; report findings; make suggestions or put forward ideas.

Usually, a report will conclude by making recommendations for action. Reports can be classified according to whether they are routine, such as an Annual Company Report to Shareholders, or special, such as a Royal Commission to investigate the problem of child poverty. Reports do not have to be concerned with such major subjects and can be quite short, for example, in the case of a sports club treasurer's report on the club's financial position and the ways in which it can be improved. Reports can also be classified as formal or informal, although both must be structured.

Formal and informal reports

Formal reports are more heavily structured and generally longer than informal reports. The greater the level of detail in a report, the greater the need for structure. Representing a work of research, argument and recommendation, report writing is a significant test of anyone's communication skills. Because every report identifies its author and may be circulated to colleagues and superiors, it can be highly influential in making or breaking a person's reputation in an organisation. A highly structured report may contain the following sections:

  (i)   Title page.

  (ii)   Contents page.

  (iii) Summary of recommendations.

  (iv) Introduction and Terms of Reference (the objectives of the report).

  (v)   The information on which the report is based.

  (vi) Conclusions.

  (vii) Recommendations.

  (viii) Appendices.

  (ix) Reference section (references to information sources on which the report relies).

Routine and special reports

Reports which are produced routinely, for example, to give annual sales figures or report balance of trade figures are generally standardised and ideal for production by computer systems Routine reports are normally built into a business's information systems, to be output on demand or automatically at regular intervals or specified times.

Special reports, by definition, are not about standard issues and the structure tends to be less standardised. All reports, however, must be based on Terms of Reference or objectives. A special report be sequenced as follows:

  (i)   Terms of Reference.

  (ii)   A logically presented statement of facts or arguments concerning the subject of the investigation.

  (iii) Findings. These identify possible solutions to the problem, giving the benefits and drawbacks or each solution.

  (iv) Reasoned recommendations.

Draft report

A 'draft report' is the report before it has been put in its final presentation form. At this stage, the author is concerned with getting the content right, rather than obtaining a highly polished report. Its conclusions may also not be completely finalised and may be altered following further consultation and feedback from those who have commissioned the report. The term 'draft' can be used to refer to any document which is not yet in its final form.

Communicating by e-mail

E-mail etiquette (netiquette)

The word 'etiquette' refers to rules of correct behaviour in society or amongst members of a profession. These rules are not about being 'stuffy' but about observing courtesies which communicate respect and consideration for others. Of course, as society changes so do the rules of etiquette and today many people are happy to be addressed without titles or formality. This is not a problem in face-to-face communication because gestures, body language, facial expression and eye contact can all be used to communicate respect, consideration and friendliness without the constraints of more formal forms of address. Even on the telephone, tone of voice can be used to express feelings and emotions which are difficult to put directly into words. When writing to a stranger, you may have no way of knowing how they wish to be addressed or how they will respond to your usual style of writing, which may convey friendliness or cold formality. Either may be appropriate or inappropriate depending on the recipient of your document. Preparing a document for delivery by 'snail mail', that is, conventional post, takes preparation and effort and provides plenty of time for redrafting or even a decision not to send it at all. If the document is contentious in any way, such as a letter of resignation, or a complaint then the adage "sleep on it" is good advice; a difficult situation often appears very different the next day. E-mail is electronic and once a message is transmitted it may be in the recipient's mailbox seconds later. The first 'netiquette' rule of e-mail is "Think before you send." Some other important rules are:

❑   Check your e-mail regularly to ensure that you respond quickly to messages. Of course this applies to normal letter communications as well.

❑   If you can't reply immediately, send a quick acknowledgement.

❑   If you don't use encryption, be careful about what you say. A building society has been sued for libellous comments e-mailed by one of its employees. Laws on copyright, personal privacy, libel, pornography and incitement of racial hatred also apply to electronic communication.

❑   Use your words carefully, especially if you are angry or irritated. As explained earlier, e-mail does not provide the opportunities for body language or voice intonation to 'fine-tune' what you say. If you write something in jest, for example, "You are bone idle, you haven't replied to my e-mail", it is wise to use a 'smiley' (see later) to indicate that you are only joking.

❑   Keep your messages fairly brief. If you need to communicate a large amount of information send it as an attachment.

E-mail writing style

E-mail communications are encouraging informality, but you should always try to use wording and style which communicate respect. Because the medium is so quick, many e-mail users become very careless about spelling and grammar, which is probably acceptable between friends but is still unwise in business communication. Abbreviations are common, for example, BTW for "By the way", FAQ for "Frequently asked question", FWIW meaning "For what it's worth" and IMO for "In my opinion".

Smileys

These are ASCII or plain text characters formed into facial expressions to convey a variety of emotions. Suppose that you sent the following message:

> "She has gone on holiday."

You might mean

> "SHE has gone on holiday" (said with bitterness")

> "She HAS gone on holiday" (confirming something that had been in doubt)

> " She has gone on HOLIDAY" (said incredulously)

Even with capital letters, each of these could indicate different emotions from those suggested. Here are some examples of smileys which may help to more accurately express the emphasis in what you want to say. To get the effect you need to turn your head to view them sideways. (They look best in the Courier New font.)

```
:-)     Happy face - don't take what I said too seriously.
;-)     The smile with a wink implies sarcasm or irony.
:-(     The frown means that you don't like what was said to you.
8^0     The open mouth and wide eyes suggests that you are shocked.
```

Proofing documents

Some of the most commonly used proofing signs are shown in Figure 1.9.

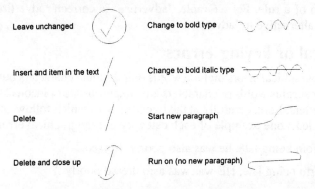

Figure 1.9. *Standard proofing symbols*

To produce readable and presentable documents you need to develop the skill of *proofing* or searching for errors. Generally, except for very short documents, it is very difficult to carry out all proofing on screen and you will probably need to print a draft copy to read. With hard copy, you can use a ruler to guide your eye as you scan each line. If someone else is to carry out the corrections, it is helpful to use standard correction signs which are recognised and used by those involved in writing and publishing.

Proofing requires concentration and systematic searching for several types of error which commonly occur. They are detailed below, together with examples.

Spelling

You may have little trouble with spelling, but most people have a 'blind spot' with certain words and some common errors are listed below.

Correct spelling	Common misspelling
sep*a*rate	separate
station*e*ry	stationary (if referring to paper)
station*a*ry	stationery (if you mean stopped/not moving)
sincer*e*ly	sincerly
lia*i*son	liason
person*n*el	personel
revers*i*ble	reversable
com*m*ittee	comittee

Apart from checking for misspellings, you should try to be consistent where a word has more than one acceptable spelling. Frequently, for example, you will find that the letter '*s*' can sometimes be used in place of '*z*'. The Oxford English Dictionary will give you the word 'organization', but you will frequently see it spelt as 'organi*s*ation'. Similar examples include, 'specialize' or 'speciali*s*e', 'emphasize' or 'emphasi*s*e'. These are only examples and not demonstration of a rule. For example, 'adverti*s*e' is correct, 'adverti*z*e' is wrong and 'advi*z*e' is *not* an alternative to 'advi*s*e'.

Typographical or keying errors

Categories of typographical errors include words or individual characters out of order (*transposed*), missing or surplus words or characters and inappropriate or inconsistent use of lower case and capital letters. Look carefully at the two sentences which follow and you should be able to identify at least one example of each category of typographical error.

"Apart from being late, he was also poorly dressed."

"apart form being late, HE was was aslo dressd poorly ."

Punctuation errors

You need to look for incorrect and missing punctuation. Some rules, such as the use of a full stop at the end of a sentence, are absolute. Rules on the use of, for example, commas are less clear. Generally, they are used to improve the readability of a document and are often a matter of personal judgement. For example, the sentence

> "Apart from being late he was also poorly dressed."

would not be incorrect but would be more readable if a comma was used as follows.

> "Apart from being late, he was also poorly dressed."

Spacing errors

This relates to the incorrect omission of space or the inclusion of surplus space between words, sentences, lines or paragraphs. Generally, you should leave a single space between words and between a full stop and the beginning of the next sentence. You should also leave a blank line between paragraphs. (Alternatively, you can format the paragraph style to include additional space after each carriage return). Your word processor may provide the option to display characters which are normally *hidden*. These include spaces, tabs and carriage returns, and can make proofing for spacing errors easier.

Figure 1.10 shows some hidden characters, with a space represented by a • and a carriage return by a ¶. Two possible consequences of erroneous spacing can be identified in the Figure.

- ❏ 'Centred Heading' is off centre because the preceding spaces are taken as characters and included as part of the heading.

- ❏ The lack of a space after a comma means that the word before and after it, and the comma itself, are taken as one word; this would mean, for example, that the word processor's spell checker would highlight 'Generally,you', in Figure 1.10, as a misspelling. To correct it you would have to insert the required space.

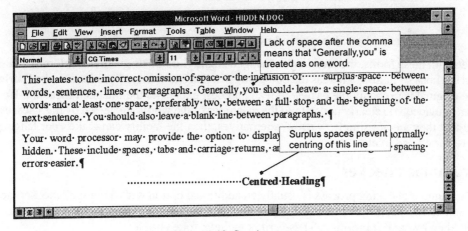

Figure 1.10. *Spacing errors*

Spellchecker

All word processors and many other packages include a *spell checking* facility. You may find that, for example, it throws up words like 'organization' as being incorrectly spelled and indicates that only 'organisation' is correct. This does not mean that you cannot use the 'z' form. It simply means that the spellchecker's rules have not allowed for it. Spell checkers will identify as misspelled any word that does not appear in its *dictionary* (stored on disk). Thus, you may find that proper names, such as 'Wilkinson', or abbreviations like 'VCE', as well as many specialist technical terms, are highlighted as being incorrect. Most spell checkers allow you to add words to the dictionary, so that they are not identified as misspellings. If you mis-spell a word and it happens to be the correct spelling for another word, then the computer will not detect it. For example, 'stationery' and 'stationary' are both correctly spelled but have en-tirely different meanings. Such errors can only be found by careful proofing.

Thesaurus

Apart from a built-in spell checker, your word processor may also have a *Thesaurus*, which allows you to check the meanings of words and suggests alternatives. This facility should be used with great care, to avoid the use of unusual words which may obscure what you are try-ing to say. Further, it should only be used to jog your memory for an alternative word. If you use a word with which you are not familiar, you may discover that the word has a similar, but not identical, meaning to the original. For example, the meaning of the following sentence is quite clear.

"She was studious and passed all her examinations."

If you checked the Thesaurus for the word 'studious', it may throw up the suggestions such as, assiduous, diligent, industrious, determined, hard-working, busy, contemplative, intent and tireless. The adjectives do not necessarily relate to the activity of studying. To keep the meaning similar, you could change both adjectives to adverbs and keep the verb 'to study'. Possible alternatives of this form are shown below.

"She studied industriously and passed all her examinations."

"She studied diligently and passed all her examinations."

"She studied assiduously and passed all her examinations."

Even with these forms, the meaning is changed slightly. In the original, it is inferred that she was studious by nature, whereas the others suggest that she was studious for a limited period. The original is probably the easiest to read and best expresses the intended meaning. How-ever, provided you clearly understand the meanings of the words suggested by the Thesaurus and that they are not simply 'wordy' alternatives, then the facility can make your language more varied and lively.

Grammar checker

The grammar checking process is usually an additional option within the spellchecker facil-ity and can be useful for picking up some of the more obvious errors, which could also be picked up by careful proofing. These errors include, for example:

❑   using two full stops at the end of sentence;

❑   using a lower case letter at the start of a sentence;

❑   repeating the same word in succession.

Generally, however, the grammar checker should be used with extreme care as it will often make suggestions which may conform to the rules of grammar but if adopted would make complete nonsense of what you are trying to say. The grammar tool is only useful for identifying possible errors and you need to be confident in your use of grammar in order to determine whether an error actually exists. After the grammar checker has completed scanning a document it can be set to display readability statistics, as shown in Figure 1.11.

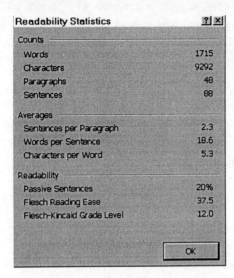

Figure 1.11. *Readability statistics*

The 20% 'Passive sentences' figure relates to the use of sentences such as:

> An example is shown in the next Figure.

To use the 'active voice', which many word processors encourage, you would have to say:

> The next Figure shows an example.

Either is acceptable and which you use is a matter of personal preference but using the active voice can improve readability. Sometimes, the active voice is completely inappropriate, and you need to know when to ignore the grammar checker's warning against the passive voice. For example, the sentence

> You calculate the area of a rectangle by multiplying the width by the length

is in the active voice but if I don't wish to address the reader directly, I would write

> The area of a rectangle is calculated by multiplying the length by the width.

Each of the US readability measures (Flesch Reading Ease and Flesch-Kincaid) is based on the average number of syllables per word and words per sentence. Readability also has to do with choice of words and the ways in which sentences are constructed, but the measures do provide a crude guide to readability. Again you need to use your own judgement in assessing readability and only shorten sentences or use words with fewer syllables if it will not destroy the flow and style of your writing. As explained earlier in this chapter, you need to tailor your style to suit the reader. For example, you would not expect to achieve the same readability score for a document aimed at university professors as you would for one aimed at young children.

✍ Self-test questions

1. Using illustrative examples, suggest two reasons why correct spelling is important.
2. What is meant by proofing and why is it an important process?
3. a.   Briefly describe the operation of a spell checker.
   b.   With the aid of suitable examples, explain the limitations of a spell checker for proofing purposes.
4. Identify **three** types of document when a personal writing style may be important and **three** types of document when it would not be relevant.
5. Distinguish between a *serif* and *sans-serif* font, giving an example of each.
6. What rules concerning content should you bear in mind when summarising a document.
7. What is the purpose of meeting minutes.
8. What standard items would you expect to see on an agenda?
9. List the sections would you expect to see in a curriculum vitae to support a job application.
10. Suggest items of information you would expect to see in a job advertisement.
11. List the main components of a formal letter.
12. a.   Give three examples of information gathering which would be suited to the use of questionnaires.
    b.   Give an example of a question which can be answered using an opinion scale.
    c.   Give an example of a leading question.
13. Distinguish between a bar chart and a pie chart and give an example of numerical information for which each would be appropriate.
14. List the main headings you would expect to find in a formal report.
15. What is a *draft* document?
16. Give two examples of e-mail etiquette.
17. What is a smiley?
18. a.   When would you use a Thesaurus?
    b.   When may a Thesaurus be of little use?
19. With the use of examples, distinguish between the 'passive voice' and the 'active voice'.
20. Suggest why a word processor's grammar checker cannot be wholly relied upon for correct grammar.

Chapter 2

Designing and creating documents

This chapter describes the various aspects of a document which contribute to its style and the presentational facilities provided by a typical word processing package. Word processing describes the activity of writing with the aid of a computer. The term 'writing' is used in its widest sense and includes, for example, the production of personal or business documentation, such as letters, reports and memoranda, legal documents, articles, books and even the addressing of envelopes. Most word processors include tools for the production of columns and tables, as well as the inclusion of graphics.

Page layout components

Before you start entering text, or at some point before you print the final document, you may need to work through a *page set-up* procedure. This allows specification of the margin sizes, paper size and orientation that the printer will use when it prints the document. Even though the package has a *default* page specification (Figure 2.1), you should check that it conforms to your requirements and if necessary, adjust the appropriate settings. Figure 2.2 shows the location of the various margins referred to in Figure 2.1, for an A4 page in *portrait* orientation. Landscape orientation simply rotates the page through 90°.

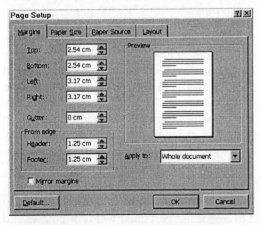

Figure 2.1. *Page setup for unbound document*

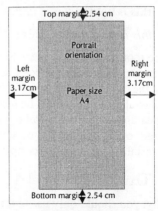

Figure 2.2. *Portrait orientation*

The *top margin* sets the amount of space the printer leaves at the top of the page before print-ing text. The *bottom margin* determines the amount of space that the printer will leave at the end of a full page. The *left margin* and *right margin* are the offsets from the left and right sides of the paper and determine the limits of the print line. Printer margins are usually mea-sured in inches or centimetres.

Figure 2.3 shows example page settings for a bound document. Note the reference to inside and outside margin instead of left and right margin. The inside margin refers to the margin closest to the binding and is set wider so that the page contents are not obscured. Also, a value can be entered for the gutter to allow for the binding. To enter these settings, you must first select the 'Mirror margins', as shown in Figure 2.3. The location of the margins and the gut-ter are shown in Figure 2.4.

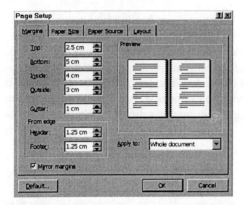

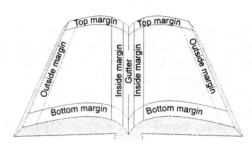

Figure 2.4. *Location of mirrored margins and gutter*

Figure 2.3. *Page setup with mirrored margins*

Text format and font style

All types of printer allow the printing of a range of text formats. Some common examples are given below.

this is bold   *this is italic*   ~~this is strike through~~   this is underline

this is bold italic   this is ^{superscript}   this is _{subscript}

There are thousands of text *fonts* to choose from, the most common including Times New Roman (the font used for the body text here), Arial and Courier. It is likely that only a small subset of the thousands of available fonts will be installed on the computer, so if you wish to use additional fonts, they must be installed first. Most fonts are True Type, which means that their appearance on screen matches almost exactly their printed appearance and that they can be re-sized to any height. If you wish to have a wider range of fonts to choose from, they must be installed first. Some example font styles are given below (size is measured in *points*).

This is Parade 14   This is HandelGotDLight 14

Generally, you should only use text formatting when it contributes to the impact and clarity of the document. For example, if you use bold to emphasise particular words or phrases and its use extends to, say, every other line on the page, its impact will be lost. The number of font styles in a document should be restricted to two or three and care should be taken in mixing the more flamboyant font styles used for headlines. The following example illustrates the point.

Sale Monday 20th June 2000 at 2.00 pm

Bargains Galore

Don't miss it!

Bargain Basement Stores, York Road, Stockton-on-Tees

Figure 2.5. *Poster using four different fonts reduces readability and visual impact*

Greater impact is obtained by using only two font styles as follows.

Sale Monday 20th June 2000 at 2.00 pm

Bargains Galore

Don't miss it!

Bargain Basement Stores, York Road, Stockton-on-Tees

Figure 2.6. *Poster using only two font styles, thereby improving readability and visual impact*

Of course, it is even more important to choose appropriate fonts for formal documents, such as reports and business letters. Generally, a serif font (such as Times New Roman) is effective for the main body text and a sans-serif font (such as Arial), suitably enlarged and emboldened or underscored, is appropriate for paragraph headings.

A business document can look very unprofessional, as well as a little silly, if you use too many font styles. You may use bold or underlined characters to emphasise and italics for a quotation.

WYSIWYG (What You See Is What You Get)

All modern word processing packages are WYSIWYG in that a document can be viewed as it will appear on the printed page. Thus, lines can be seen as centred, characters can be viewed as bold, *italic*, <u>underlined</u>, and in

different sizes and FONTS.

Apart from the package's WYSIWYG facilities, your screen must have the necessary graphics capability and *resolution*.

Paragraph style elements

Any line or group of lines, with only one carriage return at the end of the last line, is treated by a word processor as a paragraph. Following standard practice, even when typing continuous prose, you should insert a blank line by pressing the ENTER key a second time, after each paragraph. Alternatively, you can specify that spacing, measured in *point* (pt) size, is left after a paragraph, once you press the ENTER key. Figure 2.7 shows a dialogue box indicating selection of a 6 pt space after a paragraph.

In preparing a more lengthy document, such as a booklet, or magazine article, it is advisable to make use of styles, which may be pre-defined, or which you have defined yourself. A style defines a number of features concerning text, including paragraph alignment (left, right, centred and justified - straight left and right margins), paragraph indent, bullets or numbering, line spacing, character font and size. See Styles and Style Sheets later.

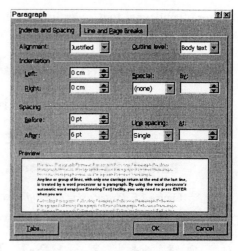

Figure 2.7. *Paragraph format settings*

Paragraph alignment

Paragraph alignment can be set, either for a complete document or for individual paragraphs, in relation to the left and right margins. Paragraphs can be aligned as follows.

Left aligned

In preparing a more lengthy document, such as a booklet, or magazine article, it is advisable to make use of styles, which may be pre-defined, or which you have defined yourself. A style defines ....

Right aligned

In preparing a more lengthy document, such as a booklet, or magazine article, it is advisable to make use of styles, which may be pre-defined, or which you have defined yourself. A style defines ....

Justified

In preparing a more lengthy document, such as a booklet, or magazine article, it is advisable to make use of styles, which may be pre-defined, or which you have defined yourself. A style defines ....

Centred

In preparing a more lengthy document, such as a booklet, or magazine article, it is advisable to make use of styles, which may be pre-defined, or which you have defined yourself. A style defines ....

Hyphenation

There may be occasions when you need to split a word at the end of a line, to prevent words being too widely spaced. This can only occur when paragraph alignment is justified. It is more likely to happen if you have set wide margins, or are using multiple columns, and the line length is particularly short. The problem is illustrated in Figure 2.8 with a two column layout example and Figure 2.9 shows the result of using hyphenation. You can choose to have a document automatically hyphenated or let the word processor suggest hyphenation points which you can choose or reject.

The data communications industry has always had to deal with problems of *incompatible* standards. Standards have to do with all aspects of a communications system, including, for example, the *hardware devices*, the *encoding* of data and the forms of *signals* used.

Figure 2.8. *Excessive word spacing in justified paragraph (2 columns)*

The data communications industry has always had to deal with problems of *incompatible* standards. Standards have to do with all aspects of a communications system, including, for example, the *hardware devices*, the *encoding* of data and the forms of *signals* used.

Figure 2.9. *Hyphenation to remove excessive word spacing*

Indents and hanging indents

An *indent* is a starting point for text which is not in line with the left (or occasionally, the right) margin. You can choose to indent the first line only in a paragraph, a complete paragraph, or all but the first line of a paragraph. This last form is known as a *hanging indent*. The three forms are shown below. To set up an indent may involve the use of menu options and/or the ruler.

First line indent

An *indent* is a starting point for text which is not in line with the left (or occasionally, the right) margin. You can choose to indent the first line only in a paragraph, a complete paragraph, or all but the first line of a paragraph. This last form is known as a *hanging indent*.

Paragraph indent

An *indent* is a starting point for text which is not in line with the left (or occasionally, the right) margin. You can choose to indent the first line only in a paragraph, a complete paragraph, or all but the first line of a paragraph. This last form is known as a *hanging indent*.

Hanging indent

An *indent* is a starting point for text which is not in line with the left (or occasionally, the right) margin. You can choose to indent the first line only in a paragraph, a complete paragraph, or all but the first line of a paragraph. This last form is known as a *hanging indent*.

Line spacing

By default, your word processor should leave a single line space between each line of text, as part of automatic *word wrap*. Most word processors provide an option which automatically inserts two and sometimes one-and-a-half blank lines between each line in a paragraph. This option may be helpful in the preparation of a notice or advertisement, in combination with a larger font . Sometimes, your tutor may ask for work to be double line spaced to make marking and the insertion of comments easier. Figure 2.7, earlier in this chapter, shows a dialogue box for the selection of line spacing preferences.

Tabulation

Tabulation is particularly useful for typing lists in columns, or text and figures in table form. If you wish to begin text entry to the right of the existing left margin, you can change the margin setting, but this will mean that word wrap or pressing the ENTER key will always place the insertion point at the new margin setting. To move the insertion point for a single line of text, use the TAB key. The screen ruler probably has some default TAB settings, possibly set every $0 \cdot 5$ inch or $1 \cdot 27$ centimetres.

Each time you press the TAB key the insertion point is moved to the next TAB point. You can either begin typing at that point or press the TAB key to move to the next position. Once you reach the right margin, the insertion point may be moved to the first TAB position on the next line or to the preceding one on the same line. If you have chosen the exact tabulation settings, then it is better to clear the default settings and insert tabulation points as required. This may be achieved through a menu option if they are to be regularly spaced. If the spacing is irregular, your word processor will allow you to set and move them on the ruler (usually by double clicking at each required position). Figure 2.10 shows a tabulated document with the normally hidden TAB characters displayed. The TAB markers are shown on the ruler at 1cm, 5cm and 11cm from the left hand margin.

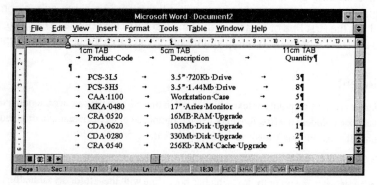

Figure 2.10. *Tabulated document with TAB markers shown on ruler*

Bullets and numbered lists

Bullets and numbers can be used to emphasise or sequence items in a list. Two examples are given below.

Example bullet list

This pack includes the following items:

☑ assembly instructions

☑ colour illustrations

☑ components for assembly

Example numbered list

The tasks should be carried out in the following order:

(i) initial investigation;

(ii)   analysis;

(iii) design;

(iv)   implementation.

In the second example, the numbering sequence is carried out automatically and a variety of number styles may be available, using Arabic or Roman numerals, or letters of the alphabet.

Style palettes

Styles can be applied, not only to headings and paragraphs, but also to *tables* (see later). An example paragraph style definition is detailed below.

```
Style: Heading 2
Font: Arial, 12 pt
Format: bold italic
Paragraph alignment: flush left
Spacing before: 14 pt
Spacing after: 10 pt
```

The location of the spacing settings is illustrated below.

This is the preceding paragraph.
   14 point space before ↑

Heading 2, Arial 12pt, bold italic, flush left
   10 point space after ↓
This is the following paragraph.

You should make use of different text styles to emphasise, for example, titles, chapter headings, sub-headings or body text. The word processor will normally have a set of named styles, which you can use immediately. You can modify any of these styles and keep the same names or you can create new styles and name them yourself. The ready-made styles are held in what is often referred to as the *style palette*. Figure 2.11 shows a variety of user-defined styles with some of the style names displayed in the pull down palette. To apply a style, you would need to place the insertion point within the relevant paragraph and then use the pointer tool to select the appropriate style from the palette. Styles which you create can be added to the palette, but they will only be available for the current document, unless you make them part of a *document template* (known as a *style sheet* in desktop publishing programs). Style sheets are also used in other presentational applications, including those for slide presentations (Chapter 3) and Web site development (referred to as *cascading style sheet* or CSS).

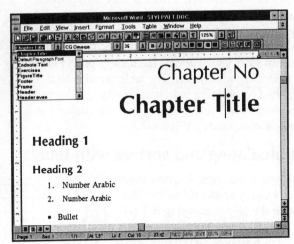

Figure 2.11. *Example styles and style palette*

Columns

Typically, when you start your word processor you will be presented with a default page with a single column, spanning the width available between the left and right margins. Column layout is suitable for documents such as news sheets, newspapers and magazines. You can choose to create columns before or after the entry of text and the width of each can be altered at will. You can choose to have the columns the same width and equally spaced, or vary the column widths and the spacing between columns according to preference. Figure 2.12 shows a two column layout.

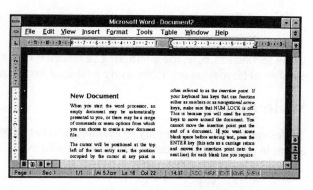

Figure 2.12. *Two column layout*

Tables

If you need to present text in a tabular way, you can use tabulation, but a *table* tool allows much greater control over layout. It may also provide extra features to enhance presentation and even allow simple calculations on numeric items. To define a basic table, you need to specify the number of *rows* and *columns*. Each entry point in the table is known as a *cell*. The table can also be formatted by defining individual border widths and colours and cell shading or by using an *autoformat* facility (Figure 2.13).

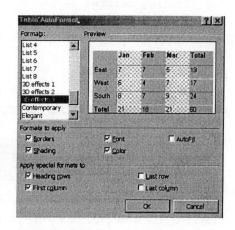

Figure 2.13. *Table autoformat facility*

Calculating and sorting with tables

If you have used a spreadsheet package, you should be familiar with the idea of carrying out calculations automatically, with the use of formulae. Word processor tables provide a number of simple functions, such as SUM, to add the contents of a range of cells and PRODUCT, to multiply the contents of cells. Figure 2.14 shows a table with the results of the SUM(ABOVE) formula at

Name	Units sold
Jones	15000
Avia	22000
Wiemann	33500
Anderson	23800
Fung	14200
Total	108500

Figure 2.14. *Using a formula to total a column of figures*

the bottom of the Units Sold column. The formula dialogue box is shown alongside.

A word processor may also allow you to treat the table as a simple database and sort rows, as if they were records, using one or more columns as sort keys. Figure 2.15 illustrates the sorting of the Name column in ascending order. Sorting can be grouped, so that for example, a staff list could be sorted according to Department and within each department, be sorted by Surname. The topic of sorting is examined in more detail in the Database Design Unit.

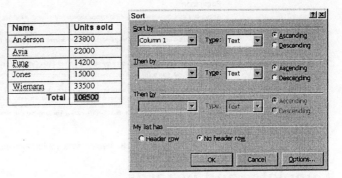

Figure 2.15. *Sorting a table using a single column as the key*

Text box

A text box can be used to position text on a page, independently of any accompanying text.

Normal paragraph text can be made to flow around the frame, or it can be split by it. Figure 2.16 shows a text box and the settings for text to flow around it. Once you have positioned a text box within the paragraph text, you can assign it an exact position on the page, or allow it to move with the text. In the latter case, inserting new text above the text box will move the text box forward as the new text is entered.

Text inside a text box (or a table cell) can be rotated through 90° as shown in Figure 2.17.

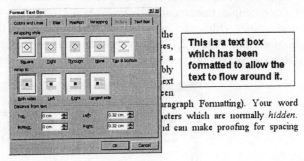

Figure 2.16. *Bordered text box with text flowing around*

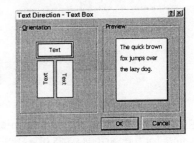

Figure 2.17. *Altering text direction*

Watermark

A text box can also be used to create a watermark, which can sit behind or in front of the text on a page. Typically, the former option is used to give a document a corporate image using the company name on every page. Provided that the text is in a light colour it should not obscure the main contents of the document. A watermark may sit on top of the contents, for example, when it is important to emphasise that it is a 'DRAFT ONLY' or 'HIGHLY CONFIDENTIAL'. A watermark can also be formed from a graphic. In Microsoft Word, watermarks must be created within a header or footer, formatted as required and position on the page before the header or footer is closed. Figure 2.18 shows an example watermark in the background of a document.

Pagination

As you develop a document, the word processor automatically inserts a *soft* page break each time you add another page. The word processor usually displays such breaks on screen, or you may only find out where they occur when the document is printed. The point at which a soft page break is inserted depends on the length of the page as defined in *page set-up* (see Page Set-up). Normally, you will select one of a number of standard sizes, such as A4 or A5. If you return to edit an earlier part of a document, perhaps to add or remove text, then the pagination process recalculates the amount of text on the page and adjusts subsequent soft page breaks accordingly.

A soft page break may occur at an inconvenient point, perhaps immediately after a heading or in the middle of a table and in such an event you can force a *hard* page break at a more suitable point. Subsequent soft page breaks are again adjusted accordingly. Generally, you should leave the insertion of hard page breaks until you are satisfied that your document is complete and does not require any further revision. This is because hard page breaks are not moved in the automatic pagination process and after further editing you may have to remove certain hard page breaks or relocate them.

Figure 2.18. *Watermark in background*

Templates and wizards

Templates contain the features of style sheets, plus additional tools to support development of, for example, documents of various types, including invoices, reports, memos and slide presentations. Other packages, such as spreadsheets and drawing packages, also contain template facilities. Figure 2.19 shows the dialogue box for template selection in Microsoft Word, with separate tabs for each category of document and the Memo tab currently selected.

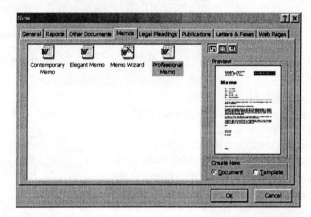

Figure 2.19. *Template selection in Microsoft Word with Memo template highlighted*

Effectively, a template provides pre-defined entry points for the various parts of a standard document and standard styles, although these can be modified. The style list associated with the Memo template is shown in Figure 2.20. Standard templates provided with a package are useful for generating standard documents quickly, but it is unlikely that such documents would meet the precise 'in-house' style requirements of an organisation without some modification. However, once a document has been created in the particular in-house style, it can be saved as a template and used to ensure consistent presentation of that particular document throughout the organisation.

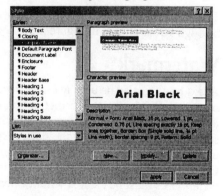

Figure 2.20. *Style list for Memo template*

A special template (often referred to as *normal.dot*), is used to set the default layout and formats, for a new document. Typically, templates of various forms may be available for immediate use (you can modify a template if it does not fit your need exactly). They may include, for example, memorandum, invitation, bulletin, report, dissertation and invoice templates. Apart from simple templates, the word processor may provide a number of document *wizards*; a wizard takes you through a number of dialogue boxes, taking information on the data to be included in the document. Typical examples include wizards for the production of calendars, agendas and faxes. To produce an agenda, for example, the design and main headings are provided by the wizard, so all you have to provide is the *variable* data, such as meeting title, location, times, topics and so on.

Longer documents

For documents of more than three or four pages, it is usual to use additional elements to help the reader. These elements may include: a table of contents, page headers (and possibly, footers), footnotes and an index. Some packages provide an outline feature, which is useful for planning and re-arranging the content of a document.

Outlining

Figure 2.21 shows an example of the *outline* view of a document. The indentation represents the hierarchy of the topics. The full document is concerned with the topic of word processing and the main divisions of the topic are 'Introduction', 'Creating a Document' and Editing Guidelines'. Sub topics are identified by their level of indentation from the main list. The title 'Creating a Document' has six sub-topics, one of which has its own sub-topic, 'The Word Processor Screen'.

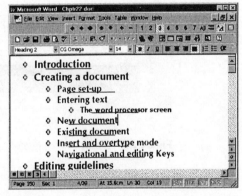

Figure 2.21. *Outline view of a document*

Thus, if you are planning the contents and structure of a report, you should find an outlining facility extremely useful. Even if your word processor does not provide such a facility, you would be wise to plan an outline on paper before starting on the report. The outlining facility in Microsoft Word relies on the use of the built-in heading styles (Heading1, Heading 2 ...), stored in a style palette (see earlier). Complete sections can be copied, deleted or moved within the hierarchy by dragging the relevant heading to its new position; any text and subtopic which is located beneath a dragged heading is also moved

Headers and footers

A *header* is descriptive text which appears above the top margin on every page. For example, a header may include the page number, date, report title and the author's name. A *footer* serves a similar function except that it is located beneath the bottom margin on each page. You only have to enter a header or footer once and the word processor automatically places it on each page when the document is printed. Creating a header or footer is a separate operation from normal text entry and you can only create, edit or remove one through the relevant package commands. If you do not wish to place a header or footer on every page, there is normally a facility, for example, to exempt the first page or assign a different header or footer to the odd or even pages.

Figure 2.22 shows the Layout tab in the Page Setup dialogue; the 'Different first page' selection allows for no header on the first page, which is standard practice.

The 'Different odd and even' option is not selected, so every page has the same text (obviously page numbers are not affected by this and will increment automatically.

Figure 2.23 shows a header with automatic page number and a fixed header text, together with the header and footer toolbar (includes formatting facilities).

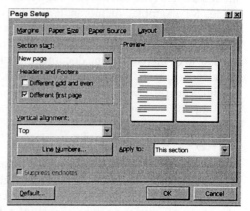

Figure 2.22. *Page layout tab showing header and footer display settings*

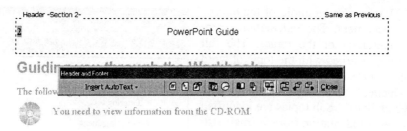

Figure 2.23. *Header with automatic page numbering and fixed for all pages*

Running heads

There are occasions when a fixed header text for all pages is not appropriate, as in this book, for example. When header contents change to take account of current chapters and topics, they are known as *running heads* and we will use this book to illustrate their features:

❑ for the first page of a chapter, the header is hidden;

❑ each left-hand page has a page number, a unit number, a chapter number and the chapter's title. The words 'Unit' and 'Chapter' are entered directly into the header, but the page number and the chapter number and the chapter title are entered as *field codes* which then pick up the current values for page number. Figure 2.24 shows the entry of a field code called StyleRef and the associated style 'Chapter Title' it is to use to determine the value which appears in the header.

❑ each right hand page header displays the current main heading. This is achieved by entering a field code (as for the left-hand page) in the header, using one of the document styles. For example, using Heading 1 as the field code automatically picks up the most recent occurrence of that style in the document. When a new Heading 1 paragraph appears on a page, the header value is automatically altered.

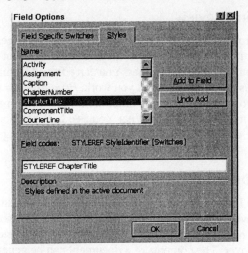

Figure 2.24. *Entering the field code "styleref" to enable automatic entry of current Chapter Title*

Footnotes and endnotes

Footnotes are useful if you want to briefly explain a word or phrase, without including the explanation within the main body of the text. Instead, a reference number is placed next to the relevant word or phrase and the explanation is put at the foot of the page, identified by the same reference number. Here is an example, to explain the word *endnote*[1].

Pagination, widows and orphans

As you develop a document, the word processor automatically inserts a *soft* page break each time you add another page. The word processor usually displays such breaks on screen, or you may only find out where they occur when the document is printed. The point at which a soft page break is inserted depends on the length of the page as defined in *page set-up* (see Page Set-up). Normally, you will select one of a number of standard sizes, such as A4 or A5. If you return to edit an earlier part of a document, perhaps to add or remove text, then the pagination process recalculates the amount of text on the page and adjusts subsequent soft page breaks accordingly. A soft page break may occur at an inconvenient point, perhaps immediately after a heading or in the middle of a table and in such an event you can force a *hard* page break at a more suitable point. This may be the case if the *widows* and *orphans* control is not set. This control prevents the first line of a paragraph (orphan) being left alone at the bottom of the page and the last line of a paragraph (widow) being left by itself at the top of the page. Subsequent soft page breaks are again adjusted accordingly. Generally, you should leave the insertion of hard page breaks until you are satisfied that your document is complete and does not require any further revision. This is because hard page breaks are not moved in the

---

1   This a footnote, but an endnote appears at the end of a document

automatic pagination process and after further editing you may have to remove certain hard page breaks or relocate them.

Page view and print preview

These two facilities allow you to view a document as individual pages. *Page view* shows you the edges of the page, if the 'zoom' is set to 'page width'. You can see the bottom and top edges as you scroll from one page to another. You can edit and format the text while in page view and see the effects of re-pagination as you work. *Print preview* shows you each page of the document (one, two or more pages at a time) in miniaturised form as they will appear on the printer. These are true WYSIWYG (What You See Is What You Get) features. The results of pagination are easy to see and the points at which hard page breaks are needed are clear.

Generating a contents table

As explained earlier, a Table of Contents is essential for longer documents, particularly if it is divided into sections which may be accessed directly. Of course, some documents, such as novels or essays don't need a Contents table because they are designed to be read in their entirety, form cover to cover. The contents of a document can be generated automatically and Figure 2.25 shows a typical Table of Contents, together with a dialogue box for choosing the presentation style and the number of levels to be included.

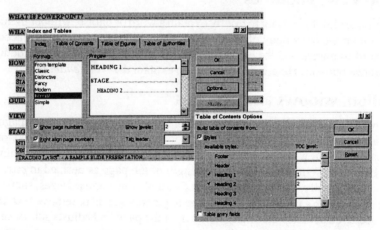

Figure 2.25. *Generating a table of contents automatically by selecting heading styles*

The Options dialogue, also shown in the Figure, allows the selection of heading styles (including user-defined) which are to be picked up for each level in the table and thereby determine the contents of the table.

Generating an index

The process for creating an index automatically is similar, but first requires the marking of text which is to be indexed. Figure 2.26 shows the dialogue box for creating the marked text 'printer' and the resulting field code, { XE "Printer" } in the document (can be viewed by displaying hidden characters)

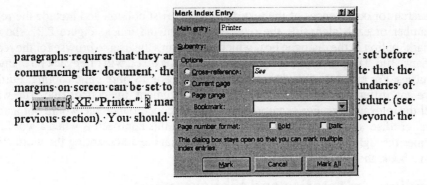

paragraphs·requires·that·they·ar [...] ·set·before·
commencing·the·document,·the [...] te·that·the·
margins·on·screen·can·be·set·to [...] ndaries·of·
the·printer⌐·XE·"Printer"·⌐·mar [...] :edure·(see·
previous·section).·You·should· [...] beyond·the·

Figure 2.26. *Marking an index entry*

The index generation process then scans the document for the index markers, placing the entry and the relevant page number within the alphabetical order of the index. The Index creation dialogue and a section of a typical index are shown in Figure 2.27.

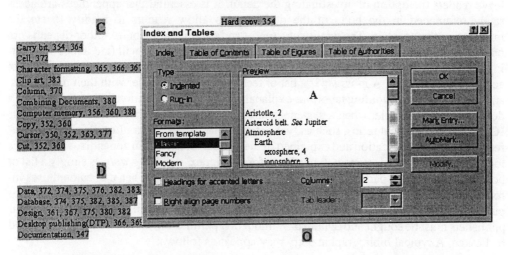

Figure 2.27. *Creating an index*

Using a concordance file

For the index to contain relevant entries, it is best to mark text for inclusion as described above, but for a very large document it may be quicker, though less satisfactory, to have the word processor *automark* the document from a *concordance file*. In Microsoft Word, this consists of a two-column table with text values to be marked in the first column and the desired index label in the second column. An example is shown in Figure 2.28.

The word processor then uses the concordance

laser	printer
ink jet	printer
dot matrix	printer
printer	printer
cartridge	disk storage
disk	disk storage
platter	disk storage
floppy	disk storage
zip	disk storage

Figure 2.28. *Example concordance file for automarking index entries*

file to search for occurrences of the text items in the first column and include the relevant page number of each alongside the relevant entry in the index. Figure 2.27 shows the 'Automark' option in the dialogue box, which then allows the user to browse for the required concordance file. The problem with a concordance file is that it will often pick up many irrelevant entries. For example, the phrase 'optical' may refer to fibre optic cabling. Further, if there are any differences in spelling or phrase arrangement, the concordance file will not mark all the relevant text. For example, the example concordance file would not automark 'printers' or 'disc' or 'inkjet'. Another difficulty with this approach is when a word occurs many times throughout a document. For example, imagine automarking the word 'file' or 'data' in a book about ICT.

Appendices, glossaries and bibliographies

Appendices appear at the end of a document and are a valuable way of maintaining its readability without omitting vital content. For example, a report on a company's sales performance over the last five years may include an appendix containing a detailed analyses of products and customer feedback. The report body will draw conclusions from this data and leave readers the option of investigating the detail. It is essential that appendices are accurately referenced in the body of the document to allow readers to readily locate the information they contain. The quality of a report and the reputation of its author depends not only on its content but also on its structure and readability. A reader will find it most frustrating if he or she has to thumb through a document looking for information because it is not accurately referenced. A *glossary* is a list of technical terms, together with their definitions, and is useful way of avoiding laborious explanations and their repetition within the body of a document. For example, when a systems analyst prepares a Specification of Requirements (Chapter 22), technical terms, such as 'validation', 'file server' or 'multi-tasking' can be referred to in the specification and explained in the glossary. As with an appendix, a glossary is located at the end of a document, typically before the index. A *bibliography* is simply a list of books or articles on a particular subject or by a particular author. When a document uses information from other sources, the sources must be acknowledged. If the document is to be published, that is, made available to the public then the permission of the authors or their publishers must be sought and obtained. Without that permission, the law of copyright would be broken. A typical bibliographic entry may appear as follows:

Knott, Geoffrey & Waites, Nick, *BTEC Nationals Computing*, (Brancepeth Computer Publications, 2000).

An entry may also identify the page numbers from which the information is taken. A bibliography is normally located at the end of a document, before the index.

Using graphics, shading and colour

In a world where people are used to viewing information through multi-media, including film, television, computer games and the World Wide Web, printed documents, such as publicity flyers and advertisement posters need to make use of graphics, colour and shading if they are to make an impact on their target audiences. Of course, illustrations, colour and shading also make a document more attractive and this is important, even for utilitarian documents such as invoices, order forms, questionnaires, reports and text books. Graphics are also important for simplifying and clarifying processes and structures, as the following examples illustrate.

❑ A business may issue maps to guide customers, deliveries and sales representatives to their retail outlets, warehouses and offices, as appropriate.

❑ A systems analyst produces flow diagrams and charts to illustrate processes and procedures in a Requirements Specification.

❑ A text book uses illustrations to help explain important ideas and processes.

❑ A computer manufacturer provides buyers with graphical guides to the assembly of their computer systems.

Border, line, shading and fill

Borders can be placed around a page, a table, individual cells within a table, paragraphs and selected text, as illustrated in Figure 2.29. Cell shading is also illustrated.

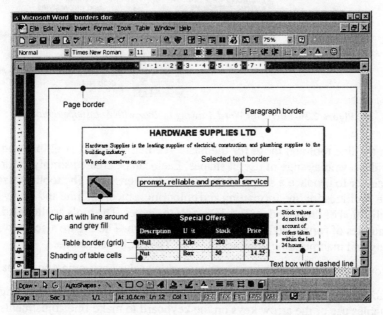

Figure 2.29. *Use of borders, lines and shading with a variety of page elements*

Microsoft Word distinguishes between borders and *lines*. Figure 2.29 refers to lines in respect of text boxes and graphics objects because the package procedures for formatting them are different from those relating to page, paragraph and text. The clip art graphic of the hammer has a line around it and a grey *fill* has also been applied. A text box also counts as a drawing object and can be filled with a colour in the same way.

Graphics tools

Although you may use a specialist graphic design or drawing package to produce illustrations and diagrams, word processors provide drawing tools, which are adequate for most purposes. Figure 2.30 shows part of a typical drawing toolbar and some arrow autoshapes.

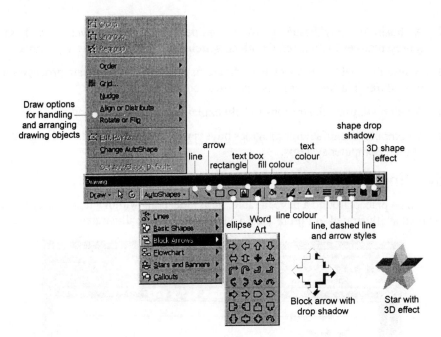

Figure 2.30. *Microsoft Word drawing toolbar with Autoshape options*

Apart from the line tool and those for the basic geometric shapes of ellipse and rectangle, Word provides a whole range of useful shapes. Each can be created simply by dragging the cross-hair cursor to produce a shape of the required dimensions. The toolbar also includes, for example, facilities for line formatting and colouring, object fill, line and arrow formatting and the application of drop shadow and 3D effect to shapes. The tools are labelled in the Figure and examples of formatted autoshapes are also shown. The Figure also shows the menu for arranging and manipulating graphics objects. The facilities include:

❑   grouping. Objects can be grouped to enable easier positioning on the page.

❑   nudging. Rather than using the mouse for precise positioning the nudge option enables use of the arrow keys on the keyboard to make fine adjustments.

❑   ordering. Objects can be layered, that is placed on top of one another. The order of layering can then be altered, moving objects towards the front or the back.

❑   rotation. Objects produced with the drawing tools can be rotated (freely or though 90°) or flipped horizontally or vertically. Imported graphics, such as clip art cannot be rotated. If you produce a graphic in another package and wish to rotate it, you must do so in the source package before importing.

❑   align and distribute. Multiple drawing objects can be selected and then aligned, for example, to the left, right, centre, top, middle or bottom, They can also be distributed, for example, evenly across the space between the first and last object in the group.

Importing text and graphics

Although modern word processors include facilities normally associated with desktop publishing, graphic design and drawing packages, it is sometimes necessary and desirable to import images from a specialist package. Similarly, although a word processor may include facilities for simple spreadsheet-type calculations (see Tables) and simple database sorting, you are likely to use specialist spreadsheet and database packages for such work. It is important that data can be transferred from one package to another, to avoid any re-entry or editing of data. For example, if you are preparing a report on personnel issues in an organisation and need to include some actual data from a personnel database, you should be able to import that data into your document. Commonly, imported images are either *objects* or *pictures* (depending on their format).

Clip art

Microsoft Word refers to all clip art files as pictures, although some are *bit map* and others are *vector* images which differ in the ways in which they can be manipulated and edited. These types of file are described in the following paragraphs. The Clip Gallery in Microsoft Word also gives access to photographs (which are always bit maps), video sequences and sounds.

Bit maps

Bit maps include some clip art images, drawings produced with 'paint' software and other digital images, such as scanned pictures, photographs taken with a digital camera and individual frames captured from a video sequence. Also, graphics produced with a *vector-based* (see later) drawing package, such as CorelDRAW, can be *exported* as bit maps. A bit map comprises a fixed number of *pixels* (or picture elements), and the computer sets each one to a particular colour, to form the image. In the case of greyscale images, each pixel is set to a black, white or one of a number of shades of grey. There are numerous file formats used to store bit map images. These formats are often named according to the *file extension* (*.ext*) which is attached to the filename when a file is saved in a particular format. Common examples include:

❑ *.bmp* files can be stored using a variety of colour depths: black and white; 256 shades of grey; 16, 256, 16 million and 6.8 billion colours. The memory occupied by the latter format is much higher than those using, for example, 16 or 256 colours. Figure 2.31 shows a bitmap image using 256 shades of grey.

Figure 2.31.
Bitmap image

❑ *.pcx*. This is the file format for Windows Paintbrush;

❑ *.jpg*. (JPEG - Joint Photographic Experts Group). This type uses a standard for still-image compression, known as the JPEG algorithm and is widely used on the Internet. It allows the use of 16 million colours which makes it suitable for digitised photographs. JPEG images can be compressed but with loss of quality. A Web page designer has to strike a balance between obtaining a good quality image and a file size which will not take too long to download. It is common practice to use a very small 'thumbnail' image which appears almost immediately and which the Web user can click on to download an enlarged image.

❏   *.gif* (Graphic Image File). This type was promoted by CompuServe, a major Internet service provider, and is still widely used for still images on the Internet. A maximum of 256 colours can be used, which is adequate for images made up of blocks of colour, but photographs and images with graduated shading are not suitable for .gif format. Images can be made transparent, which allows the background colour to show through a specified colour within the image. Word processed document pages or Web pages with a background colour other than white will use

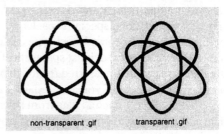

Figure 2.32. Opaque and transparent .gif images

transparent images to achieve this effect. Otherwise, the image will always appear within a rectangle. Figure 2.32 shows the results of using a transparent and non-transparent GIF on a coloured background.

❏   *animated .gif.* Used extensively in web pages, an animated gif contains one file with multiple frames and each frame contains a different image (or different aspect of the same image). The effect of animation is achieved by cycling rapidly through the frames (the speed can be varied), which is the basis of all traditional cartoon animations.

Vector graphics

Vectored images are drawn by setting coordinate points, or vectors. A two-dimensional (2-D) drawing requires the setting of y-coordinates (the vertical position) and x-coordinates (the horizontal position). A three-dimensional image (3-D) needs a third vector for the depth, a z-coordinate. An image consists of a number of lines drawn between a number of x, y and, in the case of 3-D, z coordinates. By altering vector values, an image can be re-scaled and for animation purposes, moved around the screen. Figure 2.33 shows a vector clip art image and the separate drawing objects after *ungrouping*.

Figure 2.33. Vector clip art image and ungrouped objects

Manipulating clip art

Figure 2.34 shows an imported clip art picture and the Picture toolbar in Microsoft Word for formatting and manipulating the image. Note the *transparency tool* which achieves the same effect as a transparent gif. The ways in which the image can be manipulated are limited to re-sizing and *cropping*; any imported object or picture will be placed at the current position of the insertion point and can only be moved freely on the page if a 'float over text' option is chosen. Clip art images cannot be rotated within Microsoft Word, although the operation could be carried out in a drawing or graphic design package before importing the image. Graphics produced with the word processor's own drawing tools can be rotated.

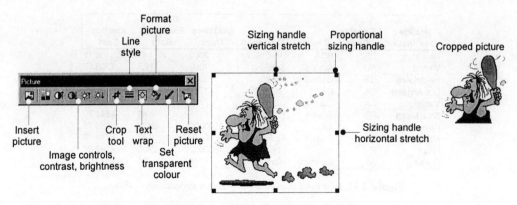

Figure 2.34. *Clip art and formatting tools*

Importing drawing objects and object linking

Figure 2.35 shows a drawing produced with CorelDraw and then imported into this document and the same drawing after re-sizing. Modern operating systems allow you to edit an imported object without quitting the word processor, or separately loading the drawing package. Double clicking on the drawing automatically opens the drawing application and the drawing can be edited; when editing is finished and you return to the document, the image is automatically updated (you can choose that this does not happen). This *object linking and embedding* (OLE), as it is known, can be carried out with any package which supports this type of operation.

Figure 2.35. *Imported CorelDraw object and re-sized image*

Word Art

Text can be entered as an artistic image, rather than as normal paragraph text. It is treated as an object, in the same way as other imported images, even though the program which produces it (Microsoft WordArt) is accessed from within the word processor itself. Figure 2.36 shows an examples of this 'word art'. As with other objects produced within the word processor itself, Word Art images can be rotated.

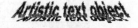

Figure 2.36. *Word Art example*

Importing spreadsheet and database files

The simplest way to import spreadsheet and database data into a document is to use the *clipboard* which allows cutting, copying and pasting. The relevant data is highlighted within the relevant package, before the copy command is executed. The data is then pasted into the document within the word processor; you can switch between the applications using the operating system's multi-tasking facility. Table 2.37 shows imported data from the Excel spreadsheet.

Holiday Destination	Country Code	Country	Currency	Currency Cost	Current Exchange Rate	Sterling Cost
New York	US	USA	US Dollar	2000	1.42	£1,408.45
Vienna	AU	Austria	Schilling	4000	17.5	£228.57
Heidelberg	GE	Germany	Mark	3600	2.5	£1,440.00
Los Angeles	US	USA	US Dollar	1750	1.42	£1,232.39
Vancouver	CA	Canada	Can. Dollar	2750	1.9	£1,447.37
Strasbourg	FR	France	Fr. Franc	5175	8.46	£611.70
Florence	IT	Italy	Lire	1600000	2425	£659.79
Marseilles	FR	France	Fr. Franc	6275	8.46	£741.73
Milan	IT	Italy	Lire	1850000	2425	£762.89
Frieberg	GE	Germany	Mark	1245	2.5	£498.00

Figure 2.37. *Imported (linked object) Excel spreadsheet table*

If the data can been pasted into the document as an *object of the source application* (the spreadsheet or database), it can be edited by double clicking on the object. Depending on the package you are using, the editing may be *embedded* (see Figure 2.38) within the word processor, or the application may be opened in a separate window.

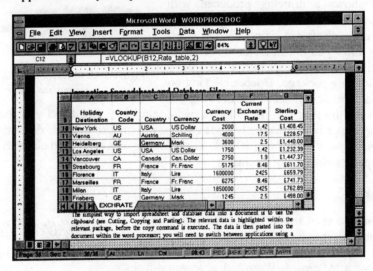

Figure 2.38. *Spreadsheet object being edited within the word processor*

If you paste the data simply as text, the spreadsheet cells are converted to a word processor table and the contents can be edited within the word processor. However, no link is established with the source package. The same applies to records pasted from the Access database.

✍️Self-test questions

1. List and briefly explain the function of the components you would expect to find in Page Setup.
2. What is a *true type* font and what particular benefit does the type provide?
3. Explain how paragraph formatting can remove the need to insert blank lines between paragraphs.
4. What is the role of hyphenation in justified text?
5. Distinguish between a first line indent, a paragraph indent and a hanging indent.
6. Suggest a document type which may make use of tabulation.
7. What is the function of a style palette?
8. Suggest example documents which may make use of multiple columns.
9. Explain the variety of ways in which a table can be formatted.
10. a. List and briefly describe the features of word processing tables which you would expect to find in a spreadsheet.
    b. Identify any limitations inherent in the spreadsheet functions which your word processor includes.
11. Identify the options for text flow in respect of text boxes.
12. Suggest circumstances when a watermark would be used.
13. a. With the aid of an example, describe the basic operation of a document wizard.
    b. Why may a document wizard not meet a user's exact requirements?
    c. Explain the different options for the creation of a document template.
    d. How can templates support the maintenance of an organisation's corporate image?
14. Explain the operation and benefits of a word processor's *outline* facility.
15. Suggest typical contents of a left and right page headers in a multi-page document.
16. What is meant by the term 'running heads'?
17. When would you use a footnote or endnote? Give an example.
18. Define the terms *widow* and *orphan*.
19. Distinguish between a *hard* and a *soft page break*.
20. Briefly describe the process of creating a contents table using your word processor's automatic facility.
21. What is an index marker?
22. What are the benefits and drawbacks of using a concordance file to automark index entries.
23. Describe the function of an
    a. appendix;
    b. glossary.
24. Define the graphics terms: grouping; nudging; ordering; rotation; align; distribute.
25. When is it useful to use a *transparent gif* image?
26. What is OLE and why is it useful?

Chapter 3

Designing slide presentations

A slide presentation package, such as Microsoft PowerPoint, enables the user to create, assemble and run slide shows on a computer screen, either automatically, or under user control. Apart from on-screen presentations, individual slides can be printed with a conventional printer, or be transferred to acetate sheets for display on an overhead projector, or be output as 35mm slides. It has to be said that significant communication impact is lost if on-screen display is not used. On-screen displays are dynamic and can include text, graphics, animations, video sequences and sound, as well as hyperlinks (text or images which can be mouse clicked to jump to another part of the presentation, to a different presentation or indeed, to other sources of information, such as a Web site). A presentation can be viewed passively or with user interaction. Colour, movement and sound can all contribute to get your message across. Facilities also include various screen 'wipes', 'zooms' and 'dissolves' (commonly available with camcorders). Images can be produced or taken from a library within the package, or they may be produced in another application and then imported. The three Figures show some of the features of a sample slide show.

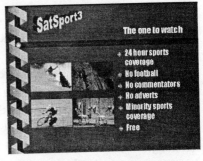

Figure 3.1. *Opening slide*

Figure 3.2. *Second slide*

Figure 3.3. *Closing slide*

The main facilities you need are:

❏ *Backgrounds.* You can select a background from a library provided with the package, or create your own. Most of the backgrounds in the library are only suitable for screen presentation, because, that is the way they are meant to be used.

If you do want to print them, you should probably design one of your own, using only limited shading; heavy use of colour and shading does not print well in monochrome. A colour printer, on the other hand, should produce satisfactory results. The package may provide in-built facilities for you to create your own backgrounds, or you may have to create them in another graphics package and then import them using OLE (Object Linking and Embedding), to allow access to the source package and editing of the image.

❑ *Graphics objects from other packages*. This includes clip art and other images created with other software. The appropriate import filters must be available to convert one form of image to another.

❑ *Text entered within the package*. The usual text formatting facilities are available, including the facility to add bullets to listed items.

❑ *Sound and animation.* The package may allow the inclusion of sound objects and animation sequences created with a package, such as CorelMOVE.

❑ *Slide sorter*. This facility allows you to insert or delete slides and change their sequence.

❑ *Run screen show*. This starts the display, one after another, of the slides you have included in your show. You can set a standard time for the display of each slide or use a *timeline* to set individual timings for each slide.

❑ *Transition effects*. These are commonly available with camcorders and provide various screen 'wipe' or 'dissolve' modes to smooth the transition between slides.

The following features are specific to PowerPoint, but illustrates the ways in which presentations can be developed.

❑ PowerPoint provides a number of standard slide layouts, with text boxes and places to insert pictures. These can be altered or you can create your own. Alternatively, a slide can be set up with preset entry points for text and graphics, using an AutoLayout. A standard layout can be altered by moving, resizing, deleting or inserting text boxes or graphics frames.

❑ Animations can be applied to both text and picture objects.

❑ When you insert a blank slide, it will use the same template as the others and have the same background, thus ensuring consistency across the presentation.

❑ Clip art, photographs, sounds and video sequences are all accessible through the Insert | Picture menu.

Slide presentation design

A presentation needs to be carefully designed to take into account its content and the target audience. It is helpful to consider the following questions and guidelines.

1. Is the user going to browse through and control the flow of the presentation or will the show be controlled by a presenter with spoken commentary? The answer to this question will affect the content of slides - if there is spoken commentary,

supplementary information can be provided without cluttering up the slide with too much information.

2. Is the information provided in the presentation regarded as important or of real interest to the audience? Careful use of animation and, where possible, sound can provide impact and prevent the audience from slipping into a deep sleep. On the other hand, fancy effects can distract the audience from the content of a message.

3. Images should be carefully chosen to suit the subject and the target audience. Cartoon images can add a little humour, but may distract from a serious message. On the other hand effective use of cartoon images can 'lighten' the presentation of what is otherwise a serious subject.

4. Text font styles and sizes should be consistent and appropriate to the presentation. A wild array of several font styles will simply make the text more difficult to read.

5. Don't pack too much information onto one slide and keep the font size large enough for the audience to read, taking into account the distance that they will be from the screen.

6. Good use of colour is more difficult for some, but provided colours are not too garish and text fonts contrast sufficiently with the background to make text legible, then the effect should never be too objectionable.

7. Timing of slide changes and animations within slides is also important if the user is not controlling its progress. You will need to check time delays to give the audience time to absorb the message on each slide. Excessive delays between slide changes are likely to be irritating.

✎ Self-test questions

1. A company uses a presentation package to produce slide shows for use in its training programmes. The package includes many features to aid the construction and running of a show, including *master slide*, *transitions*, *buttons*, *hotspots*, *backgrounds*, *templates*, *text*, *graphics* and *animations*.
    a. Define each of the italicised terms.
    b. Explain the options for controlling a slide presentation and comment on the benefits and drawbacks of each option.
2. List the types of object which can be included in a slide presentation.

Chapter 4

Managing information

All organisations need to transmit information internally, for example, from sales to accounts departments and to external agencies and individuals, such as the Inland Revenue, suppliers, customers and clients. Although each organisation is likely to have some specialist information requirements, there are some document forms and standards which are common to most. They include, for example, invoices, formal letters, order forms, credit notes, Annual Accounts statements and memoranda.

There are also certain organisations, for example, engineering companies, architects and component manufacturers that make extensive use of technical drawings and illustrations, whilst most organisations make use of illustrations, pictures and art work for advertising and the promotion of their products and services.

The preceding chapters in this Unit have concentrated on the presentation of information for a variety of purposes and audiences. This chapter is concerned with managing information from its point of collection to its transmission to the end user. Through the use of a business scenario, we examine:

❑ the need for presentation standards for internal and external communication;

❑ the types of information organisations need to operate effectively and the documents they use to gather, present and communicate each type;

❑ the need to acknowledge receipt of information;

❑ typical uses of illustrations, technical drawings, pictures and art work;

❑ the methods of presenting a corporate image.

Scenario: Eco Holidays

Eco Holidays is a holiday company specialising in eco-friendly holidays, that is they are not all-inclusive, but make use of privately owned accommodation and eating places rather than hotels owned by multi-national corporations. Their holiday researchers are native to the holiday destinations and have the local knowledge to ensure that holidays are organised in a way which harmonises with and is not offensive to the local populations. Activities on the holidays are particularly designed to avoid damage to the environment.

The company is producing a publicity flyer for the new season and a number of departments are involved, directly or indirectly, with the process. The flyer is to be sent to all the major travel agents and holiday operators in the UK.

Figure 4.1 illustrates the various types of information which have to pass between staff and departments and between Eco Holidays and external bodies.

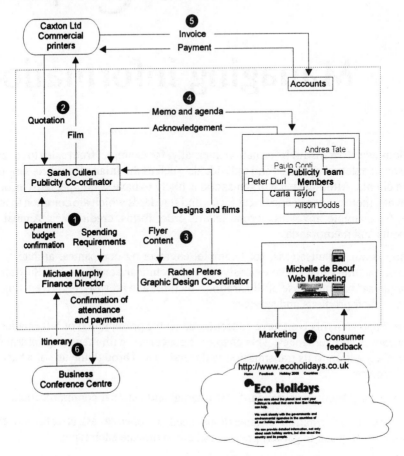

Figure 4.1. *Information flows in Eco Holidays*

The following sections explain the information flows (numbered from 1 to 7 in the Figure). Each explanation includes an illustration of the documents used, comments on their content, major components, layout and style. Appropriate methods of communication, such as e-mail and fax are also identified.

The order of the sections does not necessarily reflect the likely order of events in the scenario.

1. Cash budget and memorandum

Sarah Cullen, Publicity Co-ordinator sends details for her spending requirements for the year to Michael Murphy, Finance Director. To allow the calculation of totals, the information could be produced in a spreadsheet and then imported into a word processor for final document production. As this is a purely internal matter and urgent, she decides to send the budget details by e-mail as a spreadsheet attachment. The e-mail is shown in Figure 4.2 and the spreadsheet budget in Figure 4.3.

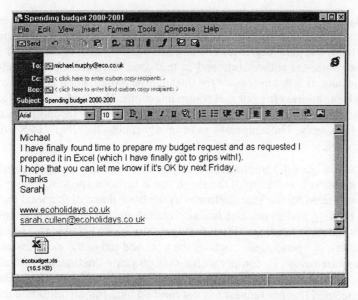

Figure 4.2. *E-mail from Sara Cullen to Michael Murphy concerning spending budget*

The email reads:

> Michael
> I have finally found time to prepare my budget request and as requested I prepared it in Excel (which I have finally got to grips with!).
> I hope that you can let me know if it's OK by next Friday.
> Thanks
> Sarah
>
> www.ecoholidays.co.uk
> sarah.cullen@ecoholidays.co.uk

Attachment: ecobudget.xls (16.5 KB)

Microsoft Excel - Publicity Budget.xls

C5 = Printing

Sarah Cullen - Publicity Co-ordinator

Anticipated Spending Requirements Apr 2000 - Mar 2001   £ 19,965

Stationery	Photo copying	Printing	Postage	Travel Expenses	Hospitality	Leasing PCs x 6
£ 1,825	£ 1,160	£ 9,000	£ 335	£ 3,700	£ 645	£ 3,300

	Apr	May	Jun	Jul	Aug	Sep
Stationery	£ 200	£ 200	£ 200	£ 200	£ 100	£ 75
Photocopying	£ 120	£ 120	£ 120	£ 120	£ 80	£ 60
Printing	£ 500	£ 500	£ 500	£ 3,000	£ 500	£ 300
Postage	£ 35	£ 35	£ 35	£ 35	£ 35	£ 20
Travel Expenses	£ 750	£ 300	£ 200	£ 750	£ 50	£ 50
Hospitality	£ 25	£ 25	£ 25	£ 25	£ 25	£ 70
Leasing PCs x 6	£ 200	£ 200	£ 200	£ 200	£ 200	£ 200
Monthly Totals	£ 1,830	£ 1,380	£ 1,280	£ 4,330	£ 990	£ 775

	Oct	Nov	Dec	Jan	Feb	Mar
Stationery	£ 75	£ 75	£ 150	£ 150	£ 200	£ 200
Photocopying	£ 60	£ 60	£ 90	£ 90	£ 120	£ 120
Printing	£ 2,000	£ 300	£ 500	£ 300	£ 300	£ 300
Postage	£ 20	£ 20	£ 20	£ 20	£ 30	£ 30
Travel Expenses	£ 50	£ 50	£ 200	£ 750	£ 400	£ 150
Hospitality	£ 80	£ 25	£ 25	£ 40	£ 200	£ 80
Leasing PCs x 6	£ 350	£ 350	£ 350	£ 350	£ 350	£ 350
Monthly Totals	£ 2,635	£ 880	£ 1,335	£ 1,700	£ 1,600	£ 1,230

Sheet1 / Sheet2 / Sheet3

Figure 4.3. *Spending requirements for Publicity Department*

The writing style in the e-mail is informal, partly because the medium tends to encourage informality, but more importantly because the communication is internal and few organisations today use personal titles. The important components in the e-mail are the recipient's e-mail address, the subject line and in this case, the attached spreadsheet file. The signature at the bottom is not necessary for this internal e-mail, but it is useful to include the company's web site address for external communications. The sender's e-mail address helps to reinforce the corporate image established by the domain name (ecoholidays.co.uk) and is not necessary for a reply. The recipient would simply choose the 'Reply to Sender' option in the e-mail software.

The spreadsheet in Figure 4.3 emphasise the importance of setting out facts clearly. The most important information is at the top of the sheet, that is the total spending figure Sarah anticipates that she will need for the year, followed by the breakdown of that total into areas, such as stationery, printing and so on. She has also made careful use of borders and shading to highlight totals and main headings. The monthly details are included so that Michael Murphy can see the pattern of spending throughout the year and judge the department's cash flow (Chapter 11) requirements. To comply with e-mail etiquette ('netiquette'), Michael Murphy should acknowledge Sarah's message as soon as he has checked his mailbox. Otherwise, Sarah may be concerned that her request has not reached him. For an important matter such as the approval of a departmental budget, it is likely that Michael will also reply with a printed document, probably a memo as shown in Figure 4.4. It is not essential for a memo to be signed, but in this case Sarah Cullen needs to know that her budget is properly authorised.

MEMORANDUM

TO: Sarah Cullen, Publicity Co-ordinator   Date: Feb 24, 2000

FROM: Michael Murphy, Finance Director

SUBJECT: Departmental budget 2000 - 2001

I am pleased to confirm that your anticipated spending figures have been accepted and that your budget for 2000 - 2001 is **£20,000**. As usual, you will need to submit details of actual spending every two months, beginning with 31 May 2000.

Michael Murphy

Figure 4.4. *Memorandum confirming budget figure for Publicity Department*

2. Quotation and hand-written note

Caxton Ltd have sent a quotation to Sarah for the printing of 2000, A4, double-sided, full colour flyers, which are being designed in-house. The quotation is shown in Figure 4.5 and has been faxed to Eco Holidays. Caxton do work regularly for Sarah, hence the informal close "Regards, Anna Kalenski". However, as an offer to make a contract, the detail is precise and an order number is provided.

```
13-04-00 14 : 32 Caxton Commercial Printers Ltd   ID=01207 356288
```

Press House, King's Mews, SE16 1LJ,
Phone: 01207 356217, Fax: 01207 356288

Caxton Commercial Printers

Fax

To:	Sarah Cullen, Eco Holidays	**From:**	Anna Kalenski
Fax:	01207 3138854	**Date:**	July 1, 2000
Re:	A4 Full colour, leaflet	**CC:**	

☐ **Urgent**   ☐ **For Review**   ☐ **Please Comment**   ☑ **Please Reply**   ☐ **Please Recycle**

Dear Sarah,

Our prices for the printing of full colour, A4, double-sided leaflets on 150gsm white gloss artpaper are as follows.

Price for: 2000   £275.00

The above price does not include artwork unless stated. VAT will be charged at the standard rate where applicable. We would need three days notice and would complete the work in 5 days. If this is acceptable, please quote Order No: 00313 when you send the film.

Regards,

Anna Kalenski

Anna Kalenski

Figure 4.5. *Printing quotation sent by fax*

In response to the quotation, Sarah simply rang Anna to accept the quotation and confirmed that she would send the film (needed for printing the leaflets) by courier. To ensure that the film is identified correctly, she will attach a covering note on the Company's headed paper, quoting the Order Number 000313. The regular contact between the businesses allows for a degree of informality and Sarah will simply write the note by hand (but still takes care with spelling and grammar).

3. Draft and final design of flyer

Sarah Cullen and her team have been working on the content for the publicity flyer and will be meeting again once the designs have been prepared by the graphic design team. A member of Sarah Cullen's team has produced the draft flyer in a word processor, and the design team will then import the text into a desktop publishing package; this is to enable the production of the necessary film for printing.

The draft and final flyer designs are shown in Figures 4.6 and 4.7, respectively. The Publicity team are concerned primarily with content, so little time has been spent on layout and presentation, which are part of the design team's function. Apart from the text, the draft indicates the location of the main graphics, which have already been chosen, but will require some processing by the graphics team. The final designs have to be approved by Sarah Cullen before the films are produced and sent to Caxton Commercial Printers.

<Company logo>

Holiday 2000

Experience the excitement of South Africa and its wildlife at the

Simbamili Lodge in the Sabi Game Reserve

Simbambili is to be found on the Sabi Sand Game Reserve by the Manyeleti River.

<picture elephant>

The luxury, air-conditioned and glass-fronted chalets give fine views across the river bed (it is dry sometimes) and the watering holes visited by a great variety of wildlife, including elephant, giraffe and lion.

Figure 4.6. *Part of draft content for publicity flyer*

Eco Holidays ²⁰⁰⁰

Experience the excitement of South Africa and its wildlife at the

Simbamili Lodge
Sabi Game Reserve

Simbambili is to be found on the Sabi Sand Game Reserve by the Manyeleti River. The luxury, air-conditioned and glass-fronted chalets give fine views across the river bed (it is dry sometimes) and the watering holes are visited by a great variety of wildlife, including elephant, giraffe, and lion.

Figure 4.7. *Part of finished flyer*

The writing and presentation style is restrained as is appropriate to the market at which the flyer is aimed and the image of the company. Publicising a theme park or beach holiday would require a much more flamboyant and 'punchy' style and the use of 'fun' graphics and colours.

4. Memorandum and agenda

Having received the flyer proofs from the Rachel Peters, Sarah Cullen calls a meeting of her publicity team. She has prepared special e-mail stationery using an extract from the flyer (coded in HTML, which is used to control the appearance of Web pages), partly to let the team have a 'sneak preview', but primarily because she intends to use e-mail to further emphasise the corporate image of Eco Holidays. The flyer image is a demonstration of how this can be done. The e-mail is sent with an attached agenda to all the team members.

Figures 4.8 and 4.9 show the e-mail and agenda, respectively.

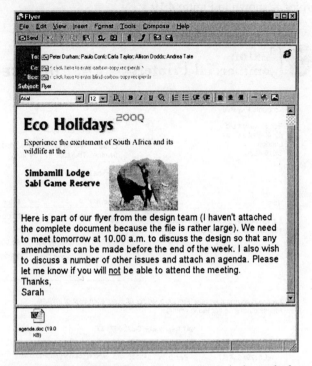

Figure 4.8. *E-mail with HTML stationery and attached agenda document*

Publicity Team Meeting, Room A32, 10.00 a.m. Board Room

AGENDA

1. South African safari flyer

2. Spending budget 2000 - 2001

3. Annual leave

4. A.O.B.

Figure 4.9. *Agenda for Publicity Team meeting*

The format is similar to the example of a Parish Council agenda in Chapter 1, but less formal. The above example makes no mention of minutes, although this is not the usual practice. Presumably, the management of the company do not require formal minutes when the primary purpose of a meeting is the giving of information. Apart from the discussion of the flyer design, the other items are not matters for discussion.

5. Invoice and payment

Having completed the printing of the flyers, Caxton Commercial printers send an invoice to Eco Holidays for the quoted amount. The invoice is processed by the Accounts department, but before paying it they need to reconcile the amount with the quotation. To allow for this,

Sarah sends a copy of the quotation and confirmation of its acceptance to the Accounts department. The invoice is shown in Figure 4.10

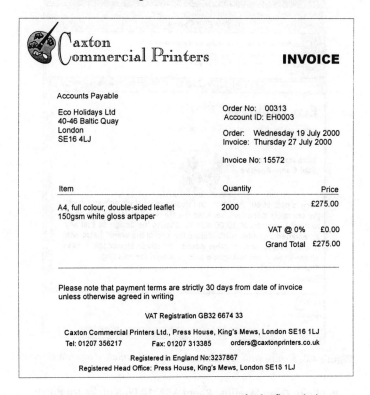

Figure 4.10. *Invoice requesting payment for leaflet printing*

The layout of the invoice is fairly standard and contains a number of important items of information.

❑ Accounts payable. The name and address beneath this item identifies the person or organisation who must settle (pay) the invoice.

❑ Order No. This enables the Accounts department at Eco Holidays to match the invoice to a particular order. The original quotation from Caxton quoted the same Order No.

❑ Account ID. This indicates a credit account, that is one whereby Caxton allow the customers a period of credit (30 days in this case) to settle the invoice. It may be that Eco Holidays have more than one such account with Caxton.

❑ Order date and invoice date. The invoice date can be used to determine when payment should be made, in this case 30 days after 27 July 2000.

❑ Invoice No. If Eco Holidays contact Caxton about the invoice, they should quote that number and use it when they send payment. This allows Caxton to match the payments they receive with particular invoices and accounts.

- [ ] Item, quantity and price. There may be several items beneath which are then totalled before adding VAT.

- [ ] VAT @ 0%. Value Added Tax is charged on certain goods, although in respect of printing it is generally zero rated. The VAT registration number must be recorded on all Caxton's business stationery.

- [ ] 'Please note that payment terms .....'. These are known as Credit Terms and indicate the time the debtor is given to settle the invoice.

- [ ] Company details. As an incorporated limited company, the details at the bottom of the invoice must be included on all company stationery.

6. Itinerary

Michael Murphy is attending a conference in Zurich and has asked for an itinerary from the conference organisers. Basically, this tells him the route and the times of connections between the various forms of transport he needs to use. The itinerary is shown in Figure 4.11 and is incorporated in a formal letter.

Euro Currency Conference, Zurich, 18 August 2000		
Delegate: Michael Murphy, Eco Holidays Ltd		
17 August check in 0930	Heathrow Airport	Flight BA 3645 Zurich
17 August arrive 1130	Zurich Airport	
17 August	Taxi to Zee Hotel, Zurich	
18 August 0830	Taxi to Conference Centre	
18 August 1730	Taxi to Zee Hotel, Zurich	
19 August 0830	Taxi to Zurich Airport	
19 August check in 1000	Zurich Airport	Flight BA 3525 London, Heathrow
19 August arrive 1300	Heathrow Airport	

Figure 4.11. *Itinerary*

7. Web site and feedback form

Eco Holidays has a web site, primarily to promote the image of the company, to provide potential customers information holiday services and to gather valuable marketing information. This type of site is commonly referred to as a 'brochure' site. There are plans for the development of an e-commerce element to allow on-line booking and payment for holidays. In keeping with the company's image, the Web site home page (Figure 4.12) is uncluttered and simple.

The promotional flyer for the South African safari holiday centre is also featured on the site. Helen de Boeuf is developing a Web marketing strategy for the company and a Feedback page is included to gather information from visitors to the site. It is hoped that responses will suggest new ways in which holiday requirements of consumers can be met, within the company's ethical policy. Once the e-commerce site is operational, then on-line bookings will be an important way of gathering vital marketing information. The Feedback form is shown in Figure 4.13. To encourage visitors to complete the form, Eco Holidays is offering information packs on the countries

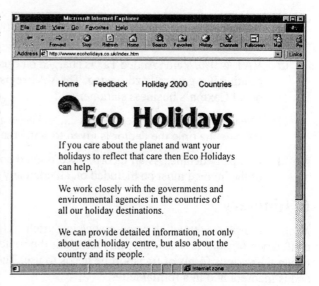

Figure 4.12. *Home page of www.ecoholidays.co.uk*

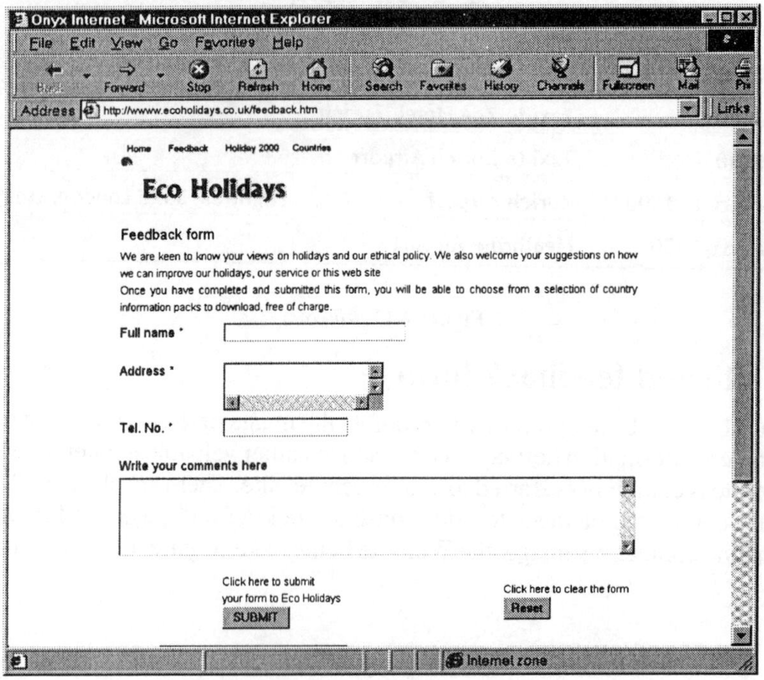

which they use as holiday centres. These packs can be downloaded from the site once the form has been completed. When the 'submit' button is clicked, the form's contents are transmitted as an e-mail to Helen de Boeuf's department.

Figure 4.13. *Feedback form*

Self-test questions

1. Suggest ways in which e-mail be used re-inforce a company's corporate image.
2. What is an e-mail attachment? Give three examples.
3. Comment on the advisability of using a word processor table to prepare the budget illustrated in Figure 4.3.
4. Identify one benefit and one drawback of using fax as opposed to e-mail.
5. What is the purpose of preparing a *draft* document?
6. The Purchasing Department of Acme Systems places an order with a supplier and sends a copy of the order to Acme's accounts department. Why is this necessary?
7. List four categories of information you would expect to find on an invoice.
8. What is an *itinerary*. Briefly describe an example.
9. Suggest two benefits of using a web site for marketing.

Chapter 5

Standard ways of working

Work organisation

If you organise your thinking, your time and your filing systems, the creativity, imagination and hard work you put into a task are more likely to achieve the results you want. Without organisation, some efforts will be wasted, work will often be completed behind schedule and the final product will be poorer. In employment you will be expected to complete tasks to a certain standard, possibly using particular procedures and to schedule. If you are self-employed, you will need to impose these standards on yourself.

Analysing the task

This requires a detailed analysis of the task objectives, to determine the solutions to achieve them. It is helpful to break the task down into smaller component parts, identify possible solutions, evaluate them and either accept or reject them. For example, you may need to produce some vector graphics and have the options of using a word processor's built-in drawing tools or those of a specialist drawing package. If much of the task involves use of the word processor and the graphics are not complicated, then you may decide on the first option. In any event, it is important that you think ahead and try to identify, if possible, the most efficient route.

Task analysis is an *iterative* process, as decisions on one aspect of the task may require a re-examination of other aspects. The formal method of analysing a problem into progressively smaller components is known as *top-down design*, a method you will use in many aspects of ICT work. When planning the production of a report, for example, you can use the outlining (Chapter) facility which may be provided by your word processor.

Analysis also requires that a sequence of activities is identified for the achievement of each task component, as well as the resources which are needed (such as programs and information sources) at various points in the sequence. This is known as *scheduling*.

Planning a schedule

The aim of a schedule is to plan the timing of events, activities and resource usage, such that a particular aspect of your task is competed at a particular time. A task is likely to consist of several separate 'strands', each occupying a slice of your time and attention. These 'strands' of work need to be co-ordinated, or properly related. If we say that someone is uncoordinated, we mean that their various physical movements do not properly relate to one another. Lack of physical co-ordination manifests itself in clumsiness, and for example, an inability to dance or do gymnastics. Co-ordination of your work, therefore, means ensuring that the various task 'strands' on which you are working, are related and complement one another. Loss of co-ordination may mean that you work extremely hard on one 'strand' which bears little relation to and does not properly contribute to, the progress of the whole task.

Organising your filing system

A system of directories or folders allows you to manage the storage of information on you computer. The Microsoft Windows 9x operating system provides Windows Explorer for accessing, creating, renaming, copying and moving folders and files held within them. You need to ensure that your folder structure reflects your work needs and if others share your files, the structure should be agreeable to you all. In general, you should ensure that there is a logic to the structures and that the folder and file names you use reflect and remind you of their contents. 'Jokey' file names may be amusing but do not give an image of competence and professionalism.

To allow efficient access to files through applications, it can be helpful to set the 'file locations' setting within the package to the folder which you most frequently need to access. For example, if you are working on a spreadsheet project over a number of weeks, it makes sense to direct the 'Open File' dialogue box to the directory where the project files are held.

Allowing for modification

A major benefit of computer-produced information is that it can be readily modified. This benefit can be made even more important if you develop your documents and other projects in ways which allow them to be easily modified. The use of styles and templates is key to simple modification. For example, altering the appearance of a lengthy document which uses Heading and Body Text styles is simple if all you have to do is alter the style definitions. If, on the other hand, you have formatted each heading separately, you will have make each alteration separately. Layout modifications are also simplified if proper use is made of, for example, tabulation and tables. This means, for example, aligning items in a list by using tab positions or a table, rather than the space bar. To alter the alignment of tabulated items simply requires movement of the tab position on the ruler (Chapter 32) or a column position in the table.

Keeping information secure

It is important that you:

❑ prevent loss of data files caused by software or procedural errors, or by physical hazards;

❑ protect data from accidental or deliberate disclosure to unauthorised individuals or groups;

❑ protect the data from accidental or deliberate corruption or modification. This is known as maintaining *data integrity*;

❑ protect the rights of individuals and organisations to restrict access to information which relates to them and is of a private nature, to those entitled or authorised to receive it. This is known as *data privacy*.

Potential causes of data loss

Data loss may be caused by:

❑   environmental hazards such as fire, flood and other natural accidents;

❑   mechanical problems, for example the danger of storage media damage caused by a drive unit malfunction;

❑   software errors resulting from programming error;

❑   human error, for example, loading of the wrong file, using the wrong program version, mislaying or physically damaging storage media;

❑   malicious damage. It is not unknown for people to intentionally damage storage media or to misuse programs at a terminal.

❑   computer virus. There are literally thousands of viruses designed to create nuisance or destroy data.

Measures to prevent data loss

There are a number of measures which you can take to minimise the risk of data loss and these are described in the following paragraphs.

Security backups

Make frequent backup copies of important data files and keep program disks secure. Although most software is now provided on CD-ROM and can not be damaged by magnetic fields, the recording surfaces are still delicate and should be kept in a suitable case to prevent scratching.

Keep backup copies of data files in a secure place, both to prevent damage from the hazards outline earlier and to prevent loss or theft. Make sure that you save your work regularly to avoid accidental loss. Sometimes software 'hangs up' - it just stops working and you have to restart your computer. If this happens you will very likely lose any changes that you have made to your work since you last saved it. Saving work regularly reduces the amount of work that you have to redo if this happens.

If you are developing a document or program, it is also a good idea to keep copies of it under different names as it evolves. For example, you might think of a way to improve a macro. So you record it again making the changes and then save it using the same name as before. Then you find that the 'improvement' wasn't such a good idea, or it doesn't work and you want to return to the original version. Effectively, you have lost data because you replaced the original by the new version. Using a different name for the new macro would have prevented this problem from arising.

Make important files 'read only'. In Windows Explorer, for example, right clicking on the selected file reveals a pop-up menu from which you can choose 'Properties'. To make the file 'read only', check mark the relevant attribute box. You will then be able to load the file into its application, but you will not be able to make alterations without removing the read only attribute. You can still delete the file in Windows Explorer, but you will given a warning prompt and asked to confirm the action.

Computer virus protection

A computer virus is program code designed to create nuisance for users, or more seriously, to effect varying degrees of damage to files stored on magnetic media. Files downloaded from *bulletin boards* on the Internet may be infected and uncontrolled use of these services is likely to result in the receipt of viruses.

A feature of all viruses is that they replicate themselves. Once into the computer's memory, it transfers from memory on to any integral storage device, such as a hard disk and commonly conceals itself in the boot sector (and sometimes in the partition sector where it is less likely to be traced), from where it can readily infect any other media placed on line in that computer system, whether it be stand-alone or networked. Naturally, any write-protected media cannot be infected.

Some virus codes are merely a nuisance, whilst others are developed specifically to destroy, or make inaccessible, whole filing systems.

Boot sector virus

This type of virus stores itself in the boot sector of the hard drive and so is activated when the system is started up. From there the virus can carry out various types of damage to files on the hard drive and copy itself to any disks accessed from floppy drives. Some are able to change their form to avoid detection by virus detection software. One such virus, Hare, only affects Windows 95 systems and is picked up from Usenet News on the Internet. It activates when an infected machine is booted on the 22nd August or the 22nd September and overwrites the contents of the hard disk.

Macro virus

This is probably the most common type of virus, new ones being reported almost daily. It embeds itself in documents created with general-purpose packages, such as Microsoft Word and Excel, each of which provides its own *macro language* (a type of programming language). The language can be used to automate certain procedures, such as formatting a document in a particular way, or customising the package for a specific application. Macro viruses have the following features.

❏ Once a macro virus has infected a machine, it embeds itself in all documents subsequently created with that machine.

❏ Macro viruses may change or delete file contents, or prevent subsequent saving or opening of a file.

❏ It spreads quickly because so many people use these packages and exchange files on portable media, such as floppy disks and increasingly via e-mail as attachments..

❏ Some macro viruses are of the 'Trojan' variety. They do not reproduce themselves, but destroy or corrupt the data in the infected document as soon as it is opened.

Largely because of the widespread use of Internet e-mail, the macro virus now presents the greatest threat of system infection.

Trojan horse virus

Named after the wooden horse at the siege of Troy, this type of virus does not reproduce it-self, but pretends to be a real application program. Ironically, one such program claims to remove viruses, but in fact introduces viruses into a computer system.

Virus protection software

Figure 5.1 shows an example of a virus protection program, Command Antivirus for Windows.

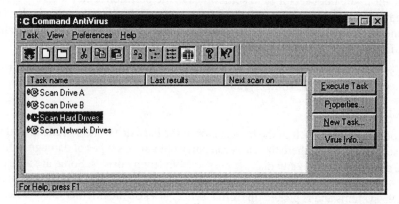

Figure 5.1. *Virus protection software*

As the Figure shows, the software is designed to scan all types of drive connected to a computer system. This means reading and checking the contents of all files, systems and applications, on each disk. Figure 5.2 shows the options available for the scan process. The scanning options allow:

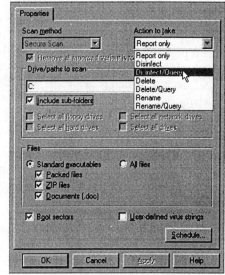

❑ scanning of a particular drive, folder or sub-folder;

❑ the checking of all files, or just executable (program) files. Executables can include zipped or compressed files and .doc files for macro viruses;

❑ checking of the boot sector for viruses of that type;

❑ alternative actions, for example to simply report viruses or report and remove them.

Figure 5.2. *Scan options*

New viruses are continually being produced, so a virus protection program soon becomes out of date. It is vital to have a contract with the software producer, to obtain frequent updates which take account of the latest viruses. Deciding when and how frequently to scan the computer system depends on the level of risk of infection. If users commonly insert floppy disks from other machines, or regularly download information from the Internet, scans should be more frequent than for a system controlled by a single user. Apart from virus protection software, the following safeguards are helpful.

❏ Only use proprietary software from a reliable source.

❏ Disks used for reading purposes only should be write protected.

❏ Use diskless workstations on networks.

❏ Control access to portable media and forbid employees to use their own media on the organisation's computer system.

Controlling access

An obvious way of protecting computer data is to limit access to the computer systems that store it. Access can be restricted physically and methods include, for example, security staff, locks, alarms and video surveillance. Access can also be restricted by procedures. For example, employees must obtain authority, such as a signed form, to obtain access to files which they do not access regularly as part of their jobs and identity cards with photograph and signature must be worn by staff in the building. Software protection examples include:

❏ Swipe cards. These could be identity cards with a magnetic strip, containing personal details and a personal identification number (PIN). Doors may only be opened with the swipe card and keypad entry of the matching PIN. This method is used to control access to service tills at banks.

❏ Personal characteristics. For example, voice recognition or fingerprint comparison provide excellent methods of personal identification.

❏ Password controls. Access to machines, networks, files or programs can be restricted with passwords.

Password protection

To protect all or part of a system against unauthorised access, applications or the operating system may use a password

Figure 5.3 shows the Windows Password Properties tabs.

There are two tabs, one to change passwords and the other detailing the uses of the passwords. There are two options:

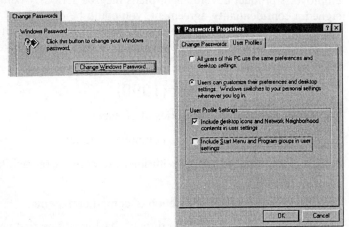

Figure 5.3. *Windows 9x password protection options*

❑   one that all users require the same desktop settings;

❑   that individual users can tailor the desktop to personal requirements, but will be asked for a user-id to log on and a password to gain access. The personalised settings are loaded when a user logs on.

More importantly, password protection may also be used to share a computer's resources (files and programs) between users.

Fault logging and reporting

A common cause of data loss is failure of equipment or software. It is important, therefore, to keep a log of faults, ensuring that each one is attended to as soon as it occurs; you will be able diagnose and deal with some faults yourself, but you should know when to report them to others.

For example, during a file processing operation, you may receive an error message indicating that an attempt to read a particular file has failed. On the assumption that the error is reported by the application rather than the operating system, you are unlikely to receive an exact diagnosis. Assume further that you repeat the operation and at the second attempt not error is indicated. You then decide that it is not worth reporting and the following day the error recurs and the file is lost. If you have made a backup copy, you may recover the file but it is also possible that your backup file is corrupted. It depends on whether the file or the disk storage medium is corrupted.

Maintaining a log of faults and procedures followed to correct them may help to identify fault patterns and avoid similar problems in the future.

Maintaining confidentiality

Confidentiality is important for the protection of personal privacy and in the case of organisations, commercial advantage. For example, informing a competitor organisation about your employer's product development plans may be seriously damaging. Even if you have not signed a confidentiality agreement, you could be disciplined or dismissed from your job. Breaking confidence for monetary gain would be a prosecutable offence. The following paragraphs details the legislation which exists to deter computer crime and protect personal privacy.

Computer Misuse Act (1990)

The Act identifies three categories of offence:

❑   Unauthorised access to computer material.

❑   Unauthorised access with intent to commit or facilitate commission of further offences.

❑   Unauthorised modification of computer material.

The Act deals with the general crime of 'hacking'. The first category of offence deals with unauthorised access to a computer system, its programs and data. An offence is committed if a person performs any computer function with the <u>intent</u> of securing unauthorised access to any program or data held in any computer. The second category covers the offence of persistent hacking. The third category covers the alteration of data to which a hacker has gained access. These crimes are punishable by prison sentences.

Computer fraud and protection measures

Computer fraud is invariably committed for financial gain, but unlike some forms of fraud, the perpetrator(s) will make considerable efforts to prevent discovery of any loss by the victim. The rewards for such efforts may be complete freedom from prosecution, or at least a delay in discovery of the fraud and a consequent chance of escape. Unless proper controls and checks are implemented, computer systems are particularly vulnerable to fraudulent activity, because much of the time processing and its results are hidden. The following section examines some methods for committing fraud and the measures which can be taken to foil them. To extract money from a financial accounting system requires its diversion into fictitious, but accessible accounts. To avoid detection, appropriate adjustments must be made to ensure that the accounts still balance. Sometimes, fraudulent activity may involve the misappropriation of goods rather than cash. Frequently, the collusion of several people is necessary to effect a fraud, because responsibility for different stages of the processing cycle is likely to be shared. Some common methods of fraud are given below.

❏　Bogus data entry. This may involve entering additional, unauthorised data, modifying valid data or preventing its entry altogether. Such activity may take place during the data preparation or data entry stages.

❏　Bogus output. Output may be destroyed or altered to prevent discovery of fraudulent data entry or processing.

❏　Alteration of files. For example, an employee may alter his salary grading in the payroll file or adjust the amount owing in a colluding customers account.

❏　Program patching. This method requires access to program coding and a detailed knowledge of the functioning of the program in question, as well as the necessary programming skill. By introducing additional code, in the form of a conditional subroutine, certain circumstances determined by the perpetrator can trigger entry to the subroutine, which may, for example, channel funds to a fictitious account.

❏　Suspense accounts. Rejected and unreconciled transactions tend to be allocated to suspense accounts until they can be dealt with; fraud may be effected by directing such transactions to the account of someone colluding in the crime. Transactions can be tampered with at the input stage to ensure their rejection and allocation to the suspense/personal account.

An organisation can minimise the risk of computer fraud by:

❏　controlling access to computer hardware; in centralised systems with a limited number of specialist staff access can be readily controlled. On the other hand, if power is concentrated in the hands of few staff, then the opportunities for undetected fraud are increased. Distributed systems or centralised systems with remote access, for example through the Internet, may increase the number of locations where fraud can be perpetrated;

❏　auditing of data and procedures; until hard copy is produced the contents of files remain invisible and a number of auditing techniques can be used to detect fraudulent entries or changes.

❏ careful monitoring of the programming function; program patching can be controlled by division of the programming task, so that an individual programmer does not have complete responsibility for one application program. Unauthorised alterations to existing software can be detected by auditing utilities which compare the object code of an operational program with an original and authorised copy.

Data Protection Acts (1984 and 1998)

The Data Protection Act of 1984 states that a business or other organisation which holds personal information on their computer system must register with the Data Protection Registrar, the body that administers the act. The registration process requires identification of the classes of data held and the purposes for which they are to be used. For example, a business may hold personal data which includes information on lifestyle and income which it uses to target its marketing campaigns.

A new UK Data Protection Act, passed in 1998 and which came into force on 1 March 2000, specifically concerns the processing of personal data on the Internet. The main provisions of each Act are given in the following sections.

Data Protection Act (1984)

Since the 1960s, there has been growing public concern about the threat that computers pose to personal privacy. Most countries, including the UK, have introduced legislation to safeguard the privacy of the individual. The Younger Report of 1972 identified ten principles which were intended as guidelines to computer users in the private sector. A Government White Paper was published in 1975 in response to the Younger Report, but no legislation followed. The Lindop Report of 1978 was followed by a White Paper in 1982 and this resulted in the 1984 Data Protection Act. Apart from public pressure concerning the protection of personal privacy, a major incentive for the Government to introduce the Act stemmed from the need to ratify the Council of Europe Data Protection Convention. In the absence of this ratification, firms within the UK could have been considerably disadvantaged in trading terms through the Conventions provision to allow participating countries to refuse the transfer of personal information to non-participating countries. The principles detailed in the Younger Report formed the foundation for future reports and the Data Protection Act. They are listed below.

❏ Information should be regarded as being held for a specific purpose and should not be used, without appropriate authorisation, for other purposes.

❏ Access to information should be confined to those authorised to have it for the purpose for which it was supplied.

❏ The amount of information collected and held should be the minimum necessary for the achievement of a specified purpose.

❏ In computerised systems which handle information for statistical purposes, adequate provision should be made in their design for separating identities from the rest of the data.

❏ There should be arrangements whereby a subject could be told about the information held concerning him or her.

❏ The level of security to be achieved by a system should be specified in advance by the user and should include precautions against the deliberate abuse or misuse of information.

❏ A monitoring system should be provided to facilitate the detection of any violation of the security system.

❏ In the design of information systems, periods should be specified beyond which information should not be retained.

❏ Data held should be accurate. There should be machinery for the correction of inaccuracy and updating of information.

❏ Care should be taken in coding value judgements.

The White Paper which followed the Younger Report identified certain features of computerised information systems which could be a threat to personal privacy:

❏ The facility for storing vast quantities of data.

❏ The speed and power of computers make it possible for data to be retrieved quickly and easily from many access points;

❏ Data can be rapidly transferred between interconnected systems.

❏ Computers make it possible for data to be combined in ways which might otherwise not be practicable.

❏ Data is often transferred in a form not directly intelligible.

The 1984 Data Protection Act sets boundaries for the gathering and use of personal data. It requires all holders of computerised personal files to register with a Registrar appointed by the Home Secretary. The holder of personal data is required to keep to both the general terms of the Act, and to the specific purposes declared in the application for registration.

Terminology

The Act uses a number of terms which require some explanation:

❏ Data. Information held in a form which can be processed automatically. By this definition, manual information systems are not covered by the Act.

❏ Personal data. That which relates to a living individual who is identifiable from the information, including any which is based on fact or opinion.

❏ Data subject. The living individual who is the subject of the data.

❏ Data user. A person who processes or intends to process the data concerning a data subject.

Implications

The requirements of the Act may result in an organisation having to pay more attention to the question of security against unauthorised access than would otherwise be the case; appropriate education and training of employees are also needed to ensure that they are aware of their responsibilities and are fully conversant with their roles in the security systems. The Act also provides the right of a data subject (with some exceptions) to obtain access to information concerning him or her. Normally, a data user must provide such information free of charge or for a nominal charge of around £10.

From the individuals point of view, the Act can be said to have a number of weaknesses:

❑   Penalties for infringement of the rules are thought to be weak and ineffective.

❑   There are a number of exemptions from the Act. Some holders do not need to register and there are exceptions to the right of access to ones own file. There are also limits to confidentiality.

The Registrar is appointed by the Home Secretary and cannot therefore, be wholly independent.

Data Protection Act (1998)

"An Act to make new provision for the regulation of the processing of information relating to individuals, including the obtaining, holding, use or disclosure of such information." [16th July 1998 Data Protection Act]. The Act defines 'data' as information which is automatically processed, or is gathered with that intention, or is held in a structured filing system which is not automatically controlled. In other words, the Act covers manual filing systems which were not covered in the 1984 Act.

The Act also refers to:

❑   the "data controller" as the person or persons who determine the purposes to which the personal data is put and the manner in which it is processed;

❑   the "data processor", meaning any person (other than an employee of the data controller) who processes the personal data;

The terms "data subject" and "personal data" retain the same meanings as stated in the 1984 Act. The 1998 Act additionally refers to "sensitive personal data", meaning personal information relating to racial or ethnic origin, political opinions, religious or similar beliefs, trade union membership, physical and mental health, sexual life, offences or alleged offences and court proceedings for such offences. There are a number of exemptions to registration, for example, when the data is held for national security, crime prevention or detection and certain tax purposes.

Respecting copyright

A computer program can now obtain the status of literary work and as such, retains protection for 50 years from the first publishing date. Computer software is now covered by the Copyright Designs and Patents Act 1988 and infringements include:

❑   the pirating of copyright protected software;

❑   the running of pirated software, in that a copy is created in memory;

❑   transmitting software over telecommunications links, thereby producing a copy.

The major software producers have funded an organisation called FAST (Federation Against Software Theft) which successfully lobbied for the inclusion of computer software into the above-mentioned Act.

The law also covers material published on the World Wide Web, including images and materials used as part of a Web site's design. For example, you would be committing an offence if you copied images of products from a manufacturer's on-line brochure. Technically, an offence is also committed if you place a link in your own Web site to another site which contains copyright material, without the copyright holder's permission. It is wise to assume that material is copyright protected unless there is a statement to the contrary. In the UK, copyright is created by the mere act of publication, although it is usual to include a notice of copyright ownership. You should make it standard practice to acknowledge the sources of information you include in your assignments, even though they are not to be made available to the public. If you produce material for publication, even through a web site, you must obtain permission from copyright holders for any material you include, such as published directories, extracts from reports or pictures taken, for example, from another web site or scanned from a manufacturer's catalogue.

Respecting the rights of others

ICT is a powerful tool for the production and dissemination of information and the World Wide Web, in particular, illustrates its use for good and ill. As a user of ICT, it is your moral and often legal responsibility to avoid, casually or deliberately, producing material which:

❑   incites racial hatred or religious intolerance;

❑   does not respect the spiritual, moral and religious beliefs of others;

❑   is libellous (defames a person's character in written material);

❑   breaks personal privacy laws;

❑   releases information which you have a responsibility to keep in confidence. This may relate, for example, to commercially sensitive information about your employer's business.

Health and safety

Although a computer is not inherently dangerous, users should be aware of a number of potential risks to their safety and general health. Most employers have obligations (under Section 2 of the Health and Safety at Work Act, 1974) to protect the health, safety and welfare of their employees, by ensuring safe equipment, work systems and working environment. This legislative protection applies to work with a computer *workstation* (a visual display unit and its associated equipment and furniture), as it does to other work. In 1993, specific legislation was introduced to implement European Directive 90/270/EEC, "on the minimum safety and health requirements for work with display screen equipment".

This section examines the potential hazards of using a computer workstation and the steps that can be taken to avoid them. The 1993 legislation recognises that good work organisation and job design, and the application of established *ergonomic* principles, can largely avoid the hazards to health and safety.

Ergonomics

Ergonomics is the "study of efficiency of workers and working arrangements" (Oxford English Dictionary). Although a separate science in its own right, certain aspects of ergonomics are being applied increasingly to the design of:

❑   furniture associated with office computer systems;

❑   computer equipment for person/machine interfacing, for example, screen displays and keyboards;

❑   office and workstation layout.

It is generally recognised that, if workstation facilities and the working environment are inadequate, computer users will tend to be inefficient and may suffer from general fatigue and boredom. The increased emphasis on ergonomic design has come about because of the large increase in the number of computer users. The term *user* includes not only computer specialists, but also non-specialist users, such as data entry operators, clerks, accountants and managers.

Hazards to operator health and efficiency

In designing a suitable workstation, the designer needs to be aware of a number of potential hazards, which are described in the following paragraphs.

Visual fatigue

Various symptoms may indicate the onset of visual fatigue: sore eyes; hazy vision; difficulty in focusing when switching vision between near and distant objects; aching behind the eyes. Certain workstation features and user behaviour can contribute to visual fatigue. The screen display and the positioning of documents that are being transcribed, typically contribute to this fatigue. More specifically, the fatigue may be caused by one or more of the following.

❑   screen glare;

❑   poor character-definition on screen;

❑   excessive periods of screen viewing and consequent short distance focusing;

❑   screen flicker;

❑   screen reflection;

❑   insufficient or excessive ambient (surrounding) lighting;

❑   frequent, excessive eye movement when switching between screen and document.

Bodily fatigue

Tense and aching muscles or inflamed nerves, generally in the shoulders, neck, back, wrists or hands may result from:

❑   adopting a poor seating posture;

❑   bending frequently to reach various parts of the workstation;

❏ using a keyboard which is not at a comfortable height. *Repetitive strain injury* (RSI), or *carpal tunnel syndrome*, is now recognised as a disabling condition, which can result from intensive keyboard work. Products are available to support wrists and help users to avoid the injury. The nerves which lie down the edge of the hand can also become inflamed and painful, a condition known as *ulnar neuritis*.

❏ holding the head at an awkward angle to view the screen or a document.

Other hazards to health and safety

The proper design and positioning of a workstation can help prevent a number of potential hazards, generally relating to the use of equipment. The hazards may include:

❏ *electric shock*. A person may receive a live electric shock, from faulty equipment (such as incorrect earthing of the power supply), and from incorrect use of equipment (such as the removal of the machine's casing, without first isolating the machine from mains power). This form of electric shock will persist until the person breaks contact with the machine, or else the power is cut. Clearly, this hazard is life threatening, and although this is the primary concern, it will probably also cause damage to the machine.

❏ *static electric shock*. This is caused by the sudden discharge through any conducting material of static electricity, which may have built up in the body. The equipment earths the static electricity which the person has accumulated. A person may build up static electricity by walking on a nylon carpet. Sometimes, static electricity accumulates on the computer screen and a shock may be received when it is touched (the person acts as the earth). If the screen is cleaned with special anti-static wipes, this problem should be avoided. Static electric shock is momentary and, whilst in exceptional circumstances it may injure someone, it is more likely to damage the equipment and, possibly, the stored data.

❏ *injury from impact*. For example, someone may bump against the sharp corner of a desk, be injured by dropping equipment when attempting to move it or be cut by sharp edges on equipment;

❏ *muscular or spinal strain*. Lifting heavy equipment may cause strained or torn muscles, or spinal injuries such as a 'slipped' disc;

❏ *burns, cuts or poisoning caused by equipment breakdown*. These injuries may result from fire or overheating of equipment.

Designing an appropriate workstation

A number of workstation features are considered in the overall design and together can contribute to a good working environment.

Work surface

Height. A user should have thigh clearance amounting to at least 180mm, measured from the front surface of the seat, to the underside of the work surface. Obviously, this measurement can be obtained if the chair is adjustable in height and the work surface height does not require seat adjustment below its minimum height. The minimum clearance may be insufficient for someone to sit cross-legged, a position which he or she may wish to adopt for short periods, so some extra thigh clearance may be desirable.

Typical heights of manufactured workstations are either 710mm for fixed or between 520mm and 750mm when adjustable. The standard 710mm which manufacturers use for a fixed height desk is based on the ideal writing height for an average male and does not take account of keyboard thickness.

Area. The work surface area required obviously depends on the nature of the work being carried out at the workstation. If transcription work is to be carried out, a *document holder* can be attached to one corner of the mobile workstation. Where more space is available, users may prefer that the document holder is positioned between the keyboard and the screen to reduce the amount of eye movement when alternately viewing the screen and the document. As with all computer equipment, a *matt surface* is desirable to avoid screen reflection and possible eye strain.

Chair

Where a fixed height desk of, say, 710mm is bought, then it is particularly important that the chair's height is *adjustable* and that a footrest is available for persons of small stature. This is obviously necessary for a comfortable keying height. At the same time, support is provided for the feet (if they are not supported, blood circulation in the legs may be impaired as pressure is exerted by the edge of the seat on the back lower thighs). The footrest should allow the thighs to be slightly raised above the front edge of the chair, thus avoiding 'pins and needles' in the legs and feet. An adjustable chair should be variable in height from 340mm to 520mm. Invariably, manufacturers produce computer workstation chairs which are adjustable for height and back, particularly lower back, support.

Screen display

In workstation design, the screen display has to be judged for its *quality* and its *position* in relation to the operator. Screen quality is measured for the clarity and steadiness of the images it displays. A high *resolution* screen is generally desirable, even for word processing work, but is of paramount importance if it is used for detailed design work. Several precautions can be taken to minimise eye strain if a poorer quality display is being used:

❑   appropriate lighting; this is examined in the next subsection;

❑   comparisons can be made with other screen displays (the clarity may deteriorate with age) and any deterioration reported;

❑   the use of a higher resolution screen, appropriate to the application and colour where graphical work is involved;

❑   the correct adjustment of contrast and brightness controls. Filters can cut glare and improve character definition by preventing screen reflection from inappropriate lighting. However, their quality is highly variable and a good quality screen should avoid the problem of glare.

There are two major concerns regarding the *positioning* of the screen. First, there is an optimum viewing range. Second, its location should be aimed at minimising excessive head and eye movement. The distance between the user's eyes and the screen should, ideally, fall somewhere between 450mm and 500mm and the design should try to achieve a viewing distance within this range. However, eye strain is more likely to result from repeated re-focusing for lengthy periods, whilst attention is switched from the screen to a document on the desk top. This can be avoided by attempting to position documents approximately the same distance away as the screen. A document holder can be useful in achieving this aim, even if it is positioned to one side and thus requires some head movement to view the document. Some head movement helps to keep the neck and shoulder muscle loosened and avoids stiffness and aching in those areas. A user should try to look away from the screen occasionally, perhaps to the other side of the office, to avoid eye strain which stems from constant focusing at one distance.

Lighting

Natural light falling through office windows may, at times, be adequate for healthy and efficient working but there will be many occasions when it is either too dark or too bright. It is generally necessary to supplement the natural light with artificial lighting and control the entry of bright sunshine with window blinds. The detailed study of lighting is beyond the scope of this text but the following points provide some basic guidelines as to the artificial lighting requirements for a workstation;

❑ attempt to avoid glare. This can result if there is insufficient lighting and the screen's brightness contrasts sharply with the ambient level of brightness;

❑ reflection on screen can make it difficult to see the displayed characters and cause eye strain. The use of window blinds and non-reflective work surfaces and equipment can help.

Cabling

Cabling is needed to power individual systems, connect the component parts of system unit, printer, keyboard and screen and for communications purposes when separate systems are networked. Loose cable trailing beneath desks or across the floor can result in injury to staff who trip over it. If, in the process, hardware is pulled from a desk onto the floor, it is likely to be damaged and may result in loss of data and temporary loss of system use. Cabling should be channelled through conduit or specially designed channels in the workstation. Cable 'bridge' conduit is specially designed to channel cable safely across floor areas.

Floor covering

It is important to choose the right type of floor covering and a number of considerations concerning choice are given below.

Noise. Staff generally prefer an office floor to be carpeted because it makes the room feel more 'comfortable'. Carpet also serves to absorb some office noise and results in a quieter environment than would prevail with a tiled floor.

Chair movement. If operator chairs are on casters then the carpets should be sufficiently firm and smooth to allow the operator to move easily while still seated. Movement should not be so easy that the operator has difficulty in maintaining position. A chair with casters is difficult to control on a tiled floor.

Static electricity. Carpets made with a large percentage of man-made fibre tend to cause rapid build-up in body static. The static is caused through friction as a person walks across the carpet. Woollen carpets produce less static electricity but are more expensive than the synthetic variety. An alternative is to use anti-static mats to cover carpet areas around workstations. An anti-static mat is earthed and designed to drain away body static when a person stands on it. Another way of preventing static is to spray a special chemical solution onto the carpet every six months.

Office layout

If the designer has the luxury of starting from 'scratch', then the simplest approach to design-ing the layout is to make a scale drawing of the office on which the location of equipment and furniture can then be marked. Designated work positions should also be indicated. Numerous drawing and computer aided design packages make experimentation easy. Libraries of stan-dard symbols (representing office equipment and furniture) are available, which the designer can select and locate on screen. The designer has to take into account a number of constraints which will dictate the location of some furniture and equipment. Fixed items should be placed on the drawing first so that those with fewer constraints can be tried in different loca-tions until an optimum layout is achieved. Ideally, the designer should present two or three alternatives for consideration by management and office staff, whose opinions ought to be paramount. A number of factors should be taken into account when choosing the location of workstations:

❑ staff should not be obliged to work in areas which are subject to extremes of temperature, for example, next to radiators or near a frequently used door which creates a draught each time it is opened;

❑ computer equipment should not be placed next to a radiator as overheating may cause the system to malfunction;

❑ computer screens should be protected from direct sun-light which causes screen reflection and glare;

❑ there should be sufficient space for staff to move around the office without moving equipment or furniture;

❑ workstations should have sufficient space to allow routine maintenance and cleaning to be carried out;

❑ there should always be easy access to fire fighting equipment and fire exits should be kept clear.

Self-test questions

1. Briefly explain the process of using top-down design to analyse a task.
2. Suggest two benefits to be gained from scheduling the completion of a task.
3. Explain ways in which the facilities of an applications package and Windows Explorer can be used to make you work organisation efficient and effective.
4. Suggest two ways in which you can use a word processor's facilities to make future modifications of a document more straightforward.
5. A business is making extensive use of e-mail and the Internet in general and has experienced some minor problems from nuisance viruses. It is concerned that it may be suffer real damage from viruses in the future.
   a. What is a computer *virus*?
   b. Describe the main types of computer virus.
   c. Explain the measures which can be taken to minimise the risk of virus damage.
6. a. Identify three *costs* which may be incurred by a mail order business if a disgruntled employee causes a system fault which prevents access to its customer records for a week.
   b. Briefly outline two measures which can be taken to allow *recovery* from system failure or loss.
7. Research and describe products which provide *physical protection* against unauthorised access to information systems.
8. What benefit may be provided by fault logging and reporting. Briefly describe an example.
9. Identify one category of offence covered by the Computer Misuse Act (1990).
10. Use an example to illustrate the importance of maintaining confidentiality of personal information.
11. What is a *program patch* and how may it be used to commit fraud?
12. With the use of suitable examples, explain two of the data protection measures included in the Data Protection Acts in the UK.
13. Define the terms *data subject*, *data processor* and *data controller*, as used in the Data Protection Acts.
14. Describe two circumstances when UK copyright law may be broken in respect of electronic material.
15. Define the term ergonomics and use an example to illustrate the importance of ergonomics for health and safety protection.

Developmental Exercises

Wordprocessing

All the activities in this set of exercises should be completed within the same document. Use the following settings and standards.

- ❑ The relevant page settings are as follows: *paper size* A4; *orientation* is portrait; *top margin* 2.49 cm; *bottom margin* 5.99 cm; *left margin* 3.5 cm; *right margin* 2.49 cm; *header* 1.25 cm from top edge; *footer* 1.25 cm from bottom edge.

- ❑ The *default font* is Times New Roman, *point size* 11 and *paragraph alignment* is justified (unless indicated otherwise in the text).

- ❑ Use only one space between words, after a comma and after a full stop. Leave one blank line (or 8pt paragraph space) after a heading or between paragraphs. Use single line spacing.

- ❑ These exercises covers a range of character formatting facilities, simple table construction, as well as general editing.

Activity 1

Enter the text between the headings 'Start of unformatted text' and 'End of unformatted text' as shown, computer spellcheck it and save the file as 'baretext'. Print the file and proof it against the original. Make any necessary corrections and save the file again.

Start of unformatted text

Character Formatting

All dot matrix (impact, ink jet and thermographic) and laser printers allow the printing of a wide range of character styles. Some common examples are given below.

bold italic

strike-through

underline

bold-italic

For some word processing work, these variations are quite sufficient and your printer may well have a control panel to select a different font, but any such selection will be applied to the whole document. Typically, your printer may offer

courier, roman, condensed

Variable sizing of character fonts is a common feature of word processing programs. Some examples are given below (size is measured in points).

This is Arial 18.

This is Arial 14.

WYSIWYG Packages

WYSIWYG stands for What You See Is What You Get, which means that the results of paragraph and character formatting commands are seen on screen. Thus, lines can be seen as centred, characters can be viewed as bold, italic, underlined, or even in different sizes and fonts.

Apart from the package's WYSIWYG facilities, your screen must have the necessary graphics capability and resolution.

Bullets and Numbered Lists

Bullets and numbers can be used to emphasise or sequence items in a list. An example of a bulleted list is given below. This pack includes the following items: assembly instructions; colour illustrations; components for assembly.

End of unformatted text

Activity 2

Load the file "baretext", completed in Activity 1 and format it to appear as shown in the following version. *Instructions appear in this form and are not to be included in the text.*

Save the file as "poshtext" and print it.

Compare it with the original, correct as necessary, re-save the file and print a finished copy.

Start of formatted text

Character formatting

1. Define Heading 1 style as Times New Roman 14 and apply to first heading

All dot matrix (impact, ink jet and thermographic) and laser printers allow the printing of a wide range of character styles. Some common examples are given below.

bold	*italic*	~~strike through~~	<u>underline</u>	***bold italic***

2. Create table with grid border

3. Insert words in table and format as shown

For some word processing work, these variations are quite sufficient and your printer may well have a control panel to select a different font, but any such selection will be applied to the whole document. Typically, your printer may offer

courier, roman, condensed

Variable sizing of character *fonts* is a facility which is a common feature of wordprocessing software. Some examples are given below (size is measured in points).

4. Format fonts as stated

This is Arial 18
This is Arial 14

5. Apply Heading 1 style, already defined

WYSIWYG Packages

WYSIWYG stands for What You See Is What You Get, which means that the results of paragraph and character formatting commands are seen on screen. Thus, lines can be seen as centred, characters can be viewed as **bold**, *italic*, <u>underlined</u>, or even in

6.   *Format fonts as indicated*

7.   *Arial 13, Arial 14 and Tahoma 18, centred*

different sizes and fonts.

Apart from the package's WYSIWYG facilities, your screen must have the necessary graphics capability and resolution

8.   *Apply Heading 1 style already defined*

Bullets and numbered lists

Bullets and numbers can be used to emphasise or sequence items in a list. An example of a bulleted list is given below.

9.   *Arial 10, bold*

This pack includes the following items:

10.   *Apply bullets, Arial 9, indented*

❑   assembly instructions;

❑   colour illustrations;

❑   components for assembly;

End of formatted text

Activity 3

Load the "poshtext" file and insert a right aligned title, using Arial, point size 18, bold. Insert page numbers to appear as a footer on the right hand side of each page. At the left side of the footer, insert your own name, the file name and the date on which you completed this document.

Activity 4

Create a new document and illustrate use of the various drawing tools (simple demonstrations of each will do). If your word processor does not have drawing tools, you will have to use a graphics package and then import, or paste, the drawing into the document. Also insert a clip art image into the document. Use text boxes, to annotate the drawings (for example, circle, square, ellipse and so on).

Writing style

Actvity 5

You are a trainee graphic designer in a large organisation and wish to draw attention to a potential safety hazard. Shortage of power outlets in your office sometimes means that power cables to computers are trailed across the floor. Your office colleagues are not bothered about the situation and it is left to you to write a memorandum to your Head of Department. Write a suitable memo explaining the reasons for your concern and asking for extra power outlets to be installed.

Activity 6

Study the four advertisement examples (Figures 1.1, 1.2, 1.3 and 1.4) in Chapter 1 and design four of your own advertisements (for different products) which reflect the presentation and writing styles used in each of the examples. You should pay careful attention to your choice of image, colour and writing style and layout. Write a short justification for each design, explaining how you have used each element (graphics, colour, layout and writing style). Ask your colleagues to comment on the suitability of each design for its stated purpose.

Activity 7

Word process your curriculum vitae and keep it up to date.

Activity 8

Following the merger of Silicon Software with Omega Business Systems, the first board meeting of the new company, Silicon Business Software Limited, resulted in a number of important changes being implemented. One of the changes is to establish a Human Resources department. Previously, neither company had operated corporate personnel systems, but had left personnel matters to indvidual departments. You have been transferred to this new department, where your job involves you working as a senior assistant to the Human Resources Manager, Ann Robinson. After your initial meeting with Mrs Robinson, at which a variety of issues were discussed, you received the following internal memorandum.

Memorandum

To: Senior Personnel Assistant

From: Human Resources Manager

Re: Establishment of corporate materials

Date: 14 June 2000

I have given thought to our conversation on the need for standardised letters and forms to meet the functions of the new department. I am satisfied that we cannot standardise job advertisements, but want you to provide me with drafts of the following:

Forms:

   a job application form that all job applicants would have to complete (I would want it to contain sufficient information to enable me to use it as an employee record form).

   a staff appraisal form to record job performance.

Letters to fulfil the following tasks:

   invite applicants for job interviews;

   inform an applicant that he/she is not being called for interview;

   inform an interviewee that he/she is not being offered the job;

   offer the job to the successful interviewee;

   issua formal warning to an employee who is guilty of misconduct, stating that dismissal will result from a repetition of the conduct complained of;

issue a dismissal;

inform an employee that he/she is being made redundant;

I am aware that this is a substantial task but would ask you to complete it as a matter of urgency.

1. Draft the forms and letters requested in the memorandum, using a content, tone and style appropriate to each of them.
2. Write a memorandum to the Human Resources Manager indicating that you expect the work to take considerable time to complete.
3. Obtain examples of some of the above documents, letters and forms used by public and private sector organisations in your area. Compare these in order to produce a dossier containing an example of each document, letter or form which combines the examples of best practice in each.

Meeting documents

Activity 9

Draw up and word process an agenda for a meeting to discuss an issue relating to your course. For example, you will probably appoint one or more of your fellow students as representatives to attend Course Team meetings and will need to inform them of matters which you wish to pass on to Tutors. You should appoint a chairperson and minutes secretary (this job can be taken by a different person for each meeting). The minutes should be word processed by the minutes secretary after each meeting and be distributed to the rest of the group before the next meeting. As minute taking is a difficult skill, you will need to record the main points only and the name of the person who made each contribution. At the next meeting, the minutes of the previous meeting will be checked for accuracy before being signed by the chairperson.

Questionnaires

Activity 10

This activity concerns the design and use of a questionnaire to do a survey on some area of interest.

1. Design a questionnaire to survey opinion on an area of interest to you. Think carefully about the aims of the survey, the size of the survey and how the results ae to be analysed, because these factors will greatly influence the design of the questions an how they are to be coded.
2. Apply the questionnaire to a suitable population or sample of a large population.
3. Calculate the percentages of response to each question and present the calculations in tabular form for easy reference.
4. Calculate any other useful statistics, such as means, medians or modes.
5. Produce appropriate statistical charts to illustrate the results of the survey.
6. Write a report describing the results of your survey and explain the reasoning behind your conclusions.

Unit 2

ICT serving organisations

Chapters

Assessment Evidence

You need to produce

☐ a case study analysing a suitable organisation.

To achieve a grade E your work must show:

☐ clear descriptions, with the aid of diagrams, of the main function(s) of the organisation, its associated customers (or clients) and suppliers, the function of each department, the structure of the organisation and the relationships between the main departments and outsiders

☐ descriptions of the ICT provision for each of the organisation's departments (or functions) and identify possible extensions or improvements to the use of ICT that would benefit the organisation

☐ using diagrams, clearly how information essential to successful operation moves within the organisation and to and from outsiders

☐ detailed descriptions of the purpose and operation of an important ICT application used within the organisation, including examples of input and output data and the job functions and personnel involved

☐ that your case study is presented clearly as a coherent report and is checked for meaning and accuracy.

To achieve a grade C your work must show:

☐ a well-structured case study, fluent use of technical language, appropriate conclusions and suitable references to the information sources used

☐ detailed explanations of how information used in the organisation is processed including details of the data capture techniques, any processing or calculations involved and the specification and style of data output that you can work independently to produce your work to agreed deadlines.

To achieve a grade A your work must show:

☐ detailed explanations, with the aid of diagrams and definitions of the data, of how information moves from a customer or client through the organisation to result in the delivery of a product or service

☐ use of examples to recommend improvements to the organisation's internal ICT systems (this may cover items such as integration of existing systems, specialised equipment or software, database development, LAN or WAN systems)

☐ detailed description of how the organisation might benefit from more extensive use of new communication technologies, such as the Internet, mobile communications, e-mail, e-commerce or EDI

☐ description of how the organisation might use a management information system to monitor or control activities, improve decision.

Chapter 6

Organisations

Need for organisations

The society in which we live is complex and sophisticated. As consumers we demand a variety of goods and services to enable us to maintain the quality of life we enjoy. In order to satisfy these demands, suppliers must produce the goods and services which the consumer wants by combining factors of production such as land, labour and capital in the most efficient manner. By this we mean producers must hire workers, rent or buy premises, perhaps invest in plant and machinery and purchase raw materials, and then organise the manufacture of the final product in such a way that they will make a profit. Society may also gain, as its scarce resources are being used in the way consumers wish rather than being wasted in producing things people do not need. Suppliers under such a system are known as commercial organisations. Many public sector organisations also provide goods and services to society and, in the same way as commercial organisations, these public sector bodies must employ staff, occupy premises and raise capital. The fundamental difference between these two types of organisation lies in the objectives they seek to fulfil. The private sector tends to be motivated by profit, while public sector organisations will often have a much less mercenary motive, such as providing for the public good and improving the state of society. If we wish to see society ordered and governed in such a way that individuals are free to express their demands and producers are able to meet such wants, it becomes necessary to form organisations to control and regulate society through a variety of administrative structures. These are the bodies which make up the organisations of the state. In the UK, these are Parliament, the Government and its Executive, the Civil Service, the Local Authorities and the Courts and justice system. These bodies are required to carry out legislative, administrative and judicial functions.

If you examine the nature and range of individual demands in an industrialised society you soon realise that most of them cannot be met other than by organisations. Individually we lack the knowledge, skills and physical resources to manufacture products that fulfil our needs, whether these are simple or sophisticated. It would be as difficult for us to make a biro or a floppy disk as it would a television or a computer. Admittedly, some goods and services can be supplied by an individual working alone. A farmer may be able to grow sufficient food to satisfy himself and his family without any help from others. But what if he requires other goods and services? It is unlikely that the farmer will also have the ability or resources to produce his own combine-harvester or tractor. If he did not have such products which are manufactured by others, his life would be much simpler, but no doubt much harder.

A similar situation exists in the supply of services. A strong and resourceful individual may try to protect himself and his property from the dangers imposed by thieves or vandals. If he cannot, however, then he may turn to the state to demand protection. Recognising that a failure to respond to such demands from its citizens would lead to an anarchic system, the government must accept the responsibility and establish a legal system incorporating law enforcement agencies to provide the protection being sought.

How, then, are these goods and services produced? It is clear that individuals working independently would be unable to meet our complex physical and social needs. Therefore society has developed a system where people join together to form organisations. These bodies are extraordinarily diverse. They manufacture products, which they distribute and sell. They also provide all the services that we need. Thus, both the BBC and the Ford Motor Company are organisations, although their products are very different.

Clearly, then, if individuals within society are to have all their various needs satisfied, there must be co-operation between workers. Each must specialise in a certain aspect of the supply process. These workers must be organised and allocated a specific role in which to perform co-ordinated tasks. These tasks are normally organised with the aim of producing a given product or service, although there are some organisations which do not specialise and which make an extremely diverse range of products. In the private sector of the economy, such businesses will usually have the objective of making a profit for their owners. Of course, this is just one example of an organisation. As we have already noted, the state is another form of organisation which is clearly more complex than a business, and it has a variety of objectives, such as increasing the wealth of citizens, improving their quality of life and protecting them if they are threatened. We are all members of organisations, some of which are formal while others are informal. Your family is an example of an informal organisation, as is the group of friends you mix with. Other more formal organisations to which you may belong or may have belonged are the school you attended as a child, your employing body, or your trade union.

The tendency to form groups is a characteristic of human nature. Human beings are highly socialised, they need to 'belong' and will generally find it uncomfortable and disturbing if they cannot find 'acceptance' within a social group. An employee who is capable and confident in his or her job, and who is in turn regarded by the employer and the rest of the work force as a professional, gains a 'role' satisfaction through identifying as a vital part of the group. So organisations have an important role to fulfil in meeting the social needs of man. However, perhaps more important in the context of this course of study is the function of organisations as the satisfiers of needs. They allow individual workers to develop their specialist skills, and this in turn allows productive capacity to increase.

Since differing organisations concentrate on the supply of different goods and services, there must be a system established whereby products can be distributed to the consumers. Thus shops, wholesalers, transport companies and so on must all be involved. The fabric of the social and economic environment is based on a process whereby individuals form organisations which are dependent upon other organisations to survive. In just the same way as the needs of the individual cannot be met by that individual alone, so the same also holds true for organisations. They are interdependent. Organisational activity involves a perpetual interaction, one organisation with another, as society steadily evolves in a direction that individually and collectively we try to guide. However, as we shall see, even though the overall aim of society is the advancement of our physical well-being, the methods for achieving this are the subject of much disagreement.

Characteristics common to all organisations

The specific reasons for the formation of organisations are many and varied, and may not, of course, always be clearly defined. Some are the result of the need for individuals to find company for a social or leisure reason, for example by forming a sporting or working-men's club. Others are formed with a more precise economic objective in mind, such as the desire to make a profit for the person who has established a business organisation. Some, such as the organisations which make up the state and government, evolve as a result of the emergence of particular needs in society which require government intervention. For example, the Government established the National Health Service in 1946 to meet the needs of society for a high standard of free health care, available to all. Nevertheless, most formal organisations have some common characteristics. These may be simply stated as follows:

(i) The establishment of an organisation is usually for a specific purpose.

For example, the Automobile Association was founded with the precise objective of promoting the interests of motorists within this country. Other organisations may be launched with one prime aim, but may later diversify in order to follow alternative causes or objectives. For instance, Guinness, the brewery company, was established to produce alcoholic drinks, but now has subsidiaries making a variety of products such as fishing tackle boxes and cassette cases. This illustrates how a business may try to evolve as the commercial environment changes and new commercial opportunities emerge.

(ii) Organisations usually have a distinct identity.

People belonging to a specific organisation can identify themselves as being part of a group either as a result of where they work or of what they do. A Manchester United footballer wears a red shirt to show he is part of the particular organisation. A member of a trade union is given a membership card to signify he belongs to that union. Manufacturing companies promote their brand names through advertising. This sense of identity, which we have already seen is an important need for most people, can produce extreme loyalty to the organisation.

(iii) Most organisations require some form of leadership.

We have seen that organisations are normally formed for a specific purpose. In order to achieve this purpose, it is necessary to co-ordinate the efforts of the members of the organisation. This requires management, or leadership. Formal organisations such as companies or a club have a specified management hierarchy which may be appointed by the owners of the organisation. For instance, the shareholders of a company appoint the directors. Alternatively, the leadership may be elected, as in the case of a club or society where the members vote to have a chairman, secretary and committee. However, once appointed this management team has the responsibility for ensuring the organisation achieves its objectives.

(iv) Organisations are accountable.

Such accountability applies both to those the management team deals with and those it employs.

Objectives of organisations

The objectives of an organisation are the targets it hopes to achieve. Clearly the objectives which are set will vary considerably between different types of organisation. As we shall see later in this section, the objectives of commercial organisations will largely be based around the goal of profit. For organisations within the public sector, profit may not be the sole aim. Factors such as benefit to the community or the creation of jobs may also feature as targets for the public sector. It should be noted, however, that the profit motive has grown substantially in importance in recent times.

A classification of organisations

Initially, it is convenient to categorise organisations as follows:

❑   public service;

❑   commercial and industrial.

Public service organisations

Many public services are provided by central and local government (the public sector) Central government takes responsibility for a wide range of services and has specific organisations, referred to as Departments, to manage each. Thus, there are separate departments, each responsible for the provision of, amongst others, health, education, defence and social welfare services. The role of local government is continually changing as successive governments pursue policies which tend to centralise power, or devolve it to locally elected council bodies. The provision of water, electricity and gas services used to be provided by 'public utilities', but they have been 'privatised' and now operate as commercial and industrial businesses. Some services, traditionally provided by the public sector, are now partly in the private sector; for example, some prisons are privately owned and private companies may carry out the work of refuse collection. Even so, overall control of such services is still the responsibility of central and local government departments. Table 6.1 lists some major central government organisations and briefly describes the responsibilities of each. Table 6.2 does the same, in respect of local government.

Government departments	Responsibilities
Education	Schools
Transport	Road and building
Home Office	Law and order, police and prison services policy
Health	Hospitals,
Trade and Industry	Business and industrial policy
Social Security	Benefits such as income support.
Treasury	Economic policy
Defence	Armed Forces

Table 6.1. *Central Government Departments and areas of responsibility*

It should be noted that although the government departments retain overall responsibility for the areas listed in the Table, private companies carry out some of the work. For example, some hospitals, prisons and schools are privately owned. As part of the government's 'privatisation' programme, local councils have to allow private businesses to tender for (compete for) work traditionally carried out by their own departments; this is called Compulsory Competitive Tendering (CCT).

For example, private businesses can tender for contracts to carry out street sweeping or refuse collection. In addition, some schools have 'opted out' and receive their funding directly from central governments.

Local Government departments	Responsibilities
Social Services	Home helps, children's homes, meals on wheels, day nurseries, residential homes and day centres for the mentally ill.
Education	Nursery, and secondary schools.
Housing	Council housing provides affordable accommodation for those who cannot buy their own homes.
Environmental Services	Refuse collection and disposal, street sweeping and pollution control.
Police and Fire Services	Although there is co-operation between forces, these services are still locally controlled.
Planning and Building Control	Consider applications for local building and enforce regulations on building standards.

Table 6.2. *Local Government Departments and areas of responsibility*

Industry and commerce

The term 'industry' covers a wide range of organisations which form part of a country's economy. We tend to link factories with the idea of industry, but the term also covers: *extraction* industries, such as coal-mining and fishing; *manufacturing* businesses which take raw materials and process them into finished products, such as cars and clothing, as well as those assembling ready-made components into, for example, computers and televisions; *retail* and *wholesale* businesses, concerned with buying, selling and distributing goods for personal and business consumption; *service* industries, such as hotel, catering, travel and banking. The word 'commerce' overlaps with 'industry' and includes all forms of trading organisation and those which support trade, such as banking and insurance.

Organisational structures

A structure can be defined as having component parts, which are connected in a particular way. Structures are designed to fulfil purposes. For example, a house is a structure, consisting of rooms, windows, floors, ceilings, doors and connection passages; the mix of these component parts and the way they are put together determines the design of the house. Two main types of organisational structure are considered here: *hierarchical*; *flat*.

Hierarchical structure

An organisation with a hierarchical structure includes different levels of authority and responsibility. Heads of Department may be directly responsible to one of the Directors. For example, the Accounts Department Head may be subject to the authority of the Financial Director. Such authority relates to the operation of the organisation and enables tasks to be completed. There may be Section Supervisors who are responsible to their respective Heads of Department for particular functions within departments. Each section supervisor may have authority over a number of clerks. Generally, there are more 'workers' than 'bosses', so a hierarchical structure can be viewed as a pyramid, as shown in Figure 6.1; the lower down the pyramid you descend, the larger the number of staff you are likely to find employed. The jobs at the top of the pyramid carry the most authority and the greatest responsibility for the success or failure of the organisation. Operatives and clerical staff are unlikely to have any authority in the organisation, but they have responsibility for the completion of their own jobs.

Downward communication

Figure 6.1 shows that, within the pyramid, communications go up and down. Policy decisions taken at board level by the directors are implemented by instructing the relevant departmental heads to see that the policy is carried out. The heads of department brief their middle managers and the final stage in the process is the communication between middle managers and their subordinates.

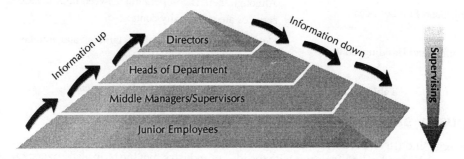

Figure 6.1. *Hierarchy of authority, responsibility and information flow*

Upward communication

The communication also passes from the bottom upwards. Staff provide feedback to their seniors. This may take many forms; it may involve monitoring shortages of materials, absences of staff, production problems, grievances and suggestions for improving work methods. Anything which requires the authority or approval of someone further up the organisational hierarchy and which has been generated or identified below, will pass back up the system. Only in extreme circumstances is it likely that an issue arising at the bottom of the pyramid will pass right back to the top for consideration and decision. For the most part, an immediate senior is likely to have sufficient authority to make a decision; ultimately however, it is a question of the extent of *delegated* responsibility held by senior employees that determines whether they can deal with it personally, or must pass it back to their own superiors. As organisations grow bigger it is inevitable that communications have much further to travel. This is not ideal since it is likely to take longer to transmit information and there is greater distancing between the giver and the receiver, which can lead to a 'them and us' view of the organisation by junior staff. However, it is clear that as the organisation grows, so its communication system must be become increasingly refined. Information technology support is crucial to the efficiency of communications.

Flat structure

In contrast to a hierarchy, a flat structure generally has a single level of management, as shown in Figure 6.2. Except for the smallest organisations, very few will have an entirely flat structure. It is possible, that an organisation wishes to avoid a cumbersome hierarchy and attempts to keep the number of management levels to a minimum; they are thus aiming for a 'flatter' structure. As mentioned earlier, hierarchies with many levels of authority can make communication difficult. A flatter structure can encourage 'team spirit' through the avoidance of the 'them and us' feelings, which can be characteristic of hierarchies

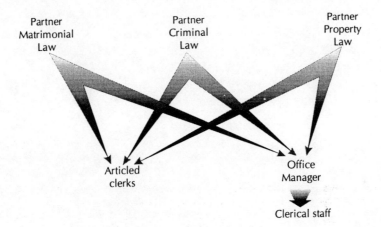

Figure 6.2. *Flatter structure*

Figure 6.2 represents a firm of solicitors, where each partner has the same level of authority and responsibility, specialises in a particular aspect of the law and has joint authority over the Office Manager and articled clerks ('apprentice' solicitors). The Office Manager is responsible for supervision of the clerical staff. Although there are hierarchical elements in the organisation, its structure is fairly 'flat'.

✍ Self-test questions

1. Choose three formal organisations with which you are familiar and for each:
   (i)   identify its main *purpose*;
   (ii)   select an aspect which gives it its distinct *identity*;
   (iii) briefly describe how it is *lead* - its top management structure;
   (iv)   identify to whom the management are ultimately *accountable*.

2. The water industry used to be in the public sector, but is now run by private companies, overseen by a regulator (OFFWAT). Briefly list features which allow the privatised water company to be classified as both commercial and public service.

3. (i)   Choose a hierarchically structured organisation with which you are familiar and using Figure 6.1 as a guide, draw a pyramid structure to show the main levels of authority.

   (ii)   Identify two benefits and two drawbacks of the structure for the chosen organisation.

Chapter 7

Functional areas of organisations

This Chapter investigates some of the main functional areas to be found in organisations, namely:

- ❑ financial accounting (sales, purchasing and general ledger);
- ❑ invoicing and stock control;
- ❑ marketing;
- ❑ payroll and personnel;
- ❑ design and production;
- ❑ ICT services.

Financial accounting

Financial accounting or 'book-keeping' is the process of recording financial transactions arising from the day-to-day operation of a business. The sale of goods to a customer and the subsequent settlement of the debt are two examples of financial transactions. More detailed information on financial accounting systems is provided in Chapter 9.

Sales accounting

When credit sales are made to customers, a record needs to be kept of amounts owing and paid. Payment is normally requested with an invoice, which gives details of goods supplied, quantities, prices and VAT. Credit sales are usually made on for example, a 14, 21 or 28 day basis, which means that the customer has to pay within the specified period to obtain any discounts offered. Overdue payments need to be chased, so sales accounting systems normally produce reports analysing the indebtedness of different customers. Debt control is vital to business profitability and computerised systems can produce prompt and up-to-date reports as a by-product of the main application.

Purchase accounting

This function is concerned with controlling amounts owed and payments made to suppliers of services, goods or materials which are used in the main business of the company. For example, a car manufacturer will need to keep records of amounts owing to suppliers of car components and sheet steel manufacturers. Delayed payments to suppliers may help cash flow, but can harm an organisation's image, or even cut off a source of supply when a supplier refuses to deliver any more goods until payment is made.

Nominal or general ledger

The general ledger keeps control of financial summaries, including those originating from payroll, sales and purchase accounting and acts as a balance in a double entry system. Computerised systems can automatically produce reports at the end of financial periods, including a trial balance, trading and profit and loss account and balance sheet.

Other finance-related functions

Stock control

Any organisation which keeps stocks of raw materials or finished goods needs to operate a stock control system. Although stock constitutes an asset, it ties up cash resources that could be invested in other aspects of the business. Equally, a company must keep sufficient quantities of items to satisfy customer demand or manufacturing requirements. To maintain this balance a stock control system should provide up-to-date information on quantities, prices, minimum stock levels, and re-order quantities. It should also give warning of excessively high, or dangerously low levels of stock. In the latter case, orders may be produced automatically. A stock control system may also generate valuable management reports on, for example, sales patterns, slow-moving items, and overdue orders.

Sales order processing

This function will normally be concerned with:

- ❑ the validation of orders, checking, for example, that the goods ordered are supplied by the business or that the customer's credit status warrants the order's completion;

- ❑ the identification of individual items ordered. A customer may request several different items on the same order form and any particular item will probably appear on many different order forms, so the quantities for each are totalled to produce picking lists to enable warehouse staff to retrieve the goods for despatch;

- ❑ the monitoring of back orders. If an order cannot be fulfilled, it may be held in abeyance until new stocks arrive, so all outstanding back orders need to be available on request.

Invoicing

This function deals with the production of customer invoices, requesting payment for goods or services delivered. Information stored in the customer files and stock files is used to produce invoices, usually on pre-printed continuous stationery.

Payroll

Payroll systems are concerned with the production of payslips for employees and the maintenance of records required for taxation and other deductions. In a manual system, the preparation of payroll figures and the maintenance of payroll records is a labour intensive task. Although tedious and repetitive, it is a vitally important task. Most employees naturally regard pay as being the main reason for work and resent delays in payment or incorrect payments, unless of course it is in their favour! The repetitive nature of the task makes it a popular candidate for computerisation, especially with organisations which employ large numbers of people. The automatic production of reports for taxation purposes also provides a valuable benefit. Smaller organisations with only several employees probably do not regard payroll as a high priority application for computerisation. The benefits are not as great if the payroll can be carried out by one or two employees who also carry out a number of other tasks.

Human resources

The human resources (personnel) function is responsible for the selection (usually by interview), recruitment, training and development of staff. Personnel records will store all the information needed by Salaries and Wages to make the correct payments to employees; this will include details of, for example, gross salary, tax code, statutory sick pay and holiday entitlement. Depending on the size of the organisation, information may also be held concerning: qualifications, courses attended; personal and career development plans.

Design

The design function is present where an organisation develops its own products and services; a trader who simply buys and sells goods has no need of a design team. Design is part of the research and development R& D) function, which is vital to organisations wishing to radically develop their product range. The nature of design teams depends on the product or service being designed. The skills and talents of a car design team are clearly very different from those of a team designing a cover for a magazine.

Production

The production function should, ideally, be driven by the market for the business's products. In other words, it should be geared to produce the necessary mix and quantities of products required by customers. If goods are perishable within a short time, and large reserve stocks cannot be held, then production should be flexible and responsive to the day-to-day sales requirements. Of course, this is an ideal and production plans cannot always be changed at short notice; ships and other large items take months or years to build.

The production department must know exactly what is required and when; it must also have the staff with the necessary skills and any machinery must have the appropriate facilities and production capacity. For example, a production department which is geared to produce 1000 units of a product per day, will probably find it difficult to produce 2000 units, without modification of the system of production.

Marketing

A marketing function is a vital part of many large national and international businesses; it aims to generate information, from a wide range of data sources, to support marketing decisions. Three such decision areas are:

(i)   *strategic* and relating to, for example, expansion of the company's existing market share and the identification of new marketable products;

(ii) *tactical*, for example, planning the marketing mix;

(iii) *operational*, for example, day-to-day planning of sales calls and ad hoc promotions.

At the operational level, for example, data gathered from sales invoices, sales force staff and accounting information can be used to establish customer types. Thus, customers can be classified as 'low', 'medium' or 'high' volume users according to the frequency and volume of their orders. This information can help sales staff to target particular categories of customer and to plan the timing of sales calls. At the tactical level, invoices provide information on sales variance between different market segments over time or sales projections based on current patterns.

Distribution

Distribution concerns the delivery of a company's products to its customers and is obviously of great importance. An organisation can have the best products in the world and the most effective marketing campaigns, but if it cannot distribute its goods efficiently it will fail. Distribution systems include the management and control of a company's own delivery vehicles and drivers, the scheduling of deliveries to ensure rapid response to orders and efficient use of the transport fleet. If a company does not have its own vehicles, then it must arrange for suitable contracts with other companies, such as Parcel Force, UPS and Securicor. Systems must also be in place for the handling delayed deliveries and customer complaints, order tracking (buyers can check on the progress of their order) and the return of unwanted or damaged goods.

Controlling the costs of distribution, which can be considerable, is of major importance. For example, the breakdown of distribution costs across manufacturing industry is typically as follows: administration 17%; transport 29%; handling 8%; packaging 12%; warehousing 17%; stock control 17%.

Administration

Administration systems provide support and services across the organisation. They include, for example, the handling of telephone switchboard and fax and photocopying services, document production, room booking (for meetings etc), requisitioning of equipment and consumables, and general secretarial support. ICT services are part of that administration support service.

ICT Services

Apart from small firms, most organisations need specialist staff to develop, introduce, maintain and update the various systems which make use of information technology. The term 'information communication technology' covers all computer-based information processing systems, plus those which make use of data communications, such as computer networks, fax machines, photocopiers and telephone systems. The responsibilities of ICT Services are, therefore, much broader than those traditionally held by wholly centralised computer services or data processing departments. The development of cheaper and more powerful microcomputer systems, which can be networked with one another, as well as with larger mini and mainframe systems, has resulted in computer facilities being distributed more widely. For this reason, ICT Services needs to provide a much more flexible service and support user systems at the point of use. For example, users of network workstations need support when equipment, such as a shared printer, breaks down or they may require help in the use of software on the network. This contrasts with a centralised department, which holds all the computer equipment, carries out all computer processing and restricts user access to specialised applications, run through dedicated terminals. ICT Services may be known variously as Computer Services, Management Information Services or less commonly now, the Data Processing Department.

Role of ICT Services

ICT Services fulfils a servicing function for the whole organisation. In larger organisations, there is a centralised computer facility, possibly in the shape of a mainframe or minicomputer system, with the responsibility for major applications, such as payroll and stock control. User departments may have access to the centralised facility through attached terminals or networked microcomputers. Individual members of staff may also use stand-alone microcomputer systems or portable devices, such as notebooks and personal digital assistants (PDAs). ICT Services staff need to support users in the use of these distributed facilities, as well as control the operation of any centralised system. IT Services provides facilities to satisfy both *operational* and *managerial* information needs.

Operational requirements

Each functional area has its own operational information needs. For example, Wages and Salaries need payroll details and payslips, and Sales Order Processing require the production of customer invoices. Common examples of routine operations include:

❑ keeping stock records

❑ sales accounting and purchase accounting;

❑ payroll;

❑ invoicing and production of delivery notes;

❑ routine costing;

❑ filing of customer orders.

Managerial requirements

Routine processing work forms the bulk of the activity within ICT Services, but there is an increasing demand for management information. This includes assistance with functions which require management involvement and thinking, but which can be partially automated or assisted by computers. Examples of such functions include:

- ❑   production planning;

- ❑   short term and long term forecasting;

- ❑   setting of budgets;

- ❑   decision-making on financial policies;

- ❑   marketing decisions and sales management;

- ❑   factory maintenance and management;

- ❑   price determination;

- ❑   selection of suppliers.

Function of ICT Services

Figure 7.1 shows the typical functions within an ICT Services department.

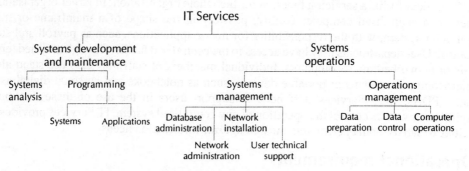

Figure 7.1. *Typical structure of ICT Services department*

Systems development

This function relates to the development of new computerised systems and the maintenance of existing ones. This function is staffed primarily by *systems analysts* and *programmers*. In small organisations, hybrid skills are often needed, so job titles such as *analyst programmer* may be used.

Systems analysis

Systems analysis is a process used in the design of new systems, as requested by corporate management. Systems analysis follows stages of *investigation*, *design* and *implementation*. Each stage should involve close consultation with potential users, in the various functional areas of the organisation, to ensure that their information and operational requirements are met.

The design stage should produce a *system specification* which, rather like an architect's plans for a building, details all necessary materials and procedures needed to fulfil the specification. The specification should detail the necessary clerical procedures, hardware requirements and the inputs, processing and outputs required of the computer software.

After implementation of a system, it will require continual monitoring and probably, occasional modification, when the operational or information requirements of users change. This maintenance task is the responsibility of the systems analysts,

Programming

Programming lacks some of the creative aspects of systems analysis and involves the use of a programming language (for example, C++, COBOL, Visual BASIC) to code the necessary computer programs. The program requirements are detailed in the *program* or *software specification*, which forms part of the system specification prepared by systems analysts.

Most programmers who work in an ICT Services department are likely to be *applications programmers*, responsible for the development or modification of applications, such as stock control or payroll. Systems programmers are concerned with the development of operating systems and utilities, which are normally developed by large computer manufacturers or software companies, such as Microsoft. An ICT Services department may also employ *systems programmers*, but they are likely to have a more limited role than applications programmers. Much software is now in commercial package form, but not all applications can be satisfied by such means and applications programmers continue to be needed for tailoring of programs specifically for their employer.

The growth of network use has created the need for *network programmers*, who have specialist knowledge of such systems. Apart from specialising in systems, applications or network programming, a programmer is likely to be skilled in the use of one or more programming languages. An organisation seeking to employ programmers will specify the language or languages they require.

System operations

This broad function is concerned with the operational, rather than the developmental aspects of the ICT systems. It is divided into *systems management* and *operations management*.

Systems management

This function deals with the general operation of all the ICT systems and is not directly concerned with particular applications.

There are a number of separate areas within this function: *network installation*; *network administration*; *intranet and extranet management*; *user technical support*; *database administration*.

Network installation and administration

Computer networks are a feature of most organisations and tasks of selecting, purchasing and installing the hardware and software, both systems and applications, may be carried out by specialist staff in this area. Staff employed in this area need to be familiar with the network operating system and its utilities. They are responsible for setting up and managing network user accounts, controlling passwords, managing printer queues, allocating and maintaining and backing up network storage and monitoring the performance of the network.

User technical support

The distribution to users, of computer resources through networks, desktop and portable computer systems has hugely expanded the need for ICT user support. Users often have access to a range of different devices, such as printers, scanners, plotters and fax modems and apart from needing initial training in their use, they also require occasional support when things go wrong. Support staff may also give guidance in the use of software and help trouble-shoot problems which users will inevitably encounter at some stage. User technical support is extremely important if users are to use ICT resources efficiently and for the benefit of the organisation.

Database administration

If applications are implemented through a database system, then specialist staff, known as database administrators, are employed to control access to the database by applications and ensure consistency in the use of data within it. Systems analysts and programmers involved in the development of database applications need to work closely with the responsible *database administrator* (DBA).

Operations management

This function, led by an operations manager, has three main areas of responsibility: *data control*; *data preparation*; *computer operations*; *media library*. These responsibilities relate particularly to centrally controlled applications.

Data control

Data control staff are responsible for the co-ordination and control of data flowing through the operations section. For example, data received from Salaries, to update the payroll master file and produce payslips, have to be controlled to ensure their accuracy and completeness at all stages of processing.

Data preparation

Batch processing systems require the transcription and encoding of data gathered from source documents, such as order forms or invoices, on to magnetic storage. The input is then effected directly from the magnetic tape or disk on which the data has been accumulated. On-line, transaction processing systems, do not usually require this data preparation stage.

Computer operations

Computer operators are responsible for the day-to-day running of the computer hardware. In the case of mainframe computer systems, their responsibilities include the loading and unloading of magnetic tape reels or magnetic disk packs, according to the on-line requirements of applications currently in use. For example, before a payroll run, the media containing the master and transaction files have to be loaded onto the relevant devices, so that they can be accessed by the computer which is running the payroll program. The computer hardware is under the control of operating system software and an operator needs to communicate with the operating system regarding jobs to be processed and to deal with error conditions which may arise. A separate terminal is normally dedicated as an *operator console* and access to it is restricted both physically and through software-controlled passwords.

✍️Self-test questions

1. Machem Ltd is a large manufacturing business. It buys in raw materials from a number of suppliers and uses the raw materials to produce its range of specialist outdoor clothing and equipment, which it sells to retailers. It has a warehouse next to the factory, to store the stocks of raw materials and finished goods.

   (i)   Explain the circumstances when Machem Ltd is a *debtor* and when it is a *creditor*.

   (ii) Explain circumstances when Machem will receive *invoices* and when it will issue them.

   (iii) List the processes involved in invoicing a retailer and settlement of the debt.

   (iv) Identify features of a typical *stock control* system which Machem Ltd could use to maintain sufficient, but not excessive levels of stock.

   (v)   Machem Ltd is planning to extend its range of products and needs to ensure that there will be sufficient demand for the new products to make a profit. As well as its production function, the company has its own research and development (R&D) and marketing departments. Suggest ways in which these three functions may co-operate to maximise Machem Ltd's chances of success.

2. Machem Ltd has its own *ICT Services* function, employing systems analysts, programmers, network engineers, network administrators and user technical support assistants.

   Briefly outline the likely role of each of these categories of staff at Machem Ltd.

Chapter 8

Information in organisations

Role of information

In business, making decisions or taking actions without all the relevant information can be risky. For example, if a company decides to increase the price of a product because the product is selling well and ignores information that competitors have launched similar products, it is acting without all the relevant information. Similarly, fulfilling a customer order without checking their credit record risks an increase in bad (unrecoverable) debt). Information can vary in quality and to provide the best possible basis for decision-making, organisations should attempt to control the quality of the information they use. If it is to act with any purpose, an organisation needs information about itself, its customers (or clients) and suppliers (if any) and the *environment* in which it operates. Environment includes influences which are external to an organisation, such as government legislation and bank lending rates. Without such information, an organisation cannot properly plan for the future (*strategic planning*), or control and monitor its present performance (*operational control*).

Strategic planning

Planning for the future is never risk-free, but with a range of appropriate information the risks of decision-making can be minimised. Suppose, for example, that a manufacturing company is planning its production output for the next month; it needs to specify the particular product mix and the number of units of each product to be manufactured. In making these decisions, it is likely to draw on two main sources of information:

- ❏ past sales figures;
- ❏ market research results.

Decisions of this nature are likely to be made at corporate (Board of Directors) level and fall into a category known as *strategic* decision-making.

Operational control

When a company monitors its production figures, its stocks of raw materials and finished products, its is controlling its day-to-day, manufacturing operations. Other functions in the company, such as sales, payroll and accounts require similar operational control. Operational information permits day-to-day control to be exerted and allows measurement of present performance, as opposed to future prospects. Common examples of operational information include:

- ❏ balances of customer accounts;
- ❏ invoices for customer sales;
- ❏ delivery notes for goods received from suppliers.

Periodic monitoring through Annual Accounts

The production of statements, such as a Trading and Profit and Loss Account and Balance Sheet, provides information on the financial health of a company, at the time the statements are produced. These statements are a legal requirement for all but the smallest businesses, but are useful for periodic monitoring of performance. Accounting records are essential to effective decision-making and also produce information demanded by, for example, shareholders, the Inland Revenue or the VAT authorities. Not all information generated within or used by an organisation can be categorised as wholly operational or corporate. Information which is classed initially as operational can become part of corporate information. For example, the operational information that a customer has failed to pay their account in two successive months may result in a suspension of further credit. Subsequently, this information may be combined with details of similar customer accounts to produce a bad debts report, which results in a corporate decision to alter customer credit and debt collection strategy.

Information systems

The production of information needs to be a controlled process, exercised through the use of information systems. An organisation can be divided into a number of *internal* functions, such as Sales, Marketing, Production and Accounts and each function requires its own information systems or sub-systems. The information system for any one functional area should not be considered in isolation, because it forms only part of an organisation-wide information system. This is made particularly clear when database systems are used. The various information systems within an organisation interact and affect one another. An organisation also interacts with and is influenced by organisations, such as banks and the Inland Revenue, in the surrounding environment; these are *external* functions. Co-ordination of an organisation's separate information systems or sub-systems is essential if its common aims are to be achieved.

Information needs

To operate, different functions within an organisation need access to particular types of information, some examples of which are briefly described below.

Design specifications; before a product is manufactured a specification is produced detailing, for example, the types, qualities and quantities of required materials, physical features, performance requirements (such as for a car) and so on. Some products, such as computer software, need to include design features concerning, for example, the user interface.

Construction drawings. As the term indicates, these are used to guide the person or persons building or constructing the product. An architect produces construction drawings for the house builder to follow; design specification details are also included, so that the builder knows the types and quantities of materials.

Market research. This information is often gathered through surveys, either using question-naires or monitoring consumer buying patterns. A company should carry out market research before beginning the production or sale of a new product in its range.

Advertising is essential to any organisation wishing to promote its image or product range. Advertising uses market research information to target the most appropriate areas of the population. For example, market research may indicate that a product is most likely to be bought by professional people living in the south of England; advertising can be directed, perhaps through mails shots, to that section of the population.

Sales orders detail customer order requirements, including item details, quantities and delivery dates; *purchase orders* detail the organisation's purchase requirements from suppliers.

Payments and receipts. These may relate to sales orders or purchase orders. Receipts are amounts received from debtors. Payments are made by a business to settle debts with creditors (suppliers to the business).

Transport requirements. This information will detail, for example, a goods list, the delivery address, special requirements, such as refrigeration and possibly the route to be taken.

Information flow diagrams

Figure 8.1 illustrates some information flows within a typical manufacturing and wholesaling organisation.

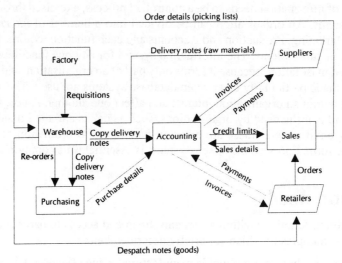

Figure 8.1. *Information flows between functions*

An examination of Figure 8.1 shows that each functional area is dependent on one or more other areas for the information it needs to operate. For example, to charge the retail outlets (their customers) for the goods supplied, the Accounting function requires the necessary sales information, which is supplied by the Sales function. The information allows the Accounting function to prepare the necessary invoices to send to customers. Similarly, Purchasing must be kept informed by the Warehouse (stock control) of raw materials which need re-ordering from suppliers, to replenish stocks.

These examples of *operational* information allow day-to-day decisions to be made on the operation of the business. To keep the diagram fairly simple, certain vital functions, such as Production Control and Marketing, are not shown. Obviously, their inclusion would increase the number of information flows and the complexity of the diagram.

The information flows shown in Figure 8.1 are all 'triggered' by *events*. For example:

(i)   a customer order is generated when a customer orders goods;

(ii)   credit limit details flow from Accounting to Sales, when a customer order is checked;

(iii) an invoice is raised when goods are despatched to a customer;

(iv)   a payment to a supplier is triggered when the invoice payment falls due.

An information flow diagram may also illustrate the transmission medium or method used for each flow. For example, an interaction between two functions may be face-to-face, by e-mail, a video conferencing link, fax, electronic point-of-sale (EPOS), web site, or one of several other methods outlined at the end of this chapter.

ICT support of information flows

Teleconferencing

This service allows users to support a discussion over the telephone with a shared computer application, such as a word processor, spreadsheet or drawing package and a common whiteboard (an area of the display screen) visible to the conference users. The whiteboard is a comment or drawing area which users can use to illustrate points they wish to make. Each user has the ability to control the application, allowing co-operative development of, for example, a drawing or a spreadsheet model. Of course, such application sharing needs to be carefully managed and controlled to avoid inefficiency and time-wasting, which may result if users have different views on how the drawing or model should develop. The voice communications may be carried out over a conventional telephone network or over the Internet as part of the teleconferencing package. Microsoft's NetMeeting is built into the Explorer browser and supports all these facilities.

Video conferencing

Using computers with attached video cameras, microphones and speakers, conference participants are able to see and hear one another. The audio and video signals are carried over the Internet for real-time display as the conference takes place. The availability of cheap mini video cameras has radically increased the popularity of this service. Both tele and video conferencing have the potential to make significant savings for organisations in staffing, travel and accommodation costs. The main cost derives from local rate telephone charges.

Bibliographic databases

These databases provide information on specialised or widely ranging subjects. For example, BLAISE, which is provided by the British Library, gives information on British book publications. Euronet Diane (Direct Information Access Network in Europe) provides information extracted from publications, research documents and so on, which may be of interest to specialists, such as scientists, engineers, economists and lawyers. Each extract provides the relevant bibliographic references to allow users to access the original sources more fully.

Bulletin boards

A bulletin board (BB) is simply a means by which users can, for example, exchange ideas, pass on information and buy or sell items to one another. Frequently, no charge is made. Chat lines are often included; this means that two users can carry on a conversation, through the use of screen and keyboard.

Telex

Telex is a well established communications system which, rather like the public telephone network, allows subscribers to communicate with one another. There are over a million subscribers in this country at present. Each subscriber is given a telex code (you will often see it at the top of business letter headings next to the telephone number) and must have a teleprinter which is a combination of keyboard and printer. There is no screen, so all messages sent or received are printed onto hard copy.

The transmission rate of approximately 6 characters per second is slow compared with more modern telecommunications systems, but the limitations of keyboard entry and printer speed on the teleprinter, make any faster speed unnecessary. The main benefit of telex is that a permanent record of communications is kept and the receiver does not have to be on the spot when the message arrives. Its main disadvantage is that there is no storage facility for messages. Any transmission has to be printed as soon as it is transmitted so that if the receiver is faulty, the system comes to a halt. Although it is inferior to e-mail (see next paragraph), it is still the only method (apart from telephone) of instant communication with less developed countries, where Telex machines are still widely used.

Electronic mail (e-mail) services

E-mail systems based on computer networks are paper-less (except when a user requires hard copy). A major advantage is the facility for message storage if a destination terminal is busy, or has a temporary fault. When it is free, the message can be transmitted. Certain basic features can be identified as being common to all e-mail systems:

❑   a terminal for preparing, entering and storing messages. The terminal will be intelligent, possibly a microcomputer, mainframe terminal or dedicated word processor. In any event, it should have some word processing or text editing facilities to allow messages to be changed on screen before transmission. A printer may also be available for printing out messages received over the system;

❑   an electronic communication link with other workstations in the network and with the central computer controlling the system;

❑   a directory containing the electronic addresses of all network users;

❑   a central mailbox facility (usually the controlling computer) for the storage of messages in transit or waiting to be retrieved.

Ideally, the following facilities are available to e-mail users:

- messages are automatically dated upon transmission;

- messages are automatically acknowledged as being received when the recipient first accesses it from the terminal;

- multiple addressing, that is the facility to address a message to an identified group, without addressing each member of the group individually;

- priority rating to allow messages to be allocated different priorities according to their importance.

Networks require two particular features in order to support e-mail:

- a message storage facility to allow messages to be forwarded when the recipient is available;

- compatibility with a wide range of manufacturers' equipment. Devices attached to a network have to be able to talk to the communications network using protocols or standards of communication.

Benefits of e-mail

The following major benefits are generally claimed for e-mail systems:

- savings in stationery and telephone costs;

- more rapid transmission than is possible with conventional mail;

- e-mail can be integrated with other computer-based systems used in an organisation;

- all transmissions are recorded, so costs can be carefully controlled;

- e-mail allows staff to telework, that is, to work from home via a terminal;

- the recipient does not have to be present when a message is sent. Messages can be retrieved from the central mailbox when convenient.

Electronic data interchange (EDI)

Similar to E-mail, EDI allows users to exchange business documents, such as invoices, delivery notes, orders and receipts over the telephone network. EDI can drastically reduce the volume of paperwork and business can be transacted much more quickly than is possible through the normal postal system. UK examples of EDI systems are:

- Tradanet, linking manufacturers, wholesalers, distributors and retailers;

- Brokernet, which links insurance companies and brokers;

- Drugnet, linking medical practices to pharmaceutical companies, allowing the provision of current information on various products;

- Factornet allows firms to deal with *factors* who buy outstanding customer bills at a discount; the factors then obtain payment from the debtor. Small firms find this service particularly useful as it enables them to improve their cash flow.

Web site

The World Wide Web has made possible new ways for a business to communicate with its customers. Some sites are 'brochure' sites and are simply another way of promoting a business's corporate image, whilst some e-commerce (Chapter 9) sites are the basis of the entire business. Amazon.com is probably the most famous of such sites, selling books, CDs and other publications entirely through the Web.

Intranet and extranet

Some organisations may use their internal networks to form an intranet, effectively a private Internet. Its appearance is that of the Web and the familiar browser is its user interface. 'Out of the box' Web servers provide a convenient and relatively cheap method of developing internal network requirements and many organisations have built intranets as part of their overall Internet strategy. Employees are usually familiar with the Web and require little training to access the resources they need on the company intranet.

Web tools, such as HTML (code for developing Web pages) editors, are relatively cheap and application development only becomes expensive when large and complex databases are needed, as in the case of an on-line store's product database.

To provide access external access to their intranet a company may use its Web site, with suitable access controls, including the use of *firewalls* (software protection), encryption (scambling of incoming and outgoing messages) and passwords. As an intra/extranet, outside access only requires the use of a Web browser, which is generally available. Extranets can be a valuable way of providing customer support and services. For example, the progress of a project can be monitored by the client, products can be developed by sharing information with partner organisations, customers can check on product availability, or the status of a delivery.

New generation mobile phones

Apart from voice transmission, mobile phones can be used to transmit text messages and those that support Internet Protocol (IP) or the newer WAP (Wireless Application Protocol) can be used to access Internet services, albeit very slowly. The delivery of Internet services through mobile networks is hampered by the mobile phone itself, with its slow processor, poor battery life, mono display and awkward keypad, as well as by limited bandwidth. The development of *broadband* mobile networks and more sophisticated phones will full potential of the Internet's multimedia content is to be made as accessible through a mobile phone as it is through a PC. In the meantime, services are largely text-based and perfectly adequate for the viewing of such information as travel, weather, sport results, share prices and the delivery of bank, ticket and message services. New generation mobile phones are making use of larger flip-up screens with touch-sensitive input and handwriting recognition as additions to the usual keypad.

EFTPOS (electronic funds transfer at point-of-sale)

This service provides for the automatic debiting of customers' bank accounts at the checkout or point of sale. Many garages now have a device for reading the magnetic strip details on bank and credit cards. The system saves considerable time when contrasted with payments by cheque and as an alternative to cash, reduces the likelihood of theft. The retailer also has the assurance that the payment is authorised before the sale is made. Usually, a retailer will have a floor limit, or amount above which a telephone call needs to be made to the credit card company for authorisation of payment.

EFT (electronic funds transfer)

This system is used to transfer money between the branches of the same bank and between different banks. In the UK, the system is known as the Bankers Automated Clearing Service (BACS). The service is not restricted to bank use; organisations can pay their employees salaries directly into their bank or building society accounts. Business accounts can also be settled through this EFT system. Apart from the banks, other users usually link into the pstn through a dial-up connection (unless the volume of data justifies a leased line).

Facsimile transmission (FAX)

This service allows the transmission of facsimiles or exact copies of documents or pictures through a data communications network. Using a fax machine connected to a telephone line, the user simply dials the fax number of the recipient, waits for the correct signal and the document is fed though the fax machine and transmitted. The fax machine sends picture elements or pixels obtained by scanning the document in a series of parallel lines; a synchronised fax machine at the other end prints a facsimile from those pixels. Fax/modems allow computer communication by fax with other fax modems or with conventional fax machines.

Example of ICT support of information flow

To illustrate the role of ICT in managing information flow, we use a simple example of a small electrical company, Wingrove Electrical Ltd, based on the outskirts of London. It employs 38 people and produces electrical components for use in central heating equipment. The following examples of activities and information flows are used to show the potential benefits of using IT.

An enquiry from a potential buyer

A telephone enquiry from a potential customer is received by the company's telephonist, who attempts to connect the caller with the company sales manager, who is out of the office. She makes a note of the caller's name and the nature of the enquiry and promises to pass these details on to the sales manager when she returns to the office. Unfortunately, the paper with the message is lost and so is the potential order. Clearly, the system could have been improved by a number of methods.

If Wingrove had a local area network, the telephonist could have obtained sufficient product information to meet the initial enquiry of the potential buyer. The message could have been transmitted through the electronic mail system, for the sales manager to access when she returned. If the sales manager used a notebook computer, she could download such messages remotely, through the telecommunications or mobile phone network.

It is also possible that the customer's enquiry could have been satisfied through the company web site. Information on products, prices, anticipated delivery times, technical support details and the answers to frequently asked questions (FAQs) can be stored and kept up to date through customer support pages.

Receipt of an order

Wingrove receives a substantial order by post. The manual procedures involve copying the order, sending a copy to Accounting and a copy attached to a 'job sheet' to Production. When the order is completed and despatched, Accounting will invoice the customer and await payment. Unfortunately, when the customer eventually pays, he submits a cheque for an incorrect amount, but the clerk fails to notice that the amount on the invoice and the amount on the cheque do not agree; as a result, he processes the invoice as paid. Wingrove has thus lost some of its profit.

The company could improve its financial control by installing a computerised order processing and invoice verification system. As each order is received into the company, the appropriate details, such as customer, item, quantity, price and so on, are entered into its computer, which automatically generates an invoice, statements and increasingly harshly worded reminders, until the customer settles the debt. When the cheque arrives, its value is also entered and the program automatically checks to ensure that the amount matches both the original price quoted and the invoice value. As protection against the miskeying of the cheque amount, a further check involves the automatic reconciliation, each month, of totals for paid and unpaid invoices.

Production of a quotation

Wingrove's managing director is informed that Birmingham City Council is intending to replace the central heating systems in all its public buildings, over the next three years and is seeking tenders for the component parts of the system. Wingrove would very much like to gain the contract and decide to submit a detailed quotation document. The quotation is 28 pages long and contains an extensive amount of technical detail, as well as product specifications, prices and delivery details. Typed manually, reference would have to be made to numerous files for component specifications and prices and the inevitable modifications to the tender would involve extensive re-typing. The following improvements are possible.

Using a word processor and quotation template, the task can be completed much more quickly. Layout alterations and editing can easily be done before a final copy is printed. A high quality printer, possibly with colour facility, will contribute to a highly professional appearance and improve the image of the company. Component specification and price data can be imported from the company's database of such information, directly into the document. If speed is important, the document could be faxed or e-mailed to Birmingham City Council.

ICT applications for strategic decision-making

Management information systems (MIS)

Although computers can perform routine processing tasks very efficiently, it is generally recognised that limiting a computer's use to the processing of operational information constitutes a waste of computer power. An MIS is designed to make use of the computer's power of selection and analysis to produce useful management information. An MIS has a number of key features:

  ❑   it produces information beyond that required for routine data processing;

❑   timing of information production is critical;

❑   the information it produces is an aid to decision-making;

❑   it is usually based on the database concept.

The claims for MIS are sometimes excessive. It is rarely the complete answer to all a company's information needs, but when successfully implemented, it provides a valuable information advantage over competitors.

Decision support systems (DSS)

A DSS aims to provide a more flexible decision tool than that supplied by a MIS which tends to produce information in an anticipated, pre-defined form and as such, does not allow managers to make ad hoc requests for information. DSS tend to be narrower in scope than MIS, often making use of general-purpose software packages. Examples of DSS include electronic spreadsheets, such as Microsoft Excel and relational database management systems such as Access and Paradox. Additionally, *financial modelling* (Chapter 11) and statistical packages are considered to be DSS tools. A major benefit is the independence they allow for information control by individual managers and executives. When, for example, a sales manager requires a report on sales figures for the last three months, a microcomputer with database package may provide the report more quickly than a centralised data processing department.

✎ Self-test questions

1. Study the information flow diagram in Figure 8.1 and answer the following questions.
    (i)   When a customer places an order with Sales, to which function must they refer for a credit limit?
    (ii)   When a customer order is accepted why are the details passed to Accounting?
    (iii) What information does accounting need from the Warehouse function before paying an invoice sent from a supplier?
    (iv)   What use does the Warehouse function make of the requisitions it receives from the Factory?
2. With the use of suitable examples, explain the role of e-mail, video conferencing in supporting communications within and between organisations.
3. Distinguish between an *Intranet* and an *Extranet* and indicate how each can be used to improve the way an organisation communicates internally and with its customers and suppliers.
4. Distinguish between EFT and EFTPOS.
5. Suggest one benefit and one drawback of using a mobile phone to access the World Wide Web.
6. List the key features of a Management Information System (MIS).
7. A Sales Manager uses a spreadsheet to identify sales patterns across each of the five areas for which she is responsible. The data will be used to identify one area which is to be targeted for a special sales drive. What is the general term for this type of information system>

Chapter 9

ICT applications in business

Financial accounting systems

The following section describes the various financial accounting systems of a typical business and the main features of accounting software. To begin with some associated terminology is defined and some basic concepts are explained.

The ledgers

Business accounts are needed to record:

❏ *debtor* transactions; debtors are people or organisations who owe money to the business for goods or services provided (credit sales);

❏ *creditor* transactions; creditors are people or organisations to whom the business owes money, for the supply of goods (credit purchases).

These transactions are recorded in the *sales ledger* and the *purchases ledger* respectively. A third ledger, the *nominal* (or *general*) *ledger* is used to record the overall income and expenditure of the business, with each transaction classified according to its purpose.

Sales ledger

General description

The purpose of the sales ledger is to keep a record of amounts owed to a business by its trading customers or clients. It contains a record for each customer with a credit arrangement. Most businesses permit their customers to buy goods on credit. The goods are usually supplied on the understanding that, once payment has been requested, the debt will be paid for within a specified period of, for example, 14 or 30 days. Payment is requested with the use of a customer addressed *invoice*, which contains details of goods supplied, the amount owing and credit days given. Once a customer order has been accepted and processed, the total amount due for the order is recorded in the relevant customers account in the sales ledger and the balance owing is increased accordingly. When a payment is received from the customer, the amount is entered to the customer's account and the balance owing is decreased by the appropriate amount. There are two main approaches to sales ledger maintenance, *balance forward* and *open item*.

❏ Balance forward. This method provides: an opening balance (the amount owing at the beginning of the month); the transactions for that month, giving the date, type (for example, goods sold or payment received); the amount of each transaction; a closing balance. The closing balance at the end of the month is carried forward as the opening balance for the next month. A *statement of account*, detailing all the transactions for the month will normally be sent to the customer and a copy filed away for business records. The customer's account in the sales ledger will not then contain details of the previous month's transactions so any query will require reference to the filed statements of account.

☐ Open item. The open item method is more complicated in that each invoice is identified by a code and requires payments from customers to be matched against the relevant invoices. All payments received and relating to a particular invoice are recorded against it until it is completely paid off. This method can make control difficult as some customers may make part payments, which cannot be tied to a particular invoice. If a customer does not specify to which invoice a particular payment relates it is normally assigned to the oldest invoice(s). Once an invoice has been completely settled it is cleared from the ledger and any subsequent statements of account.

Package requirements and facilities

Customer master file

When setting up the Sales Ledger system, one of the first tasks is to open an account for each customer. These accounts are maintained in a sales ledger *master file*, which is updated by sales and account settlement transactions. A typical package should provide as a minimum, the following data item types for each customer record:

☐ *account number* - used to identify uniquely a customer record;

☐ *name and address* - this will normally be the customers address to which statements of account and invoices are sent;

☐ *credit limit* - the maximum amount of credit to be allowed to the customer at any one time. This is checked by sales staff before an order is authorised for processing;

☐ *balance* - this is the balance of the customer's account at any one time.

A choice is usually provided to select the form of sales ledger required, either *open item* or *balance forward* (see previous section). Normally, when the file is first created, a zero balance is recorded and outstanding transactions are entered to produce a current balance. An open item system stores details of any unpaid invoices. Each invoice can be associated with a particular customer account through the account number.

Transaction entries

Transactions may be applied directly to customer accounts in the sales ledger (*transaction processing*) or they may be initially stored as a transaction file for a *batch* updating run. Whichever method the package uses, it should allow for the entry of the following transaction types:

☐ *invoice* - this is sent to the customer requesting payment concerning a particular order. The amount of the invoice is debited to the customer's account in the sales ledger, thus increasing the amount owing;

❑ *credit note*. If, for example, goods are returned by a customer or there is a dispute concerning the goods, a credit note is issued by the business to the customer. The amount of the credit note will be credited to the customer's account in the sales ledger, thus reducing the balance owing. Credit notes are often printed in red to distinguish them from invoices;

❑ *receipt* - this is any payment or remittance received from a customer in whole or partial settlement of an invoice. Such an entry will be credited to the customer's account and reduce the balance owing accordingly.

The following data may be entered with each type of transaction:

❑ *account number* - essential to identify the computer record. Although some packages allow for the entry of a shortened customer name (if the account number has been forgotten) the account number is still necessary to identify uniquely a record;

❑ *date of transaction* and *amount of transaction*;

❑ *transaction reference* - this is the invoice number to which the transaction relates.

Outputs

The following facilities may be expected:

❑ *single account enquiry* - details of an individual customer's account can be displayed on screen. Retrieval may be by account number or a search facility, using a shortened version of the customer name. If more than one record is retrieved by this method they may be scanned through on screen until the required record is found;

❑ *customer statement printing* - it is essential that the system can produce monthly statements for sending to customers;

❑ *debtors age analysis* - this provides a schedule of the total amounts owing by customers, categorised according to the time various portions of the total debt have been outstanding (unpaid). It is important for a business to make financial provision for the possibility of *bad debts*. These are debts which are unlikely to be settled and may have to be taken out of business profits. From their own experience of the trade, the proprietor of a business should be able to estimate the percentage of each debt that is likely to become bad. Generally, the longer the debt has been outstanding, the greater the likelihood that it will remain unpaid;

❑ *customers over credit limit* - this may form the basis of a black list of customers. Any new order from one of these customers has to be authorised by management. On the other hand, the appearance of certain customers on the list may suggest that some increased credit limits are needed. When a business is successful, it often needs more credit to expand further;

❑ *dormant account list* - if there has been no activity on an account for some time, it may warrant removal from the file. Alternatively, it may be useful to contact the customer to see if further business may be forthcoming.

Validation and control

The package should provide for careful validation of transactions and the protection of records from unauthorised access or amendment. Generally, for example, a customer record cannot be removed from the sales ledger while the account is still live (there is a balance outstanding). More details of validation and control are given in Chapter 24.

Purchase ledger

General description

The purchase ledger function mirrors that of the sales ledger, except that it contains an account for each *supplier*, from whom the business buys goods. When trading with a supplier, it is usually through credit arrangements, similar to those provided by the business for its own customers. Thus, the business receives an invoice requesting payment, within a certain period, for goods purchased. The amount of the invoice is credited to the supplier's account and the balance owing to the supplier is increased accordingly. When payment is made to a supplier, in full or part settlement of an invoice, the supplier's account is debited by the appropriate amount and the balance is decreased.

Most purchase ledger systems operate on an open item basis. Each supplier invoice is given a reference number and when payment is made to a supplier, the reference number can be used to allocate the payment to a particular invoice.

Package requirements and facilities

Supplier master file

The supplier master file contains the suppliers' (*creditors'*) accounts. It is updated by supplier invoices and payments to suppliers.

A typical package should provide, as a minimum, the following data item types for each supplier record:

❑ *account number*- used to identify uniquely a supplier record;

❑ *name and address* - the name and address of the supplier business;

❑ *credit limit* - the maximum amount of credit allowed to the business by the supplier at any one time. A check should be kept on this to avoid rejection of orders;

❑ *settlement discount* - this is the amount of discount given by a supplier if an invoice is settled within a specified discount period;

❑ *due date* - the system may issue a reminder when payment is due. A report may be printed, on request, listing all invoice amounts due for payment within, say, 7 days;

❑ *balance* - the current balance on the account.

A choice is usually provided to select the form of purchase ledger required (either open item or balance forward).

Transactions

Transactions may update the supplier accounts directly (transaction processing) or they may be initially stored as a transaction file for a later updating run. A purchase ledger package should allow for the following transactions:

❑ *supplier invoices* - before entry, each invoice must be checked against the appropriate order and then against the relevant delivery note, for actual receipt of goods. The balance on a supplier's account (the amount owed to the supplier) is increased by an invoice entry. Some packages allow unsatisfactory (there may be doubt about the delivery of the goods) invoices to be held in abeyance until cleared;

❑ *approved payments* - once an invoice has been cleared for payment, a voucher may be raised to ensure payment, on or before a due date, and discount for prompt payment. The entry of the payment value decreases the balance of a supplier's account and thus the amount owed by the business to the supplier. Cheques may be produced automatically on the due date, but there should be some checking procedure to ensure that payments are properly authorised;

❑ *adjustments* - to reverse entries made in error.

Outputs

The following output facilities may be expected:

❑ *single account enquiries* - details of an individual supplier's account can be displayed on screen; retrieval may be through a supplier code;

❑ *payment advice slip* - this may be produced to accompany a payment to a supplier. Each payment slip details the invoice reference, the amount due and the value of the payment remitted. Payment advice slips help the supplier, who may be using an open item sales ledger system;

❑ *automatic cheques* - the package may, with the use of pre-printed stationery, produce cheques for payment to suppliers, as and when invoices fall due. There must be a careful checking and authorisation procedure to prevent incorrect payments being made;

❑ *unpaid invoices* - a list of all outstanding invoices, together with details of supplier, amount owing and due date;

❑ *creditors' age analysis* - this is the supplier equivalent of debtors' age analysis. The report provides a schedule of total balances owing to suppliers, analysed according to the time the debt has been outstanding. The report may be used to determine which payments should be given priority over others.

Nominal ledger

General description

The nominal ledger is used to record the income and expenditure of a business, classified according to purpose. Thus, for example, it contains an account for *sales*; sales totals are entered on a daily basis. The sales ledger analyses sales by customer, whereas the   *sales account* provides a cumulative total for sales, as the accounting year progresses. The *purchases account* in the nominal ledger fulfils a similar purpose for purchases by the business. Other income and expenditure accounts recorded in the nominal ledger may include, for example, *rent*, *heating* and *wages*. If some items of income and expenditure are too small to warrant separate analysis, there may also be *sundry income* and *sundry expenditure* accounts. The information held in the nominal ledger accounts is used to draw up a *profit and loss account*. This account provides information on the trading performance of the business over the year. A *balance sheet* can then be produced to give a snapshot view of the assets and liabilities of a business, on a particular date.

Package requirements and facilities

Nominal accounts master file

When an account is opened in the nominal ledger, the following data item types should be available:

❑ *account code* - each account is given a code, to allow the allocation of transactions. For example, an entry for a gas bill payment may be directed to the Heating account by the code 012;

❑ *account name* - for example, Sales, Heating, Rent;

❑ *balance*.

Associated with each account are a number of transactions processed during the current accounting period.

Transactions

❑ *sales and purchases* - these may be entered periodically as accumulated totals or, in an integrated accounts system, values may be posted automatically, at the same time as they update customer and supplier accounts in the sales ledger and purchase ledger;

❑ *other income and expenditure* - entries concerning, for example, wages, rent, rates or heating.

Outputs

Typical output facilities include:

❑ *trial balance* - this is a list of debit and credit balances categorised by account. The balances are taken from the nominal ledger and the total of debit balances should agree with the total of credit balances;

❑ *transaction report* - a full list of transactions which may be used for error checking purposes, or as an audit trail, to allow the validity of transactions to be checked by an external auditor.

❑ *trading and profit and loss account* - a statement of the trading performance of the business over a given period;

❑ *balance sheet* - a statement of the assets and liabilities of a business, at a particular date.

The major benefit of the computerised nominal ledger is that these reports can be produced easily and upon request. The manual production of a trial balance, trading and profit and loss statement and balance sheet can be a laborious and time consuming task. Many small businesses, operating manual systems, have difficulty in completing their annual accounts promptly for annual tax assessment.

Apart from the basic ledgers described in the previous section, there are other applications which can benefit from computerisation. They include:

❑   stock control;

❑   sales order processing and invoicing.

Stock control

General description

Different businesses hold different kinds of stock. For example, a grocer holds some perishable and some non-perishable stocks of food and a clothing manufacturer holds stocks of materials and finished articles of clothing. Any trader's stock needs to be controlled, but the reasons for control may vary from one business to another. For example, a grocer wants to keep the full range of food items that customers expect, but does not want to be left with stocks of unsold items, especially if they are perishable. A clothing manufacturer's stocks will not perish if they are unsold, but space occupied by unwanted goods could be occupied by more popular items. On the other hand, if the manufacturer runs out of raw materials the production process can be slowed or even halted. Apart from such differences, there are some common reasons for wanting efficient stock control:

❑   excessive stock levels tie up valuable cash resources and increase business costs. The cash could be used to finance further business;

❑   inability to satisfy customer orders promptly because of insufficient stocks, can often lead to loss of custom.

It is possible to identify some typical objectives of a stock control system and these can be used to measure the usefulness of facilities commonly offered by computer packages:

❑   to maintain levels of stock which will be sufficient to meet customer demand promptly;

❑   to provide a mechanism which removes the need for excessively high safety margins of stock to cover customer demand. This is usually effected by setting minimum stock levels which the computer can use to report variations outside these levels;

❑   to provide automatic re-ordering of stock items which fall below minimum levels;

❑   to provide management with up-to-date information on stock levels and values of stock held. Stock valuation is also needed for accounting purposes.

Stock control requires that an individual record is maintained for each type of stock item held. Apart from details concerning the description and price of the stock item, each record should have a balance indicating the number of units held. A unit may be, for example, a box,

500 grammes or a tonne. The balance is adjusted whenever units of that particular stock item are sold or purchased. Manual or computerised records can only give recorded levels of stock. Physical stock checks need to be carried out to determine the actual levels. If there is a difference between the recorded stock level of an item and the actual stock of that item, it could be because of pilferage or damage. Alternatively, some transactions for the item may not have been applied to the stock file.

Package requirements and facilities

Stock master file

The stock master file contains records for each item of stock and each record may usefully contain the following data item types:

❑ *Stock code or reference* - each stock item type should have a unique reference, for example, A0035. The code should be designed so that it is useful to the user. For example, an initial alphabetic character may be used to differentiate between raw materials (R) and finished goods (F) and the remaining digits may have ranges which indicate particular product groupings. The stock file may also be used to record any consumable items used by a business, for example, stationery and printer ribbons. The initial character of the stock code could be used to identify such a grouping. The number and type of characters in a code, as well as its format, are usually limited by the package because the code will also be used by the software to determine a record's location within the file;

❑ *Description* - although users may become used to referring to individual products by their codes or references, a description is needed for the production of, for example, purchase orders or customer invoices;

❑ *Analysis code* - this may be used in conjunction with sales orders so that they can be analysed by product group. If, for example, a clothing manufacturer produces different types of ski jacket, it is important for production planning purposes to know the relative popularity of each type;

❑ *Unit size* - for example, box, metre, tonne, kilo;

❑ *Re-order level* - this is the stock level at which an item is to be re-ordered, for example, 30 boxes. Reaching this level may trigger an automatic re-order when the appropriate program option is run. Alternatively it may be necessary to request a summary report which highlights all items at or below their re-order level. The decision on what the re-order level should be for any particular item will depend on the *sales turnover* (the number of units sold per day or week) and the *lead time* (the time taken for delivery after a purchase order is placed with a supplier). Seasonal changes in sales figures will require that re-order levels for individual items are changed for time to time;

❑ *Re-order quantity* - this is the number of item units to be re-ordered from a supplier when new stock is required;

❑ *Bin reference* - this may be used to indicate the physical location of stock items within, for example, a warehouse;

❏ *Minimum stock level* - when an item falls to this level, a warning is given that the stock level of the item is dangerously low. As with the re-order level, the warning may be produced by a request for a special summary report which highlights such items. Even though the re-order level warning may have already been given, it is possible that no new stocks were ordered or that the supplier was unusually slow with deliveries;

❏ *Cost price* - the price paid by the business for the stock item;

❏ *Sale price* - the price charged to the customer. The package may allow the storage of more than one sale price to differentiate between, for example, retail and wholesale customers;

❏ *VAT code* - different items may attract different rates of Value Added Tax (VAT);

❏ *Supplier code* - if orders can be produced automatically, then the supplier code may be used to access a supplier file, for the address and other details needed to produce an order;

❏ *Quantity issued* - generally, several values may be entered, so that the turnover of an item can be viewed for different periods, for example, from 3 months ago to date, the preceding 3 month period and so on;

❏ *Stock allocated* - a quantity may not have been issued but may have been allocated to a customer order or factory requisition;

❏ *Quantity in stock* - the current recorded level of stock. This will change whenever an issue, receipt or adjustment transaction is entered.

Transactions

❏ *Goods received* - stock received from a supplier;

❏ *Goods returned* - for example, stock returned by a customer or unused raw materials returned from the factory;

❏ *Goods issued* - this may result from a customer order or from a factory requisition, if the business has a manufacturing process;

❏ *Stock allocated* - this will not reduce the quantity in stock figure but the amount allocated should be used to offset the quantity in stock when judging what is available;

❏ *Amendments* - for, example, there may be amendments to price, re-order level or supplier code.

The method used to update the stock master file will depend on how up-to-date the figures need to be (this will depend on how tight stock levels are) and how often the data entry operator can get at the computer. To keep the file up-to-date throughout the day, physical stock changes have to be notified immediately to stock control and the transactions have to be entered as they occur. Unfortunately, this means that a single-user system would be unavailable to any other users, such as sales staff, who needed to know quantities in stock. A networked system with central file storage, would allow continual updating and enquiry access. If the stock levels are sufficiently high to allow differences to arise between physical and book totals without risking shortages, then daily batch updating may be acceptable. In such a situation, an enquiry on a stock item may reveal, for example, a book stock of 200 units, when the physical stock is only 120 units (80 having been issued since the last update at the end of the preceding day).

Outputs

Typical outputs from a stock control package include:

❑ *Stock enquiry* - details concerning a stock item may be displayed on screen, or printed;

❑ *Stock out report* - a list of stock items which have reached a level of zero;

❑ *Re-order report* - a list of stock items which have fallen to their re-order level, together with supplier details and recommended re-order quantities;

❑ *Stock list* - a full or limited (for example, within a certain stock code range) list of stock items, giving details of quantities held and their value. The value may be calculated using the cost or sale price, depending on the costing method used by the business;

❑ *Outstanding order report* - a list of all purchase orders not yet fulfilled and the dates ordered. This may be used to chase up orders when stocks are falling dangerously low.

This is not an exhaustive list and some packages offer many other analytical reports which can help a business to maintain an efficient customer service and plan future production and purchasing more effectively.

A stock control case study

The Astex Homecare chain of DIY stores has branches all over the country and each branch maintains stocks of thousands of items used in the home. These items range from building materials such as sand and cement to bedroom furniture, fitted kitchens, bathroom suites, ceramic wall and floor tiles, lights and light fittings, garden materials such as plants, plant pots and garden furniture, nails, screws, paint, wallpaper and numerous other common household goods.

Each branch has its own small computer system dedicated to dealing with the *point of sale* (POS) terminals located at the customer tills. The POS terminals are used to record purchases and provide customer bills by scanning the bar code on each purchase using a hand-held scanner. The stock number contained in the bar code is fed by the POS terminal to the local computer which returns the description and price to be printed on the customers' receipts as well as the bill totals.

Each branch maintains its own stock file on the local computer but ordering stock is controlled by a mainframe computer at the Astex head office. Each Astex branch is laid out according to a *merchandise layout plan* (MLP) in which the store is organised into a large number of four foot sections, each having its own MLP code. Each item of stock is allocated to one MLP section and its computer record contains the MLP code together with the minimum and maximum stock level for that particular section of the store. When an item has been sold, the relevant information is transmitted automatically by the local computer to the mainframe at head office. The head office computer determines from the MLP data whether the item needs to be re-ordered from a supplier. It uses the MLP information regarding minimum and maximum stock levels in order to determine how many of a particular item to order.

Overnight, while the stores are closed, the head office computer transmits suggested ordering information back to the individual branches where order sheets are printed out on local laser printers, so that they can be checked manually by the appropriate personnel before stock is ordered. This manual monitoring of computer-generated information allows the information system to cope with unexpected situations and prevents the occurrence of gross errors. About ninety percent of all orders can be made electronically using communication links to the computers used by suppliers. Other suppliers not linked to the central Astex computer are contacted manually by telephone.

The security of the Astex information systems are ensured in two major ways. Firstly, because of the importance of the local computer system for producing customer bills, a backup processor is always available for use in the event of the primary processor failing. Secondly, access to the various users of the computer systems is provided on several different levels. Each person who uses the computer system has his or her own access code which provides access to only those areas he or she is authorised to use. These measures are essential to maintain the security and reliable operation of such large-scale systems.

Some sophisticated stock control systems enable the supply of materials just before they are needed for manufacture. Nissan car plants operate using this *just in time* principle, using satellite supply companies located around or near the main plant.

Sales order processing and invoicing

Sales order processing

Sales order processing is concerned with the handling of customers' sales orders. It has three main functions:

❑ validation of orders. This means checking, for example, that the goods ordered are supplied by the business or that the customer's credit status warrants the order's completion;

❑ to identify quantities of individual items ordered. A customer may request several different items on the same order form. An item will probably appear on many different order forms and the quantities for each need to be totalled to provide lists (picking lists) for warehouse staff to retrieve the goods;

❑ to monitor back orders. If an order cannot be fulfilled it may be held in abeyance until new stocks arrive. The system should be able to report all outstanding back orders on request.

The efficient processing of customer orders is of obvious importance to the success of a business and in whatever form an order is received, the details should be immediately recorded. Preferably, the details should be recorded on a pre-designed order form which ensures that all relevant details are taken. The order details should include:

❑ the date the order is received;

❑ the customer's order number;

❏ a description of each item required including any necessary stock references or codes;

❏ the quantity of each item ordered;

❏ the price per item excluding VAT;

❏ the total order value excluding VAT;

❏ any discount which is offered to the customer;

❏ the VAT amount which is to be added to the total price;

❏ the total order value including VAT;

❏ the delivery date required.

Invoicing

The invoice is the bill to the customer, requesting payment for goods or services supplied by the business. The following section describes typical package facilities which allow the integration of the sales order processing and invoicing systems.

Package requirements and facilities

To be effective, the sales order processing system needs to have access to the customer file (sales ledger) for customer details and to the stock file, so that prices can be extracted according to stock item codes entered with the order. This latter facility means that the system may also be integrated with invoicing.

Files

❏ *Customer file.* When a customer account number or name is keyed in with an order, the package usually accesses the customer file and displays the address details, so that the operator can confirm the delivery address or type in an alternative address if this is required. The process also ensures that all orders are processed for registered customers;

❏ *Stock file.* As stock item codes are entered from an order form, the system accesses the price and displays it on the screen for confirmation by the operator. Access to the stock file also ensures that only valid stock codes are used;

❏ *Completed order file.* This is used for the generation of invoices after an order's completion;

❏ *Back order file.* This is needed to ensure that orders which cannot be fulfilled immediately are kept on file and processed as soon as goods become available.

Transactions

❏ *Sales order* - details concerning an individual order, including customer number, items required (by item code), quantity of each item, delivery date, discount allowed and the date of the order.

Outputs

❑ *Invoice* - an invoice can be generated by using the details of customer number, stock codes and quantities from the order, together with information retrieved from the customer and stock files;

❑ *Back order report* - a report can be requested detailing all unsatisfied orders. This is useful for planning production schedules or generating special purchase orders;

❑ *Picking list* - a summary of the quantities required of each item ordered. These are used by warehouse staff to extract the goods needed to make up orders for delivery;

❑ *Sales data* - details of each customer's order need to be extended to include the financial ledgers (sales, purchase and nominal ledger). Such integration should not usually be attempted all at once but full integration does reduce the number of inputs necessary and automates many of the updating procedures described in this chapter.

Payroll

The task of calculating wages for a large company having hundreds or even thousands of employees is an enormous task. It involves taking into account some or all of the following factors:

❑ number of hours worked;

❑ amount of overtime;

❑ bonus payment;

❑ sickness leave;

❑ type of employee (for example, waged or salaried, shop floor or management);

❑ deductions (for example, national insurance contributions and union fees);

❑ holidays;

❑ tax code;

❑ tax rate;

❑ cash analysis.

The gross pay is calculated from the hours worked and hourly pay rate, for weekly paid employees, and is a standard sum for salaried employees. Added to this gross payment are any allowances from overtime or bonuses, for example. Tax is calculated and subtracted from the total earnings and other deductions such as national insurance, union fees and pension contributions are also taken from it. Thus the total calculation is quite complicated, and it will probably be different for each employee. Producing payslips manually is therefore very time consuming and prone to error, so computers are particularly well suited to the task. Most computerised payroll systems use batch processing in which long-term employee information held on a master file is used in conjunction with a transaction file containing recent information such as hours worked and overtime details. The transaction file changes from

a

week to week or month to month but most of the information on the master file either does not change at all or changes only occasionally. If employees are paid weekly, at the end of each week details of hours worked, bonus payments, overtime payments and deductions are recorded on a payroll transaction file which contains a record for every employee. This sequential transaction file is then sorted into employee number order so that it is in the same order as the payroll master file. The two files are then used by the computer to calculate and print the payslips, and to update the master file which must keep track of such things as tax paid to date, total national insurance contributions and holiday and sickness leave for each employee for the current tax year. A *systems flowchart*, as illustrated in Figure 9.1, is often used to describe business data processing systems such as this.

The systems flowchart shows the computer operations involved in a payroll run. Payroll systems normally use batch processing when the majority of the employees need to be paid. This lends itself to the use of magnetic tape devices (the flowchart does not specify the medium) which are restricted to sequential access. The payroll data is first stored on the payroll transaction file using keyboards as the input devices.

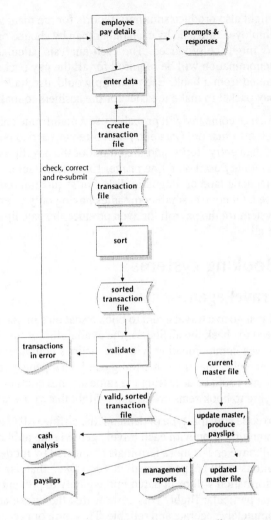

Figure 9.1. *Systems flowchart for payroll system*

Each employee's pay information is stored in a separate record identified by employee number. Because the master file records are stored on tape in order of employee number, the transaction file must also be sorted into the same order. This is to avoid having to search for matching master file and transaction file records for each employee - because both files are in the same order, the next record in each file should be for the same employee. The sorted transaction file must be validated by the computer before processing the payroll data to produce payslips. This process performs various checks on the transaction file to ensure that only correct data will be processed. Any errors detected at this stage must be corrected before the payslips are generated.

Finally, the validated and sorted transaction file is processed against the payroll master file in order to produce the payslips. In addition to updating the master file, the payroll system might also produce summary reports for the management personnel of the company, and, if employees are paid by cash rather than by cheque or transfer to a bank account, a *cash analysis* might be produced. The cash analysis calculates exactly how many of each currency denomination will be required for all the pay packets, so that the correct money can be obtained from a bank. Each payslip would also have a corresponding breakdown for a single pay packet to make it easier for the cashiers to make up the pay packets.

A large company will probably use a mainframe computer for the task of processing the payroll information. Data entry will often be carried out using key-to-tape systems by a number of data entry clerks, and the output of the payslips will probably be by means of pre-printed stationery used on a line printer for speed. Backing storage will normally be in the form of magnetic tape or magnetic disk, but sequential *batch processing* will almost invariably be used. Of course, small companies having only a few employees might use a microcomputer system for the payroll, or even produce the payslips manually without the use of a computer at all.

Booking systems

Travel agents

If you go to a travel agent to book a seat on a major international airline, the travel agent will need to check the airline for the availability of the flight that you require. This normally involves communicating with the airlines computer to obtain up-to-date flight information. Remember that the same thing can be happening from all over the world: numerous travel agents could be accessing the same airlines computer at the same time, several of them even trying to book seats on the same flight that you want.

To cope with this type of demand, the airline will use a mainframe computer allowing on-line communication with each travel agent via the public telephone network. Each travel agency will have one or more terminals connected by modem to the airlines computer. Flight reservations will be performed in *real-time*, that is, the mainframe's flight and passenger information will be updated immediately to prevent the possibility of double-booking a seat on a particular flight. This ensures that the information that the travel agent obtains will be completely accurate and reliable. This form of processing, where a master file is updated immediately, is called *transaction processing*.

The process of reserving a seat on a flight is further complicated by the fact that several airlines might have scheduled flights to your destination, each offering different flight times, facilities and costs. Rather than contacting each one separately, a process that could take a considerable amount of time, the travel agent links into a wide area network(WAN) which connects the main computers of the different airlines. This allows the agent to choose the most appropriate flight for you and book it immediately. Though each airline in the system might have a different passenger reservation information system, the network software presents the same information format to the travel agents and takes care of transferring data in the correct format to the individual computer systems of the airlines.

When you have decided on your choice of airline and flight, your details are entered at the travel agent's terminal. While this is happening, other travel agents are prevented from accessing that particular flight record. On completion of the reservation, the flight record becomes available again. Booking cancellations and changes are handled in the same way.

Your ticket, which will have been produced by the airline's computer, is usually sent out to you a few days prior to the departure date. Individual airline's computers also produce passenger lists automatically for use at the departure airports.

An airline's master passenger reservation and flight information file will be held on a high-capacity magnetic disk drive. For backup purposes, in case the master file is in some way lost or partly erased, or the disk drive fails, a separate disk drive will be used to hold an exact duplicate of the master file, and this duplicate file will be updated at the same time as the other master file. This duplication is necessary because the master file will be in constant use, night and day, and there will be no opportunity to stop updating it in order to make a backup on magnetic tape. For the same reasons of security, there will also be a duplicate main computer immediately ready to be used if the other one fails for some reason. Because of the importance of the fast response time required of the system, it will almost certainly be used exclusively for passenger booking purposes, and it will have been designed to operate without break, 24 hours a day, every day of the year.

Similar real-time systems are used by holiday firms, some of which are able to offer thousands of holidays all over the world. Travel agents must have access to accurate information regarding the availability of all the holidays on offer. Again it is important to ensure that exactly the same holiday is not sold to more than one customer, so the booking file held on the holiday company's main computer must be completely up-to-date.

Hotel booking

Hotels frequently use booking systems for keeping track of room reservations made by guests. These systems generally provide additional facilities relating to hotel management, typically keeping track of guests accounts and producing hotel room usage information.

When someone reserves a room in the hotel, a record is created in the guest file. The file contains three types of data:

- details of the guest, such as name, address, telephone number;

- room details, such as type (single, double etc.), number, period of occupancy;

- charges incurred by the guest during the stay at the hotel. For each charge, the item code, cost and date will be recorded.

The first two types of data are entered at the time the reservation is made; items and services bought by the guest during his or her stay, such as telephone calls, drinks, newspapers and extra meals, are recorded as and when they occur. When the guest leaves, the hotel system calculates the total bill and prints out an itemised list that the guest can check.

A hotel management system such as this can easily be implemented with a microcomputer system, though large hotel chains might also have a large central computer at their headquarters for general accounting purposes (such as producing financial reports covering the whole chain of hotels, and for payroll calculations).

Library systems

Dotherstaff College is a split site college of further and higher education. Each site has a large library which has recently been supplied with a microcomputer network for a library automation system called Alice, produced by a software company called Softlink. The software has a number of interlinked modules covering all aspects of typical library operation.

❑ Catalogue and Classification - managing the book database;

❑ Circulation - managing borrowers;

❑ Enquiries - information retrieval;

❑ Acquisition - ordering books;

❑ Reports and utilities- producing reports of publishers' details, author details and library usage figures;

❑ Periodicals- managing the ordering of magazines.

Catalogue and classification

This module is mainly used for the addition of new titles to the book database. Book details can be created, edited and deleted, as well as allowing the file to be browsed through, or searched.

Circulation

The circulation module is used for managing borrowers' details. To borrow a book from the library a borrower must produce his or her ticket on which there is a unique bar code. This bar code is scanned by a librarian and the borrower's record then appears on the screen. When the bar code of the book is scanned, the code is stored in the borrower's record. To return a book, the bar code of the book is scanned or typed in and the book is automatically removed from the borrower's record. The system also allows the display of all books currently borrowed by any person. Periodically, about every two weeks, the borrower file is searched for overdue items so that reminders can be generated automatically.

Enquiry

The enquiry module is used by staff and students to search the book database for books satisfying certain criteria. For example, a user can type in the name of an author and obtain a list of all books in the library written by that person. The title of a book, or part of the title can be entered and a list of books closely matching the title will be displayed. Alternatively, one or more keywords can be used to produce a list of books which contain the keywords in the title. The book information retrieved by an enquiry is summarised on the screen in several sections containing such things as the book titles, subjects covered and author(s). Any book selected from the list can have its full details displayed on screen or printed. This type of enquiry facility can save a great deal of time searching shelves or catalogues for specific information.

The network used for the library information system currently supports about 20 terminals, but it is also linked to the main college networks which provide access to other software such as word processors and spreadsheets.

E-commerce

Many businesses including, for example, supermarkets, travel agents, wine merchants, booksellers and car sales companies now sell their products through e-commerce web sites. With a computer, Internet connection and Web browser, consumers can visit these virtual stores and view, select and pay for goods which can often be delivered within 24 to 48 hours. Until the 1960s it was common practice for shops to make home deliveries on orders taken over the telephone and Internet shopping has the potential to reduce the volume of traffic visiting, for example, out of town shopping centres. It is extremely unlikely that demand for conventional 'bricks and mortar' will disappear because Internet shopping provides no social interaction and many consumers will wish to view and handle many types of goods before buying.

More formally, e-commerce can be defined as *"conducting business transactions over electronic networks"*. E-commerce is fundamentally changing the way business operates. Because of e-commerce, businesses of all sizes are changing their internal operations and their relationships with suppliers and customers. When properly implemented, e-commerce can improve the efficiency of all stages of the business process, from design and manufacture to retailing and distribution.

E-commerce is playing a major role in the establishment of a global economy. The major catalyst for the expansion of international electronic retailing is the Internet. Its users, the number of which is rapidly increasing, can communicate with the Web sites of countless organisations all over the world, and it is through these *World Wide Web* sites that companies can provide 'on-line stores'. The Web-based on-line stores are accessible by Web browsers, such as Microsoft Explorer and Netscape Communicator and a standard feature of all modern home computers. An Internet store provides all the facilities that the customer needs, including a product catalogue, a 'virtual shopping basket' and a secure credit card payment system.

Application objectives

A number of general objectives can be identified as being of relevance to most applications, in most organisations:

- ❏ Improved *operational efficiency*. *Speed* and *accuracy* of operations should be radically improved. This is not automatic as the computer-based system may be badly designed and the staff may be ill-trained, but given proper design and implementation, administrative systems will normally be more efficient.

- ❏ Better *control of resources*. Administrative systems such as those for financial control and the control of resources such as staff and raw materials, benefit particularly from the rapid production of up-to-date information by computer.

- ❏ Improved *productivity*. Redundancy does not always follow computerisation, particularly if the organisation is an expanding business. Computer-based systems should permit large increases in the volumes of business which can be handled without the need for extra staff.

- ❏ Improved *security of information*. With proper physical security, clear operational procedures to restrict access to computer facilities to those properly authorised, and with sophisticated use of software control mechanisms such as passwords, information can be made more secure than equivalent manual systems.

- ❏ Opportunities to *share data*. This is most likely where database systems and networked computer systems are employed.

- ❏ Improved *quality of information* for *decision taking* at the operational, strategic and corporate levels in an organisation. *Operational decisions* concern day-to-day operations, such as handling of customer orders or delivery of new stocks. At the *strategic level*, decisions may relate to issues such as production planning and the selection of suppliers. *Corporate decision* examples include the setting of prices, targeting of markets and the manufacture of new products. Most systems generate a range of management information reports, drawn from the routine processing of transactions and these are primarily of use at the strategic level, but may also help with corporate decisions. Accounts software, for example, produces reports on outstanding debts, potential bad debtors, dates when payments to suppliers are due and analysis of sales patterns.

❏ Improved *external image*. An organisation can improve its external image by the improved presentation of correspondence and by an improved service to its customers or clients, but badly designed procedures can also make life more difficult for them.

❏ Improved *working conditions*. This is highly debatable in respect of an office environment, but computer-based manufacturing systems usually provide a less dirty and dangerous environment for employees, as much of the work is done by robots and other computer-controlled machinery.

Self-test questions

1. Which *ledger* would a business use to record:
   (i)   balances owing by customers for goods bought on credit?
   (ii) expenditure on heating, light and wages?
   (iii) balances owing to suppliers for goods bought on credit.?
2. Name the type of document which is sent to a customer:
   (i)   requesting payment for goods bought on credit;
   (ii) to show a refund on their account to the value of goods returned.
3. Which accounting package report would be useful for identifying potential *bad debts*?
4. Which report details the assets and liabilities of a business on a particular date?
5. Which report shows the profit made by a business over a specified period?
6. Which fields in a stock record are concerned with maintaining optimum levels of stock?
7. List three transaction types which may be entered into a stock control system.
8. (i)   Assuming a fully integrated financial accounting system, identify the files which would need to be accessed to produce an invoice.
   (ii) What data would be extracted from each file identified in (i), to produce the invoice?
9. List the components an organisation needs to support an e-commerce operation.

Developmental Exercises

Industrial and Commercial IT

Activity 1

Produce *two tables* (use the word processor's table facility), one giving general descriptions of *commercial system* examples and the other, general descriptions of *industrial systems* examples. The commercial examples to be included could be: *booking systems; electronic funds transfer; electronic point of sale; stock control; order processing; payroll processing.* The industrial examples to be included could be: *design; process control; robotics; environmental control; traffic control.*

Activity 2

As a team of 4, produce a report on two *commercial* and two *industrial* systems. The report should:

1. Analyse each system, in terms of: purpose; hardware; software; data; people; processing activities; inputs; outputs; advantages; limitations; impact on environment.

2. Evaluate each system using the following criteria: comparison with an alternative system; costs; benefits (speed, efficiency, accuracy, quality), identification of potential improvements.

   a. **Arrange** a team meeting to agree upon the *allocation of responsibility*.

   b. You will have been given a deadline for the completion of the project, so you need to **prepare** a schedule of work to ensure, not only that the separate parts of the work are completed, but that there is sufficient time to integrate the separate contributions into a cohesive final report.

   c. As a team, **design** and **produce** a document template which you can all use. You need to agree at the outset on the format of the final document, so that each member's word processed document is consistent with the others when they are merged into one document.

   d. **Investigate** your assigned area and **prepare** your contribution (using the designed template).

   e. As the work progresses, team meetings should **monitor** the team's work and comments should be sought from the tutor (and acted upon)at each stage.

   f. **Merge** the separate documents into a single file, secure and print it.

   g. **Record** *your assessments* of your contribution and those of other team members.

   h. **Study** the contribution of *another team member* and **use** *presentational graphics software* to **prepare** a presentation which summarises the main points of their contribution to the report. **Present** this to the rest of the class and be prepared to answer questions on the content.

Information Flows

Activity 3

This activity requires a general examination of a wide range of organisations and then a more in-depth study of two particular organisations.

a. Produce a table (use word processor table facilities) of various examples of *commercial*, *industrial* and *public service* organisations, for example: commercial bank; insurance company, chemical engineers; supermarket chain; leisure centre; accountancy firm; electricity generating company; university. Include, at least, *two* examples of each type. Also indicate whether the organisation *tends towards* a *hierarchical* or *flat structure*. The table should have three columns, headed: *example organisation*; *category* (industrial, commercial or industrial); *structure* (hierarchical or flat). Save two copies of the table, one with the organisations *sorted according to category* and the other *sorted by structural type*.

b. Draw, using vector drawing tools, *two* organisation charts, one showing a *hierarchical* structure and the other a *flat* or *'flatter'* structure. The charts should show *areas of responsibility* (which may be indicated by job title) and a *clear division* between *the major functional areas* (for, example, sales, personnel). Use two of the example organisations for this purpose. Each organisation chart should include features of its *corporate image*, including a *graphic logo*, *organisation title* and Head Office *address*.

c. Explain, by example, the *three* main forms of information: *verbal*, *documentary* and *electronic*. Gather examples of commonly used documents, for example: orders; invoices; account statement; price list. Store them in your file for use in Systems Analysis.

d. Select two organisations (of *different type*) from the table produced in A. For each organisation:

   (i)   (identify at least three *internal* and two *external* functions;

   (ii) (identify *at least three types* of information, which are used by the selected functions. You must include at least one *example* for *each form* of information (one *verbal*, one *documentary* and one *electronic*).

   (iii) (For each organisation draw (using vector drawing tools) one *information flow diagram*, showing *all the functions* identified in D; the information flows between them should include the example information types identified in D.

e. Present all your work in a word processed document, with embedded graphics and a consistent format throughout.

Information systems

Activity 4

This activity (which could usefully be undertaken as a team project) requires some research into the functional areas of a large clearing bank (you can choose another type of large organisation, with which you are familiar) to determine the data handling systems the bank is likely to use. For example, customer services comprise a number of different, but related systems: on-line telephone banking (touch tone or voice processing), account statement maintenance and production, charges calculation, personal insurance and mortgage services. Some of these services can be provided by home visits from a personal account manager, who will make use of a notebook computer for the provision of information and completion of application forms.

a. Produce a table (using a word processor's table facility) of the systems you identify and for *each system*, indicate, with reasons, which processing method (*batch* or *transaction*) it would use. Use an example system to explain the batch and transaction processing methods and place the explanations beneath the table of systems already described.

b. Using several bank system examples, explain what is meant by a *single user* and a *multi-user* system.

c. Define the terms *centralised* and *distributed processing* and suggest reasons why modern banks favour a measure of distributed processing. Use the systems you have identified to support your suggestions.

d. Explain the function and general operation of the following types of data handling system and identify the applications of these systems in the clearing bank organisation: *bookings, payroll, ordering, invoicing, stock control, personal records*.

e. For each of the following methods of data capture, identify a bank system which could benefit from its use (briefly explain why it is used in preference to another method): *keyboard, mouse, keypad, bar code reader, OMR, MICR, magnetic strip reader, voice processor, touch tone telephone* (the list is not exhaustive and you should be able to identify others)

f. For each of the following *methods of processing*, identify a bank system which would use it (the same system may use several). Briefly explain the *nature* of each processing method and its *application* in the identified system(s): *calculating, converting, sorting, searching, selecting, merging, grouping*.

g. Select two data handling systems from those already identified and compare the data capture method(s) used. Explain how the data capture method used by each system contributes to the achievement of the identified system objectives. These should be drawn from the following: *speed, accuracy, cost, decision-making support.*

h. Review the performance of both systems against their identified objectives and suggest how they might be improved.

i. Present all your findings in a word processed report.

Security and privacy

Activity 5

This activity requires a *team* approach, to investigate and report on security and privacy issues. It also requires the *merging* of separate document files of a consistent format and the use of *presentational graphics* software to summarise main points in your investigation. A team could have three members, one being the team leader responsible for the co-ordination and integration of the work of individual team members. The terms of reference for the investigation are:

❑   the *types of data* held on *individuals* and *organisations* and the reasons for the protection of such data (confidentiality, legal, moral).

❑   *obligations of system users* (at least 4): confidentiality of data; accuracy; rights of individuals under personal privacy legislation; copyright protection for software and data; responsible attitudes to uncensored or private materials (consider difficulties of Internet).

❑   *System security methods* (at least 4) to: control access; identify users; prevent and recover from computer virus attacks. The methods should be appropriate to the threat and the circumstances of the organisation and deal with, for example, back-up and recovery procedures, passwords, audit trails, forced recognition of security (official secrets legislation, signing non-disclosure agreement). Categorise the methods into logical and physical.

One area is allocated to each team member. Each team should **relate its investigation** to one, particular kind of organisation. In other words, although the investigation is wide ranging, comments should be included stating the relevance, or otherwise, of an issue to the chosen organisation. Examples are provided in the next table (this allows for six teams).

clearing bank	college or university
national manufacturing company	hospital
national estate agency chain	government department (e.g. Social Security)

a. **Arrange** a team meeting to agree upon the *allocation of responsibility*. The *terms of reference* identify 3 areas of investigation.

b. You will have been given a deadline for the completion of the project, so you need to **prepare** a schedule of work to ensure, not only that the separate parts of the work are completed, but that there is sufficient time to integrate the separate contributions into a cohesive final report.

c. As a team, **design** and **produce** a document template which you can all use. You need to agree at the outset on the format of the final document, so that each member's word processed document is consistent with the others when they are merged into one document.

d. **Investigate** your assigned area and **prepare** your contribution (using the designed template).

e. As the work progresses, team meetings should be used to **monitor** the team's work and comments should be sought from the tutor (and acted upon) on the work you have completed at that stage.

f. **Merge** the separate documents into a single file, secure the new file and print it for submission.

g. **Record** *your assessments* of your own contribution and those of other team members.

h. **Study** the contribution of *another team member* and **use** *presentational graphics software* to **prepare** a presentation which summarises the main points of their contribution to the report. **Present** this to the rest of the class and be prepared to answer questions on the content.

Unit 3

Spreadsheet design

Chapters

Assessment Evidence

You need to produce

☐ a spreadsheet solution to meet specified user requirements, involving the use of at least six of the more complex spreadsheet facilities

☐ user and technical documentation, including a test report

To achieve a grade E your work must show:

☐ a clear design specification that meets user requirements, including appropriate selection of more

☐ complex facilities, details of sources of data, outline screen data entry forms, calculations required, user aids to operation and how output is presented

☐ suitable data entry facilities including input messages and macros that reduce keystrokes and improve user efficiency

☐ suitable printed or screen output that makes appropriate use of cell formats, charts or graphs, page or screen layout and graphic images

☐ clear technical documentation identifying formulae and functions used, and screen and printed report layouts

☐ clear user documentation with copies of menus andscreens and examples of input and output

☐ testing of your spreadsheet against the designspecification and careful checking of the accuracy of the data used and the output generated.

To achieve a grade C your work must show:

☐ a good understanding of spreadsheet design and attention to detail by creating an imaginative customised spreadsheet that makes good use of design and layout facilities

☐ detailed test specifications together with examples of afull range of acceptable and unacceptable input, associated expected output and any associated error messages

☐ that you can work independently to produce your work to agreed deadlines.

To achieve a grade A your work must show:

☐ a good understanding of the purpose and value of more complex facilities by using them effectively in your spreadsheet design

☐ customised data input using facilities such as forms, dialogue boxes and list boxes that are clear, well laid out, suitably labelled and validate data input

☐ comprehensive records of spreadsheet drafting, testing and refinement that show how the spreadsheet was developed and how any problems were resolved

☐ high-quality, clear user documentation making good use of graphic images in detailed instructions for use together with examples of menus and data input screens, types of output available and possible error messages.

Chapter 10

Spreadsheet features and facilities

Spreadsheet packages are designed, primarily, for the manipulation of numerical information. The term *spreadsheet* is not new and has long been used to describe the computerised system's manual equivalent, commonly used by accountants to prepare, for example, budgets and financial forecasts. A manual spreadsheet is a large sheet of paper with a grid of intersecting rows and columns; a computerised spreadsheet adopts the same layout. Apart from financial applications, spreadsheets are used for statistical analysis and data modelling. Spreadsheet packages provide a graphics facility for the construction of graphs and charts (see Spreadsheet Graphics).

Spreadsheet features

When you load your spreadsheet program, the screen displays a *worksheet*, as shown in Figure 10.1. a number of functional features can be identified.

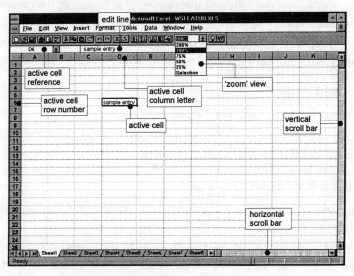

Figure 10.1. *Main features of a worksheet*

The features labelled in Figure 10.1 are described on the next page.

Cells. These are formed in a *grid*, each one being identified by a *column letter* (sometimes, columns may be numbered) and a *row number*. A worksheet provides hundreds of columns and thousands of rows, typically 256 and 16,384 (2^7) respectively, so more than the 26 letters of the alphabet are needed to uniquely identify each column. The problem is overcome by using two letters (AA, AB, AC ... AZ and then BA, BB, BC ... BZ and so on), from column Z onwards. The grid of cells is marked out by *gridlines* and your package may allow you to hide or display them. Each cell is a separate data entry point. The types of entry you can make are described later in the section titled Entering Data.

Active cell. The spreadsheet's cursor is the cell highlight (in Figure 10.1, it is D6 and contains the text 'sample entry'), which, like the insertion point in a word processor, indicates where the next entry will be made. So, if you want to make an entry into a particular cell, you first have to move the highlight to it. This can be done, either with the arrow keys or by clicking on the relevant cell with the mouse.

Active cell reference. This provides visual confirmation of the current location of the cell highlight. It is a more reliable method of identification than scanning the column and the row to identify the relevant letter and number.

Edit line. The contents of the active cell are displayed here. Through an appropriate operation (such as clicking the mouse on the edit line) the contents can be altered and then confirmed.

'Zoom' view. The grid of cells which you can see is only a small part of the complete worksheet. The vertical and horizontal *scroll bars* or arrow keys allow you to view other parts of the worksheet as necessary. As with other types of package, you can 'zoom' to see more rows and columns, in a condensed form, or magnify the image at the cost of seeing a smaller section of the worksheet. Figure 10.1 shows that the current selection of 100% can be magnified to 200% or condensed to 75%, 50% or 25%. If variations, such as 15% or 70% are required, then you can simply type in the value. It is important to mention that, although you may not be able to see all the cells and their contents at one time, the computer is holding them all in its main memory or RAM.

Worksheet selection. You may be able to store (under one filename), several worksheets and be able to switch attention between them without further reference to backing storage.

Types of data

Figure 10.2 identifies three main types of cell entry.

❑   a *label* or *text* entry consisting of alphanumeric characters. This sort of entry is used for headings which identify numeric contents of another cell or group of cells. The italicised entries in Figure 10.2 are all textual. Text entries cannot be used in any numerical calculation;

❑   a *numeric value*, used in calculations and sometimes, for other special types of entry, such as dates.

❑   a *formula*, which normally makes reference to and performs calculations on other cells. A formula can comprise a single cell reference or refer to several, interspersed by arithmetic operators. Thus, for example, to multiply the contents of cell B6 by those of B7 and B8 and place the result in B9, you would enter the formula =B6*B7*B8 into cell B9 (the active cell). Figure 10.2 shows a formula, on the edit line, which makes use of a *function*. The formula in the active cell, D15 (shown on the edit line) uses the SUM function to add the contents of cells D5 to D13, inclusive. The same function is used to total the adjacent columns, B, C, E, F and G.

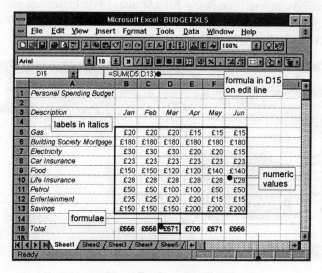

Figure 10.2. *Types of cell entry*

Using formulae

The main power of the spreadsheet lies in its ability to use formulae which cause values contained in individual cells to be made dependent on values held in other cells. Any changes in cells referred to in a formula are reflected in the cell containing the formula. For example, if you look at the worksheet in Figure 10.2, you should see that any changes in the contents of cells within the range *D5* to *D13* would result in a change to the value displayed in cell *D15*, which contains the formula *=SUM(D5:D13)*. This formula automatically totals the contents of cells *D5* to *D13* and displays the result in cell *D15* where the formula is located. Similar formulae are contained in the adjacent cells, A15, B15, C15, E15, F15 and G15.

Whenever changes are made to *numeric* values (which may themselves be generated by formulae) in the worksheet, any dependent formulae reflect these changes in the values they display. This automatic calculation is usually referred to as the spreadsheet's '*what if*' facility. It is possible to set up complex combinations of inter-dependent factors and see 'what' happens to the final results 'if' one or more of the factors is changed. More complex examples are provided in Chapter 12, to illustrate the power of the spreadsheet for the solution of *predictive modelling* problems.

Typical spreadsheet facilities

Highlighting a range of cells

If you wish to process a number of cells at once, you can highlight them, so that they can be treated as a single unit. However, the cells must be adjacent and the range must be a rectangle. This is illustrated in Figure 10.3. In terms of cell references, a range is identified by the extreme top left and bottom right cells which border it. Typically, you will highlight cells for special treatment, such as deleting the contents, moving them elsewhere, altering the font, or perhaps adding shading or borders. Figure 10.3 shows a highlighted range of cells, containing costs of various expenditure items, for a holiday; a dialogue box shows selection of a currency format, which will prefix all the amounts with the £ sign. The dialogue shows how the first cell in the range will look (£85), as a sample.

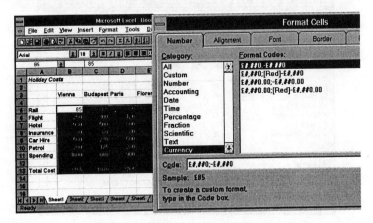

Figure 10.3. *Highlighted cells and format dialogue*

Pointing

A formula often includes reference to another cell and, frequently, to a range of cells. For example, you may enter the formula =SQRT(B12) into cell A4. This has the effect of displaying in cell A4 the square root of the value held in cell B12. Similarly, you may wish to display the result of adding a range of cells by entering a formula, such as =SUM(F5:F14). Typically, you may be able to enter a formula by:

❑   typing the complete formula, including any cell references;

❑   *pointing*. This facility allows you to point (using the arrow keys or the mouse) at the cells as you want them to appear in your formula. When the highlight is moved to the relevant cell, its reference appears on the edit line as if you had keyed it in. If you need to refer to a range of cells, as with the formula =SUM(F5:F14), you can use the mouse to click on the first cell in the range and then drag down to the last cell in the range. Figure 10.4 shows this process, as a SUM formula is entered to add cells ranging from B5 to B11. The first part of the formula is keyed in as =SUM and then the appropriate range of cells is selected by pointing and dragging (Figure 10.4 shows a broken line surrounding the range of cells and the mouse pointer (a white cross, in this case) indicating the last cell in the range.

Figure 10.4 also indicates the Autosum tool, which automatically enters the =SUM() function and also selects the range of contiguous (no blanks or non-numeric entries in between) numeric entries above it or along side it. All you have to do is ensure the selection range is correct, before confirming the entry. Autosum would not work for the example in Figure 10.4, because the range of cells is separated from the formula cell by a text entry.

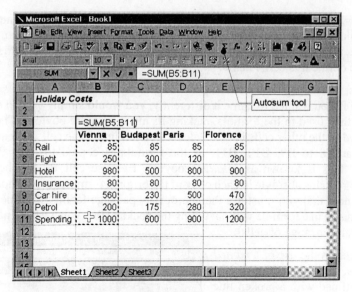

Figure 10.4. *Entering Sum formula by pointing*

Pointing has two particular benefits. First, it reduces the likelihood that you will make a mistake in entering cell references. Second, pointing is helpful if you wish to refer to cells that are not within view; in other words, you cannot scroll the worksheet to see them and check their references, without losing sight of the cell where you are entering the formula.

Naming cells

You can make a spreadsheet formulae more readable by *naming* a cell or range of cells. Naming may be used for another purpose, which is to make reference to a cell or cells *absolute*, before copying a formula to other cells. The circumstances when this is necessary are explained below, but in more detail in the section on Copying Data.

In Figure 10.5, cell B4 (the shaded cell) contains the unit price of a product sold by the four salespersons.

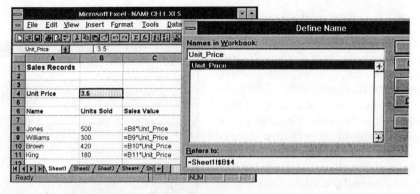

Figure 10.5. *Naming a cell*

The formula =B8*Unit_Price, in cell C8 (the result of the calculation would normally be displayed) calculates the value of sales made by Jones. Instead of referring to the unit price by its cell reference, it has been *named*, in this case, as 'Unit_Price'. Figure 10.5 also shows the dialogue used to define this cell's name.

As it happens, the package has picked up the label in cell A4 and suggested its use as the cell name for B4. If you wanted to name it differently, you would simply type in another name. The name is then used in the formula, making its meaning more obvious. The formula can then be copied to the other cells in the 'Sales Value' column. The cell reference B8 is automatically changed to B9, B10, B11, as the formula is copied to rows 9, 10 and 11, respectively. This is known as *relative* copying. Because cell B4 has been named as Unit_Price, it remains absolute in each copy of the original formula (it does not change). It is important to note that you must use the appropriate package facility to name the cell. You cannot use a name in a formula without telling the package that you wish the name to refer to a particular cell (or range of cells).

Figure 10.6 shows the use of a *named range* of cells. The cells (C8, C9, C10 and C11), outlined with a broken line and showing their displayed values, have been named as 'Total_Sales' and this name has been used in the SUM formula which adds the individual sales figures, to produce a total sales value. Before naming the group of cells, you need to highlight them. There is no need for an absolute reference to this group of cells, so the name is used simply to make the SUM formula more meaningful.

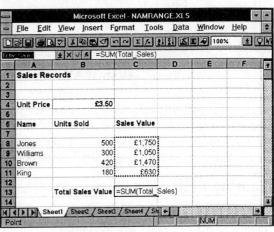

Figure 10.6. *Named range of cells*

Formatting

There are various ways in which you can tailor the appearance of a worksheet and the values contained in them. They are described in the following paragraphs.

Currency, fraction and percentage formats

You can format the way that a number is displayed, although its internal representation does not alter. So, for example, money amounts can be displayed with a £ sign prefix, in other words, in *currency* format. Similarly, if the amounts included pence, they could be displayed with two decimal places. Altering the displayed precision (the number of decimal places) of a number does not affect its internal precision. Consider the cell entries in Figure 10.7. Cell C2 contains a formula =B2*A2 (shown on the edit line)

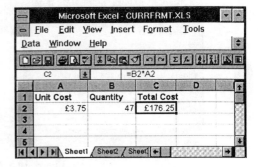

Figure 10.7. *Currency format*

and the stored result, accurate to 2 decimal places, is as shown. If, however, you formatted cell C2 as integer, you would only see £176, which would appear to be wrong. The internal value would be correct, but you could not see it.

The VAT amount, shown in Figure 10.8, is formatted as currency, with two decimal places and is thus displayed as £30.84. Its internal value, accurate to 5 decimal places, is 30.84375, but that degree of accuracy is not necessary here. Displayed as an integer, however, it would appear as £31 (rounded to the nearest £); this would be unacceptable if the £31 Figure 10.8 is used to draw up a customer invoice. When you create a formula which uses values stored elsewhere on the worksheet, you should use the appropriate cell references and not their displayed contents (this will also mean that if the contents of cells referred to in a formula alter, the formula can reflect those changes). The displayed precision required depends on the

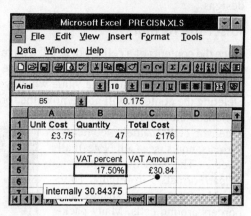

Figure 10.8. *Precision of values*

application. When quoting the attendance figures at a football match, the nearest thousand or five hundred would suffice, but displaying product prices (ranging from, say, £1.00 to £95.00), rounded to the nearest £10, is certain to be unsatisfactory. Figure 10.8 also shows cell B5 displaying a value of 17.50%, but the edit line shows a decimal fraction of 0.175. This is because the value is stored as a decimal fraction but formatted as a percentage; the formatting process multiplies the contents by 100 to produce a percentage figure.

Date and scientific formats

❑ *date*. Typical example display formats are:

day-month-year month-day-year day-month-year month-day-year month-year

23-Jun-1993   Jun-23-1993   23-06-93   06-23-93   Jun-1993

Each date has an internal value which equates with the number of days since 1st January 1900 (value 1). This allows dates to be compared, sorted, or used in formulae and calculations.

❑ *scientific*. Numbers output from computers are frequently presented in scientific or *standard index form*, but using the letter 'E' to separate the decimal part of the number (usually called the *mantissa*) from the *index* (usually called the *exponent*). The following are examples of numbers represented in this form.

$$-4.365982E+07 \text{ which means } -4.365982 \times 10^7 = -43659820$$

$$7.025E-3 \text{ which means } 7.025 \times 10^{-3} = 0.007025$$

The format is useful for the display of either very large integers or fractional numbers to great precision.

Other built-in formats include *special*, for the display of telephone numbers and post codes and *custom* for the display of a variety of number, date and time values. Formats can be applied to the whole worksheet, a single cell, or a range of cells. An Autoformat facility allows the application of built-in table designs, similar to those in a word processor. To ensure consistency in your own projects, you can also create styles from your own worksheet designs.

Resetting formats

Once the contents of a cell are deleted, you may wish to reset the cell to the default format, or to another format and this requires a separate operation. For example, if you assign currency format to a cell, any numeric value which you place in there will use the currency display. Deleting the contents will not remove the format. Figure 10.9 shows a menu command with

options to clear various aspects of a cell or cells, namely: contents; formats; notes (see Cell Notes); all three. The menu option 'Clear/Formats', in Figure 10.9, would also include shades and borders around cells. Many packages allow the format to be changed by the form of any new entry. Thus, for example, keying 20% into a cell automatically applies a percentage format, but stores it as a decimal fraction; this means that the internal value is 0.02 and for display purposes, this figure is multiplied by 100.

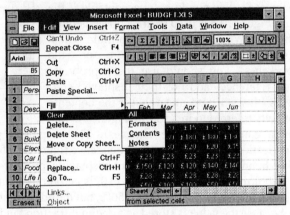

Figure 10.9. *Clearing cell contents, formats and notes*

Column widths and alignment

Figure 10.10 is a worksheet extract which illustrates some of the different circumstances when you need to change the width of individual columns and align (left or right) or centre labels.

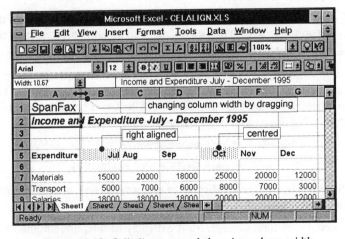

Figure 10.10. *Cell alignment and changing column width*

A column has a default width, but you can change it if the displayed entry requires more space. Remember, however, that even if the full entry is not displayed, it is stored in RAM in its complete internal format. Note from the Figure 10.10 that:

❏ The title 'Income and Expenditure July - December 1995' spans several columns. The entry is in stored in cell A2, but is displayed as spilling over into other cells. If you want to edit the entry, you would have to make A2 the active cell by moving the highlight to it. Figure 10.10 shows A2 as the active cell and so the text appears on the edit line. Because there are *no entries in the cells to the right* you do not need to change the column width to the length of the label entry. If there were an entry in cell B2, it would obscure the overspill from A2 (in which case, you would increase the width of A2 accordingly, or use a text wrap facility).

❏ The heading 'Expenditure' in A5 has more characters than any of the entries beneath it, so it dictates the width of the column. It is necessary to change the column width, because unlike the entry in A2, the cells to the right are occupied and the entry in B5 would obscure any A5 characters in excess of the column width. Figure 23.10 shows the column width being altered by dragging, although it can also be altered through a menu and dialogue, for entry of a precise measurement.

❏ The month headings are shorter than the numbers beneath, and it is the longest entry in a column which dictates its width. Therefore, you would need to use a column width to suit the maximum value to be stored in the column.

All the *label* entries (except for B5 and E5) are, by default, *left aligned* in their cells, but *numeric* values are *right aligned*. So that you can see the differences, the label 'Jul' in B5 has been right aligned and 'Oct' in E5, centred, using a formatting command. Either of these alterations improves the alignment with the numbers beneath. As a general rule, it is advisable to change the alignment of labels to suit the position of numbers in the same column. This is because altering the alignment of numbers with a fractional part can result in vertical 'zigzagging' of the place values (units, tens, hundreds etc.) and, if they have fractional parts, the decimal points. Figure 10.11 illustrates the problem.

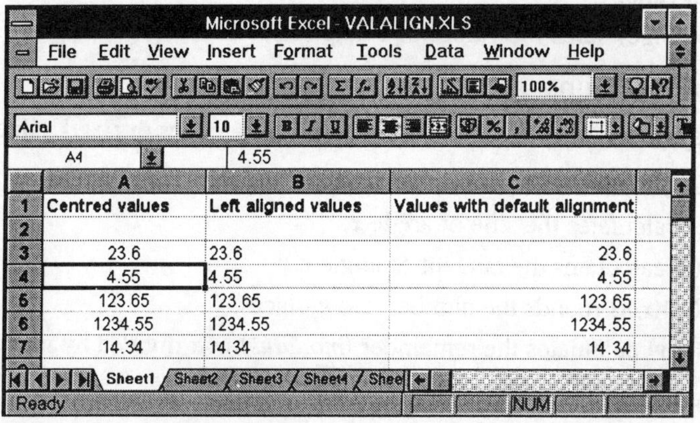

Figure 10.11. *Misalignment of place values by left alignment and centring*

Vertical alignment and wrapped text

Cell contents can also be aligned vertically, or at varying angles and to avoid excessively wide columns, contents can be made to wrap around within the available width.

Colour, borders and shading

These facilities are the same as those for the formatting of tables (Chapter) in a word processor and allow the use of built-in Autoformats and the formatting of individual cells and groups of cells.

Using functions

Functions provide you with in-built facilities, which allow you to execute a range of processes. A function requires one or more *arguments*, normally bracketed after the function name. For example, the =SUM function requires a cell range to be specified. Thus, to add the contents of cells F23 to F36, requires the function =SUM(F23:F36). The function =AVERAGE (A3:K3) calculates the average of the values stored in cells A3 to K3.

Other functions require different arguments. The function =PMT requires three arguments, *principal*, *interest* and *term* and calculates the periodic payment required to pay off a loan, given a particular periodic interest rate and number of payment periods. For example, the function =PMT(30000, 15%, 25) relates to a loan (the principal) of £30000, with interest charged at 15% per annum, repayable over a 25 year term. Typically, a spreadsheet package will provide *statistical*, *mathematical*, *financial*, *lookup* and *logical* functions. The function names used here are not necessarily the same as you may find in the package you use, but you should be able to identify related functions from the examples which follow.

Statistical functions

❏   =AVERAGE*(range)* which averages the values in a range of cells.

❏   =MAX*(range)* which finds the largest value in a range of cells.

❏   =MIN*(range)* which finds the smallest value in a range of cells.

❏   =STDEV*(range)* calculates the population standard deviation of the values in a range of cells.

❏   =SUM*(range)* sums the values in a range of cells.

Mathematical functions

The arguments symbolised by x, y and n may be cell references or fixed values.

❏   =SQRT(x) calculates the square root of x.

❏   =SIN(x) calculates the sine of angle x.

❏   =TAN(x) calculates the tangent of angle x.

❏   =ROUND(x,n) rounds the number x to n places.

❏   =MOD(x,y) calculates the remainder (*modulus*) of x divided by y.

Financial functions

❏   =NPV*(interest, range)* gives the net present value of a series of future cash flows, discounted at a fixed interest rate.

❑ =FV(*payments*, *interest*, *term*) computes the future value of money invested in equal periodic payments, at a given interest rate, over a given term.

Lookup and reference

❑ =HLOOKUP(*lookup_value, array, row_index)* Looks up a search value in a table (array) and returns an associated value from another row in the array. The function is described in detail later, with examples.

❑ =VLOOKUP(*lookup_value, array, column_index*). This is the same as HLOOKUP, except that the array is organised in columns (vertically as opposed to horizontally).

❑ =CHOOSE(*index_no, value1, value2,...*), uses an index number to choose a value from a list of values.

Logical

❑ =IF(*logical_test, value_if_true, value_if_false*). Alternative values are returnable depending on whether the result of a logical test is true or false. Examples of logical tests are: B3>25; Salary<15000 ('Salary' would be a *named* cell - see Naming Cells). The function is described in detail later.

❑ =AND(*logical_test1, logical_test2,...*). Returns logical *true*, if all logical tests are true. It can be used in combination with IF. The function is used as part of examples illustrating the IF function, later.

❑ =OR(*logical_test1, logical_test2,...*). Returns logical *true*, if any of the logical tests are true. Forms part of the group of logical functions, commonly used in combination with the IF function, which include, AND, OR, NOT.

Copying and moving data

You can copy (original is left in place) or move (original is deleted) numbers or labels to other cells. The contents are copied without change, unless the spreadsheet software detects a pattern, such as days of the week or number patterns (see Autofill later).

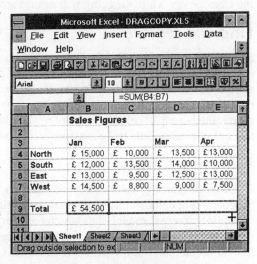

You can copy a formula, *relatively*, to another cell or range of cells. This is necessary if you want the same calculation to be carried out in a different row or column, by referencing a different group of cells. Thus, for example, the formula in Figure 10.12, =SUM(B4:B7), which totals a group of values for the month of January can be copied to succeeding columns to the right for February as =SUM(C4:C7), for March as =SUM(D4:D7), for April as =SUM(E4:E7) and so on. The

Figure 10.12. *Copying by dragging*

formula is logically the same but the column references change according to the position of the formula.

If you wish part of a formula to remain unchanged, you must make the relevant cell reference *absolute.* Typically, the software prefixes the row and column reference with a $ sign when you make it absolute. Thus, for example, the formula =(B3+C3)*$A$6 would add the contents of B3 and C3 (because the brackets give the expression precedence) and then multiply the resulting sum by the contents of A6. The $ prefixes will ensure that when the formula is copied, the reference to A6 remains constant. Thus when copied to, for example, rows 4 and 5 the formula becomes =(B4+C4)*$A$6 and =(B5+C5)*$A$6 respectively.

If you *name* a cell or range of cells (see Naming Cells) the reference is normally made absolute automatically, but you may have to make it so by a separate operation. Figure 10.5, earlier, provides an example which uses an absolute cell reference (by naming) to refer to a price, which is multiplied by a series of sales figures. Absolute cell referencing is also used in later examples, to fix reference to a table (an array of cells) used with the HLOOKUP and VLOOKUP functions (see Using Functions).

The copying process may require a series of operations which identify what is being copied (which may be a single cell or range of cells), and the cell or range of cells to which the copy is directed; this is similar to the *copy* and *paste* operation in a word processor. The process is often simplified and allows you simply to drag a 'handle' on the cell (or highlighted group of cells) being copied, over the group of adjacent cells, where you wish the copy to be directed. An example of the process is illustrated in Figure 10.12.

Autofill

This Excel facility automatically completes series or sequences into adjacent cells. For example: 9.00 copies to 10.00, 11.00, 12.00....; Week1 copies to Week2, Week 3 .....; Aug copies to Sep, Oct, Nov....... Using a group of cells, a pattern can be repeated. For example, two cells containing 9 and 11 (both selected) will copy 13, 15, 17.... to adjacent cells. The feature can be disabled through menu options, but to suspend it for single operations, holding the Control key while dragging will ensure absolute copying.

Find and replace

Spreadsheets provide a *cell find* option, similar in operation to the *text find* facility in a word processor. A particular cell or set of cells can be found by quoting, either specific data contents (*wild cards* can be used if you are unsure of the precise contents) or specific types of data (for example, all formula cells). The range of search can be the whole worksheet or a highlighted group of cells. A *find and replace* facility may also be available, to allow the contents of particular cells to be replaced with new data.

Protecting cells

If you are developing a worksheet to be used by someone else, then it may be useful to protect the contents of certain cells from being overwritten or erased. For example, you may develop a cashflow forecast model, into which the user has only to enter the anticipated amounts of monthly payments and receipts. Clearly, the cells used for the storage of these figures must remain accessible, but the cells which contain text headings and your formulae need to be protected. Many spreadsheet packages allow you to specify ranges of cells as *locked* ('read only') or unlocked. In Microsoft Excel, these settings only take effect when the worksheet protection is enabled. It must be emphasised that if the user of your cashflow model knows the commands to unprotect cells, then unless you assign a password to this operation, there is little that you can do if he or she chooses to change the settings and alter the contents of the related cells. To allow recovery of your work in such an event, you should be maintaining backup copies. Proper staff training and adherence to standard procedures should prevent corruption of data accidentally or through tampering.

Inserting and deleting rows, columns and cells

You may find that, having constructed part or all of a worksheet, you need to insert one or more rows or columns. Rows are moved down to make room for inserted rows. Columns are moved to the right to make way for inserted columns. When you delete rows or columns, the space is closed up. Before removing rows or columns, you should make sure that the process will not destroy the contents of cells currently out of view. If you simply wish to remove the entries in a row or column, you should use the clear contents facility, rather than removing the entire row or column. Individual cells can be inserted or deleted, adjacent cells being moved as necessary.

Freezing titles

You may wish to keep one area of the worksheet in view whilst scrolling to another part. For example, you may have titles which you want to keep in view while you enter associated values along the same rows. You can freeze the column(s) or row(s) containing these headings so that they remain in view, while adjacent rows or columns are scrolled. Figure 10.13 illustrates a column of frozen titles (Column A); you can see that columns B, C, D and E are missing and that column F is now adjacent to A. This is because, as the worksheet is scrolled right, successive columns appear to pass underneath the frozen column. When the sheet is scrolled left, they will reappear, one at a time. You can do the same with any row or column.

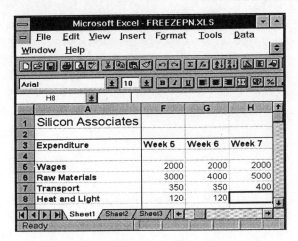

Figure 10.13. *Splitting a window into panes*

Self-test questions

1. Give and example of a label, numeric value and formula cell entry.
2. What is meant by a spreadsheet's "What if" facility. Give an example of an application which may use it.
3. Identify three spreadsheet operations which would require highlighting of cells.
4. When entering a formula, explain the process of pointing as an alternative to simply keying in cell references.
5. Identify two spreadsheet operations when you would drag the mouse pointer.
6. With the use of an example explain two benefits of naming a cell or range of cells.
7. List three different cell formats which affect the display of numeric values. Explain the benefits of using date and time formats.
8. Explain the options for displaying text in a single cell when it exceeds the default columns width.
9. Give one example of each of the following function types
   - ☐ Statistical
   - ☐ Mathematical
   - ☐ Lookup and reference
   - ☐ Logical
10. Distinguish between relative and absolute cell referencing and given an example when each would be used.
11. Give 3 examples of data types which can be entered using Autofill.
12. Explain the operation of *worksheet protection* and *cell locking*. Suggest circumstances when the facilities would be used.

Chapter 11

Spreadsheet development

In this chapter, we use a cashflow forecast model to illustrate the principal stages you should follow to produce a working spreadsheet which meets user requirements. Although some presentation features, such as borders and shading are used, this chapter concentrates on the basics of determining user requirements, planning layout, using formulas, testing spreadsheet operation and producing documentation.

Determining user requirements

For simple models, user requirements can be simple to meet. For example, if a client asks for a spreadsheet which will output an average value of 100 numbers entered in a single column, the options for varying the design are very limited. However, questions you may need to ask include:

"Do you want to restrict the range of values which can be entered, or perhaps exclude negative and fractional numbers?"

"If fractional numbers can be entered, do you want them to be rounded and displayed as integers?"

"Will users know how to enter the numbers or will they need guidance?"

Clearly, this is a trivial example, but it serves to illustrate the difficulties of precisely determining what a client wants you to produce. It is also possible that the client will not fully understand what a spreadsheet can do and will, therefore, not be in a position to draw up a specification without considerable help from the developer. This dilemma is precisely why packaged solutions, designed to meet a broad range of user requirements, are so successful. Imagine if you wanted to buy a spreadsheet program but first had to specify all the features and facilities you wanted it to include, in precise detail. A tailor-made solution is always more expensive, precisely because it can require a lengthy analysis, specification, design, testing and documentation process.

A cash flow model specification

Suppose that you work for Lucre Manufacturing in a general ICT support role with additional responsibility to tailor packages for user departments. The Accounts Manager, Fred Lucre, has asked you to produce a computer-based cashflow forecast model to replace the present manual system. It is assumed that you only have a vague idea of the model's purpose and that the process of drawing up a specification will require explanation from Fred Lucre and some questioning by you. First, Fred Lucre explains the project.

"A cash flow model is used to make judgements about our future cash requirements. You probably use the model without thinking. For example, if you know that your car has to undergo major repair next month, you will know that you are probably going to have less cash to spend, unless your income or regular spending commitments change. It may mean you have to approach the bank for a temporary overdraft. You might also know that in three months time you will be receiving a tax rebate which will restore you finances to normal and your bank account to credit. It is the same for a company, except in the business world future income is not guaranteed, like a salary at the end of the month. A cash flow forecast is a series of educated guesses as to the amount of cash we will have or the amount of overdraft we will need each month for, say, the next four months.

To be a cash flow model, the balance (credit or debit) at the end of any particular month is carried forward and taken into account in the calculation of the next month's balance. This means that changes in anticipated income or expenditure, at any point before the end of the cycle, have to be reflected in all the figures which follow. In other words, the model will allows us to judge what happens to the cash flow, when certain income or spending alternatives are placed into it. I am sure that a spreadsheet can simplify my task."

Fred then shows you the model he uses and has produced in a word processor. The model does not make use of formulae and all calculations are carried out manually (his mental arithmetic skills are good).

Lucre Manufacturing		Cash flow forecast		
	Jan	Feb	Mar	Apr
Cash receipts				
Sales	£300,000	£ 94,000	£395,000	£520,000
Rent	£ 15,000	£ 15,000	£ 15,000	£ 17,500
Interest	£ 4,600	£ 4,600	£ 4,300	£ 3,800
Total cash receipts	£319,600	£ 113,600	£414,300	£541,300
Cash outflow				
Raw materials	£130,000	£ 275,000	£125,000	£230,000
Wages and salaries	£ 32,000	£ 32,000	£ 30,000	£ 42,000
Factory overheads	£ 3,400	£ 3,400	£ 3,900	£ 4,700
Transport and distribution	£ 2,300	£ 3,400	£ 3,000	£ 6,000
Interest on loans	£ 2,400	£ 2,800	£ 3,200	£ 4,700
Total cash outflow	£170,100	£ 316,600	£165,100	£287,400
Balance b/f	£ 27,000	£ 176,500	−£ 26,500	£222,700
Balance c/f	£176,500	−£ 26,500	£222,700	£476,600

Figure 11.1. *Fred Lucre's cash flow forecast model*

Assuming that you understand the general principles, you now need to ask a few questions.

Q.   Can you explain to me what calculations you make and where they are located on the sheet?

A.   Yes. In the 'Total cash receipts row' I add the income we receive each month from sales, rent and interest (on investments). In the 'Total cash outflow' row I add the amounts we spend each month on raw materials, wages, overheads, transport and interest on loans. Before I explain the bottom two rows, 'b/f' stands for 'brought forward' and 'c/f' stands for 'carried forward'. The first amount in the 'Balance b/f' row (£27,000 in the example) is not the result of a calculation, but our cash balance at the start of the first month in the model (January in the example); I enter the amount as it appears on our bank statement. The other entries in the 'Balance b/f' row I copy from the previous month's 'Balance c/f'. For example, January's balance c/f for £176.500 becomes February's balance b/f and February's balance c/f becomes the balance b/f for March and so on. I calculate each figure in the bottom row by adding, for each month, the Balance b/f to the Total cash receipts and then subtracting the Total cash outflow figure. In other words, it is the balance we start with, plus our income, minus our spending.

Q.   What aspects of the model give you most difficulty?

A.   The calculations aren't really a problem and they only take me a few minutes. However, when I do the 12 month forecast, the process is rather tedious. Also, when future income and spending predictions change, for example, when a new contract comes in or a machine needs replacement, I have to do some calculations again. If the change is in the final month, then it only means re-doing the calculations in one column, but if the change is towards the beginning, it affects every balance c/f and balance b/f from there to the final month. Basically, what I want to be able to do is type in the new income or spending figures and see the results immediately.

Drawing up the specification

Given the example model and the information provided by Fred Lucre, you should be in a position to put some of the details into the specification. A possible analysis is given below.

Output requirements

The variable outputs are illustrated by the following areas extracted from the sample model.

Total cash receipts	£319,600	£ 113,600	£414,300	£541,300
Total cash outflow	£170,100	£ 316,600	£165,100	£287,400
Balance b/f	£ 27,000	£ 176,500	−£ 26,500	£222,700
Balance c/f	£176,500	−£ 26,500	£222,700	£476,600

N.B. The shaded areas are label entries and will not change. The bordered entry is an input value which represents the opening cash balance taken from the company's bank statement.

Current method of obtaining output

The values are all calculated manually. Clearly, spreadsheet formulae can be used to produce these figures automatically.

Sources of input data

All the figures are projections of likely spending and income and are drawn from a variety of sources. The following analysis is probably not necessary in this case, because Fred Lucre already has systems set up to obtain the information, but the details serve to illustrate the specification process.

Sales	£300,000	£	94,000	£395,000	£520,000

The sales figures are taken from the previous year's figures for the same months, although adjustments may be made on knowledge of changes in the market for the company's products.

Rent	£ 15,000	£	15,000	£ 15,000	£ 17,500

The rent value is not a prediction because the agreement with the landlord lasts for two years and is negotiated in advance. The rent figure is taken directly from the company accounts.

Interest	£ 4,600	£	4,600	£ 4,300	£ 3,800

Interest rates vary and the company may draw on or add to its investments, causing a fall or rise in the amount of interest received. The company draws on its investments to buy new equipment so any planned purchases can be used to adjust the interest on investments figure.

Raw materials	£130,000	£	275,000	£125,000	£230,000

Raw materials purchases are directly linked to anticipated sales of the company's products. For example, Product A has a recipe which states that each unit of the product is made from X quantity of raw material B and Y quantity of raw material C. The company uses these recipes to predict its raw materials requirement and it is the monthly costs of these planned purchases which are used in the cash flow model.

Wages and salaries	£ 32,000	£	32,000	£ 30,000	£ 42,000

Salaries are not difficult to predict as the company tries to maintain its salaried staffing levels for a full year at a time. No overtime is paid to salaried staff. Waged staff, on the other hand, are paid overtime when necessary and may be on 'short' time when production levels drop. The wages part of the figure is thus more difficult to predict.

Factory overheads	£ 3,400	£	3,400	£ 3,900	£ 4,700

Factory overheads include, for example, heat, light and maintenance and vary according to production levels.

| Transport and distribution | £ 2,300 | £ 3,400 | £ 3,000 | £ 6,000 |

Transport and distribution costs are directly linked to those of sales.

| Interest on loans | £ 2,400 | £ 2,800 | £ 3,200 | £ 4,700 |

Interest on loans varies for similar reasons to interest on investments.

Data capture methods

Even for a cash flow forecast of 12 months, the number of entries to be made is small and does not really justify the automatic entry of values, even those which are clear (such as rent). However, if predicted values are generated in Accounts and other departments, they could be transferred electronically to Fred Lucre. To generate a cashflow directly from those figures would require that the model was part of an integrated Management Information System (MIS).

Processing requirements

At this point you need to convert Fred Lucre's explanations of the calculations into spreadsheet formulae. At this stage each can be just an indication, not an actual formula. The relevant output rows are shown.

| Total cash receipts | £319,600 | £ 113,600 | £414,300 | £541,300 |

  =sum(range)in each cell

| Total cash outflow | £170,100 | £ 316,600 | £165,100 | £287,400 |

  =sum(range) in each cell

| Balance b/f | £ 27,000 | £ 176,500 | −£ 26,500 | £222,700 |

  = cell reference of previous month's Balance c/f cell

| Balance c/f | £176,500 | −£ 26,500 | £222,700 | £476,600 |

  = Total cash receipts plus Balance b/f minus Total cash outflow

Facilities for input

If Fred Lucre is the only person who is to use the model then he is unlikely to need much guidance or support, but you do suggest that all cells except for the data entry areas should be locked to prevent the model from being modified. Shading could be used to highlight the data entry cells.

If Fred Lucre is likely to modify the model, perhaps adding further rows or columns then he would need to know how to switch the worksheet protection on and off.

Model appearance

You may suggest to Fred Lucre that the appearance of the model could be improved with the use of some shading and cell borders and perhaps a different font style for main headings. This would certainly aid readability of the model and provide a more professional image for presentation to, for example, the bank manager.

Creating the model

As there is little presentation design work to be done you can use the layout provided by Fred Lucre. If a layout has not been prepared, you may need to experiment with various arrangements to see which works best. Generally, it is best to complete the label areas first, but whether you decide to enter some sample data or the formulae first is really up to you. The model with formulae displayed is shown in Figure 11.2.

	A	B	C	D	E
1	Lucre Manufacturing		Cash flow fore		
2					
3		Jan	Feb	Mar	Apr
4	Cash receipts				
5	Sales	300000	94000	395000	520000
6	Rent	15000	15000	15000	17500
7	Interest	4600	4600	4300	3800
8	Total cash receipts	=SUM(B5:B7)	=SUM(C5:C7)	=SUM(D5:D7)	=SUM(E5:E7)
9					
10	Cash outflow				
11	Raw materials	130000	275000	125000	230000
12	Wages and salaries	32000	32000	30000	42000
13	Factory overheads	3400	3400	3900	4700
14	Transport and distribution	2300	3400	3000	6000
15	Interest on loans	2400	2800	3200	4700
16	Total cash outflow	=SUM(B11:B15)	=SUM(C11:C15)	=SUM(D11:D15)	=SUM(E11:E15)
17					
18	Balance b/f	27000	=B19	=C19	=D19
19	Balance c/f	=B18+B8-B16	=C18+C8-C16	=D18+D8-D16	=E18+E8-E16

Figure 11.2. *Layout of cash flow model with formulae displayed*

The only formula that may need explanation appears first in cell C18. Note that it consists of a single cell reference, B19. This ensures that the 'balance c/f' figure is displayed in the next month's 'balance b/f' cell. Like all formulae in the worksheet example, this formula has been copied to the other relevant cells. Note from Figure 11.2, the spreadsheet's ability to copy formulae *relatively* (the same formula, but changing any cell references used to take account of a formula's new position).

The completed model with some formatting is shown in Figure 11.3.

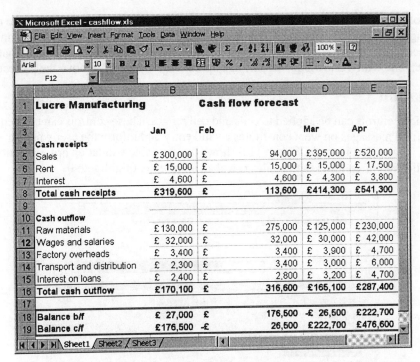

Figure 11.3. *Completed cash model with formatting to highlight data entry areas*

Worksheet protection

Figure 11.4. shows a highlighted data entry area being formatted as 'unlocked' and then the setting of worksheet protection (with password).

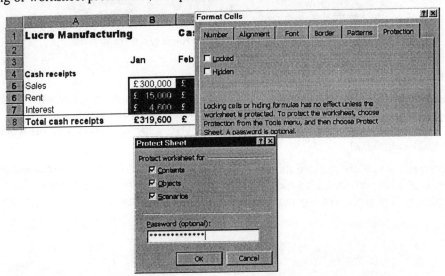

Figure 11.4. *Formatting data entry cells as unlocked and setting worksheet protection*

Microsoft Excel allows a worksheet to be protected from modification, but specific cells or cell ranges can be formatted as 'unlocked' when the protection is set. At the time the worksheet protection is set, a password can be entered. A password is essential in that, without it, anyone with a knowledge of package operation can simply remove the protection.

Validation

Validation controls can be applied to cells and cell ranges. These controls can be used to display helpful messages on what constitutes a valid entry and inform the user when an attempt to enter invalid data is made. Figure 11.5 shows the available validation criteria options and the application of controls to the Sales row data entry cells (highlighted).

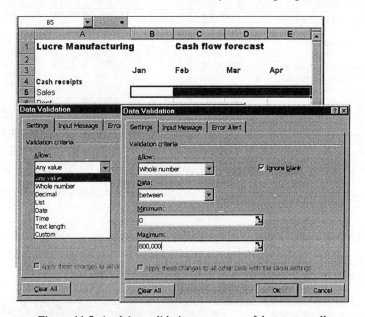

Figure 11.5. *Applying validation to a range of data entry cells*

Validation criteria

In the example, the criteria for the cell range require that each entry must be whole number between 0 and 800,000. This would prevent entry of numbers with a fractional element, negative numbers and any number greater than 800,000. As a logical expression this would be '>=0 AND <=800,000'.

The alternatives to 'between' are shown in Table 11.1 with an example expression and an explanation of what constitutes invalid data. The whole number criterion is assumed for all the examples, so it is given that any numbers with a fractional element will also be rejected.

Relational operators	Sample expression	Invalid data
not between	<0 OR >800,000	Zero, 800,000 and other positive numbers between those values
equal to	=500,000	Any number other than 500,000
greater than	>800,000	800,000 and any number less than 800,000
less than	<0	Any positive number
greater than or equal to	>=0	Any negative number and zero
less than or equal to	<=800,000	Any positive number greater than 800,000

Table 11.1. *Validation criteria*

Apart from 'whole number' there are other validation criteria options shown in Figure 11.5 and these are explained in Table 11.2.

Criteria option	Explanation
Decimal	Allows real numbers, that is, integers and fractions
List	Applies a list box to the cell and contains entries which are referenced in the same worksheet, workbook or external source.
Date	Relational expressions can then be applied to dates in the same way as for whole number. The cell should still be formatted as date type to ensure correct display of contents.
Time	Relational expressions can be applied to times in the same way as for whole number. The cell should still be formatted as time type to ensure correct display of contents.
Text length	Allows control over number of characters (including spaces) which can be entered. The cell should still be formatted as text type to ensure that the contents appear exactly as entered.
Custom	This allows the entry of expressions, using formulae and functions to provide validation controls which cannot be applied using the standard options.

Table 11.2. *Validation criteria options*

Examples of the use of these other options are provided later in this chapter.

Input and validation error messages

Figure 11.6 shows the completed Input Message and Error Alert tabs for this range of cells.

Figure 11.7 shows the displayed input message when a validated cell is selected and an error message when an invalid entry is attempted.

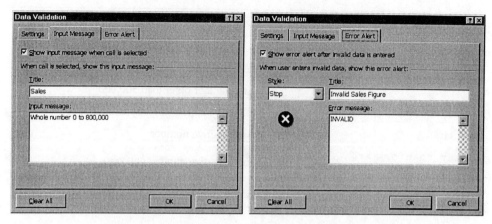

Figure 11.6. *Completed Input Message and Error Alert tabs*

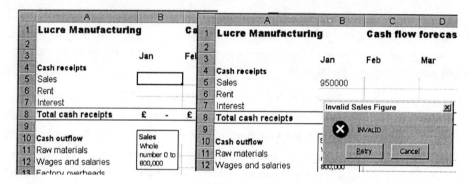

Figure 11.7. *Input message and validation error message*

Spreadsheet testing

General principles

Any ICT system you develop needs to be tested to determine that it meets the client's specification and that it performs as expected. There are general principles for the testing of all ICT systems and all are based on the design of appropriate test data. In the context of a spreadsheet project, your test data should ensure

- ❏   that every operation and facility within the spreadsheet is executed at least once;

- ❏   the effectiveness of every control devoted to detecting invalid input is verified;

- ❏   every possible sequence of spreadsheet operation is tested at least once;

- ❏   the accuracy of any processing carried out by the spreadsheet is verified;

- ❏   the spreadsheet operates according to its original design specification.

There are three general categories of test data:

1.   *Normal data.* This includes the most general data for which the spreadsheet was designed to handle.

2. *Extreme values.* These test the behaviour of the spreadsheet when valid data at the upper and lower limits of acceptability are used. The process of using extreme values is called 'boundary testing' and is often a fruitful place to look for errors. For numeric data this could be the use of very large or very small values. Text could be the shortest or longest sequence of characters permitted.

3. *Exceptional data.* A spreadsheet can be designed to accept a certain range or class of inputs. If invalid data is used, that is data which the spreadsheet is not designed to handle, the spreadsheet should be capable of rejecting it rather than attempting to process it. This is particularly important when the spreadsheet is to be used by people other than the developer, since they may be unaware of what constitutes invalid data. A developer should from the outset assume that incorrect data will be used with the spreadsheet.

Testing the cashflow model

The testing can be divided into two main areas. One aspect deals with the formulae which calculate total cash receipts, total cash outflow, balance b/f and balance c/f. As you have been provided with example data with outputs which have been calculated manually, you can compare them with the outputs of your spreadsheet version and thereby test the operation of the formulae. The second aspect concerns validation. Fred Lucre has only provided you with data which the model is designed to accept, so you need to create test data which will test each controlled cell for data which it is not designed to accept. To do this, you need to follow the guidelines in the preceding paragraphs. All the data entry cells in the cashflow spreadsheet are for integer numeric values and the only variation should be in the number ranges which are permitted in each row. Table 11.3 shows a test plan for the Sales row, our example for validation control.

Input	Type	Comments
100	valid	All numbers between 0 and 800,000 are valid, so it is sufficient to test it with one such number.
0	valid	This tests the lower boundary of permitted values.
800,000	valid	This tests the upper boundary of permitted values.
-5	invalid	All numbers less that zero are invalid, so it is sufficient to test it with one negative number.
500.85	invalid	Only whole numbers are permitted so it is sufficient to test it with one number containing a fractional element.
A456	invalid	Non-numeric characters should be rejected
123A	invalid	Non-numeric characters should be rejected. This test is advisable as some software may accept the initial digits and ignore the trailing text
abcD	invalid	Text characters should be rejected

Table 11.3. *Test plan for Sales row*

Spreadsheet documentation

Technical documentation

This should include the following:

❏ A copy of the agreed design specification. This could incorporate the original cash flow forecast example provided by Fred Lucre, with the various sections labelled with the agreed formula requirements, cell protection and validation controls. Figure 11.8 illustrates how it may appear.

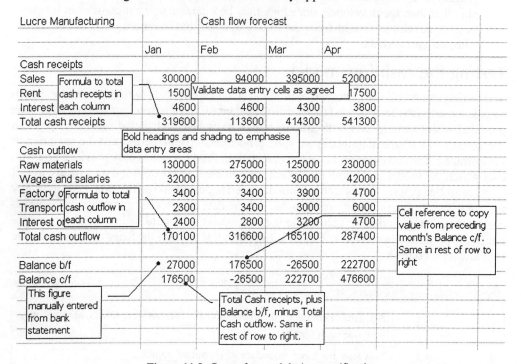

Lucre Manufacturing		Cash flow forecast		
	Jan	Feb	Mar	Apr
Cash receipts				
Sales	300000	94000	395000	520000
Rent	1500	Validate data entry cells as agreed		17500
Interest	4600	4600	4300	3800
Total cash receipts	319600	113600	414300	541300
Cash outflow				
Raw materials	130000	275000	125000	230000
Wages and salaries	32000	32000	30000	42000
Factory o	3400	3400	3900	4700
Transport	2300	3400	3000	6000
Interest o	2400	2800	3200	4700
Total cash outflow	170100	316600	165100	287400
Balance b/f	27000	176500	-26500	222700
Balance c/f	176500	-26500	222700	476600

Boxes in figure: "Formula to total cash receipts in each column"; "Bold headings and shading to emphasise data entry areas"; "Formula to total cash outflow in each column"; "Cell reference to copy value from preceding month's Balance c/f. Same in rest of row to right"; "This figure manually entered from bank statement"; "Total Cash receipts, plus Balance b/f, minus Total Cash outflow. Same in rest of row to right."

Figure 11.8. *Copy of agreed design specification*

❏ Hardware and software resources. This would specify the spreadsheet used to develop and thereafter use, the model and the minimum/recommended hardware requirements.

❏ Instructions for opening and configuring the spreadsheet. It may be necessary to modify the way the spreadsheet, for example, validates input or prints the header in a report, so details of existing configurations and procedures to change them should be documented. In this example, this would primarily concern the procedures for cell protection and validation.

❏ Calculations, functions and formulae. The purpose of this section is to allow support and simplify future modifications which may need to be made either by the developer or someone else. Particularly with more complex models, it can be difficult to remember details of how they were constructed, even a few weeks after the initial development. The screen shot in Figure 11.2 could be used for this purpose.

❑ Validation and verification procedures. Verification would require a second reference to the original sources of information to check that they had been entered accurately. The validation controls, giving details of criteria, input and error messages should be detailed. Table 11.5 details some of the validation controls and settings.

Cell range	Data subject	Criteria	Input Message	Error Alert
B5:E5	Sales	Whole number between 0 and 800,000	Whole number between 0 and 800,000	STOP. Values between 0 and 800,000
B6:E6	Rent	etc	etc	etc

Table 11.5. *Validation controls*

❑ Details of all input and output screens and printed designs. Screen shots, such as that in Figure 11.3, would be included. A sample of a printed report is shown in Figure 11.9.

December 25 2000   **2001**   *Prepared by Fred Lucre*

Lucre Manufacturing   **Cash flow forecast**

	Jan	Feb	Mar	Apr
Cash receipts				
Sales	£ 300,000	£ 94,000	£ 395,000	£ 520,000
Rent	£ 15,000	£ 15,000	£ 15,000	£ 17,500
Interest	£ 4,600	£ 4,600	£ 4,300	£ 3,800
Total cash receipts	£ 319,600	£ 113,600	£ 414,300	£ 541,300
Cash outflow				
Raw materials	£ 130,000	£ 275,000	£ 125,000	£ 230,000
Wages and salaries	£ 32,000	£ 32,000	£ 30,000	£ 42,000
Factory overheads	£ 3,400	£ 3,400	£ 3,900	£ 4,700
Transport and distribution	£ 2,300	£ 3,400	£ 3,000	£ 6,000
Interest on loans	£ 2,400	£ 2,800	£ 3,200	£ 4,700
Total cash outflow	£ 170,100	£ 316,600	£ 165,100	£ 287,400
Balance b/f	£ 27,000	£ 176,500	-£ 26,500	£ 222,700
Balance c/f	£ 176,500	-£ 26,500	£ 222,700	£ 476,600

Figure 11.9. *Printed report*

❑ Copies of the test specification (see Table 11.3).

User documentation

This should include the following:

❏ How to start the spreadsheet program, for example,

1. Click the Excel symbol on the Task Bar.

2. Click on the Open File button.

3. Select cashflow.xls from the Finance folder on the D: drive.

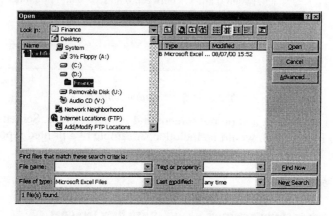

(The detail in the documentation will vary according to the requirements of the client. The above example is very prescriptive and specifies precisely where the file can be found. This is unlikely when the model may be used on different machines.)

❏ Routes through spreadsheet menus. This is not relevant here as the client will only be involved in data entry. If this is not the case, then detailed guidance facilitated by screen shots or menu sequences, such as Data|Validation, should be provided. Good examples of user guidance are provided in the tutorials in the Basic Package Skills section.

❏ Examples of input screens and data entry forms. The screen shot in Figure 11.3 would be included, or several screen shots could be used to show the model at various stages of data entry. It would also be useful to show the model with more than one data set to show its 'what if' capability.

❏ Advice on how to respond to error messages or conditions. Screen shots of the validation error messages will be useful to the user, as well as instructions on how to continue. For example, the WARN error message in Excel allows you to click Yes to apply an invalid entry or No to try again, whereas the STOP error message will not allow an invalid entry. If you know of errors in the model which you could not correct, but do not prevent the operation of the model, you can include information on how the user can avoid their occurrence. Even powerful commercial software packages contain significant 'bugs', which users learn how to cope with or 'work around'. Of course, with simpler applications, such as spreadsheet models, you should make every effort to ensure that they do operate completely as required.

❑ Examples of data output screens and printed reports. These are to be found in Figures 11.3 and 11.9, respectively.

Chapter 12

Advanced spreadsheet functions

This chapter provides further spreadsheet examples to illustrate uses of the logical IF and table LOOKUP functions. We use these applications to illustrate the use of macros, command buttons, forms, list boxes, styles, templates, 3-D referencing and a number of other spreadsheet facilities.

Logical IF function

Your spreadsheet package provides a set of *logical* functions, which allow you to test the contents of cells against defined *logical tests*. The result of the test is either *true* or *false*. The idea can be illustrated without reference to a spreadsheet.

Suppose, for example, that you are asked if you are over 25 years of age; your answer will be 'yes' or 'no'. If you answer 'yes', this equates to 'true'; you are over 25. A 'no' will confirm that you are 25 or less. The same question can be put to anyone, the answer being true (yes) or false (no), in each case. If you receive a 'no' answer, there is no need then to ask if a person is 25 or less, because the negative answer to the original question provides the information you want. Similarly, if you wish to know if someone subscribes to a superannuation scheme, you only need to ask one question, which can be phrased positively or negatively, thus: 'Do you subscribe to the superannuation scheme?' or 'Do you *not* subscribe to the superannuation scheme?'.

Concerning your spreadsheet's logical functions, you should view such questions as logical tests. The IF function has the following format. It has three arguments, separated by commas.

```
=IF(logical_test, value_if_true, value_if_false)
```

A simple example

Now consider the simple example in Figure 12.2. Column D is used to display a status message, indicating acceptance or rejection of each applicant for 'The Over 25 Club'. Only those aged over 25 are accepted.

The IF formula in cell D5 (shown on the edit line) tests the value in cell C5 (the applicant's age), to determine if it is greater than 25. The first argument is, therefore, C5>25. The value in cell C5 is 22, which means that the logical test returns *false* and that the word 'reject' is displayed. Cells D6, D7 and D8 contain the same formula, but testing the contents of cells C6, C7, and C8, respectively. The tests on C6 and C8 are found to be *true*, so the word 'accept' is displayed in the adjacent cells. The applicant Kerr, P is 25, so the logical test returns *false* and 'reject' is shown in the relevant Status cell.

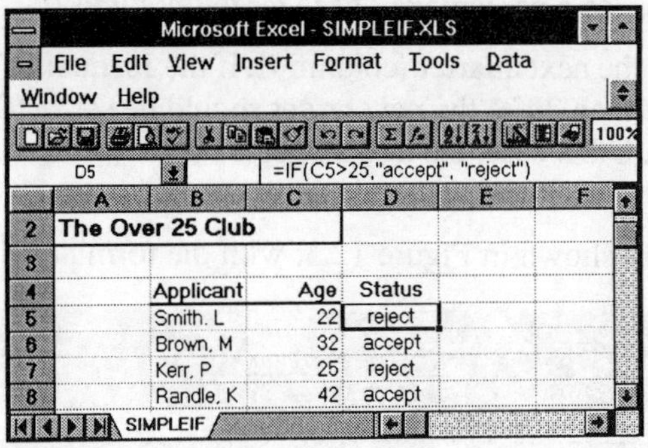

	A	B	C	D
2	The Over 25 Club			
3				
4		Applicant	Age	Status
5		Smith, L	22	reject
6		Brown, M	32	accept
7		Kerr, P	25	reject
8		Randle, K	42	accept

Figure 12.1. *Simple example using logical IF function*

A sales target model

Suppose that you are Sales Manager for the Target Corporation and wish to monitor the sales performance of the sales representatives for whom you are responsible. You set up the worksheet shown in Figure 12.2.

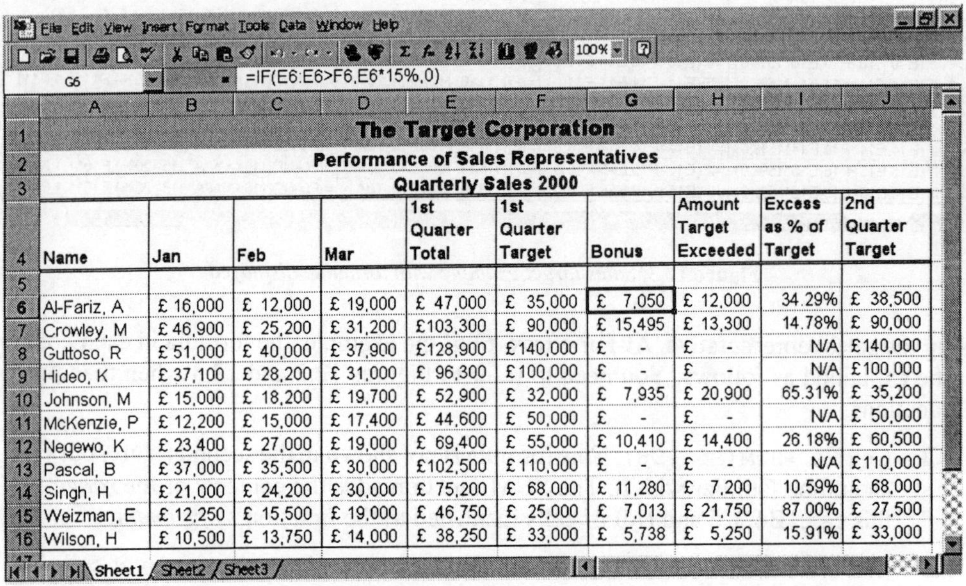

The Target Corporation
Performance of Sales Representatives
Quarterly Sales 2000

Name	Jan	Feb	Mar	1st Quarter Total	1st Quarter Target	Bonus	Amount Target Exceeded	Excess as % of Target	2nd Quarter Target
Al-Fariz, A	£ 16,000	£ 12,000	£ 19,000	£ 47,000	£ 35,000	£ 7,050	£ 12,000	34.29%	£ 38,500
Crowley, M	£ 46,900	£ 25,200	£ 31,200	£103,300	£ 90,000	£ 15,495	£ 13,300	14.78%	£ 90,000
Guttoso, R	£ 51,000	£ 40,000	£ 37,900	£128,900	£140,000	£ -	£ -	N/A	£140,000
Hideo, K	£ 37,100	£ 28,200	£ 31,000	£ 96,300	£100,000	£ -	£ -	N/A	£100,000
Johnson, M	£ 15,000	£ 18,200	£ 19,700	£ 52,900	£ 32,000	£ 7,935	£ 20,900	65.31%	£ 35,200
McKenzie, P	£ 12,200	£ 15,000	£ 17,400	£ 44,600	£ 50,000	£ -	£ -	N/A	£ 50,000
Negewo, K	£ 23,400	£ 27,000	£ 19,000	£ 69,400	£ 55,000	£ 10,410	£ 14,400	26.18%	£ 60,500
Pascal, B	£ 37,000	£ 35,500	£ 30,000	£102,500	£110,000	£ -	£ -	N/A	£110,000
Singh, H	£ 21,000	£ 24,200	£ 30,000	£ 75,200	£ 68,000	£ 11,280	£ 7,200	10.59%	£ 68,000
Weizman, E	£ 12,250	£ 15,500	£ 19,000	£ 46,750	£ 25,000	£ 7,013	£ 21,750	87.00%	£ 27,500
Wilson, H	£ 10,500	£ 13,750	£ 14,000	£ 38,250	£ 33,000	£ 5,738	£ 5,250	15.91%	£ 33,000

Figure 12.2. *Sales target model*

The spreadsheet records, in respect of each representative:

1. monthly sales (columns B, C and D) and total sales for the quarter (column E);
2. the quarter's sales target (column F);

3. a bonus of 15% of the quarter's sales total, if the target has been beaten. Otherwise, the bonus is £0 (column G).
4. the amount by which the target has been exceeded (column H);
5. the target excess, as a percentage of the target (column I);
6. a new target for the next quarter (column J). If the 1st quarter's target has been exceeded by more than 20%, the new target should be set at 10% more than the 1st quarter's target. Otherwise, the new target is to remain the same as that of the 1st quarter.

Columns G, H, I and J are shown in Figure 12.3, with the formulae displayed.

	G	H	I	J
1	poration			
2	epresentatives			
3	s 2000			
4	Bonus	Amount Target Exceeded	Excess as % of Target	2nd Quarter Target
5				
6	=IF(E6:E6>F6,E6*15%,0)	=IF(E6>F6,E6-F6,0)	=IF(H6>0, H6/F6,"N/A")	=IF(AND(I6<>"N/A",I6>20%),F6*1.1,F6)
7	=IF(E7:E7>F7,E7*15%,0)	=IF(E7>F7,E7-F7,0)	=IF(H7>0, H7/F7,"N/A")	=IF(AND(I7<>"N/A",I7>20%),F7*1.1,F7)
8	=IF(E8:E8>F8,E8*15%,0)	=IF(E8>F8,E8-F8,0)	=IF(H8>0, H8/F8,"N/A")	=IF(AND(I8<>"N/A",I8>20%),F8*1.1,F8)
9	=IF(E9:E9>F9,E9*15%,0)	=IF(E9>F9,E9-F9,0)	=IF(H9>0, H9/F9,"N/A")	=IF(AND(I9<>"N/A",I9>20%),F9*1.1,F9)
10	=IF(E10:E10>F10,E10*15%,0)	=IF(E10>F10,E10-F10,0)	=IF(H10>0, H10/F10,"N/A")	=IF(AND(I10<>"N/A",I10>20%),F10*1.1,F10)
11	=IF(E11:E11>F11,E11*15%,0)	=IF(E11>F11,E11-F11,0)	=IF(H11>0, H11/F11,"N/A")	=IF(AND(I11<>"N/A",I11>20%),F11*1.1,F11)
12	=IF(E12:E12>F12,E12*15%,0)	=IF(E12>F12,E12-F12,0)	=IF(H12>0, H12/F12,"N/A")	=IF(AND(I12<>"N/A",I12>20%),F12*1.1,F12)
13	=IF(E13:E13>F13,E13*15%,0)	=IF(E13>F13,E13-F13,0)	=IF(H13>0, H13/F13,"N/A")	=IF(AND(I13<>"N/A",I13>20%),F13*1.1,F13)
14	=IF(E14:E14>F14,E14*15%,0)	=IF(E14>F14,E14-F14,0)	=IF(H14>0, H14/F14,"N/A")	=IF(AND(I14<>"N/A",I14>20%),F14*1.1,F14)
15	=IF(E15:E15>F15,E15*15%,0)	=IF(E15>F15,E15-F15,0)	=IF(H15>0, H15/F15,"N/A")	=IF(AND(I15<>"N/A",I15>20%),F15*1.1,F15)
16	=IF(E16:E16>F16,E16*15%,0)	=IF(E16>F16,E16-F16,0)	=IF(H16>0, H16/F16,"N/A")	=IF(AND(I16<>"N/A",I16>20%),F16*1.1,F16)

Figure 12.3. *Sales target example with formulae displayed*

Using the sales representative, Al-Fariz (row 6) as the example, the formula in each column can be explained as follows. You need to refer to Figures 12.2 and 12.3 when reading the explanations.

- Cell E6. `=SUM(B6..D6)`. This formula is not shown in the second figure, but you should be familiar with it. The SUM function adds the contents of the *range* (in this case, B6, C6 and D6) of cells identified as the function's *argument*.

- Cell G6. `=IF(E6>F6,E6*15%,0)`. The logical test is a comparison of cells E6 and F6. If the first quarter's total (E6) is greater than the target (F6) a bonus of 15% of the first quarter's total (E6) is displayed. Otherwise a figure of zero is shown. In the case of Al-Fariz, the logical test returns *true* and a bonus of £7050 is displayed.

- Cell H6. `=IF(G6>0,E6-F6,0)`. Testing the bonus cell (G6) for a value greater than zero, tells us whether the target has been exceeded. Alternatively, you could use the logical test (E6>F6), from the previous formula, which calculated the bonus. If the logical test returns true, the excess is calculated by subtracting the target (F6) from the first quarter's total (E6). If false, a figure of zero is shown. For Al-Fariz, the test is true and the excess of £12000 is displayed accordingly.

❑ Cell I6. =IF(H6>0,H6/F6,'N/A'). This formula tests the value in the target excess (H6) cell to see if it is greater than zero. If true, the excess is calculated as a fraction of the target figure. The displayed percentage value is achieved with the *formatting* facility, which multiplies the fraction by 100. If false, the N/A (meaning 'not applicable') message is displayed. Note that you must enclose this non-numeric data in quotation marks. In the case of Al-Fariz, the test is true and the figure of 34.29% appears.

❑ Cell J6. =IF(AND(I6<>'N/A',I6>20%),F6*1.1,F6). This is an example of a *complex condition*. In other words, it tests the value in cell I6 to check that it is not equal to 'N/A' AND that it is greater than 20%. There is no point in checking for a percentage value if the cell contains the letters 'N/A', so both conditions must be satisfied before the value for true is returned. This is the case for Al-Fariz and the target is increased by 10% (F6*1.1) from £35000 to £38500.

There is another reason for testing for both conditions. It so happens that, for the computer, 'N/A' is greater than the value 20%. If you did not test for the 'N/A' value, you would find that the target is still increased for those cells containing the 'N/A' value. If either test returns false, the new target remains the same as the old (it displays the same value as F6). Crowley (row 7) has beaten the target, but not by 20%, so the new target remains the same as the old. The excess percentage cell for Guttoso (row 8) shows 'N/A', so the new target is not increased.

Data consolidation

The sales target example uses total sales figures for each salesperson for each month, but if it is assumed that the company sell a number of products it would be reasonable to store the figures for each product separately. If, for example, there are three products and the details are to be stored as part of the illustrated model, this would require nine further columns and thereby make it more difficult to view the entire worksheet on screen and to fit it onto a single printed page.

Instead, the sales details for each product, A, B and C, can be held in separate worksheets or files and be consolidated into the main sales target model. Data consolidation uses 3D (three dimensional) referencing, that is, formulae can refer to cells in other worksheets or external sources.

Figure 12.4 shows the use of the SUM function to consolidate the individual sales figures for each product into the main worksheet. Other functions used in consolidation include COUNT, AVERAGE, MAX, MIN and PRODUCT.

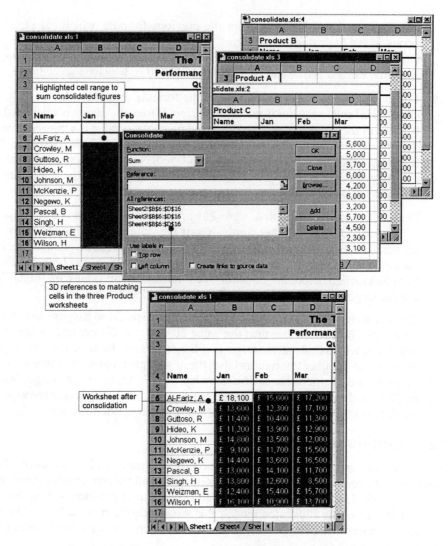

Figure 12.4. *3D referencing to sum figures from several worksheets*

LOOKUP function

This function is used to extract a value from a table by reference to another value. It is likely that you already use *lookup tables*, but not necessarily in the context of a spreadsheet package. For example, when you want the price of an item in a catalogue, you scan the product list for the relevant item and thereby find the price. Thus the product name or code is the *lookup value* and the associated price is the *extracted value*.

Similarly, banks often display a table of currency exchange rates. By scanning the list of countries, you can find the appropriate exchange rate, from one of the adjacent columns. Usually, there are four rate columns, to separately identify the rates at which the bank buys and sells notes and travellers' cheques. Once you have found the right country, you have to scan across to the appropriate column to extract the rate you want.

A spreadsheet's LOOKUP function works in a similar fashion to that described above. There are two types: VLOOKUP, for tables organised vertically, or in column form and HLOOKUP for tables which are set out horizontally or in rows. Table 12.1 shows the horizontal format, using rates of pay as an example and Table 12.2 illustrates the vertical format, with an exchange rate example.

Job Grade	A	B	C	D
Hourly Rate	£5.00	£7.50	£8.50	£12.00

Table 12.1. *Pay rates horizontal table*

Country	Currency	We buy notes at	We sell notes at	We buy cheques at	We sell cheques at
Austria	Schilling	18.0	17.50	17.95	18.22
Belgium	Bel. Franc	52.1	51.40	51.95	51.55
Canada	Can Dollar	1.95	1.90	1.93	1.92
France	Fr. Franc	8.95	8.46	8.80	8.57
Germany	Mark	2.65	2.50	2.60	2.55
Italy	Lire	2500	2425	2485	2475
Spain	Peseta	208	202	206	204
Swizerland	Sw Franc	2.20	2.10	2.15	2.12
USA	US Dollar	1.47	1.42	1.46	1.44

Table 12.2. *Exchange rates vertical table*

To identify a particular rate of pay, you need to identify the Job Grade (the lookup value is a letter in this case) from the top row and then look at the second row for the Hourly Rate, which appears beneath the letter.

Format of the LOOKUP function

The arguments for the two LOOKUP forms are shown below.

```
=VLOOKUP(lookup value, table array, column index)
=HLOOKUP(lookup value, table array, row index)
```

Note that they only differ in respect of the third argument; one refers to column and the other to row. The purposes of these arguments are given below.

1. *lookup value*. This will normally be a cell reference, which contains the value to be used to search the table. It may contain, for example, a product code to search a price table.

2. *table array*. This identifies the location of the table in the worksheet. The range of cells will be identified by the top left and bottom right cell references.

3. *column/row index*. This identifies the column or row in the table array, from

which the value is to be taken. In the earlier exchange rate example, you would use this argument to specify which exchange rate column was to be used. The Excel spreadsheet refers to the leftmost column in a table as 1 and columns to the right are identified as 2, 3 and so on. For a horizontal table, the top row is 1 and rows beneath are similarly incremented. Other packages may refer to the leftmost column as 0 and adjacent columns are referred to as *offset* column 1, 2 and so on. An equivalent pattern is used in horizontal tables. It is important to note that column and row indexes, or offsets, refer to the table array and not to the worksheet as a whole.

Note that the values in the leftmost column (for a vertical table) or the top row (for a horizontal table) must be in *ascending* sequence. Thus, alphabetic values must be in ascending alphabetical order and numeric values in ascending numerical order. Remember that the lookup value (the first argument) is compared with these values and if they are not in ascending sequence, the formula will not work properly.

Exchange rate example

Suppose that you wish to calculate holiday costs by reference to the currency table (Table 12.2). For the sake of simplicity, it is assumed that only one set of exchange rates is required. You may design the worksheet as shown in Figure 12.5.

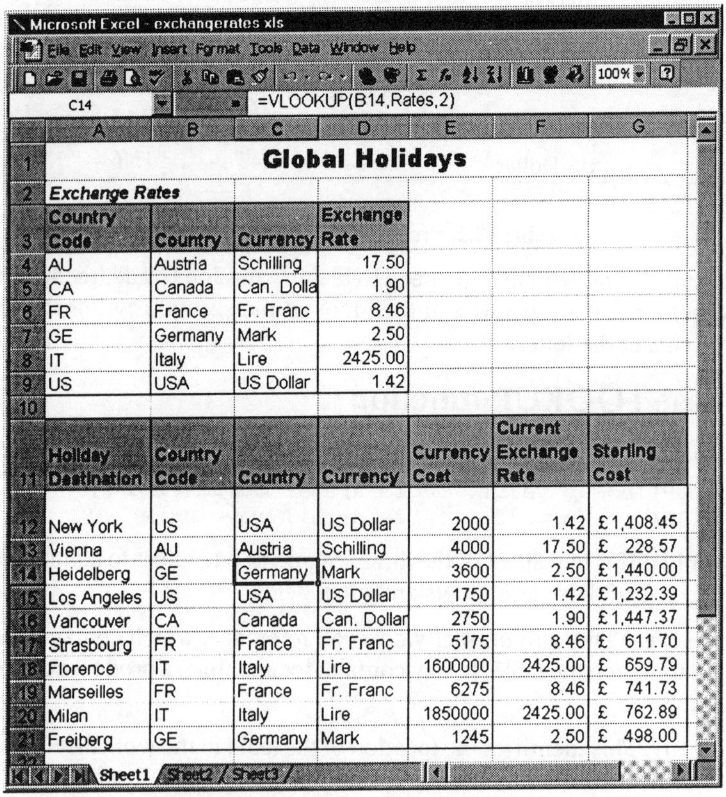

Global Holidays

Exchange Rates

Country Code	Country	Currency	Exchange Rate
AU	Austria	Schilling	17.50
CA	Canada	Can. Dolla	1.90
FR	France	Fr. Franc	8.46
GE	Germany	Mark	2.50
IT	Italy	Lire	2425.00
US	USA	US Dollar	1.42

Holiday Destination	Country Code	Country	Currency	Currency Cost	Current Exchange Rate	Sterling Cost
New York	US	USA	US Dollar	2000	1.42	£1,408.45
Vienna	AU	Austria	Schilling	4000	17.50	£ 228.57
Heidelberg	GE	Germany	Mark	3600	2.50	£1,440.00
Los Angeles	US	USA	US Dollar	1750	1.42	£1,232.39
Vancouver	CA	Canada	Can. Dollar	2750	1.90	£1,447.37
Strasbourg	FR	France	Fr. Franc	5175	8.46	£ 611.70
Florence	IT	Italy	Lire	1600000	2425.00	£ 659.79
Marseilles	FR	France	Fr. Franc	6275	8.46	£ 741.73
Milan	IT	Italy	Lire	1850000	2425.00	£ 762.89
Freiberg	GE	Germany	Mark	1245	2.50	£ 498.00

Figure 12.5. *Using VLOOKUP with an exchange rate table*

In designing the worksheet, your main aims are to minimise data entry and ensure selection of the correct exchange rate, for the calculation of individual holiday costs. To create the worksheet, you:

1. set up the Exchange Rate Table. Figure 12.5 shows that the table range extends from D3 to G8. To make your lookup formulae more meaningful, you decide to call the table 'RateTable' (see earlier section on Naming a Cell or Range of Cells). You put suitable headings at the top of each column in the table, but they do not form part of the table which is to be referenced in the lookup formulae. Placing the table above the main data entry area ensures that numerous holidays can be costed without interfering with the lookup table range. You remember to ensure that the country code values in the first column of the table are in ascending alphabetical order.

2. set up the data entry area which is to display the holiday details and costs. You place suitable headings at the top of each column;

3. enter the necessary formulae.

Figure 12.6 shows these formulae in columns C, D, F and G. Referring again to Figure 12.5, this means that, once your worksheet is set up, data entry is restricted to three items for each holiday. They are: Holiday Destination (column A); Country Code (column B); Currency Cost (column E). The information in columns C, D, F and G is generated automatically. Table values can be amended when exchange rates alter.

	C14	▼	■	=VLOOKUP(B14,Rates,2)	
	C	D	E	F	
1	**Global Holidays**				
2					
3	Currency	Exchange Rate			
4	Schilling	17.5			
5	Can. Dollar	1.9			
6	Fr. Franc	8.46			
7	Mark	2.5			
8	Lire	2425			
9	US Dollar	1.42			
10					
11	Country	Currency	Currency Cost	Current Exchange Rate	Sterling Co
12	=VLOOKUP(B12,Rates,2)	=VLOOKUP(B12,Rates,3)	2000	=VLOOKUP(B12,Rates,4)	=E12/F12
13	=VLOOKUP(B13,Rates,2)	=VLOOKUP(B13,Rates,3)	4000	=VLOOKUP(B13,Rates,4)	=E13/F13
14	=VLOOKUP(B14,Rates,2)	=VLOOKUP(B14,Rates,3)	3600	=VLOOKUP(B14,Rates,4)	=E14/F14
15	=VLOOKUP(B15,Rates,2)	=VLOOKUP(B15,Rates,3)	1750	=VLOOKUP(B15,Rates,4)	=E15/F15
16	=VLOOKUP(B16,Rates,2)	=VLOOKUP(B16,Rates,3)	2750	=VLOOKUP(B16,Rates,4)	=E16/F16
17	=VLOOKUP(B17,Rates,2)	=VLOOKUP(B17,Rates,3)	5175	=VLOOKUP(B17,Rates,4)	=E17/F17
18	=VLOOKUP(B18,Rates,2)	=VLOOKUP(B18,Rates,3)	1600000	=VLOOKUP(B18,Rates,4)	=E18/F18
19	=VLOOKUP(B19,Rates,2)	=VLOOKUP(B19,Rates,3)	6275	=VLOOKUP(B19,Rates,4)	=E19/F19
20	=VLOOKUP(B20,Rates,2)	=VLOOKUP(B20,Rates,3)	1850000	=VLOOKUP(B20,Rates,4)	=E20/F20
21	=VLOOKUP(B21,Rates,2)	=VLOOKUP(B21,Rates,3)	1245	=VLOOKUP(B21,Rates,4)	=E21/F21

Sheet1 / Sheet2 / Sheet3 /

Figure 12.6. *Exchange rate example with formulae displayed*

Using the holiday destination, Heidelberg (row 12), as the example, the formula in each cell can be explained as follows.

❑   Cell C12. =VLOOKUP(B12,RateTable,2). The first argument, B12, contains the lookup value, which in this case is 'GE' (country code). The second argument identifies the location of the lookup table. You have instructed the spreadsheet that 'RateTable' refers to the array of cells bounded on the top left by D3 and the bottom right by G8. If you did not name the range, you would use the cell references (D3:G8) as the second argument. The third argument indicates that the extracted value is to be taken from column 2 of the lookup table. Thus, for the Heidelberg example, the word 'Germany' appears in cell C12 (see Figure 23.20).

❑   Cell D12. =VLOOKUP(B12,RateTable,3). The first argument again refers to B12, which contains the country code. The second argument remains the same in all three lookup formulae. The third argument extracts the relevant value from column 3 of the lookup table. Thus, the currency is identified as the Mark.

❑   Cell F12. =VLOOKUP(B12,RateTable,4). The third argument extracts the exchange rate of 2.5 from column 4 of the lookup table and displays it in F12.

❑   Cell G12. =E12/F12. This formula simply divides the currency cost (E12), which has been keyed in, by the exchange rate (F12), which is generated by the lookup formula.

The benefits of the worksheet may seem limited, if costings are required for only a few holiday destinations. However, without the lookup table, the entry of more numerous holiday destinations, would probably require frequent repetition of the same details, concerning country, currency and exchange rate. In addition, if the exchange rate for a particular currency changes, the lookup table ensures that the costings for all relevant holidays can be amended by a single alteration to the table.

Copying the formulae

The second argument in a lookup formula refers to a particular range of cells. To ensure that reference to the table array does not alter when you copy the formula to other rows in the data entry area, you would need to make the cell references *absolute*. In the previous example, the table range has been named (RateTable) and with the Excel package, this makes the reference absolute.

Using list boxes

Global Holidays provides holidays to a limited range of cities in Europe and the United States. The Holiday Destination entries in Column A are suited to entry by list box. The full list of cities can be held elsewhere in the spreadsheet or in a different file and the data validation facilities used to link the list to each entry point in Column A.

Figure 12.7 shows the selection of the Column A cells for validation by list box and the source of each list.

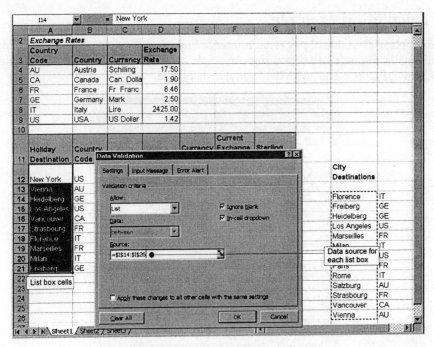

Figure 12.7. *Setting list box validation*

An open list box is shown in Figure 12.8.

Note that the City Destination list has been given a second column to hold the relevant Country Codes. The two columns can be used as a lookup table (the name `cities` has been used to define for the cell range), to allow the automatic entry of the relevant codes in Column B next to each city destination. This change means that the only data entry required is the Currency Cost in column E. The relevant section of the spreadsheet with formulae displayed is shown in Figure 12.9.

Figure 12.8. *List box*

11	Country Code	u	re	nc	nt	rli			
12	=VLOOKUP(A12,cities,2)	=V	=VI	200	=VL	=E	**City Destinations**		
13	=VLOOKUP(A13,cities,2)	=V	=VI	400	=VL	=E			
14	=VLOOKUP(A14,cities,2)	=V	=VI	360	=VL	=E	Florence	IT	
15	=VLOOKUP(A15,cities,2)	=V	=VI	175	=VL	=E	Freiberg	GE	
16	=VLOOKUP(A16,cities,2)	=V	=VI	275	=VL	=E	Heidelberg	GE	
17	=VLOOKUP(A17,cities,2)	=V	=VI	517	=VL	=E	Los Angeles	US	
18	=VLOOKUP(A18,cities,2)	=V	=VI	160	=VL	=E	Mars	lookup table	
19	=VLOOKUP(A19,cities,2)	=V	=VI	627	=VL	=E	Milan	defined as 'cities'	
20	=VLOOKUP(A20,cities,2)	=V	=VI	185	=VL	=E	New York	US	
21	=VLOOKUP(A21,cities,2)	=V	=VI	124	=VL	=E	Paris	FR	
22							Rome	IT	
23							Salzburg	AU	
24							Strasbourg	FR	
25							Vancouver	CA	
26							Vienna	AU	

Figure 12.9. *Using the City Destinations list as a lookup table*

Pay calculation example

This example uses a table of pay rates, referenced by job grade, to calculate some simplified payroll details. Figure 12.10 shows some example output for this worksheet. The worksheet is repeated in Figure 12.11, with the formulae displayed.

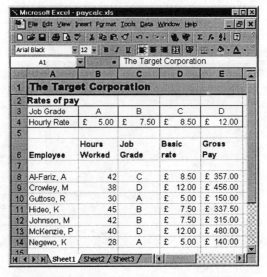

Figure 12.10. *Pay calculation using HLOOKUP*

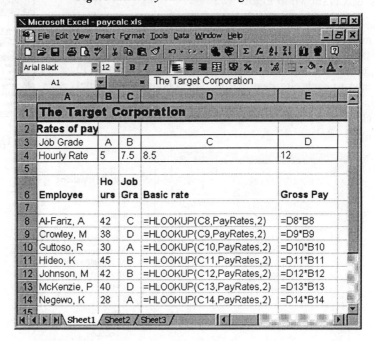

Figure 12.11. *Pay calculation example with formulae displayed*

Using the Employee McKenzie (row 13) as the example, the formulae can be explained as follows.

- Cell D13. `=HLOOKUP(C13,PayRates,2)`. The `HLOOKUP` function ensures that the table is referenced horizontally, by row. The first argument, C13, contains the lookup value. In this case it is job grade D. The lookup value is compared with the entries in the top row of the table. The second argument identifies the lookup table as the range of cells named PayRates (array B3:E4). The third argument ensures that the value associated with this grade (in this case, £12.00) is taken from the second row of the table.
- Cell E13. `=B13*D13`. This simply multiplies the hours worked figure (in B13) by the rate of pay extracted from the lookup table, to give the gross pay for McKenzie.

Lookup tables using value ranges

The examples provided so far assume that every possible lookup value (the first argument) has a precise match in a lookup table. Thus, in the first example, all Country Codes appear, and each has a set of related values. Similarly, in the payroll example, each Job Grade letter can be found in the table. Figure 12.12 shows how you can use *value ranges* in a lookup table.

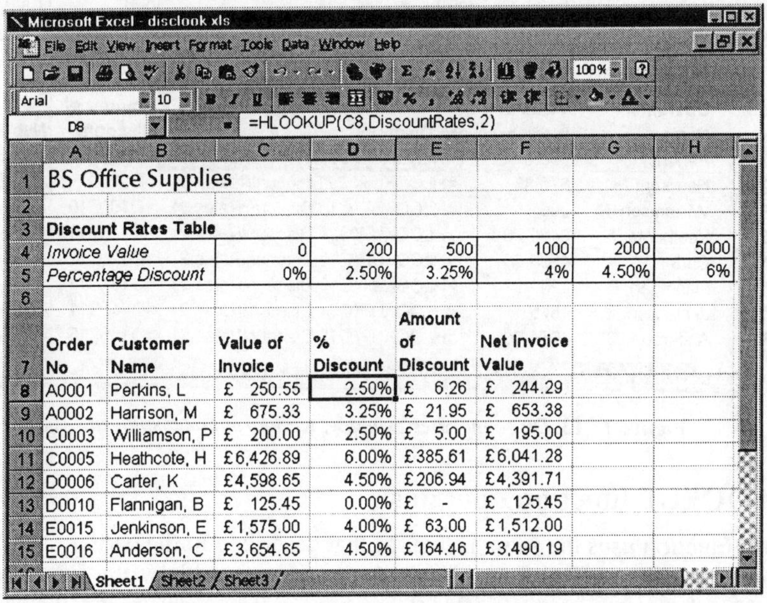

	A	B	C	D	E	F	G	H
1	BS Office Supplies							
2								
3	Discount Rates Table							
4	Invoice Value		0	200	500	1000	2000	5000
5	Percentage Discount		0%	2.50%	3.25%	4%	4.50%	6%
6								
7	Order No	Customer Name	Value of Invoice	% Discount	Amount of Discount	Net Invoice Value		
8	A0001	Perkins, L	£ 250.55	2.50%	£ 6.26	£ 244.29		
9	A0002	Harrison, M	£ 675.33	3.25%	£ 21.95	£ 653.38		
10	C0003	Williamson, P	£ 200.00	2.50%	£ 5.00	£ 195.00		
11	C0005	Heathcote, H	£6,426.89	6.00%	£385.61	£6,041.28		
12	D0006	Carter, K	£4,598.65	4.50%	£206.94	£4,391.71		
13	D0010	Flannigan, B	£ 125.45	0.00%	£ -	£ 125.45		
14	E0015	Jenkinson, E	£1,575.00	4.00%	£ 63.00	£1,512.00		
15	E0016	Anderson, C	£3,654.65	4.50%	£164.46	£3,490.19		

Figure 12.12. *Discount rates lookup table with value ranges*

Suppose that you wish to calculate discounts by reference to a table of percentage rates and according to the value of each customer invoice. You allocate discount rates on the following basis:

- invoice values up to £199.99 attract no discount;

- discount of 2.5% is given for amounts between £200 and £499.99;
- invoices for amounts between £500 and £999.99 are discounted at 3.25%;
- for amounts between £1000 and £1999.99, 4% discount is allowed;
- invoices valued at between £2000 and £4999.99 are given a discount of 4.5%;
- invoices for £5000 or more attract a discount of 6%.

These sample invoice and discount details are shown in Figure 12.12.

Figure 12.13 shows the same worksheet with the formulae displayed.

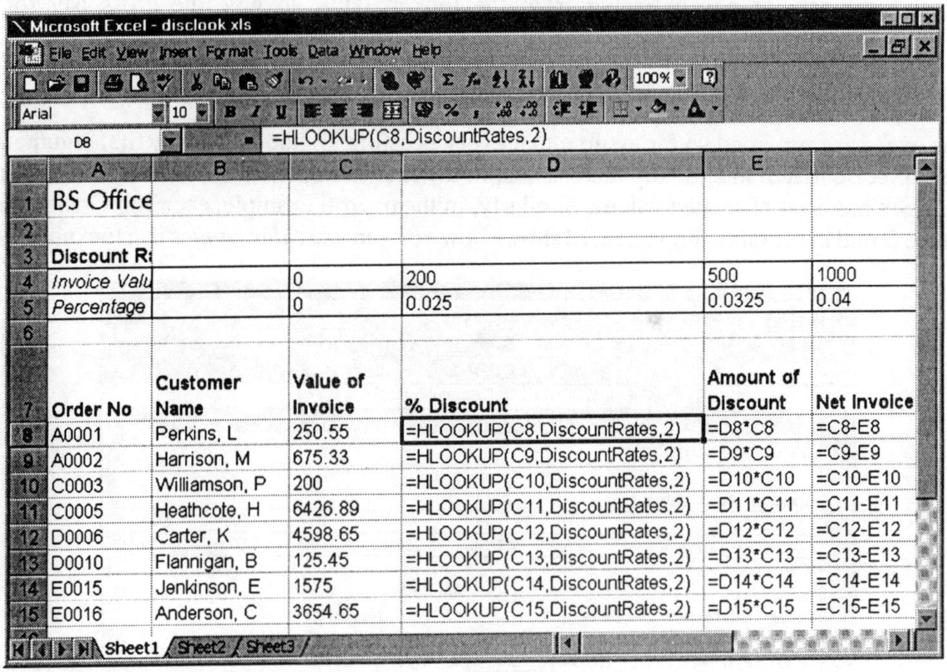

	A	B	C	D	E	
1	BS Office					
2						
3	Discount R					
4	*Invoice Valu*		0	200	500	1000
5	*Percentage*		0	0.025	0.0325	0.04
6						
7	Order No	Customer Name	Value of Invoice	% Discount	Amount of Discount	Net Invoice
8	A0001	Perkins, L	250.55	=HLOOKUP(C8,DiscountRates,2)	=D8*C8	=C8-E8
9	A0002	Harrison, M	675.33	=HLOOKUP(C9,DiscountRates,2)	=D9*C9	=C9-E9
10	C0003	Williamson, P	200	=HLOOKUP(C10,DiscountRates,2)	=D10*C10	=C10-E10
11	C0005	Heathcote, H	6426.89	=HLOOKUP(C11,DiscountRates,2)	=D11*C11	=C11-E11
12	D0006	Carter, K	4598.65	=HLOOKUP(C12,DiscountRates,2)	=D12*C12	=C12-E12
13	D0010	Flannigan, B	125.45	=HLOOKUP(C13,DiscountRates,2)	=D13*C13	=C13-E13
14	E0015	Jenkinson, E	1575	=HLOOKUP(C14,DiscountRates,2)	=D14*C14	=C14-E14
15	E0016	Anderson, C	3654.65	=HLOOKUP(C15,DiscountRates,2)	=D15*C15	=C15-E15

Figure 12.13. *Discount rates example, with formulae displayed*

How the LOOKUP function operates

The `HLOOKUP` function uses the same format as that described in the earlier examples, so is not further described here. However, it is useful to understand how the function operates when used with value ranges. As with all lookup tables, you must ensure that the values in the top row (or leftmost column, in a vertical table) are in ascending sequence.

Using the customer Perkins, L (row 8 in Figures 12.12 and 12.13) as the example, the operation of the lookup function can be described as follows.

- Cell D8 `=HLOOKUP(C8,DiscountRates,2)`. The first argument (C8) contains the lookup value, which for Perkins is an invoice value of £250.55. The function compares the lookup value with each entry in the top row of the table (or leftmost column for `VLOOKUP`), until it finds a value which is greater than or equal to the lookup value. Thus, the first entry (0) is less than the lookup value, as is the next entry of 200. Comparison with the third entry (500) brings the scan to an end. The lookup function then 'knows', according to the rules already described, that the extract value is to be taken from the second column in the table. The third argument indicates that the value is to be extracted from the second row. This results in the display of 2.50% in D8, which contains the lookup formula. Using Carter, K (row 12) as a second example, comparing the invoice total of £4,598.65 with the table entries results in the search ending when the 5000 entry is reached, which is greater than the lookup value. The extract value of 4.50% is taken, therefore, from the previous column. Finally, Heathcote, H (row 11) has an invoice value which is greater than all the entries in the top row of the table. Using the function's rules, the value (6%) is extracted from the row beneath the final entry in the table.

It is apparent from this explanation that you must understand how the VLOOKUP and HLOOKUP functions deal with value ranges, before you can properly set up the table. It should also be clear to you that the values in the top row of a horizontal table and the leftmost column of a vertical table must be in ascending sequence. As explained earlier, this rule applies to all lookup tables, whether they contain every value that is required or (as in the above example) value ranges. You also need to ensure that the minimum value (the first in the top row or leftmost column) in the lookup table must not be greater than the minimum lookup value. Thus, if the minimum lookup value is 50, then the minimum value in the lookup table must be 50 or less (that is a larger negative number).

Combined use of the IF and LOOKUP functions

In the introduction to the LOOKUP function, the example of an exchange rate table is used. The worked example in that section only allows for one exchange rate column in the lookup table. In reality, the exchange rate for any particular currency varies according to whether you are buying or selling and whether you are dealing in notes or travel cheques. Thus, a typical exchange rate table (see Table 12.2), displayed in a bank or travel agency window, has six columns. The first two columns contain the names of the countries and currencies. The other four are used for the bank or travel agency 'buy' and 'sell' rates, for notes and travel cheques.

The IF function is used to allow the LOOKUP function to select from the appropriate column. A worked example is shown in the following section.

A further exchange rate example

Figure 12.14 illustrates a worksheet which includes an exchange rate table, used as a lookup table and several example transactions which refer to it. The operation of the worksheet can be explained as follows:

1. The user enters the date of the transaction (column A), the country code (column B), the currency amount (column E) and the transaction type (column C). The transaction type consists of four codes, the meanings of which are shown in Figure 12.14.

2. Column D contains a formula to identify, from the transaction type in column C, which exchange rate column to use in the lookup table. This is done by converting

the transaction type to an appropriate column number. The error messages in row 14 are explained later.

3.   Column F contains the lookup formula to extract the rate from the table.

4.   The value of the transaction is calculated in column G, with a formula which divides the currency amount (column E) by the exchange rate (column F).

	A	B		We Buy Cheques At	We Sell Cheques At
2	Transaction Type Key	Country Code	Currency	We Buy Notes At	We Sell Notes At
3	BN=Buy Notes	AU	Schilling	18.00	17.50	17.95	18.22
4	SN=Sell Notes	CA	Can. Dollar	1.95	1.90	1.93	1.92
5	BC=Buy Cheques	FR	Fr. Franc	8.95	8.46	8.80	8.57
6	SC=Sell Cheques	GE	Mark	2.65	2.50	2.60	2.55
7			IT	Lire	2500.00	2425.00	2485.00	2475.00
8			US	US Dollar	1.47	1.42	1.46	1.44

	Date of Transaction	Country Code	Transaction Type	Table Column to Use	Currency Amount	Current Exchange Rate	Sterling Equivalent
10	23-Jan-00	US	BN	3	2000	1.47	£1,360.54
11	01-Feb-00	AU	SN	4	4000	17.5	£ 228.57
12	10-Feb-00	GE	BN	3	3600	2.65	£1,358.49
13	21-Feb-00	US	BC	5	1750	1.46	£1,198.63
14	02-Mar-00	CA	SL	invalid	2750	#REF!	#REF!
15	15-Mar-00	FR	SN	4	5175	8.46	£ 611.70
16	22-Mar-00	IT	BN	3	1600000	2500	£ 640.00
17	31-Mar-00	FR	BN	3	6275	8.95	£ 701.12
18	11-Apr-00	IT	SN	4	1850000	2425	£ 762.89
19	20-Apr-00	GE	BN	3	1245	2.65	£ 469.81

Figure 12.14. *Combined use of If and LOOKUP*

Part of the worksheet, with the `IF` and `LOOKUP` formulae displayed, is shown in Figure 12.15. Using row 10 as an example, the formulae displayed in the Figure can be explained as follows.

CellD10.`=IF(C10="BN",3,IF(C10="SN",4,if(C10="BC",5,if(C10="SC",6,"in valid"))))`. Note that, instead of the third argument (the value if logical test is false) referring to a value or another cell reference, it comprises another `IF` condition. Expressed in ordinary English, it is equivalent to saying, "If the transaction type code is 'BN', store and display the value 3; if the code is 'SN', store and display 4 and so on; otherwise display 'N/A'". You can see that there are four separate conditions, each with a different second argument (value if logical test is true). Finally, the single third argument (value if test is false) is an error message, to allow for none of the logical tests being satisfied (the `IF` conditions are nested in this example). You can see that the first of the two previous figures, includes the message 'invalid type code' in cell D14. This results from the entry of 'SL' (which is not one of the four transaction type codes) in cell C14. You should notice the four closing brackets at the end of the formula. These accord with the four opening brackets used in the formula.

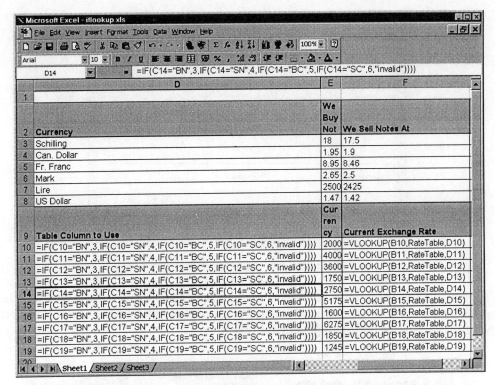

Figure 12.15. *Combined use of IF and LOOKUP with formulae displayed*

The lookup formula in column F should not need any further explanation, as it is used in earlier examples. The #REF error messages in Figure 12.14 arise because, in column F, the lookup formula has no valid first argument and in column G, the exchange rate needed in the formula is missing. These error messages can be suppressed with the use of another function, which is not dealt with in this text.

Forms and templates

As with word processed documents, spreadsheets can be prepared and stored at templates. A template is useful for any spreadsheet which is in common use, such as invoices, order forms, despatch and delivery notes. A template can be created from an existing spreadsheet design, although it is usual to remove any variable data from it first. For example, a spreadsheet used as an invoice template would not contain details of a particular sale, simply the headings and entry points for the data. A spreadsheet can also be designed to have the appearance of a form, that is a document which has certain points for data entry. The usual gridlines can be hidden, as can any formulae which are used in the form. The following example uses an order form to show the main stages in its development.

Order form example

Figure 12.16 shows the initial design for the order form (the company title at the top left is a logo image).

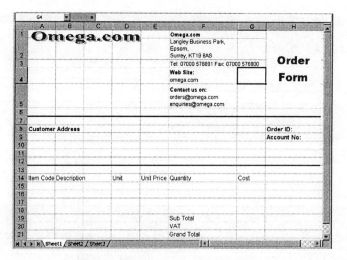

Figure 12.16. *Initial design of order form*

Figure 12.17 shows the form after some borders and shading have been added and the gridlines hidden. A *comment* has been inserted which pops up when the mouse is moved over the cell. These can be useful for guiding user input.

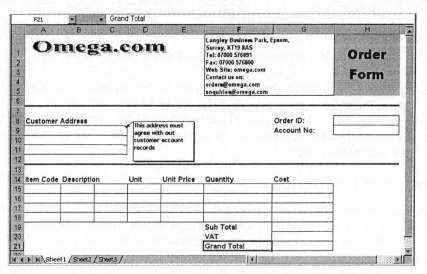

Figure 12.17. *Form after removal of gridlines and further cell formatting*

To prevent alteration of company address details, the logo and the formulae used to calculate order costs, the worksheet protection should be enabled. Before setting the protection, the data entry cells should be formatted as 'unlocked'. To allow the form to be used as a template, it should be saved as such. To prepare a new order the user simply creates a new worksheet based on the Order template (in Excel, this is done through File|New, which gives access to the templates folder). The validation controls described earlier in this chapter can be used to control data entry in the form.

✍️Self-test questions

1. Write expressions using the IF function which will test each of the following statements.
   "The value of an order is more than £100."
   "The order was place between 1st July and 30th August."
   "The customer's name is Parker."
2. What is meant by 3D cell referencing? Give an example of its use (other than that given in the chapter).
3. Give three examples of lookup tables (not within spreadsheets) which are in common use.
4. A theatre's ticket prices vary according to the seat location. Explain the operation of a lookup table by reference to this example.
5. When would it be necessary to use absolute cell referencing in respect of a lookup table?
6. With the use of suitable examples, distinguish between a lookup table containing discrete values with one containing value ranges.
7. Explain the operation of a list box and its use in validating input.
8. Describe an example of a spreadsheet designed as a form.

Chapter 13

Spreadsheet graphics

The communication of information through pictures is something with which we are all familiar. For example, a pictorial advertisement in a magazine can often convey information that, without a picture, would take a few hundred words of text. The meaning of numeric data is often made clearer and more concise, if they are represented pictorially, as *graphs* or *charts* (the terms are interchangeable, but we will use the term 'chart'). The annual financial reports of companies often include charts depicting, for example, sales performance over the year, or profits over a number of years. All modern spreadsheet packages allow you to represent numeric data in a worksheet, as a chart. Although spreadsheet packages allow you to produce a large variety of charts, in either two or three-dimensional form, there are four basic types, which are common to most: *bar* chart; *line* chart; *pie* chart; *xy (scatter)* diagram.

It is important that you are able to select the right kind of chart (sometimes more than one may be suitable) for any particular type of numeric data. Although a package may allow you to produce, for example, a pie chart from a given set of data, it may be completely meaningless. For this reason, you should make sure that you understand the function of any particular chart, and how to construct one manually, before you attempt spreadsheet graphics. Spreadsheet packages include many automated functions which you can use to make chart production simpler. It is common to provide a utility (Excel refers to it as a 'Chart Wizard') to take you, step by step, through the chart production process. It even displays the current state of the chart at each stage. This is particularly useful if you are required to make a selection, perhaps of the type of chart you want, and are unsure which to choose. You can simply try one, and if it is not what you want, select another.

Linking data to a chart

A set of numeric values which you want to use in a chart, is commonly known as a *data range* or *data series*. Various examples of such data series are shown in the figures which follow. Before you start the charting process, you should have decided (although you can change your mind later) on the type of chart you want. If you decide to produce a bar chart, then the data series you choose can also be used for a line graph (and vice versa). The following sections describe the component parts of each chart type listed in the introductory paragraph, and the procedures used to produce them.

Bar charts

A basic bar chart consists of a series of bars with lengths proportional to the quantities they represent. Bar charts are useful for depicting a series of changes in figures of interest.

Figure 13.1 shows an example *bar* chart, embedded in a worksheet which calculates the costs of various holidays. The chart's *axes* are generated from cells A3:B6. The Y-axis uses the costs in cells B3, B4, B5 and B6. The maximum value on the *Y-axis scale* has been set at £5000; the default maximum would be £4000, because the largest value in the data series is £3,505 and the scale is in divisions of £1000. The *X-axis labels* are taken from the holiday destinations of Vienna, Prague, Paris and Siena, in cells A3 to A6. *Data labels* can be used to show the precise figure represented by each bar, although the main purpose of the bar chart is to compare costs, as measured against the Y-axis scale. If data labels are not used and more precise comparison is wanted, then the Y-axis scale can be divided into £500 intervals. To generate the chart in Figure 13.1, the adjacent cells containing the X-axis labels and the Y-axis data series are highlighted. From this highlighted information, the spreadsheet can generate the basic chart, showing an X-axis with labels, a Y-axis suitably scaled to cover the range of values in the data series and bars representing each value. Other detail, such as chart title, axes titles and data labels can then be added. In Figure 13.1, the Y-axis title is 'Costs' and the X-axis title is 'Destination'.

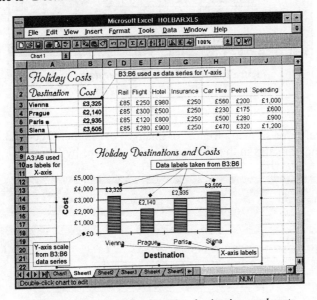

Figure 13.1. *Bar chart of holiday destinations and costs*

Bar chart with multiple data series

The chart in Figure 13.1 has only one data series. In other words, each bar relates to the cost of holidays. Figure 13.2 shows a worksheet and chart, which represent the sales figures (units sold) of three products, namely dishwashers, washing machines and cookers. This means that there are three sets of values, or data series, to represent. The process of chart construction is the same as that for the chart in Figure 13.1. The range of cells from D2 to G6 is highlighted and used by the program to generate the chart.

One feature of the chart in Figure 13.2, which is not present in Figure 13.1, is a *data legend*. This identifies each bar with the relevant product. If there is only one data series, then a legend is not necessary. You will also note that Figure 13.2 shows a bar chart, with a vertical X-axis and a horizontal Y-axis. The basic form of chart is, however, the same as that represented in Figure 13.1. Multiple bar charts are not recommended for more than four sets of figures, because more than this number of adjacent components detracts from the clarity and usefulness of the diagram.

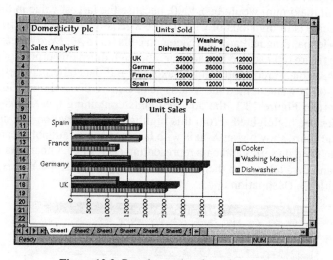

Figure 13.2. *Bar chart using three data series*

Line chart

A *line* chart is useful for showing trends, or changes over time. Figure 13.3 illustrates the movement in computer sales in the North and South regions by Home PC.

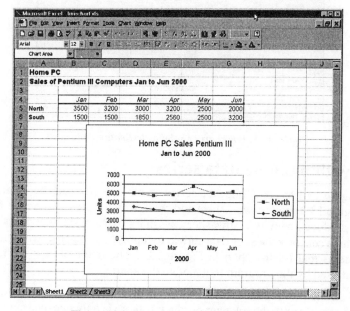

Figure 13.3. *Line chart using two data series*

Although a bar chart could have been used, the comparison of these two sets of sales figures (the data series) is more clearly illustrated with a line chart. The line joining the points marked with the diamond and square symbols help to emphasise trends, so that it is quite easy to compare the two sets of sales figures. It should be noted, however, that the connecting lines cannot be used to interpolate intermediate values; the horizontal scale does not represent a continuous quantity with meaningful values between those marked.

Pie chart

A pie chart is a circle divided into segments. The area of each segment is proportional to the size of the figure represented, and the complete 'pie' represents the overall total of all component parts. It is therefore, a convenient way of illustrating the sizes of quantities in relation to one another and the overall total.

Figure 13.4 shows a typical *pie* chart, together with the data series represented in the chart. A pie chart always contains just one data series and shows each value as a percentage of the total for the series. Each 'slice' or 'wedge' represents one value and colour or cross hatching is used to differentiate one slice from another.

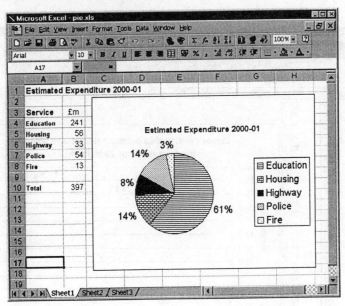

Figure 13.4. *3D pie chart showing distribution of expenditure items*

XY (scatter) diagram

A scatter diagram is particularly appropriate when two measurements are taken from some common *unit if association*, that is some common element on which the two measurements are taken, such as persons, places, or points in time. When each pair of points is plotted, the resulting graph is called a scatter diagram, or *scattergram*. For example, suppose that we have measured the height and weight of 20 subjects and the results are as shown in Table 13.1.

Subject	Height (cm)	Weight (kg)	Subject	Height (cm)	Weight (kg
1	178	85.1	11	176	79.0
2	162	73.6	12	166	75.0
3	173	78.5	13	161	72.2
4	179	79.1	14	169	81.6
5	160	62.5	15	165	71.1
6	168	72.3	16	176	85.6
7	179	82.6	17	167	75.1
8	153	63.1	18	168	75.5
9	159	74.3	19	166	79.0
10	167	73.0	20	166	72.7

Table 13.1. *Data for scatter diagram*

The scatter diagram based on this data and generated in a spreadsheet is shown in Figure 13.5.

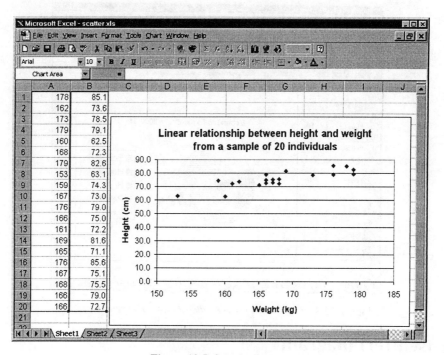

Figure 13.5. *Scatter diagram*

The scatter diagram appears to show that there is a simple linear relationship between the two measurements - there is a tendency for tall people to be heavy and short people to be light.

✍Self-test questions

1. An extract of a sales record spreadsheet is shown below.

A	B	C	D	E	F	G	H
1	Sales records				Unit Price	3.50	
2	Name	Units sold	Sales value				
3	Jones	500	=C3*$G1				
4	Guttoso	300					
5	Fariz	420					
6	McDonald	180					
7	Total						
8							

a. The formula in cell D3 calculates the value of goods sold by Jones, what value will be shown here?

b. The $ sign indicates that the reference to cell G1 is absolute. What values would appear in cells D4, D5 and D6 if the formula in C3 was replicated to those cells?

c. If the absolute cell reference was not used, how would this affect the replication of the formula to cells D4, D5 an D6?

d. Referring to your answer to (c), distinguish between an absolute and relative cell reference.

e. Write a formula (using a function) which would calculate a total for column C.

f. Should the formula you enter in C6 be copied relatively or absolutely to D6?

g. Explain how a chart is created to compare and show the total sales value achieved by each salesperson.

h. State, with reasons, which chart type would be most appropriate to display the information detailed in (g)

Developmental exercises

Spreadsheets

Activity 1

The proprietor of CompuSales wants to compare the profitability of each make of microcomputer which is sold by the firm. Use the following sample data to set up a worksheet to produce:

a. total sales revenue in respect of each model of computer;

b. total costs of the computers sold, in respect of each model of computer;

c. the gross profit (total revenue minus total cost) in respect of each model of computer;

d. the gross profit margin (gross profit as a percentage of total revenue) relating to each model of computer;

e. the total revenue from and total cost of all computers sold;

f. the gross profit and gross profit margin on all sales.

Model	Unit sale price	Unit cost	No sold
Dell P500	£829	£700	45
Dan P600	£2350	£1800	275
Compaq P400	£985	£800	95
Gateway P750	£2036	£1850	75
Toshiba 350	£1800	£1500	30
HP Brio 550	£988	£600	450

Activity 2

This activity relates to student attendance records. Each student's attendance details is to be held on a separate worksheet. Attendance is to be recorded for each separate class, identified by: day of the week; subject; start time; duration (in hours, with a maximum of two per class). The worksheet should allow the recording of attendance for a term of twelve weeks, beginning with Monday, 5th September. Some sample data are given below. Add your own to complete the week. **Design** the worksheet to allow entry of the student's *actual attendance hours* for each class throughout the term. Enter the necessary formulae to produce the following information:

Day	Class	Start time	Duration (hours)
Monday	English	9.00 am	2
Monday	Maths	11.15 am	1
Monday	Maths	1.15 pm	2
Monday	French	3.30 pm	1
Tuesday	Physics	10.15 am	2
Tuesday	German	1.15 pm	2
etc.			

a. the total *possible attendance* each week;

b. the total *actual attendance* each week;

c. the *cumulative weekly variance* (the possible weekly hours minus the actual weekly hours; accumulate these variances from week to week).The possible weekly hours total is always the same, so use a single cell entry to store it. This will mean that, before you copy this formula to all weeks in the term, you will have to make the cell reference, for possible weekly hours, *absolute*.

d. the total possible attendance over the full term, for each class; you can probably make use of the COUNT function in this formula;

e. the total actual attendance over the full term, for each class;

f. the total possible hours for all classes over the full term;

g. the total actual hours attendance for all classes over the full term;

h. item (f) as a percentage of item (g).

Activity 3

In this activity, you are required to produce various figures concerning profit. Create a worksheet to permit the entry of:

a. a single product name;

b. a single product sale price;

c. a single product cost price;

d. the number of units of the product which are sold each month, for 6 months;

e. the monthly costs of overheads, including salaries, advertising, heat, light and transport.

Enter *formulae* to produce the following information:

a. monthly sales revenue (units sold multiplied by product sale price); remember to use absolute cell referencing for the sale price, before copying this formula;

b. monthly cost of sales (units sold multiplied by product cost price); use absolute referencing for the cost price;

c. monthly gross profit (sales revenue minus cost of sales);

d. monthly overheads (the sum of salaries, advertising and general overheads);

e. monthly net profit (gross profit minus overheads);

f. monthly profit margin (net profit divided by sales revenue).

Activity 4

MicroFile is a microcomputer dealer. It needs a bank loan of £30,000 and has to present to the bank, a forecast of its repayment plans. MicroFile's quarterly costs are: January to March, £10500; April to June, £11000; July to September, £11200; October to December, £11300. These costs remain the same for each year. During the first quarter, it will sell each computer for £800; the price will then be reduced by £25 in each subsequent quarter, until a base price of £675 is reached. MicroFile expects to sell 20 computers in the first quarter and 25 in each succeeding quarter. The sales revenue for each quarter, less the quarter's costs, is to be used to reduce the loan. The loan is to be taken on the 1st of January; repayments will be made on the last day of each quarter. Loan interest of 15% on the outstanding balance is charged to the loan account at the end of each quarter.

a. **Set up** a worksheet to record this information. Following entry of the computer sale price for the first quarter, **use** a formula to produce the price for subsequent quarters. Enter formulae to calculate the gross revenue and the net revenue, which will be available for loan repayment, at the end of each quarter. Also **show** the amount of loan which is outstanding at the end of each quarter. **Show** when the loan will be fully repaid.

b. The bank may require repayment of the loan within the year. **Use** the worksheet to determine the number of computers which need to be sold to clear the loan within that period.

Activity 5

In this activity, you make use of a number of statistical functions. Use the adjacent student grades and **set up** a worksheet to calculate:

a. each mark as a *percentage*;

b. the *range* of percentage marks; this is simply the difference between the highest and lowest values (you can use the MAX and MIN functions);

c. the *mean* percentage mark (add them all together and divide by the number of marks; you can use the AVERAGE function here);

d. the *standard deviation* (use the appropriate function).

Grades	
Name	Marks (out of 75)
Smith	40
Erikson	34
Weber	50
Ricci	65
Clemenceau	27
Parker	44
Depardieu	50
Jones	70
Kahn	45

Activity 6

The Target Corporation wishes to monitor certain aspects of the business's payroll. The following information is provided:

Create a worksheet which produces the following information, in respect of *each employee.*

a. *Basic pay.* If the hours worked figure is less than that for the standard hours, the basic pay is calculated by multiplying the hours worked by the basic hourly rate. Otherwise, standard hours is multiplied by the basic hourly rate.

b. *Overtime rate.* This is one and a quarter times the basic hourly rate.

c. *Overtime hours.* If the hours worked figure is greater than that for the standard hours, the latter is subtracted from the former. Otherwise, a figure of zero is to be displayed.

d. *Overtime pay.* If overtime has been worked, multiply the overtime hours by the overtime rate. If not, display a figure of £0.00.

e. *Gross pay.* This is the basic pay, plus the overtime pay.

Save the worksheet and document it.

Employee name	Standard hours	Hours worked	Basic rate per hour
Al-Fariz, A	35	42	£5.00
Crowley, M	38	38	£5.00
Guttuso, R	35	30	£7.50
Hideo, K	40	45	£7.50
Johnson, M	38	42	£6.00
Mackenzie, P	40	40	£6.00
Negewo, K	35	28	£5.00
Pascal, B	40	47	£7.50
Singh, H	38	39	£7.50
Weizman, E	38	33	£5.00
Wilson, H	35	39	£6.00

Activity 7

Adventure Holidays want to record details of holidays sold and the amounts charged. You are given the following data.

Create a worksheet for entry of the above sample data and **enter** formulae to generate the following additional information.

Adventure Holidays				
Client	Holiday	Cost per person	Persons	Discount code
Featherstone	Andes	£1300	5	3
Cholmondley	Amazon	£1800	4	2
Carruthers	Serengeti	£2400	3	2
Scott	Antarctic	£1400	12	1
Carter	Atlantic	£1000	6	3
Fortescue	Sahara	£1350	10	1
Cousteau	Undersea	£2000	2	1

a. the gross cost of the holiday for each client;

b. the discount to be deducted from the gross cost; this is calculated with the percentage discount rate. These percentages are to be held in a table and are identified by the discount codes as follow: 1 is 2.00%; 2 is 5.50%; 3 is 6.50%;

c. a party discount. If the number of persons in the party is more than 4, then an additional discount of 3.00% is given. Otherwise, there is no party discount.

d. the net cost to each client.

Activity 8

This activity concerns the calculation of income tax. **Create** a worksheet to allow the entry of the following details relating to a single employee: name; tax code (excluding the letter); gross annual salary; superannuation rate (percentage); national insurance rate (percentage). **Use** a *lookup table* to record the tax rates (in the adjacent table), relating to gross annual salary.

Annual Salary	Tax Rate
£0 to £1999.99	0%
£2000 to £14999.99	20%
£15000 to £25999.99	25%
£40000 and more	35%

Design and **create** the worksheet to produce the following *monthly* figures:

a. gross salary;

b. superannuation (use the superannuation rate on the gross salary);

c. national insurance (use the national insurance rate on the gross salary);

d. taxable income (you need to deduct the superannuation and the month's tax allowance from the gross salary; remember that the tax code is 3 digits and has to be multiplied by 10 for the annual allowance);

e. amount of tax to be deducted (this is the tax rate pulled from the lookup table multiplied by the taxable income; remember that the tax rates in the table relate to annual taxable income). Of course, the taxable income would not all be taxed at the same rate; the first band is at 0%, the second at 20% and so on. For the purposes of this activity, assume that the extracted tax rate is to be applied to all the taxable income.

f. net salary (gross salary, less superannuation, national insurance, income tax).

N.B. Your tax calculation formula needs to be prefixed with an IF formula, to check that the taxable income is greater than or equal to £0.00. If you attempt to lookup a value less than £0.00 in the tax rate table the formula will not work; this is because the amount will be less than zero, which is not provided for in the table lookup ranges. In any case there is no point calculating tax for an employee who is not liable to it.

Activity 9

This activity concerns academic course fees, payable according to the *mode of attendance*. There are four modes: full-time (FT); part-time day (PTD); part-time evening (PTE) and block (BLO). Create a worksheet to allow the entry of a list of *student names*, *course titles* and *attendance modes* (by code). The worksheet should *automatically extract* the *fees* from a fee table (using the attendance code) and display them next to the relevant student records.

Activity 10

Suppose that you work for a small retail firm which does not make use of accounts software. Part of your job is to *monitor sales* and to *calculate revenue*. You want to use the spreadsheet to help you in this task and decide that the following information should be recorded about each sale: Product Code; Description; Unit Selling Price; Quantity; Total Price. Create a suitable worksheet.

Choose your own *product range*, *codes*, *descriptions*, *prices* and *quantities*. Bearing in mind that the details of each product will be held in a *lookup table*, it would be sensible to limit the number of products in the range to about five.

a. Set up the vertical *lookup table* and the data entry area for the sales records. Remember to minimise the need for data entry. A user should only have to enter the Product Code and Quantity for an individual sale record. The other information should be generated automatically;

b. Enter details for around thirty separate sales. This should ensure that each product code is entered several times, illustrating savings in data entry time;

c. Enter a formula to calculate the total sales revenue;

d. Save and print the worksheet.

Activity 11

This activity is concerned with a *student tutoring system*. You have been asked to develop a *worksheet* which will allow the printing of student lists, including identification of the tutor for each student. There are 4 tutors. The lookup value for each student is to be Tutor Code (uniquely identifies an individual Tutor). Use of the lookup value enables extraction of the following information: *Tutor Name*; *Tutor Location (Room No)*.

a. Set up the *horizontal lookup table*. You will need three rows in the table (Tutor Code, Tutor Name and Tutor Location).

b. Create a *data entry area* to include the following headings: Student Name; Tutor Code; Tutor Name; Tutor Location. Enter the lookup formulae to produce the Tutor Name and Location for each student.

c. Enter the *details* for around *15 students* and check that the output is correct.

d. Save the worksheet and print the student list.

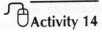
Activity 12

A particular examination board requires that assistant examiners award a percentage mark for each script they mark. They then need to be converted to literal grades (A, B, C and so on), using the adjacent scale. Set up the lookup table and a data entry area for the candidate details and marks. Enter the lookup formula to produce the literal grade for each candidate. Enter a number of candidate records and check the results. Save the worksheet and print the list of candidate results.

% Range	Grade
85% to 100%	A
75% to 84%	B
60% to 74%	C
45% to 59%	D
40% to 44%	E
30% to 39%	F
Up to 29%	U

Activity 13

A theatre called the Dominion wishes to calculate ticket costs for a new production. There are four seating zones in the theatre, labelled A, B, C and D. Each has a different standard seat price, £20, £18, £15 and £12, respectively. For senior citizens, the prices are cheaper, £14, £12, £9 and £6. For students, they are £10, £8, £6 and £4. **Design** and **create** a worksheet (using LOOKUP and IF function) to allow:

a. (the entry of a person's *name*;

b. (their *category* (standard, senior citizen or student);

c. (the *seat area*;

d. (the *number of tickets* required.

Generate a *total cost* for each ticket order.

Spreadsheet Graphics

Activity 14

This activity can be used as an introduction to *break even analysis*.

Target corporation - production costs		
Output in units	Fixed costs	Variable costs
0	500	0
100	500	200
200	500	300
300	500	350
400	500	450
500	500	600
600	500	800
700	500	1050
800	500	1350
900	500	1700
1000	500	2100

a. Enter the data (from the preceding table) on production costs and generate a total cost for each level of output.

b. Create a suitably labelled line graph showing the fixed costs, variable costs and total costs against each level of output. Save and print the graph.

Activity 15

A college wishes to show, pictorially, the relative number of students in each department, for particular academic years. A bar chart is chosen for this purpose. The following figures are provided. Use this data to construct a suitably labelled bar chart. Note that there are four data series to plot.

Department	Number of Students			
	1990	1991	1992	1993
Business	850	957	1100	1365
Management	601	675	874	900
Science	512	475	264	276
Technology	300	465	477	523
Total	4252	4556	4708	5057

Activity 16

Before trying this activity, you should have produced the payroll worksheet in Activity 8 of the Spreadsheet Study Component. In that activity, the worksheet is designed to calculate payroll details for one employee at a time; it makes use of a lookup table to extract appropriate percentage tax rates. This graphics activity requires the production of pie charts to compare the amounts (in percentage terms) of superannuation, national insurance and tax paid by employees on several different levels of salary. Therefore, you will need to modify the payroll worksheet to permit the calculation of several payroll records. The tax rates are shown in the following table. Also modify the worksheet with the following data.

Range	Rate
£0 to £14999.99	0%
£15000 to £24999.99	15%
£25000 to £29999.99	25%
£30000 to £49999.99	40%
£50000 or more	50%

a. There are 6 employees earning £18000, £28000, £45000, £60000, £80000 and £100000, respectively. Each has the same tax code of 512. National insurance is paid at 7% on the gross salary, with a maximum of £2600 per annum (you will need to use an IF formula to ensure the deduction is limited to that maximum figure). Superannuation is paid at 6% of the gross salary, with no upper limit.

b. (Once you have calculated the payroll details for each of the 6 employees, produce a pie chart for each, using the superannuation, national insurance and tax deductions, together with the net salary; the data series or range (the whole pie equates to the gross salary). Label the graphs and make observations on the varying proportions of these items at the different salary levels.

Activity 17

The table shows the inflows and outflows of male unemployment (the figures are monthly averages in thousands), for years 1970 to 1984.

a. Enter the data (or obtain more recent figures) and then graph the inflow and outflow data series for the period covered by the figures. A line graph is probably the most suitable choice. Label the graph appropriately.

b. Using stock market data from the financial newspapers, you can carry out a similar activity to show, for example, the comparative performance of particular shares and a unit trust over an extended period.

Year	Inflow ('000s)	Outflow ('000s)
1980	248	244
1981	252	236
1982	226	235
1983	207	222
1984	222	215
1985	238	208
1986	218	214
1987	203	200
1988	189	197
1989	180	183
1990	217	173

Activity 18

This activity concerns correlation; this is a measure of the strength of the relationship between two measurements. You need to know something about this topic before you can appreciate the results of this activity.

a. Collect data relating to interest rates and share prices (using the Financial Times 100 share index and the Bank of England Base lending rate). To be of value, the data will have to cover an extended period. There are financial databases and publications which will provide this data for you. The aim is to measure the degree of correlation between movements in interest rates and the performance of shares. A scatter diagram is appropriate, because the two sets of data are associated. A scatter graph is another form of XY graph, except that no line is shown, only the plotted points. You may be able to select the scatter type of graph directly, from a range of options. However, as is the case with early versions of Lotus 123, you may have to choose an XY graph and then alter the line pattern, so that it is hidden. In this way, only the plotted points are displayed. If you do leave the line in place, it will be criss-crossing, because the values in the range are unlikely to be in any recognisable sequence.

b. Repeat the exercise, perhaps with data relating to: the heights and weights of people; football statistics relating to a number of teams, such as the number of games won and the number of goals scored by each.

Unit 4

System installation and configuration

Chapters

Assessment Evidence

You need to produce

- ☐ a specification for a complete ICT system to meet user requirements, together with an operational system
- ☐ a specification for an upgrade to an ICT system that requires the installation of at least two items in the processing unit and configuration of software, together with an operational system. You must also show you can remove the installed items and use un-install procedures to restore the system to its original state
- ☐ records of set-up, installation, configuration and test activities.

Your configuration of software must include setting up a toolbar layout, a menu, a template and a macro. (Hardware installation tasks may be undertaken with a small group of colleagues.)

To achieve a grade E your work must show:

- ☐ definitions of user requirements and clear specifications for the ICT system and the upgrade, including for each full details of hardware, OS, applications software and configuration
- ☐ selection of suitable hardware and software and correct:
    - connection of hardware
    - installation of items in the processing unit
    - installation of software
    - setting of ROM-BIOS parameters
    - configuration of OS and software
- ☐ design and implementation of a suitable toolbar layout, menu, template and macro to meet the user requirements
- ☐ the upgraded ICT system correctly restored to its original state
- ☐ clear records of work done that include suitably annotated printed copy or screen prints of your toolbar, menu, template and macro, together with details of a suitable system configuration check, test procedures, problems experienced and solutions implemented.

To achieve a grade C your work must show:

- ☐ good understanding and effective use of structured analysis tools in the development of your dfds, through your records of practical work a systematic approach to specifying and constructing an operational ICT system
- ☐ clear definition and implementation of test procedures to check each task undertaken and how you overcame problems or limitations found as a result of using the test procedures
- ☐ that you can work independently to produce your work to agreed deadlines.

To achieve a grade A your work must show:

- ☐ good understanding and imaginative use of options for customising applications software, such as keyboard configuration, toolbar layout and menu design, by providing users with facilities that improve efficiency
- ☐ an imaginative use of design and attention to detail in the creation of a template and macro that clearly enable users to improve their efficiency and effectiveness
- ☐ effective use of system diagnostics, system monitoring procedures and uninstall routines, implementing adjustments as necessary to ensure correct system operation
- ☐ records kept in an organised way and indexed to enable easy reference to the problems experienced and the solutions implemented.

Chapter 14

Computer systems architecture

The term "Computer Systems Architecture" refers to the composition of computer systems and the mechanisms by which components communicate electronically with each other. A computer system is a collection of a large number of separate components. Many of these are electro-mechanical or electronic, that is physical, components collectively termed the *hardware*. The remaining components are the electronically stored *software* items that either control the hardware (computer programs) or are used by other pieces of software (data). A separate chapter is devoted to the subject of software.

Computer systems such as desktop computers (PCs) are general-purpose machines, capable of performing a wide range of data processing tasks. Computer programs make this versatility possible by controlling the hardware in different ways. For instance, many modern computer games control the components of the computer system that allow animated graphics to be displayed on the visual display unit. On the other hand, a company payroll program controls those hardware components required for processing and printing numeric and text-based data.

A knowledge of the characteristics of the many different forms of hardware and software components is essential to the task of understanding and specifying computer system configurations for specific purposes. In this chapter we provide a broad introduction to the many different forms of hardware that can be found in typical PC systems; subsequent chapters deal with some of these subjects in more detail. Throughout this and subsequent chapters in this Unit, particular emphasis is placed on hardware and software used in typical personal computer systems.

Computer System Components

The term *hardware* is used to describe all the physical devices that form a computer system. Figure 14.1 shows a few familiar examples. Although computer hardware catalogues list many examples of hardware devices, each one is likely to be concerned with a particular functional area from the following categories:

❑ input, output and backing storage devices, collectively known as *peripherals*;

❑ internal memory;

❑ motherboard and processor.

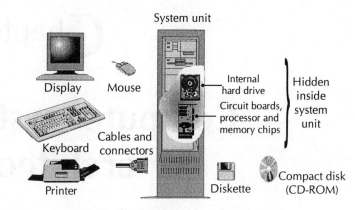

Figure 14.1. *Examples of computer hardware*

Input, output and backing storage

Figure 14.2 illustrates the functions of input, output and storage devices for communication with the central processing unit (CPU).

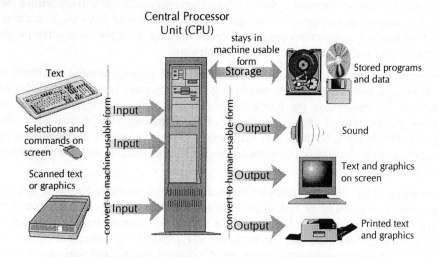

Figure 14.2. *How the CPU communicates with the outside world*

The job of each group of devices is as follows

❑ *Input* devices take data (text, graphics, sound and so on) from the outside world and convert it into the internal codes used inside the computer. Each device is designed to meet particular user requirements, so a microphone allows data entry through sound waves and a keyboard responds to keystrokes. Apart from working in a different way, they are designed to accept different kinds of data, so a microphone can accept speech input or be used to capture music. All input devices convert the data from the user's form into computer-sensible form.

❑ *Output* devices convert computer-sensible data into the forms users require. For example, a speaker converts data to sound and a screen produces a visual display.

Of course, the data must be appropriate for the devices, so a music recording cannot be output to a display screen, although with appropriate software, the sound waves could be graphically displayed.

❏ *Backing storage* devices provide permanent storage for computer programs (software) and data files. A magnetic disk, for example, allows large amounts of data to be stored in magnetic form, so data is not lost from the disk when the computer is switched off. Programs are held on backing storage and are only loaded into the computer's memory when the user needs them. Data files, such as word processed documents or a company's payroll records are also held on backing storage and are called into memory as required by the program(s) in use.

Input, output and backing storage devices are known as *peripherals* because they are outside, or peripheral to, the central processing unit (CPU). Even though disk and CD-ROM drives are usually held inside the system unit casing, they are still classed as peripherals. The topics of input, output and storage devices are dealt with in more detail in Chapters 16 and 17.

Input/output ports

Obviously, all of these types of devices must be connected to and be able to communicate electronically with the Central Processing Unit. Input/output ports are the connection points for peripheral devices, such as the mouse, printer or modem (for communication with other remote computers via a communications network such as the public telephone system).

Serial port

Microcomputers usually have at least two serial ports, one for connecting a mouse and the other for a modem. Serial ports transfer data in a single stream (one binary digit after another) as Figure 14.3 illustrates.

Figure 14.3. *A serial mouse*

Parallel port

The parallel port, known as a Centronics interface, is used to connect a printer. The port can also be used to communicate with some externally attached disk drives. The data is transferred as parallel groups of bits (each group representing a character), as shown in Figure 14.4.

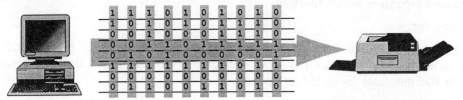

Figure 14.4. *Computer sending data from a parallel port to a printer*

Another parallel port is normally specially reserved for connecting the display screen.

PC I/O connectors

Figure 14.5 shows the rear of a typical system unit casing, with its various ports and connectors. One side of a connection is *male*, with pins and the other *female*, with holes to match the pin pattern.

Controllers and interfaces

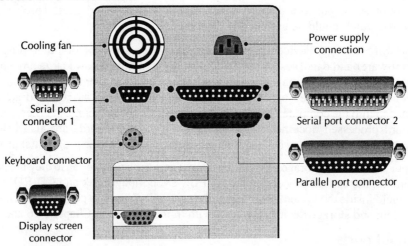

Figure 14.5. *Rear of system unit casing, showing ports and types of connectors*

Controllers

These are electronic devices that control the transfer of data between a computer and peripherals. For example, disk drives, display screens, keyboards, and printers all require controllers.

In personal computers, the controllers are often single chips. Motherboards incorporate all the necessary controllers for standard components, such as the display screen, keyboard, and floppy disk drives. Hard disk drives and CDROM drives that use the *PCI* bus have controllers built in; they communicate with the CPU via an *IDE* interface integrated within the motherboard. Some devices, including certain types of hard drives and optical storage devices, use *SCSI* interfaces that may need to be provided on expansion cards.

Controllers are designed to communicate with the computer's expansion bus (See **Buses**). Consequently extra controllers for additional devices must be compatible with a particular computer's expansion bus architecture.

IDE interfaces

The Intelligent/Integrated Drive Electronics (IDE) interface is specifically for mass storage devices, in which the controller is integrated into the mass storage device. Basic PCs usually provide IDE interfaces for up to four devices.

SCSI interfaces

Pronounced "scuzzy", SCSI (Small Computer System Interface) is a fast parallel interface standard used by PCs, Apple Macintosh computers, and many UNIX systems for attaching peripheral devices to computers. Many Apple Macintosh computers come with a SCSI port for attaching devices such as disk drives and printers. SCSI interfaces provide faster data transmission rates than standard serial and parallel ports and many devices can be linked to a single SCSI port.

SCSI devices can be attached to a PC by inserting a SCSI board in one of the expansion slots. Many high-end new PCs come with SCSI built in.

AGP interfaces

The abbreviation for Accelerated Graphics Port, *AGP* is a new interface specification developed by Intel Corporation. Based on PCI, AGP is designed especially for 3-D graphics. AGP has a number of important system requirements:

❑ The motherboard chipset must support AGP.

❑ The motherboard must be equipped with an AGP bus slot or must have an integrated AGP graphics system.

❑ The operating system must be Windows 95 (version 2.1), Windows 98 or Windows NT 4.0. Currently, many professional Macintoshes support AGP.

Internal Memory

RAM

A computer can only run a program when it is in memory or *RAM (Random Access Memory)*. Data needed by the program is also held in RAM. An important characteristic of RAM is that it is *volatile*. This means that the contents of the main memory can be destroyed, either by being overwritten as new data is entered for processing and new programs used, or when the machine is switched off. It is not practical to store data files and programs permanently in main memory because of its volatility.

Types of RAM

DRAM

Pronounced "dee-ram", DRAM stands for Dynamic Random Access Memory, the type of memory used in most personal computers. DRAM chips are available in several forms. Each is appropriate to particular types of applications. The most common forms of DRAM are:

❑ DIP (Dual In-line Package). The DIP-Style DRAM package was popular when it was common for memory to be installed directly on the computer's system board. DIPs are through-hole components, which means they install in holes extending into the surface of the printed circuit board. DIPs can be soldered in place or seated in sockets.

❑ SOJ (Small Outline J-lead), and TSOP (Thin, Small Outline Package). These are components which mount directly onto the surface of the printed circuit board. TSOP and SOJ gained in popularity with the advent of the SIMM. Of the two, the SOJ package is by far the most popular..

EDO DRAM

This abbreviation stands for Extended Data Output Dynamic Random Access Memory. Unlike conventional DRAM which can only access one block of data at a time, EDO RAM can start fetching the next block of memory at the same time that it sends the previous block to the CPU. This makes EDO RAM faster than conventional DRAM.

FPM RAM

An abbreviation for Fast Page Mode RAM, FPM RAM is a fast form of DRAM It is some-times called Page Mode Memory and is generally slower than EDO DRAM. FPM RAM is being superceded by newer types of memory, such as SDRAM.

SDRAM

SDRAM stands for *Synchronous* DRAM, a new type of DRAM that can run at much higher clock speeds. SDRAM is capable of running at 133 MHz, about twice as fast as EDO DRAM. SDRAM is replacing EDO DRAM in many newer computers.

RDRAM

Short for Rambus DRAM, a type of memory developed by Rambus, Inc. Whereas the fastest current memory technologies used by PCs (SDRAM) can deliver data at a maximum speed of about 133 MHz, RDRAM transfers data at up to 600 MHz.

Types of Memory Modules

Modern motherboards have banks of special slots for memory modules. Currently there are two main forms of these modules:

❑   SIMMs (Single Inline Memory Modules) and, more recently,

❑   DIMMs (Dual Inline Memory Modules).

Each module is a board onto which are soldered a number of memory chips. DIMMs are very high density memory modules that have two banks of chips soldered to the circuit board. Be-cause they require less space than SIMMs, they are likely to supercede SIMMs in the near future. Figure 14.6 shows an example of a SIMM containing nine memory chips. One of the chips is usually used for parity checking).

Figure 14.6. *Example of a SIMM*

The table below summarises the major characteristics of SIMMs and DIMMs. As you can see, SDRAM DIMMS are much faster than EDO DRAM SIMMs (*ns* stands for nanosecond, one thousandth of a millionth of a second). Currently, megabyte for megabyte, DIMMs are also much cheaper than SIMMs.

Type	Capacity range (MB)	Approx. access speed (ns)	Type	Pins
SIMM	8 - 64	60	EDO RAM	72
DIMM	8 - 256	8	SDRAM	168

Most new motherboards accept only 168-pin DIMMs, but some also accept 72-pin SIMMs. Motherboard documentation will specify the type of RAM that it supports: typically FP DRAM or EDO DRAM for SIMMs, or EDO DRAM or SDRAM for DIMMs.

Cache memory

Cache Memory is a special high-speed memory designed to accelerate processing of memory instructions by the CPU. The CPU can access instructions and data located in cache memory much faster than instructions and data in main memory. For example, on a typical 100-megahertz system board, it takes the CPU as much as 180 nanoseconds to obtain information from main memory, compared to just 45 nanoseconds from cache memory. Therefore, the more instructions and data the CPU can access directly from cache memory, the faster the computer can run.

Cache can be internal or external. Internal cache is built into the computer's CPU, and external cache is located outside the CPU.

ROM and flash memory

ROM is a type of memory designed to hold data more permanently than RAM. With most types of ROM, the data is built into the memory when it is manufactured and cannot be changed. For this reason it is *non-volatile*, so the contents are not lost when power is removed. ROM is used to hold the *BIOS* (Basic Input/Output System) and the *bootstrap loader*.

Flash memory also retains its contents when power is removed, but unlike ROM, its contents can be changed by software. Most modern microcomputers use flash memory to allow the BIOS to be changed automatically when new hardware devices are added.

Central processing unit (CPU)

Often referred to as the *processor*, the CPU is the heart of the computer and has two part main parts:

Control unit

The control unit:

❑ fetches program instructions from memory and decodes and executes them, calling on the ALU (see below) when calculations or comparisons need to be carried out on data;

❑ controls the flow of data both within the CPU and to and from peripheral devices such as printers, disk drives and keyboards;

❑ ensures that devices operate according to program instructions, by sending electrical control signals to them as required.

Arithmetic/logic unit (ALU)

The ALU contains circuitry to carry out important tasks such as addition, subtraction, multiplication and division of numbers fetched from RAM or held in registers in the processor. It can also, for example, compare two numbers and discover whether or not they are equal and perform logical operations, such as AND, OR and NOT.

The data-flow routes between various hardware components and the CPU are illustrated in Figure 14.7.

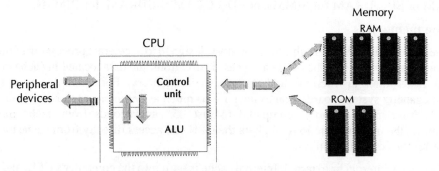

Figure 14.7. *The data flows between hardware devices*

Co-processors

In order to speed certain types of computations, a computer system might incorporate one or more co-processors. For example, a graphics accelerator card (see **Expansion Cards**) will usually include its own processor to deal with graphics computations independently of the main motherboard processor. Modern processors include a maths co-processor to deal with floating-point computations, though earlier PCs sometimes had a separate chip on the motherboard for this purpose.

Motherboard

The motherboard is the main circuit board inside a microcomputer's system casing. A number of major hardware components are plugged into it, including the CPU, the BIOS memory and RAM. It also has a number of *expansion slots*, into which plug-in circuit boards can be inserted. These are slots into which *expansion boards* or *cards* can be plugged, to add extra features to a system.

Note the following points regarding motherboards:

❑   The motherboard has printed circuits (not shown) which provide the electrical connections between all the components plugged into it. One or more *buses* are built into the motherboard to provide fast connections between components. Buses are discussed in more detail in the next section.

❑   All replaceable components must be compatible with the motherboard. This often prevents certain upgrading of the machine. For example, one type of memory called EDO RAM uses 72 pins to contact with the motherboard, but SDRAM, which allows data to be accessed more quickly than EDO RAM, uses 128 pins and therefore a different sized socket. (Memory is discussed in more detail in **Types of RAM**). In the same way, when a new processor becomes available, upgrading a machine from an older type will often mean replacing the motherboard.

❑   The processor chip plugs into a ZIF (Zero Insertion Force) socket; this allows the processor to be inserted or removed without damage.

❑   RAM chips are fixed to a small circuit board called a SIMM (Single In-line

Memory Module). For example, a 64MB SIMM has 8 × 8MB memory chips attached to it. In the motherboard map, there are two memory *banks*, each with two slots, so 4 SIMMs could be attached. If 64MB SIMMs were used, this would allow the computer to have 256MB of RAM.

❏ Modern motherboards often incorporate interfaces and functions that required separate expansion boards in the past. For example, a motherboard may include two IDE interfaces for hard drives and CD ROM drives in addition to a floppy disk interface. Many motherboards now also include sound chips that also used to require a separate card in the past.

Expansion Cards

Figure 14.8 shows the appearance of a typical expansion card. Some of these circuit boards may be used for controlling peripheral devices, but there are many other boards available for a wide range of applications. Because each pin on an expansion slot is connected to the same pin on all the other expansion slots by a printed circuit, a board can be plugged in to any compatible slot. Expansion slots are connected to the system bus (it makes electrical contact), so when an expansion card is plugged in, it becomes part of the system. Here are some common examples of expansion cards:

Figure 14.8. *A plug-in expansion card*

❏ modem cards for connection to the Internet and for receiving and transmitting faxes;

❏ graphics cards (video adapters, graphics accelerators) for accelerating graphics-based applications such as games and for capturing video sequences from external sources such as VCRs and video cameras;

❏ TV cards to allow the computer to show TV programs on the monitor;

❏ network cards to allow several computers to be linked in a network;

❏ sound cards for capturing and playing high quality sound sequences;

❏ SCSI (Small Computer System Interface) card, a fast parallel interface standard for connecting peripheral devices. (see **Controllers and Interfaces**).

Two of these, video adapters and sound cards, are described in more detail below.

Video Adapters

A video adapter is a board that plugs into an expansion slot of a personal computer's motherboard to give it display capabilities when connected to a monitor. These display capabilities depend on both the electronics provided in the video adapter and the display monitor. For example, a monochrome monitor cannot display colours whatever the quality of the video adapter. Adapters usually provide two basic categories of video modes:

❏   text mode - a monitor can display only ASCII characters;

❏   graphics mode - a monitor can display any bit-mapped image.

So that large quantities of the computer's RAM is not used for storing display data, modern video adapters contain their own memory. The amount of memory determines maximum resolution and the number of colours that can be displayed. At lower resolutions a monitor can display more colours. Some accelerators use conventional DRAM, but others have video RAM (VRAM), which enables both the video circuitry and the processor to access the memory simultaneously. A typical graphics card might contain 4MB to 8MB of VRAM. In addition, most adapters have their own graphics coprocessor for performing graphics calculations. Such adapters are often called graphics accelerators. Because of the growth of multimedia software and games requiring high-resolution graphics, most computer manufacturers now include a graphics accelerator with their systems.

Sound cards

These are expansion boards that enable computers to capture, play and edit high quality sound. As mentioned earlier, a motherboard might incorporate sound capabilities, but if not a sound card will be necessary, particularly if the computer includes a CD-ROM. Sound cards include sockets for speakers to play sound files and a microphone for recording sound on disk. Bundled software allows sound files to be loaded, edited, stored and played. The majority of sound cards support the MIDI standard for representing music electronically, and most sound cards are compatible with the Sound Blaster card which has become the standard for PC sound.

Buses

Though all computers have the same basic functional components, the architectural details in some are far more complex than in others. A particular area of variation relates to the arrangement of the bus systems which permit communication between the various parts of the computer system. A number of features concerning buses can be identified:

❏   a bus is a group of parallel wires, one for each bit of a word, along which data can flow (as electrical signals);

❏   the *system* bus comprises a number of such communication channels, connecting a computer's processor and its associated components of memory and input/output(I/O) devices;

❏   a single bus may carry data for different functions at separate times or it may be dedicated to one function. A computer will usually have several buses, used for specific purposes, for example, the I/O bus or main memory-to-processor bus;

❏   some buses are *bi-directional*, that is data can flow in both directions;

❏   the *width* of a bus determines the length of word which can be handled at one time. So, a processor which used a 16-bit bus, but required a 32-bit word to address memory, would combine two 16-bit words in two separate fetch operations.

Communication is required within a processor, to allow movement of data between its various registers, between the processor and memory and for I/O transfers. In a *single* bus system, both I/O and memory transfers share the same communication channel, whereas in a *two-bus* system, I/O and memory transfers are carried out independently; similarly, in small systems with few I/O devices, they usually share the same bus, but a larger system requires several I/O buses to ensure efficient operation.

Each of the separately identified functions of memory, register-to-register and I/O transfers (assuming that the I/O bus is shared by a number of devices), must have the use of:

- ❑ a *data bus*, for the transfer of data subject to processing or manipulation in the machine;

- ❑ an *address bus* which carries the address of, for example, a memory word to be read, or the output device to which a character is to be transmitted;

- ❑ a *control bus*, which as the name suggest, carries signals concerning the timing of various operations, such as memory write, memory read and I/O operations.

All signals on a bus follow strict timing sequences, so some operations take longer than others.

Bus architecture - a brief history

This concerns the internal structure of a computer, that is the way in which the various components are connected and communicate with one another. As technological advances improve the performance of certain components, so the architecture has to change to take advantage of these improvements. There follows a brief summary of some of the architectural standards used over the last decade.

- ❑ IBM's Micro Channel Architecture (MCA); despite the commercial power of IBM, this standard did not find general acceptance;

- ❑ Extended Industry Standard Architecture (EISA);

- ❑ Local Bus (VESA and PCI).

- ❑ Universal Serial Bus (USB)

Micro channel architecture (MCA)

MCA aimed to overcome the limitations of the old, Industry Standard Architecture (ISA), IBM AT (Advanced Technology) machines as well as a myriad of clones produced by IBM's competitors. IBM used MCA in their 32-bit PS/2 (Personal System 2) range.

System bus width and system performance

One of the many differences with the MCA approach concerns the width of the *system bus*. This bus is a communication link between the processor and system components and is an essential, but passive, part of system architecture. The active components, such as the processor, disk controller and other peripherals are the primary determinants of system performance. As long as the data transfer speed along the bus matches the requirements of these devices and does not create a bottleneck, the bus does not affect system performance. The MCA bus is 32 bits, compared with the AT's 16 bits, and the wider data path allows components within the system to be accessed twice as quickly. The MCA bus also uses bus-mastering controllers to handle data transfers more quickly. The wider bus is also compatible with the 32-bit external bus used on more recent processors. The bus can be controlled by separate *bus master* processors, relieving the main processor of this task.

MCA is also radically different from AT architecture in many other respects. For example, the expansion slots in the PS/2 range which allow the user to insert extra features, perhaps for networking or for extra memory, are physically different from those in the AT and PC machines and their expansion cards will not fit in the PS/2 machines. The problem for existing AT and PC users is that they cannot buy new PS/2 machines and still make use of their existing expansion cards. This incompatibility has also meant that few manufacturers have produced MCA versions of their expansion cards. IBM and Apricot are the biggest proponents of the MCA standard, but the fact that IBM is continuing to release ISA models is possibly an admission that MCA is unlikely to become the dominant architecture.

Extended industry standard architecture (EISA)

A consortium of IBM's competitors including Compaq, Zenith, NEC and Olivetti amongst others, established a new architecture (EISA - Extended Industry Standard Architecture) which aims to give the benefits of MCA and to retain compatibility with existing AT expansion cards. EISA also uses a 32-bit bus, thus providing the same data transfer benefits as MCA, particularly for hard disk controllers (a very important contributor to overall system performance).

Both EISA and MCA machines are more expensive than the ISA-based microcomputers, and tend to be used where extra power is needed, as *file servers* in networked systems. Most small business users find that ISA machines are adequate for their needs, particularly as the use of *local bus* technology is further increasing their power.

Local bus

A local bus is a high speed data path connecting the processor with a peripheral. Local bus design is used, primarily, to speed communications with hard disk controllers and display adapters. The need for local bus derives from the imbalance between the clock speed of a 32-bit processor (typically, in excess of 100MHz) and the ISA 16-bit system bus (operating at 8 MHz). The ISA system is illustrated in Figure 14.9.

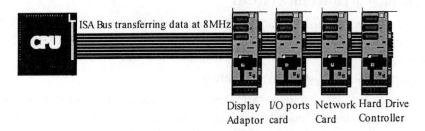

Display   I/O ports Network Hard Drive
Adaptor   card   Card   Controller

Figure 14.9. *ISA bus*

This imbalance can result in the processor idling while waiting for data to be transferred from disk, or the display adapter waiting for screen data. The widespread use of Windows, a *graphical user interface* and software packages which make intensive use of the hard disk (such as databases) and screen graphics (computer-aided design), has highlighted the deficiencies of such imbalanced computer systems. A local bus provides a wider data path, currently 32 bits and an increased clock speed, typically 33MHz or more. The first local bus systems appeared in 1992, with manufacturers following a standard referred to as *VL-bus*, developed by VESA (Video Electronics Standards Association). Figure 14.10 illustrates the broad principle of a local bus system.

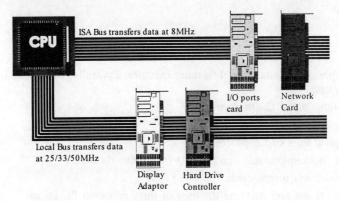

Figure 14.10. *Local bus*

In 1993, Intel backed the development of a new industry standard called *PCI*.

The PCI standard encourages the development of computer systems which allow local bus connection to any high-speed peripheral. Apart from speeding communication with screen graphics controllers, PCI local bus can be used with, for example, hard disk, network and motion video controllers (up to 10 devices in total).

USB, short for Universal Serial Bus, is a new external bus standard that supports data transfer rates of 12 Mbps (12 million bits per second). A single USB port can be used to connect up to 127 peripheral devices, such as mice, modems, and keyboards. USB also supports *Plug-and-Play* installation and *hot plugging* (adding and removing devices while the computer is running and have the operating system automatically recognise the change - also called *hot swapping*). USB is expected to completely replace serial and parallel ports.

⚑Self-test questions

1. What is meant by the term 'hardware'?
2. Name 3 types of device that are generally connected to a computer system. Give two examples of each type.
3. What two types of memory are commonly found in a computer? For each type, give an example of what it stores.
4. A CPU has two main components. Name and briefly explain the function of each part.
5. Explain the purpose of a port.
6. What is the name of the main circuit board inside a computer?
7. What is the function of a Controller?

8. Name three types of interfaces for peripherals and say for what types of peripherals each interface has been designed.

9. What do the following abbreviations mean?
   ☐ DRAM
   ☐ EDO RAM
   ☐ FPM RAM
   ☐ SDRAM
   ☐ RDRAM
   ☐ VRAM

10. Name two types of commonly used memory modules. Typically, what types of RAM are used in each case?

11. Explain the function of Cache memory.

12. What is *Flash Memory*?

13. Give two typical uses of Co-processors.

14. What are the main upgradable components of a motherboard?

15. Name 4 types of expansion cards.

16. Define a Bus. Name and describe the uses of three common PC buses.

Chapter 15

Software

The word *software* is used to describe all computer programs. *Systems software* is used to make the hardware operate as a general-purpose computer system. *Applications software* makes the computer operate in particular ways, for example, as a payroll, word processing, graphic design, route planning or games system. Figure 15.1 shows the systems and applications software groups and some of the sub-groups belonging to each.

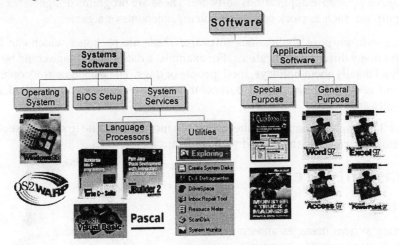

Figure 15.1. *Main categories of software, with examples*

Relevant examples of commercial software products are shown in the figure, beneath each sub-group. Some of the examples should be familiar and should help you to understand the purpose of each software group and sub-group.

Summary of software types

Referring to Figure 15.1, the following types of software can be identified.

❑ *Operating system.* This set of programs has overall control of the computer system, both hardware and applications software and acts as the *interface* between the user and the machine. Frequently the interface is graphical and known as a *graphical user interface* (GUI). Sometimes, the user may communicate through a *command-driven* interface, typing commands at a simple screen prompt.

❏   *Utilities*. These are programs to help the user carry out general maintenance tasks on the system. For example, Windows 9x provides *Windows Explorer* to manage the disk filing system, *Disk Defragmenter* to recover wasted space on disks, *DriveSpace* to create additional disk space and *ScanDisk* to find and repair disk recording problems.

❏   *BIOS* (Basic Input/Output System). The BIOS specifies the details of the installed hardware and 'fine tunes' it for best performance and user preference. Note that the BIOS software is not a category that most users deal with. The BIOS deals with the direct control of the hardware components and is normally the concern of computer manufacturers. Experienced users of computer systems may access the BIOS when installing new hardware to upgrade their system.

❏   *Development tools*. These are used by programmers to create and maintain systems and applications software. They include *programming language development tools*.

❏   *Special-purpose* applications software. These are programs designed for a single purpose, such as stock control, invoicing, accounts or a game.

❏   *General-purpose* applications software. These are packages which can be used for many different applications. For example, a database package could be used to hold details about holidays, food, people or dogs. The packages are 'content free' and need tailoring to each particular purpose. They are often called *generic software*.

The rest of this chapter examines all these topics in more detail. The first major section deals with systems software and the second with applications software.

Systems software

Operating system

An operating system manages and communicates with the resources of a computer system, as illustrated in Figure 15.2. You should recognise these resources as the hardware components that form a computer system (see Chapter 14).

❏   *central processing unit (CPU)*. The operating system controls the CPU in its different tasks, which include, for example:

   o   fetching program instructions and data from RAM;

   o   starting a data transfer from an input device;

   o   handling separate user requests for data, perhaps from the same file, in a *multi-user* system;

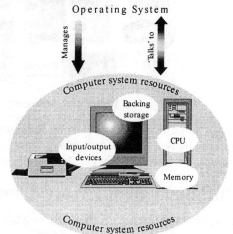

Figure 15.2. *Purpose of the operating system*

o sharing the CPU's time between several tasks in RAM at the same time, a process known as *multi-tasking*.

❑ *Memory* or *RAM*. Programs (sometimes several) have to be accommodated in RAM, together with the data they are processing. The operating system:

o loads programs (or part programs) into memory as requested;

o unloads programs (or part programs) no longer required;

o moves programs around in memory to make best use of the space.

❑ *Input/output devices*. The operating system requests the use of devices as required and checks for conflict, for example, when two user programs try to print at the same time.

❑ *Backing storage*. Programs and data files are held on backing storage and loaded into RAM as needed. The operating system:

o manages the storage space;

o supervises transfers between RAM and backing storage.

Types of operating system

Computer systems vary in size, power and the number and variety of peripherals which can be attached. The biggest computer systems are called supercomputers. Coming down the scale, there are mainframe, mini and microcomputer systems. Because the resources for each are so different and the applications for which they are used also vary widely, there is a need for different kinds of operating system. So, for example, there are:

❑ simple operating systems like MS-DOS, designed for running one program at a time for a single user.

❑ multi-tasking operating systems, which allow a user to have several programs loaded at one time. Figure 15.3 illustrates a user operating several tasks through the Windows 9x operating system.

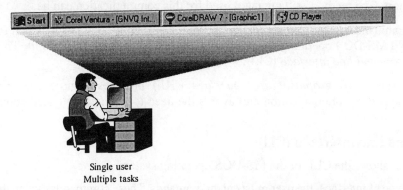

Single user
Multiple tasks

Figure 15.3. *A user multi-tasking with the Windows 95 operating system*

❑ network operating systems, such as Windows NT and Novell Netware, designed to control networked computer systems. Figure 15.4 shows several computers linked to a network using the Novell Netware operating system. A network operating system has the following features:

o   Facilities to control users' access to *shared resources*, including programs and data held on the network. They use login procedures to identify the user and request a password.

o   A user's access to the network is limited by their *network rights* and these are controlled and checked by the operating system. For example, a clerk in the personnel department may be able to view staff salary figures, but is not given access to the program which allows them to be changed.

Note from the figure that the individual workstations run their own 'local' operating system. The network operating system is designed to be able to communicate with workstations running under different *platforms*. So, for example, PCs and Macintosh workstations may be attached to the same network. There are many other operating systems, to suit every kind of use, including, for example, air traffic control, manufacturing processes and large-scale business systems such as those used by banks.

Figure 15.4. *Network controlled by a network operating system*

Operating system interfaces

An operating system is the interface for communication between the computer and its users and operators. The method or 'language' used for this communication can be:

❑   command driven. Commands are typed at a system prompt, such as that for the old MS-DOS operating system (often referred to as the C:\> prompt). This is a *command line interface* (CLI).

❑   graphical. A *graphical user interface* (GUI) provides a more user-friendly method of communication and avoids the need to learn complicated command sequences.

Command line interface (CLI)

Figure 15.5 shows the CLI for the MS-DOS operating system.

With this type of interface, the user must enter commands. These commands may instruct the operating system to carry out some action, or provide the user with some information. At the bottom of the figure, there is a lengthy command sequence to copy a file from one directory to another. It is followed by the message "1 file(s) copied", which confirms that the command has been executed successfully.

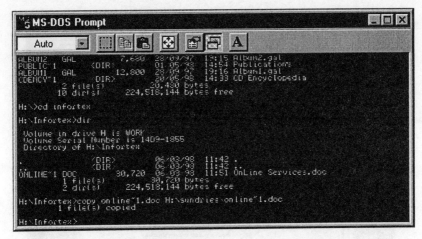

Figure 15.5. *Command line interface in MS-DOS*

The main advantage of the CLI is that the short commands, though not particularly user-friendly, are ideal for rapid, expert use.

The main disadvantages of the CLI are:

❏ it is unsuitable for novice users;

❏ the commands must be learned and remembered;

❏ it can only be used with the keyboard.

Graphical user interface (GUI)

Figure 15.6 on the next page shows the graphical user interface (GUI) for the Windows 95 operating system and illustrates the following features:

❏ a *pointer* on screen, moved by a pointing device, typically a *mouse*. The figure shows the pointer selecting a menu option.

❏ *icons* (small pictures) representing, amongst other things, programs, which can be run by pointing and clicking the mouse. The recycle bin icon is in the bottom right corner of the figure.

❏ *windows*. Applications run in their own self-contained areas called *windows*. There are three in the figure, one for Explorer, the Internet browser, another for CorelDRAW, a graphic design program and a third for Corel Ventura, a desktop publishing program. These are all examples of *applications software*.

❏ *pull-down menus* which provide access to standard functions. The figure shows such a menu in the Corel Ventura window.

Benefits of a GUI

Most users are not really interested in the technical details of a computer's operation and simply want to use it. However, to do so effectively, a user must learn routine maintenance tasks, such as creating folders, copying files and formatting disks as well as the use of the particular applications they need. A GUI is designed to make these tasks easier as follows.

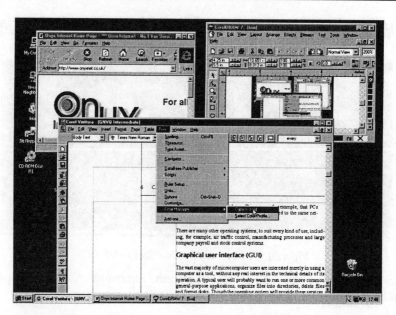

Figure 15.6. *Graphical user interface (GUI) for Windows 95 operating system*

❑ Methods of doing things are more *intuitive*. This means that a user can often anticipate what certain actions with the mouse will do. For example, selecting a file with a mouse pointer and dragging it to an *icon* (small picture) of a dustbin has the effect of deleting the selected file.

❑ Applications running under a GUI have common features, so, for example, it is easier to transfer skills learned using a word processor to those needed for a spreadsheet. The Figure 15.7 shows that two entirely different packages use several of the same menus and command buttons. As the figure also shows, common package requirements, such as creating new, opening existing and saving files, whether they relate to a spreadsheet from Microsoft or a publishing package from Corel, use the same buttons. Obviously, individual packages have extra buttons and menus which relate to their particular facilities.

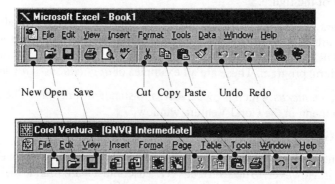

Figure 15.7. *Common menus and buttons in two packages running under Windows 9x*

Utilities

These are programs, usually included with the operating system, which do routine maintenance tasks on the computer system. The Windows Explorer, Disk Defragmenter, DriveSpace and ScanDisk utilities, provided by the Windows 9x operating system are described in this section.

Windows Explorer

Figure 15.8 shows the Windows Explorer view of a particular computer system.

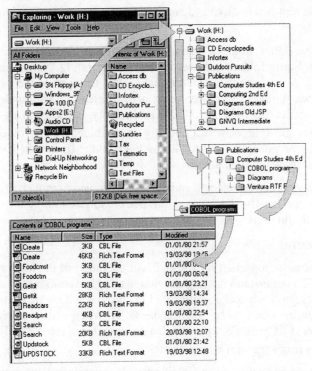

Figure 15.8. *Using Windows Explorer to view files in a particular directory (or folder)*

This Windows 9x utility allows the user to see the disk file systems attached to the computer and carry out various maintenance tasks on the files stored there. To understand the purposes of this utility, you need to know some basic principles about a Windows 9x disk file system.

❑ Each physical disk drive in the system is identified by a letter. Usually, the main hard drive is C: and the floppy drive is A:. Other drives, such as the CD-ROM take other letters, D:, E: and so on. Note that a single physical drive may be partitioned into two or more drives, each with a different letter. Also, additional, compressed drives (see DriveSpace) can be created from a physical drive, each additional compressed drive being given a different letter. Note that the example system has six drive letters:

    o   A: (floppy drive);

    o   C: (first *partition* of the main hard drive);

o   D: (a 100MB Zip drive);

o   E: (second partition of the main hard drive);

o   F: (CD-ROM drive);

o   H: (a compressed drive - see DriveSpace, later).

❑   Each drive letter can be treated as a separate disk and storage area. For example, the C: drive contains the operating system and usually the main applications programs. In the example system, the E: partition drive contains other applications programs and the H: drive all the main data files. The A: and D: drives use removable disks and are used for taking security backups of important files.

❑   Each drive letter holds a hierarchical (different levels) directory or folder structure. Some folders are created for the operating system and applications programs. A user can create additional folders to organise the data files. Figure 15.8 shows Windows Explorer being used to view the various levels on the H: drive, to access files held in the COBOL directory. Clicking on a + next to a folder reveals any sub-folders, whilst clicking on a − hides its sub-folders and clicking on a folder or sub-folder reveals its contents. In the figure, the COBOL folder is opened to show the files it holds.

❑   Files or folders can be selected and deleted, or copied or moved to other folders or drive letters. Usually, these operations use the mouse to drag the selection to the required destination.

Disk Defragmenter

This utility is extremely important for the efficient operation of the main hard drive(s) in a computer system. To understand its purpose, you need to be familiar with a number of facts relating to disk storage. Disk space is allocated in *clusters*, which are units of disk storage. For example, the cluster size may be 16 kilobytes (KB). When a file is stored on disk it takes up as many clusters as it needs. For example, if a document is of size 525 KB, it will need 525 ÷ 16 = 33 clusters (to the nearest whole cluster).

When a file is first stored on disk it is given, if possible, a *contiguous* (no gaps between) chain of clusters. Each time it is altered and made larger, it may not fit in its original place, so the extra has to be placed somewhere else. This *fragmentation* of files leads to slower disk performance, because the read/write heads may have to go to several different parts of the disk to retrieve a single file. Such a fragmented file is illustrated in Figure 15.9. Note the following points in the figure:

The figure represents a small area of disk space, with each square as a single cluster. The white squares are empty clusters. The 24 light grey squares are the clusters occupied by a particular File A. The clusters numbered 1 to 9 shows where the original version of File A is stored. Numbers 10 to 24 are clusters filled as File A has been altered and made larger. The dark grey clusters are filled by other files. Ideally, File A would be in a contiguous (without gaps) set of clusters, but each time it has been updated and made larger, the extra clusters have been taken from separate areas of the disk. The white clusters, although empty now, may not have been at the times File A was updated.

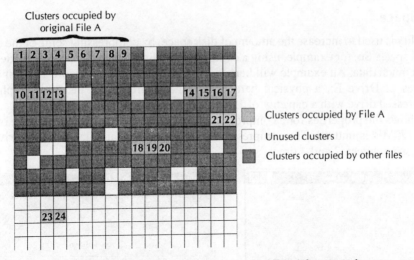

Figure 15.9. *Area of disk clusters, showing File A fragmented*

The defragmentation utility rearranges the disk space so that each file is held in a contiguous set of clusters. The empty space is also organised into a contiguous block of clusters. Figure 15.10 shows how the disk space may appear after defragmentation is complete.

Figure 15.11 shows the Windows 9x utility, Disk Defragmenter in progress, together with a legend explaining the different states of clusters on the disk. As the legend shows, the utility also identifies any damaged areas of the disk.

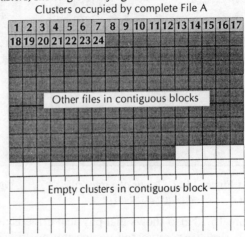

Figure 15.10. *Disk space after defragmentation*

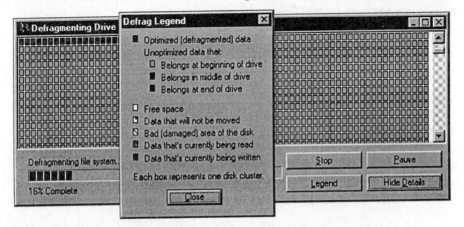

Figure 15.11. *Disk Defragmenter in progress*

DriveSpace

This utility is used to increase the amount of disk space, by compressing some of the existing physical space. So, for example, using a compression ratio of 2:1, a disk can be made to hold twice as much data. An example will help to explain what happens. Figure 15.12 shows the properties of Drive E:, a physical hard drive. The figure shows that it is a 'physical', uncompressed drive with a capacity of 1.16GB and around 379MB of unused space. Figure 15.13, shows the properties for a compressed drive H: with a capacity of 506 MB, of which around 170MB is unused. The compression ratio indicates that data stored on drive H: is compressed between 2 and 3 times.

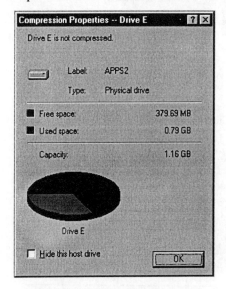

Figure 15.12. *Details of a standard, uncompressed drive*

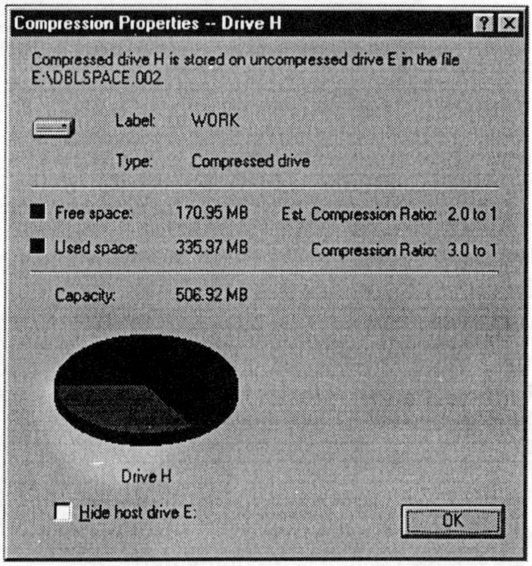

Figure 15.13. *A compressed drive H:, created from space on physical drive E:*

Figure 15.13 also shows that physical drive E: is the *host*. This means that H: is not a new drive, simply a compressed storage area on drive E:. As a result the physical space on the host drive E: is reduced because it is storing the compressed drive H:. The next figure illustrates how extra space has been created (Figure 15.14).

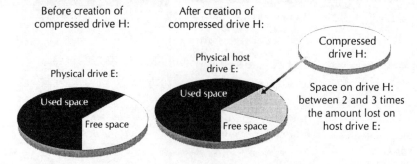

Figure 15.14. *Part of free space on physical drive E:, used to create compressed drive H:*

The amount of space gained with drive H: is, in this example, 2 to 3 times the amount of space lost to the compressed drive on drive E:. Figure 15.15 of Windows Explorer shows that a compressed drive appears to the user as just another drive.

Figure 15.15. *Windows Explorer showing drives, including compressed drive H:*

ScanDisk

This vital utility detects and repairs disk recording errors. Some locations on disk may not record data properly and if they are not found and repaired, data may be stored in those locations and be corrupted or lost. ScanDisk also finds 'lost' files. When a program 'crashes', or more seriously, when the operating system crashes, corrupted files, or bits of files, may be left on disk. These lost files take up valuable disk space and often contain meaningless information or 'garbage'. The ScanDisk dialogue box is shown in Figure 15.16. The figure shows the following options:

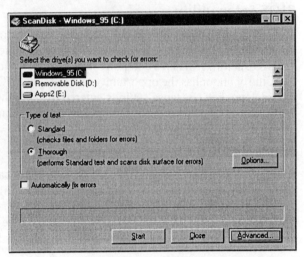

Figure 15.16. *ScanDisk with options for file and folder check and surface scan*

❏ The standard check finds files and folders for errors, including 'lost' files. It is a good idea to run this check whenever the operating system crashes.

❏ The thorough check carries out the standard check, plus a surface scan for possible disk recording errors. This check should be carried out regularly to find and fix disk recording problems before vital data is lost.

BIOS (basic input/output system)

A computer system's BIOS holds details of what hardware is installed and settings for individual components. The settings are held in CMOS RAM. This is a special type of RAM, which can retains its contents with only a tiny amount of battery power - the battery is attached to the motherboard and recharged whenever the machine is switched on. The BIOS settings are used to control the *system start-up* and carry out diagnostic checks on the hardware.

System start-up

When a computer system is 'powered on' the BIOS starts the Power-On Self-Test (POST) routine. The POST routine is in two stages:

1. The *motherboard* (also known as the *system board*) and its components (processor, RAM etc.) are checked for their normal operation. The RAM test is visible on screen while it is being carried out.
2. The hardware actually installed is checked to see that it matches with the system's BIOS (Basic Input/Output System) settings.

If an error is identified, the system reports it, either with a 'beep' or an error message on screen. The Power-On Self-Test (POST) sequence checks the hardware to see that the major components, including RAM, are present and working properly.

BIOS Setup utility

The BIOS Setup utility is held in ROM (Chapter 14) so that it is not lost when the machine is switched off. The program is used to enter details of the computer system's hardware, that is, the BIOS settings. When a computer is powered on and before the operating system starts to load, the operator has the opportunity to access the BIOS Setup utility, normally by pressing the <delete> key. Because settings entered through this program are then stored in CMOS RAM, the program menu includes options for the Standard CMOS setup and the BIOS Features (or Advanced CMOS) setup.

Standard CMOS setup

Standard CMOS Setup is used to record details of the basic hardware in the computer system. The settings are recorded when the motherboard is installed, normally by the manufacturer. This is usually the first BIOS Setup menu option. An example of a Standard CMOS Setup screen is shown in Figure 15.17 on the next page. The exact settings will vary according to the computer hardware, but note the following details labelled in the figure.

❑   The Primary Master is the main hard disk drive inside the system unit and in this example, it has a capacity of 2·5 GB. The Primary Slave, in this example, is a 100MB Zip drive, which uses removable disk cartridges. There is only one floppy disk drive, designed for 1·44 MB floppy disks.

❑   The 'Halt on' setting specifies that any hardware error will cause the powering up sequence to stop, until the error is corrected. The only other options are to ignore keyboard and/or floppy disk errors. Failure of RAM or the hard disk drive, for example, would always halt the system.

❑   The RAM total is 128 MB.

❑   The screen type is EGA or VGA. These are screen resolution standards (Chapter 3). VGA is a minimum 800 × 600 resolution.

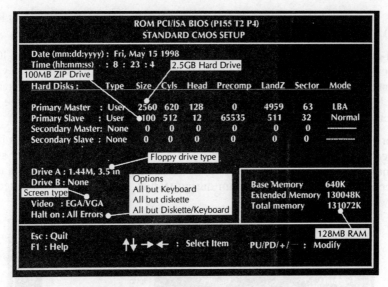

Figure 15.17. *Example Standard CMOS Setup*

The Standard CMOS Settings option would only need to be used if:

(a)   the CMOS contents are corrupted or lost, perhaps through battery failure (as can happen if a machine is switched off for a long period). It is important that the settings are written down, so that if the contents are lost or corrupted, they can be re-entered. Without the correct settings, the machine may not work properly or at all;

       or

(b)   the system configuration is altered, perhaps through replacement of the hard disk or installation of a new motherboard.

BIOS Features setup

This option is used to 'fine tune' the hardware configuration, to improve performance and to set certain user preferences. Figure 15.18 on the next page shows an example BIOS Features screen, labelled with the following four features:

1.   Boot sequence. Following a successful Power-On Self-Test (POST) routine, the BIOS loads the operating system, normally from the hard drive. The boot sequence dictates the order in which the BIOS checks the various disk drives to find the operating system. Setting the A: (floppy) drive as the first to be checked, allows for an emergency 'boot' if the operating system will not load from the hard drive. Windows 9x provides an option to create such a Startup Disk (see Figure 15.19). To carry out the emergency boot, the Startup disk is placed in the floppy drive before the machine is powered up. As soon as the BIOS finds the Startup disk boots the system from there, rather than trying to load the operating system from the hard drive. For this reason, an error message is displayed if a 'non-system' disk (one not containing special start-up files) is left in the floppy drive during start-up.

2.   Floppy disk access control. The default setting is R/W (read/write), but to prevent

users copying files from the hard drive onto floppy disk, it may be set to RO (read only). This may be done for security reasons.

3. Boot-up NumLock status. Setting the NumLock key to 'On' ensures that it is automatically on when the system is powered up. The keys on the numeric keypad then operate as such. If set to 'Off' the numeric keys have an alternate use as navigational keys (cursor left, right, page up and so on). Whatever the boot setting, the user can switch the NumLock key on or off as necessary.

4. Security option. As the earlier warning point out, altering BIOS settings has to be carried out with great care and only by someone who knows what they are doing and has the authority to do it. This option allows a password to be set. If a user tries to access the BIOS Setup program during startup, he or she will be asked for the password.

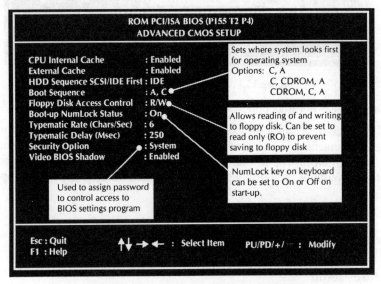

Figure 15.18. *Example BIOS Features setup*

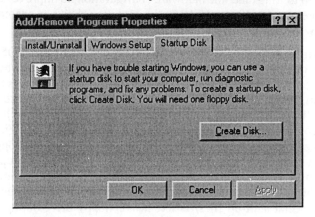

Figure 15.19. *Option to create Windows 95 Startup disk*

Plug and Play BIOS

Plug and Play operating systems use a BIOS which is automatically updated when a new device is added. On a Windows 9x machine, the BIOS details then appear in the System Properties window, as shown in Figure 15.20.

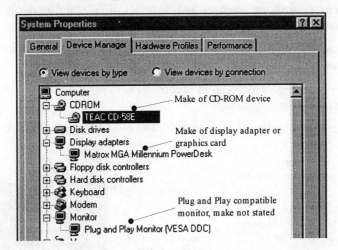

Figure 15.20. *Example BIOS details in a Windows 9x System Properties window*

The Device Manager tab lists all the categories of device attached to the computer system. In the figure, three of the items are expanded, to show details of the actual attached device:

❑   The CD-ROM is identified as a TEAC CD-58E;

❑   The display adapter, or graphics card, is a Matrox Millennium;

❑   The monitor is identified as Plug and Play (VESA DDC). 'VESA' indicates that it meets the Video Electronics Standards Association requirements for monitors.

Once a new device, such as a disk drive, or extra RAM, has been connected, the BIOS detects it during the next startup. If the device is not Plug and Play compatible, the installation settings have to be made through the BIOS setup utility.

Development tools

This is a group term for software which is used to develop applications and systems software. Examples of development tools are *programming languages* and *database packages*. To understand the purpose of development tools generally, you need to be familiar with the idea of a *computer program*.

Computer programs

The words *software* and *program* are often used to describe the same thing, but what exactly is meant by these two terms? To be usable by a computer, a program has to be in *machine code*. Machine code is *binary code*, a series of 1's and 0's, represented electrically inside the computer. A computer program consists of a series of machine code instructions which make the computer perform the required tasks.

The program is stored in memory. It is fetched, decoded and executed, one instruction at a time, by the CPU (processor) until a Halt instruction is reached. The CPU has its own *instruction set*, which it uses to understand the instructions in a computer program. The set includes instructions for:

❑ *Arithmetic operations*, such as add, subtract, divide and multiply and logical operations, such as AND, OR, NOT.

❑ *Data transfer*, to enable data to be moved between the various devices in the computer system, including input, storage and output devices.

❑ *Transfer of control*, which allows the computer to skip one or more instructions or repeat previous instructions.

The storage of a computer program in memory and its execution by the CPU are illustrated in Figure 15.21.

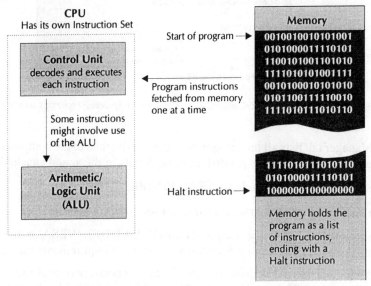

Figure 15.21. *A computer program in memory being executed by the CPU*

Writing computer programs

Although the computer needs programs to be in the binary codes it understands (according to its instruction set), it is not practical for programmers to write the same codes. Instead, programmers use *programming languages* and other development tools to write programs in a form that they understand; this is known as *source code*. The computer is then given the job of translating the source code into the machine's own code, known as the *object code*.

The next section deals with the various software development tools used by programmers.

Programming languages

C++, Visual C, Visual BASIC, Pascal, Java, Delphi and COBOL are all examples of programming languages. All programming languages can be used to produce software, although some languages are suited to particular applications. For example, COBOL is mainly for business data processing applications, while Java is particularly suited to Internet applications. Pascal is used for commercial applications, but is particularly popular in education for teaching programming skills.

Pascal

Like English and other languages, a programming language has a *vocabulary*. These are keywords which form the language. Each keyword has a particular meaning. In Pascal, for example, the keywords begin and end are used to mark the beginning and end of a program, or separate groups of instructions within it. The words if and then are used in the writing of *conditional* statements. For example, the statement

```
if age < 16 then writeln('Junior Member');
```

will display the message in quotes if a the memory location labelled *age* contains a number less than 16.

There are also rules of grammar. These are rules on the formation of program instructions. The example statement above would fail the rules for Pascal grammar if it were written as

```
if age < 16 writeln('Junior Member');
```

The word then must be used as part of an if statement. A programming language's rules for spelling and grammar are known as its *syntax*.

Program development

Programming language software includes a number of components to assist the programmer, including:

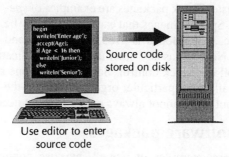

Use editor to enter
source code

Figure 15.22. *Editor used for entry and storage of program source code*

❑   an *editor* to allow entry of the source code. Figure 15.22 illustrates this process;

❑   *debugging* utilities to help find and correct errors in syntax;

❑   a *translator* to convert the source code into the object machine code. There are two main types of translator:

　o   *compiler*. This is the most common and produces a separate machine code program which the computer can use without further use of the translator.

　o   *interpreter*. This type does not produce an independent machine code program. The program must be translated each time it is run. Many versions of BASIC use an interpreter.

A translator only checks the syntax of a program, not its *logic*. Before it can be used a program must be thoroughly tested to check that it performs exactly as required. Figure 15.23 illustrates the translation process with a compiler.

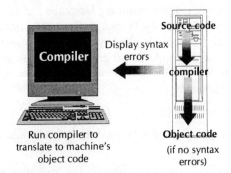

Figure 15.23. *Translating the source code to the machine's object code*

Applications software

This category of software includes all the purposes for which organisations and individuals use computers. Four examples of applications software are shown on the right.

Specific applications packages

The QuickBooks and Monster Truck packages are examples of *specific* applications package. Specific means that each one can only be used for a certain purpose. QuickBooks is used for accounts and Monster Truck is a game. Neither has any other use. Other applications in this category include, for example, payroll and stock control. Some applications software is *tailor-made*, that is, developed specifically for a particular organisation. Off-the-shelf packages, such as QuickBooks are cheaper but they cannot always meet the exact needs of an organisation.

General-purpose software packages

Word 97 and Excel 97 are examples of *general-purpose* applications packages. General-purpose means that they can be used for a range of different purposes. Word 97 is a word processor and could be used to produce any text and graphics documents, for example, letters and reports or magazines and books with colour graphics. Excel 97 is a spreadsheet package and can be used for any number-based work, such as a sales forecast or a statistical analysis of the health of a population. It can also produce graphs or charts, to present the information in different ways. Other examples include drawing and paint packages, such as CorelDRAW and PhotoPaint and desktop publishing (DTP) packages, such as Corel Ventura. There are many different such packages, but the remainder of this chapter will concentrate on the following important examples.

❑   Word processors

❑   Spreadsheets

❑   Databases

❑   Graphics, including desktop publishing (DTP), business graphics, graphic design and computer-aided drawing (CAD).

Features overlap between packages

Each type of package has a different general-purpose. For example, a word processor is mainly concerned with text and a spreadsheet with numerical data, but there is often some overlap in their features. Although a spreadsheet provides more advanced calculating facilities, a word processor also allows calculations to be made on columns of figures, as Figure 15.24 illustrates.

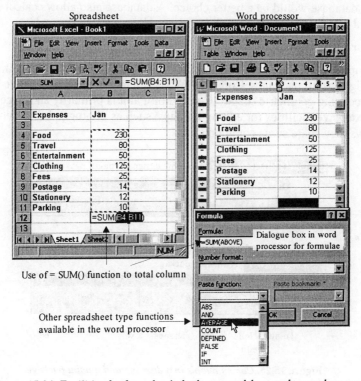

Figure 15.24. *Facilities for formulae in both a spreadsheet and a word processor*

Choosing the most appropriate package

Despite some feature overlap, choosing the most appropriate package for a particular task is not generally difficult.

Spreadsheet or word processor?

Suppose, for example, that you are required to calculate sales commission for a number of sales staff, or calculate wages. The problems are mainly numerical and best solved with a spreadsheet. If, on the other hand, you are writing a report and it includes a table of figures you could use the table and formula facility in the word processor, rather than doing that part separately with the spreadsheet.

Spreadsheet or database?

Similar feature overlap occurs between spreadsheets and databases. Data held in a spreadsheet can be sorted and extracted in much the same way as data held in a database. Choosing between the two again depends on the problem to be solved.

Suppose, for example, that you already have some sales staff records in a spreadsheet, for the purpose of calculating sales commission. If you need to sort the records by surname, or on the amount of commission earned, you can do that in the spreadsheet. Similarly, if you wanted to separately list those sales staff who earned more, say, £250 commission, that also could be done in the spreadsheet.

However, if the main requirement is to store, retrieve, sort, print and generally manage staff records the database would be a better choice. A database also allows calculations, such as totalling and averaging numerical data in its records.

Drawing or paint package?

Other examples of feature overlap occur between computer-aided drawing (CAD) and graphic design (paint) packages. CorelDRAW is primarily a drawing package with powerful tools for producing geometric shapes. Corel PhotoPaint is primarily an image editing package, with extensive facilities for editing bitmaps, such as photographs. However, as Figure 15.25 shows they share some common tools.

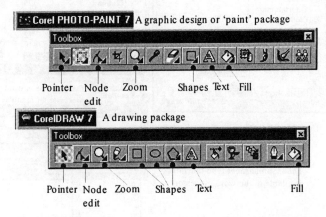

Figure 15.25. *Common tools in a drawing and a paint package.*

Of course there are many differences as well. For example, the paint package includes tools such as a spray can, brush and eraser, which are of particular use to the artist or graphic designer.

So how would you choose which package to use? As with the choices between other pairs of packages, it depends on the task. If, for example, you needed to produce a poster advertising a party, with text and some clip art you could do so with a word processor, a desktop publisher, a drawing or a paint package. If, on the other hand, you needed to produce a technical drawing with scaled dimensions a drawing package would be the best choice. If you wanted to 'touch up' some family photos taken with your digital camera you would find the most powerful features in the paint package.

Tailor-made software

There are many occasions when the specific needs of an organisation cannot be met with an off-the shelf package. On such occasions, the software must be specially developed. This means that the application to be computerised must be carefully analysed, to see how it works and what users want from it. A computerised system must then be designed and produced. The development of the software is one part of that process.

Assuming that a specific applications package that meets the need cannot be found, programmers must develop the software specially. They have to choose between a range of possible development tools (see earlier), including, for example:

❏   traditional programming languages, such as C, Pascal and COBOL;

❏   programming languages aimed at a WIMP environment (see Graphical User Interface), such as Visual BASIC and Visual C;

❏   Database packages, such as Access, Paradox and dBase. Although these packages can be used by trained users to quickly set up, for example, personnel, stock or any other kind of information system, they can also be programmed. Access, for example, includes the Visual BASIC programming language and with a special *developer kit*, software can be *compiled* to run independently of the Access package.

The main advantage of tailor-made software is that:

❏   it is designed to meet the particular needs of the user. A package may include unnecessary features and miss out some that would be useful to the user.

The main disadvantages of tailor-made software are that it

❏   takes longer to develop;

❏   is more expensive;

❏   needs extensive testing before it can be relied upon.

Self-test questions

1. What is the function of the following types of software?
    (i)   Operating system
    (ii)   Utilities
    (iii) BIOS
    (iv)   Development tools
    (v)   Applications
2. Name three operating systems commonly used on PCs.
3. What is an operating system interface?
4. What are the main features of a GUI?
5. Name and briefly describe the purpose of four types of utility software used by Windows 95.

6. What is the purpose of the CMOS settings? Typically, what information is stored by the CMOS? What BIOS settings are accessible via the CMOS?

7. Name 4 programming languages.

8. Give examples of special-purpose and general-purpose applications programs.

9. What are the advantages and disadvantages of tailor-made software?

10. Give examples of features that overlap between common general-purpose software packages.

Chapter 16

Input and output devices

Input and output devices allow users to communicate with the computer, in different ways, according to their requirements. For a given type of device, such as a printer, there are many different product specifications, each designed to meet a particular need. For example, when judging a printer specification, you need to consider its speed of output and the quality of the print it can produce. The first part of the chapter deals with input devices and the second with output devices. For each type of device there is

❑ a general description of the device and details of the main products of that type. For example, when examining printers, you need to be aware of differences between laser and inkjet products;

❑ where necessary, an explanation of technical terms found in product specifications and guidance on matching device specifications to users' needs.

Input devices

Input devices enable information to be entered into a computer for processing or storage on magnetic media. The computer can only process or store information if it is in an electronic, binary coded form, so input devices are needed to convert, for example, letters of the alphabet, digits in our number system, the sounds of the human voice or musical instruments, into the computer's code.

The most commonly used input device is the keyboard, which converts key presses into the computer's code. So, for example, pressing the 'A' key produces electrical signals which the computer uses to represent that letter. The computer uses a different code for each character on the keyboard. The ASCII (American Standard Code for Information Interchange) binary code is recognised by all computers. Similarly, a *scanner* allows typed or hand-written documents to be read into a computer and a microphone enables the entry of sounds, perhaps to give voice commands to the computer. Each input device needs its own software to make it work on a particular computer system.

Computer keyboards

A number of alternatives are available to suit different ways of working, different work conditions and special applications.

Standard keyboard

A typical standard computer keyboard is shown in Figure 16.1.

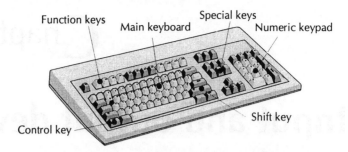

Figure 16.1 A typical standard keyboard

The arrangement of keys on the main part of the keyboard is the same as for any typewriter. This QWERTY layout comes from mechanical typewriters and has little to do with the requirements of a computer keyboard. It has continued as the favored design because many people are used to it and changing the layout of the keys would mean retraining for millions of keyboard users. The computer keyboard does have other keys, specifically designed for the computer. Function keys, for example, are programmable and are used by software packages to access particular options, such as Help menus. Some common examples of keyboard use are:

❑ entering text and numbers into the computer, perhaps using a word processor;

❑ entering keywords into a *search engine,* a type of program used to find information on the World Wide Web;

❑ controlling animated graphics characters in computer games;

❑ entering commands to an operating system such as MS-DOS.

Microsoft Natural keyboard

An alternative keyboard design has been developed by Microsoft. Its shape and main features are illustrated in Figure 16.2.

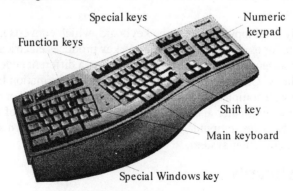

Figure 16.2. *Microsoft Natural keyboard*

The Natural keyboard splits the keys into two main areas and angles the keys slightly, allowing the user to keep a straighter, more comfortable wrist posture. The keyboard also slopes and provides palm support, which puts less strain on the wrists and allows the shoulders to relax. Repetitive strain injury (RSI) is a common complaint of keyboard users and a comfortable wrist posture helps to avoid it. The design was based on *ergonomic* research, which is the "study of efficiency of workers and working arrangements" (Oxford English Dictionary).

Membrane keyboard

This is a keyboard covered by a transparent, plastic cover, to protect the keys from dirt. Membrane keyboards are used in factories or other locations where the dirt from users' fingers or the surroundings may damage them. The membrane makes its difficult to type accurately and quickly, so these keyboards are not used in a normal office environment.

Concept keypads

In specialist applications, the standard keyboard is not always the most convenient method of input. In a factory, for example, a limited number of functions may be necessary for the operation of a computerised lathe. These functions can be set out on a touch-sensitive pad and clearly marked. This is possible because all inputs are anticipated and the range is small. The operator is saved the trouble of typing in the individual characters which form instructions.

Concept keypads are used in shops, restaurants and bars. For example, each key position on the pad can be assigned to a particular drink. Pressing a key automatically enters the charge for the specified drink. Concept keypads are also useful in education, particularly for the mentally and physically handicapped. Different overlays, which can set different areas of the keypad to different functions, allow its use for different educational programs. For example, if the responses required by a user are limited to 'yes' and 'no', the overlay is simply divided into two parts, one for each response. The cells have to be programmed to match the overlay in use. Figure 16.3 illustrates this idea.

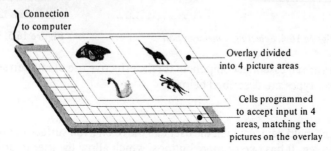

Figure 16.3. *Educational concept keypad with sample overlay*

The grid shown on the keypad is divided into a grid of 16 × 8 (128) programmable cells and the example overlay shows that the grid is to be programmed into 4 areas. Each area occupies 32 cells (128 ÷ 4) and pressure on any of the cells in one area indicates that the user has selected a particular picture. This may result, for example, in the matching word being displayed on screen. Alternatively, the input may be the user's response to the word shown on screen.

Choosing a keyboard

The desirable qualities of a keyboard are reliability, quietness and light operating pressure and in these terms keyboards vary considerably. If the keyboard is for a normal office use then a standard or Microsoft keyboard is appropriate.

Computerised tills in restaurants, pubs and hotels often use concept keypads tailored for all the items they sell. This ensures accurate pricing, as well as quicker service. Gas and electricity meter readers also use concept keypads to collect the readings. Security systems often include a concept keypad, for entry of pass codes. Dirty environments in factories or on building sites, for example, need equipment with extra protection, so membrane keyboards are used.

Pointing devices

Apart from the keyboard, which is an essential part of every computer system, pointing devices are the next most popular option for input. The devices in this group use different mechanisms and technologies, but they all allow the user to draw, erase, select and format text and graphics on screen. Figures 16.4 and 16.5 illustrate two such actions.

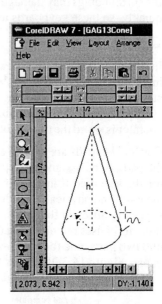

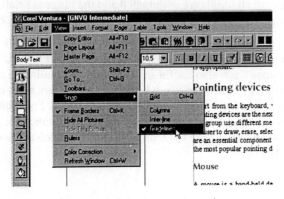

Figure 16.4. *Selecting a menu option*   **Figure 16.5.** *Drawing a line*

Pointing devices are an essential component for the effective use of modern software. Two of the most popular types are described below.

Mouse

A mouse is a hand-held device which the user can move on a flat surface to direct a pointer on the computer screen. It has two or more buttons, which allow the user to draw, erase, select and format text and graphics on screen. Most computer systems are equipped with a mouse facility and many packages, including those for art, design, word processing and desktop publishing can only be operated effectively with a mouse or similar device. Graphical user interfaces such as that provided by the Microsoft Windows 95/98 operating system, also depend heavily on its use.

Tracker ball

A tracker (or roller) ball is another variation of a mouse and is used for the same purposes. As shown here, a tracker ball is a bit like an upside-down mouse, with the ball visible on the top of the base. To use a tracker ball you simply move the ball in the required direction using your fingers. Buttons are supplied just like on a mouse. Like

Tracker ball

joysticks, tracker balls have the advantage over mice that a flat surface is not required for its operation, and for this reason they are often used with portable computers.

Other pointing devices

Although the mouse and tracker ball are very popular, they are not the most suitable for every application. Three other pointing devices are described below.

❏ *Touch screen*. A touch sensitive display allows selection of screen options with a finger. It is commonly used in banks and tourist agencies to allow customers to obtain information on certain topics.

❏ *Digitising tablet*. A stylus (pen-like device) is used to 'draw' on the tablet; the movements of the stylus are reflected on screen. Used by architects and designers, it allows more precise drawing than a mouse.

❏ *Light pen*. This pointing device is moved over the screen and uses a light sensitive tip to allow the computer to track its movements. It can only be used with cathode ray tube (CRT) displays and cannot be used with laptop or notebook computers.

Choosing a pointing device

For most users, the mouse is standard equipment, but for architects, graphic artists and other designers, the mouse does not provide the precision control possible with a graphics tablet. The light pen is a possible alternative to the graphics tablet; it is cheaper but is not capable of the same accuracy. The roller or tracker ball is suitable for a portable computer because it does not need a flat surface. Touch-sensitive screens are suited to public display information systems, because no keyboard or other input device is needed. The user simply uses a finger to touch the required option on screen.

Sensors and ADCs

Sensors are used to detect continuously varying values, such as temperature, pressure, light intensity, humidity, wind speed and so on. These sensors detect analogue signals which are not compatible with digital computers. So, apart from several other components, an *analogue-to-digital converter* (ADC) is needed to convert analogue signals into the digital values a computer can understand.

Suppose that the temperature of a washing machine is computer controlled, using a built-in microprocessor programmed for that purpose. The microprocessor can only handle discrete, that is separate, values, so the ADC in this machine takes a sample from the sensor every minute. Figure 16.6 illustrates the analogue wave form which represents the temperature variations detected by the sensor, over a 5 minute period. The figure also shows the temperature readings at each sample point (S1 to S5). For example, at the 3rd minute sample $S3 = 40^0C$.

Figure 16.7 shows a temperature sensor immersed in the water. The electrical signal (after being strengthened by an amplifier) produced by the sensor is converted by the ADC into an equivalent digital value for the microprocessor. Therefore, for each temperature sample, the microprocessor receives an equivalent digital value. It can then use these values to control the washing machine's heater.

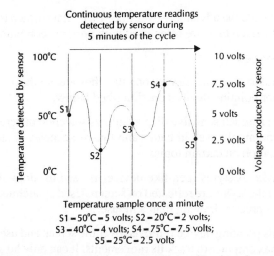

Figure 16.6. *Washing machine temperature variation, with a sample reading every minute*

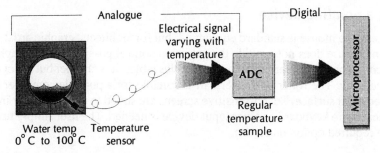

Figure 16.7. *Sensor detects variations in temperature and ADC digitises sample values*

Microphone

Just as the temperature sensor produces a voltage which varies with the temperature, so a microphone acts as a sensor, converting sound waves to equivalent electrical voltage levels. The voltages are sampled and converted by the sound card inside the system casing into the binary codes which the computer can store and process. Most personal computers are equipped with a microphone to allow, with appropriate software, sound recording or the input of commands and text. Figure 16.8 illustrates the use of a microphone connected to a computer.

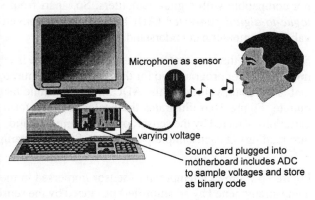

Figure 16.8. *Microphone as sensor for sound input*

Digitiser

The term *digitiser* is used to describe more complex ADCs used for capturing video sequences (the digitiser is a *video capture card*) and scanning documents. Scanners are briefly described in the next section.

Other input devices

There are a number of devices designed to capture information, in the form of pictures or text, already printed on paper. These devices include the following.

❑   *Scanners.* These devices allow whole documents to be scanned optically and converted into digital images. Text can be captured in this way and then converted for use in a word processor. The conversion is carried out by *optical character recognition (OCR)* software.

❑   *Optical mark reader (OMR)*. An OMR is designed to read simple pencil marks placed in pre-set positions on a document. A common application for OMR is a multi-choice examination paper, where the answer to each question has to be indicated by a pencil mark in one of several boxes located after the question number. The OMR can then scan the paper for the pencil marks and work out a grade. National Lottery tickets are completed and checked in a similar fashion.

❑   *Bar code readers.* Bar codes are commonly used to store a variety of data such as prices and stock codes relating to products in shops and supermarkets. A sticker with the relevant bar code is attached to each product, or alternatively, the packaging may be pre-coded. By using the data from the code, the cash register can identify the item, look up its latest price and print the information on the customer's receipt.

Output devices

Just as input devices allow human beings to communicate with computers, so output devices convert computer code into the information we can use. In this section we describe the devices that form part of typical personal computer systems, namely, *visual display units (VDUs)*, *printers* and *loudspeakers*.

Visual display unit

The most commonly used device for communicating with a computer is the *visual display unit* (VDU). The term VDU *terminal* is normally used to describe the screen and keyboard as a combined facility for input and output. On its own, the screen is called a *monitor* or *display*.

Technical features of VDUs

Screen size

A screen's size is quoted as a measurement across the diagonal, as shown. In practice, part of the screen is covered by the casing and the part of the screen you can see is usually at least an inch less, making the visible screen in the figure only 16". Some screen specifications quote this smaller measurement as the 'viewable area'.

For desktop personal computers, 14" or 15" is standard, but 17", 19" and 21" are also available. The larger screens are needed for applications such as computer-aided design (CAD). This is because the level of detail on some designs cannot be properly seen on a standard screen. Notebook computer screens, which use a different technology to desktop models, are obviously smaller and typically around 12" (12 inches) across the diagonal.

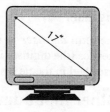

Measuring screen size

Screen resolution

A screen's *resolution* is one measurement indicating the clarity of sharpness of displayed text or graphics. Images are formed on the screen with pixels (picture elements). A pixel is one dot in a graphic image. A display screen is divided into thousands or millions of such pixels, organised in rows and columns. By varying the colours and luminosity (brightness) of individual pixels, text and graphic images are displayed. A high resolution screen packs pixels more densely to produce sharper images. A lower resolution will produce a more 'grainy' image, rather like a photograph which has been enlarged to many times its original size.

To illustrate the idea of resolution, examine Figure 16.9, showing two pictures of a puma.

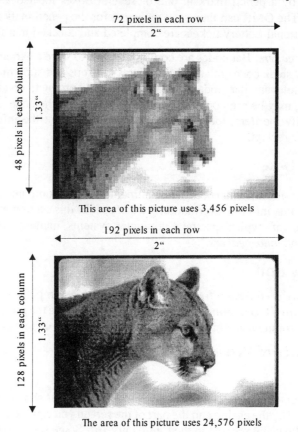

Figure 16.9. *Two pictures of the same size, but formed from different numbers of pixels*

They are both the same size, but the top picture uses fewer pixels than the other. For this reason, the top picture is much less clear than the other. In fact, the resolution is so poor that the jagged edges of pixels can be seen.

The resolution of each image is indicated by the number of pixels in each row and column. So, the top picture has a resolution of 72 × 48 and the bottom picture has a resolution of 192 × 128. Expressed as an area, the low resolution picture is formed from 3,456 pixels (72 × 48) and the higher resolution picture from 24,576 pixels (192 × 128). As you would expect the higher resolution picture is sharper, more clearly defined.

Any given screen has a *maximum resolution*. This is the number of pixels it is capable of displaying. This maximum may be reduced, depending on several other things, such as the number of colours to be used and the amount of memory on the graphics card. The software which controls the graphics card can then be used to set the screen's resolution to the user's requirements (up to the screen's maximum). Figure 16.10 shows the Windows 95 'desktop' at two different resolutions, 1024× 768 and 800 × 600.

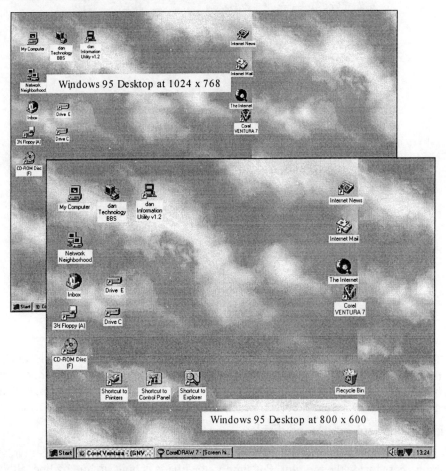

Figure 16.10. *Windows 95 desktop at two different resolutions*

Notice that the icons on the higher resolution desktop are smaller and take up less space than those on the lower resolution desktop. The higher resolution allows the user to 'zoom in' and obtain a greater level of detail. However, the higher of these two resolutions would not be useful with a screen size less than 17".

Screen size and resolution

A resolution of more than 1024 × 768 is only practical for screen sizes of 17" or larger. This is because higher resolutions on a small screen make the images too small to see.

Refresh rate

Figure 16.11 shows the 'display properties' for a monitor, including the resolution and the *refresh rate*.

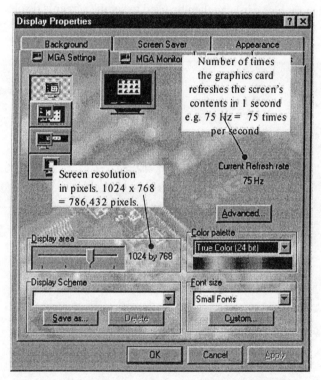

Figure 16.11. *Windows 95 Display Properties, including resolution and refresh rate*

The contents of a display must be continually refreshed, that is re-displayed. Flicker occurs when the eye can detect a gap between each screen refresh cycle. If the refresh rate is quick enough, the eye will not detect any flicker. The figure shows that the screen in question is re-freshed 75 times every second (75 Hz), which is the minimum for modern displays.

Non-interlaced and interlaced display

When a screen's contents are refreshed, as described in the last paragraph, this involves a scanning process inside the monitor. Put simply, the image is built up line by line, although the process is too quick to be noticed.

There are two main types of scanning used by monitors. Most monitors are of the *non-interlaced* type, which means that all the lines that form the complete screen image are produced in a single refresh scan. An *interlaced* screen refreshes the screen in two separate passes. Figure 16.12 illustrates the interlacing process.

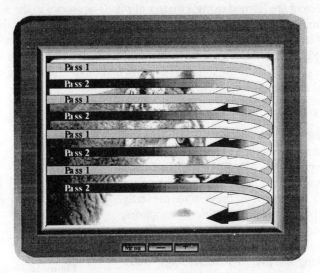

Figure 16.12. *Electronic scanning of an interlaced screen*

The number of lines is massively reduced to simplify the illustration. The lines in Pass 1 leave alternate blank lines. Pass 2 fills in these blank lines. An interlaced screen can produce the same resolution as a non-interlaced one, but does it more cheaply by only replacing half the lines each time the screen is refreshed. A disadvantage of an interlaced screen is that it takes longer to completely refresh the display (two refresh cycles). Although this is not a problem for many applications, animation, video and redraws of complex diagrams are likely to produce noticeable flicker.

Monochrome and colour

A monochrome monitor uses one colour for the text or graphic images and one for the background, for example, white, green or amber on black. Colour monitors use red, green and blue, which can be mixed together in different quantities to produce different colours. For example, when red, green and blue are mixed in exactly the same quantities, we see white light; red and green in equal quantities produces yellow; two parts red and one part green gives orange. In fact, by varying the quantities and the mixtures, any colour can be produced.

Resolution and colour range

The more colours a screen can display, the more memory is required, so graphics cards (or adapters) have their own memory. In practice, the maximum number of colours, which can be up to $16 \cdot 7$ million, is set by the graphics adapter. Higher resolutions also use more memory, so although a graphics card may allow $16 \cdot 7$ million colours at a resolution of 1024 × 768, it may only permit 256 colours when the resolution is increased to 1600 × 1200. Typically, such a graphics card would have several megabytes of its own special RAM.

Text mode

For some applications, graphics display is not needed and when operated in text mode, the computer system needs to use less power and memory. This is an advantage when numerous VDUs are controlled by a central computer. In text mode, characters are formed using a matrix of *pixels* as shown in the adjacent example and the clarity of individual characters is determined by the number of pixels used. The same principle is used in character printers, such as the ink-jet (see Printers). Selected dots within the matrix are illuminated to display particular characters. There are various main text modes, including one that displays 40 characters and another that displays 80 characters in each of 25 rows.

Dot matrix character

LCD Monitors

These monitors are very thin (about 1.5 inches thick) and occupy about a third of the space that CRT monitors require. They use much less energy than CRT monitors and because they are based on Thin Film Transistor (TFT) technology, they give off only one-third as much heat as many traditional monitors. Even more importantly, they produce virtually no electromagnetic emissions. In addition the flicker-free viewing of the TFT technology make them much easier on the eyes. Many LCD monitors swivel so that they can be used in either portrait or landscape orientation. Figure 16.13 shows two colour LCD monitors produced by IBM.

Figure 16.13. *LCD monitors*

LCD monitors are capable of high resolutions such as 1280 x 1024 and can display millions of colours. Their extremely compact dimensions and energy-efficient features make them ideal for space- or energy-conscious environments. At the moment, however, they are considerably more expensive than equivalent conventional CRT monitors, though prices are coming down as they become more popular.

Choosing a monitor

Although specific recommendations cannot be given here, it is possible to provide advice for broad application areas.

Text-based applications

These are likely to be standard applications, such as ordering, sales and stock control systems. There is no graphics requirement. You are likely to see text-based displays at supermarket checkouts or a in a car parts department.

General office applications

These include use of word processors, spreadsheets and database. They all run under operating systems such as Windows 95, through a mouse-driven, graphical interface. For general office applications, a 15" monitor is probably the norm. Although larger screens are generally better, they take up more desk space and, of course, are more expensive.

A resolution of 800 × 600 is probably the best resolution to give the necessary clarity and image size. Although the graphics card may support higher resolutions, their use may well make icons, buttons and other images so small that viewing the screen may result in eye strain. The refresh rate is important, but provided it is 75Hz or more, the screen should be flicker-free.

To obtain the cheapest alternative, an interlaced screen could be chosen, because the applications do not require complex graphics and most users will not notice screen flicker. To avoid flicker on an interlaced screen, a higher refresh rate is usual. However, a non-interlaced screen should still provide a steadier image and this is important for users' eyesight.

Graphics-intensive applications

These include computer-aided design (CAD), photo-editing, graphic design, desktop publishing, video-editing and animation. Larger monitors, from 17" to 21" are essential for these applications. Higher resolutions of 1024 × 768, 1280 × 1024 and 1600 × 1200 need greater screen areas to ensure that images are large enough to allow detailed work on them. At the two highest resolutions, a refresh rate of 85Hz is desirable, to avoid screen flicker (the higher the resolution, the more pixels that have to be refreshed).

Printers

Computer printers vary according to: the technology they use for the printing process; the quality of their printed output; the speed of printing; whether they can print in black and shades of grey, or in colour, or both.We now examine, in some detail, ink-jet and laser printers. At the end of this section, a brief summary is provided of the other types of printer.

Ink jet printers

There are two main types of inkjet, liquid and solid.

Liquid inkjet

A typical *liquid inkjet* printer is shown alongside. Ink jet printers spray high-speed streams of ink droplets from individual nozzles in the print head onto the paper to form individual characters or smooth graphical images. Individual text characters are formed by the print head as a matrix of dots, as shown on the previous page. By a series of passes and adjustments to the head's position, graphics can also be produced. Although the output quality is high, print speeds for graphical work are very slow.

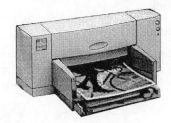

Typical ink jet printer

Liquid inkjets produce their best quality output on special paper, which is considerably more expensive than standard copier paper. The best glossy paper costs around £1 per sheet.

The fastest liquid inkjets can print 2 pages per minute (ppm) in economy mode (low resolution), but 0·5 ppm is more usual. Colour printing at the best resolutions of 600 to 700 dots per inch (dpi) is even slower. At these resolutions, near photographic quality can be achieved.

Solid inkjet

A *solid inkjet* uses sticks of ink (rather like crayons) and these are turned to liquid by being heated. In contrast to the more common liquid inkjet, the solid inkjet is quick at 3 to 4 ppm, using the base resolution of 300 dpi; this is good enough for general business graphics, but not for photographic quality. The solid inkjet achieves its high speed by using a print head the full width of an A4 sheet. Solid inkjet printers cost several thousand pounds.

Buffer memory

To enable the printer to print bi-directionally, that is from left to right and then right to left, alternately, it must have enough of its own *buffer memory* to store at least a complete line.

How colour printing works

Most inkjet printers print in monochrome, shades of grey and in colour. In colour printers, the ink is often supplied from two cartridges, one holding black ink and the other three colours (cyan, magenta and yellow) car-

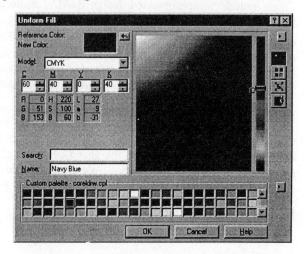

tridge. As explained in the section on colour displays, a few colours can be mixed to produce all the others. As explained in the section on VDUs, colour displays use the RGB (red, green, blue) model. Colour printing uses a different colour mode to produce the full colour range; it is called CMYK (cyan, magenta, yellow and black -K). Figure 16.14 shows a dialogue box from CorelDRAW for the CMYK model. The displayed colour is navy blue, which is produced from different proportions of cyan, magenta and black.

Figure 16.14. *CMYK model used in colour printing*

Laser printers

Laser printers are called *page printers*, because they effectively print a complete page at one time. To do this, the printer must have received the contents of an entire page from the controlling computer, before it starts printing. This is illustrated in Figure 16.15.

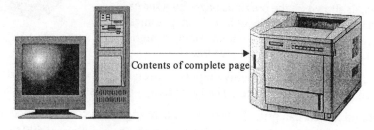

Contents of complete page

Figure 16.15. *Typical laser printer receiving complete page into its memory before printing*

Laser printers may be monochrome only or both monochrome and colour. Printing speeds are far superior to ink jet printers, with similar quality output.

Monochrome laser printer

A *personal* model will print at between 12 and 17 ppm, typically at 600 dpi, but also up to 1200 dpi. The highest resolutions are used where very high quality output is needed, for example, in publishing. Some models of *network* laser, designed to serve the printing needs of many users, can print 32ppm at 600 dpi or even 50 ppm at 300 dpi. The lower of these two resolutions in perfectly good for standard printing, including invoices and general correspondence. However, such printers are expensive and aimed at high volume use, say a maximum of 900,000 pages per month. Figure 16.16 shows an example of a large network printer.

Figure 16.16. *High volume, network laser printer*

Colour laser printer

Alongside the solid inkjet, the colour laser produces the highest print speeds, ranging from 2 to 5 ppm. Resolutions are similar to the monochrome models, up to 1200 dpi. An advantage of colour lasers over liquid inkjets is that they can produce the best quality on standard paper. The quality of liquid inkjet printing depends on the quality of paper used. As you would expect, these advantages are gained at a price, colour laser printers costing several thousands of pounds. However, the speed of the laser printer allows it to be shared on a network, so the cost per user for colour printing may be little more than that of buying a personal inkjet for each user. Running costs are also much lower than for inkjet printers.

Printer memory

As a page printer, the laser printer must be able to hold the data for an entire page at one time. If the page has a large proportion of graphics, then the memory requirements for one page can be very large. Most laser printers are equipped with a basic memory of 2MB, but this is often insufficient for complex graphical documents; extra memory can be added if necessary. Some printers also make use of the computer's own RAM and thereby remove the need for buying extra, expensive, printer memory.

Printing speeds - quoted and real

Print speeds quoted as pages per minute (ppm) in manufacturer specifications cannot be used as a rule for all kinds of printing. The following points should be noted:

❑ Print speed will vary considerably, depending on the mix of graphics and text on a page. A small logo at the top of a page may not slow the printout much, but a full-page poster is likely to reduce the printing rate drastically.

❑ Printing a text page with a little colour highlighting will mean that the entire page is printed as a colour document and will take much longer than if it were plain text.

Other types of printers

❑ *Line impact.* As the name suggests, this type of printer uses hammers to print the characters onto the continuous stationery, a complete line at a time. They are used as system printers, for internal, high volume reports and can achieve speeds of between 500 and 1400 lines per minute (lpm).

❑ *Large format (plotters)*. Used for design work, a large
format printer can handle poster images up to 150 feet
long and 54 inches wide. Monochrome and colour
models are available. Figure 16.17 shows a typical
example.

Choosing a printer

Although specific recommendations cannot be given here,
there follow some typical user examples and suggested
choices.

Figure 16.17. *Large format
printer (plotter)*

❑ Personal computer printing. The user needs to print a few letters and perhaps
produce the occasional colour poster. The choice is fairly straightforward here.
Until recently, the choice would have included the impact dot matrix (not dealt
with in this text), but the liquid inkjet provides excellent quality output, with the
option of colour.

❑ Publishing and graphics for a single user system. The user needs to print large,
monochrome publications, including some complex graphics. A laser printer is
the necessary choice for this user, because an inkjet printer would be much too
slow and the running costs too high; print cartridges have a much higher cost per
page than the toner used in a laser printer.

❑ Network monochrome printing. Again, the only choice is a laser printer. Which
model is chosen would depend on the number of users and the type of printing
required. For text documents, a printer would support more users than would be
the case for graphical work.

❑ Near-photographic quality printing. A liquid inkjet printer will produce the
necessary quality at 600 or 720 dpi, but a colour laser will do the same, much more
quickly.

If colour printing is needed by a number of users, then the higher cost of the colour
laser could be shared by placing it on a network. The alternative is to provide as
many liquid inkjet printers as there are users who need access at the same time.

❑ General-purpose colour printing. Either the solid inkjet or the colour laser printer
would provide the necessary speed and the 300 dpi quality for general business
graphics.

Self-test questions

1. Explain the need for input devices.
2. Name as many input devices as you can.
3. Why is an ADC necessary when using a sensor to capture temperature values?
4. Explain the need for output devices.
5. Name as many output devices as you can.

6. What is meant by the screen resolution of a monitor?
7. What is the difference between an interlaced and a non-interlaced monitor?
8. What advantages do LCD monitors have over traditional CRT monitors?
9. Name two types of printers commonly used. Give a typical print resolution and output speed (in pages per minute) for each one. What other factors need to be considered when choosing a printer?

Chapter 17

Storage systems

As explained in Chapter 14, backing storage is needed to hold programs and data files, from where they can be recalled as necessary by the computer. They are all *non-volatile* - their contents are not lost when power is removed. The purpose of main memory or RAM, which is volatile, is to hold programs and data currently in use - it is not a permanent storage area. A wide range of different backing storage systems is available, to suit every kind of computer system and user requirement. They vary according to:

❏   the technology they use and the way they operate;

❏   the speed with which they can record and retrieve data;

❏   capacity, that is, the amount of data they can hold;

❏   whether they are

    o   read-only - the contents cannot be changed or
    o   read-write - the contents can be changed.

The storage systems described in this chapter (there are numerous others) are those using:

❏   magnetic disk, including hard disk and removable disk media, such as floppy, Zip and Jaz.

❏   magnetic tape.

❏   optical media, including: CD-ROM (read only memory); CD-R (recordable - once only); CD-E (erasable - read and write); DVD (digital versatile disk).

A common feature of all disk storage systems is the way in which they are addressed by the computer system. Magnetic disk addressing principles are described in the following section.

Magnetic disk

All disk storage systems provide *direct access* to data. This is in contrast to tape systems where data has to be accessed *serially*, that is, in the order in which it is organised. When data is to be written to or read from disk, a specific *location* can be identified, by its *address*. Tape devices do not have locations which can be addressed, so data can only be accessed serially.

Magnetic disk addressing

In a similar fashion to the first line of a typical postal address of house number and street, magnetic disks use *sector* and *track*. This structure is illustrated in Figure 17.1.

The figure illustrates a simplified magnetic disk structure, with 8 sectors numbered 0 to 7 and a number of tracks, numbered from 0, starting with the outermost track. In reality, on a hard disk, there would be hundreds of tracks. The Figure also shows an example address, Sector 5, Track 4. To read from or write to a disk location directly, the software must specify the address.

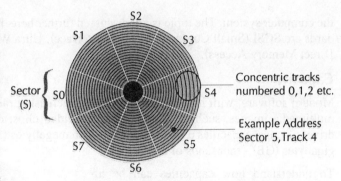

Figure 17.1. *Addressing structure on disk surface*

Hard disks and other high capacity systems use a number of disks within the one device and this makes the address structure slightly more complicated. We do not deal with this more complicated structure in this text.

Hard disk

A typical microcomputer has an internal hard disk with a capacity measured in gigabytes (GB). An illustration of its internal components is provided in Figure 17.2 . The illustration shows the top surface of a pack of hard disks on a central spindle. The disks are rotated at high speed, between 4,500 and 10,000 revolutions per minute (rpm). The read/write heads, through the use of a motor, can be moved in or out across the surface of the disk. This is how particular tracks are reached.

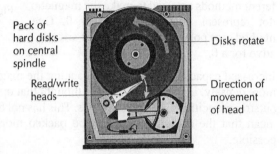

Figure 17.2. *Components of a microcomputer's hard disk drive*

Access speed

The speed with which data can be read from, or written to, a hard disk is measured as the *average seek time*, in thousandths of a second, or milliseconds (ms). This means that to access a location, the read/write heads have to move to the required track. The time taken to reach the track is known as the *seek time*. A typical average seek time is between 7 ms and 10 ms. The seek time is usually better in systems which use higher spin speeds. This means that the correct sector comes into position more quickly. Figure 17.3 illustrates seek time and spin speed delay.

Another major influence on the speed of a disk drive is its *controller*. This is the interface between the disk drive and

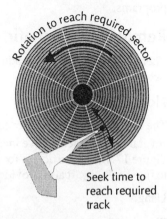

Figure 17.3. *Effects of seek time and spin speed*

the computer system. The topic is not discussed further here, but well-known interface standards are SCSI (Small Computer Systems Interface), Ultra Wide SCSI, and UDMA (Ultra Direct Memory Access).

Capacity

Modern software, with its provision of an ever-increasing range of features and the use of multimedia images, such as photographs and video clips, demands larger capacity disk drives. Typical capacities used to be measured in megabytes (MB), but are now measured in gigabytes (GB) - thousands of megabytes.

To understand how capacities can be increased in this way, you need to be familiar with some basic ideas about how the data is stored on magnetic disk. The binary codes used to represent data in a computer are stored as magnetic dots along the length of disk tracks. Figure 17.4 illustrates the tracks and magnetic dots which represent the data. Different methods are used to make the magnetic dot represent binary 1 or binary 0. One method uses polarity, positive for a 1 and negative for a 0.

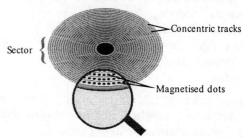

Figure 17.4. *Disk surface showing magnetic dots representing binary data*

Increased capacity is achieved by packing the magnetic dots more closely together, that is, more densely. Until recently, it was thought that optical media, such as CD-ROM would far outstrip capacities of hard disk drives. This has not been the case, because technical advances mean that the magnetic dots can be packed more densely than was previously thought possible.

Usage

The hard disk, with its huge capacity and fast access times, remains the best product for the *primary drive* in a computer system, holding the operating system and main applications programs.

Removable magnetic disk

There is a wide range of products in this category, including: floppy disk; Iomega Zip disk; Jaz disk.

Floppy disk

The floppy disk has, until recently, been the main product for securing small files. Although several developments have increased its capacity, the 1·44 MB of the 3·5" floppy disk (see Figure 17.5), is insufficient for many users. A graphics image, for example, is often too large to fit on a floppy. It also provides very slow access times, with a spin speed of only 360 rpm.

Usage

Floppy disks are extremely cheap and a 3·5" drive is still standard equipment in a microcomputer system. For many home and small business users, it is adequate for making backup copies of data files held on the primary hard drive and passing copies of data files to other users. The increasing use of e-mail, which allows the *attachment* of such files, is likely to reduce the need for this practice. For many other users, who need to produce and store multimedia data and backup large parts of their primary hard drive, the 1·44 MB floppy disk is inadequate.

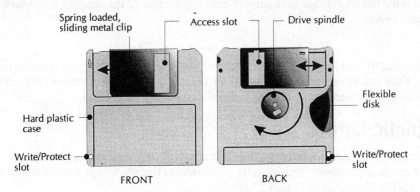

Figure 17.5. *3·5″ floppy disk*

Data compression programs

It is possible to compress files so that they will fit onto a floppy disk, through the use of data compression programs, such as WinZip. Bitmap files, in particular will compress to about 2% or 3% of their original size. Compression may allow, for example, text and graphics files with a total capacity of 50MB (which would take at least 35 disks) to be stored on around 10 disks. Backing up to even 10 disks is still a laborious task and likely to discourage the vital task of frequent and regular backup.

Iomega Zip

A Zip disk cartridge holds 100MB of data on its single platter, the equivalent of approximately 70 × 1·44MB floppy disks. The Zip drive can be attached *externally*, to the parallel printer port. The printer and Zip drive connectors can be 'piggy backed' to allow both to connect to the port. It can also be attached *internally*, as another drive, to the hard disk controller.

Access speed

Attached externally, the Zip drive is still relatively slow, but when attached internally to the main hard drive controller, it has a seek time of around 30 ms. This compares with a typical hard drive seek time of between 7 and 12 ms.

Usage

Its 100MB capacity makes it ideal for users who need to store large files, such as those producing design and multimedia presentations. The quickness of the internal drive encourages regular backup and although not matching the hard disk drive, allows it to be used as an extension to the on-line storage system. Files could be efficiently retrieved from the Zip without first copying them to the hard drive.

Iomega Jaz

A single Jaz cartridge contains two platters and will store 1GB of data (2GB with data compression). It can be attached internally or externally, but only to a SCSI drive controller.

Access speed

The Jaz drive has an average seek time of between 10 and 12 ms, making it as quick as most fixed hard disks.

Usage

Its huge capacity and hard drive performance make the Jaz drive a true extension to on-line storage. Files can be retrieved from a Jaz cartridge as quickly as from the main hard drive. It is also suitable for backing up the contents of the primary hard drive.

Magnetic tape

In contrast to disk, tape does not have locations which can be separately *addressed*. For this reason tape storage systems provide only *serial access* to data, that is, the order in which it is stored. This is illustrated in Figure 17.6.

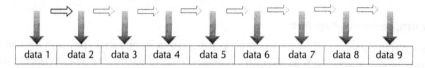

| data 1 | data 2 | data 3 | data 4 | data 5 | data 6 | data 7 | data 8 | data 9 |

Figure 17.6. *Serial access to data*

The figure shows that to reach a particular item of data on tape requires the device to read all the data that comes before it. Although magnetic tape systems can be used for some data processing applications, such as payroll, which do not need direct access, the systems described here are for backing up network servers, mini and mainframe computers.

Although the arrangement of data on tape is different from that on disk, the magnetic storage principles are the same.

Tape backup systems

To prevent permanent loss of data, it is vital that a computer system's main hard drive is regularly backed up. The more frequently the contents of files change, the more frequent should be the backups. For a single microcomputer hard drive, a single tape is often sufficient. A single tape device is often referred to as a *tape streamer*.

When several tapes are required for a complete backup, such as for a large network server a *tape library* is essential. This device includes an *autochanger*, which rather like a juke box, automatically loads the next tape. The alternative is to insert new tapes manually, which for a process that may take hours, is not desirable.

Capacity

The most popular tape backup systems use Digital Audio Tape (DAT) cartridges. For example, a 120 metre tape can store up to 4GB, and 8GB using data compression. A tape library system, capable of holding 8 such tapes, would be able to backup 64GB of data.

Data transfer rate

Typically, tape backup systems can transfer data to the tape at between 35 and 60MB per minute. If compression is being used the rate will vary during backup, because some kinds of data take longer to compress than others. At an average of 50MB per minute, a 4GB drive would take 80 minutes (4000MB ÷ 50MB).

Optical media

Instead of using magnetism to record data, optical media are read or recorded using laser light. To *record*, a high intensity laser beam burns tiny holes into the surface of the disk, each hole representing a binary 1 or a binary 0. To *read*, a lower intensity laser is used to detect the holes and the binary digits they represent.

The binary digits are recorded along tracks in a similar fashion to magnetic disk, but instead of using concentric tracks, optical disks use a spiralling track, similar to the old gramophone records. This is illustrated in Figure 17.7.

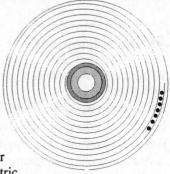

Figure 17.7. *Optical disk with spiralling track*

Compact disk (CD)

CDs are optical media and a single disk can hold approximately 650MB of data. Although data transfer rates are continually being improved, CD drives are slower than hard magnetic disks. There are three types of CD.

❑ CD-ROM (compact disk-read only memory). As the name indicates, the data is recorded during manufacture and can only be read by a CD-ROM drive. The main uses of the CD-ROM are for:

   o multimedia applications, such as games and encyclopedia.

   o software installation. The large memory requirement of many software packages means that delivery on floppy disk is impractical, whereas one CD-ROM disk is often sufficient to deliver an entire package

❑ CD-R (recordable - once only). This is a CD which can be written to once, with a suitable CD-Writer.

   o Provided the contents do not need to be updated, this can be a useful medium for archiving documentary and other material.

   o The falling cost of CD-Writers and the small cost of each disk, makes it possible for businesses and other organisations to produce their own multimedia training programmes.

❑ CD-E (erasable - read and write). Because data can be erased and updated, this type of CD is an alternative to magnetic disk, although its data transfer rates are still relatively slow.

DVD (Digital versatile disk)

Using the same basic principles as the CD, DVD packs the data more densely and can store 4.7GB, compared with the CD's 650MB. With this capacity and its quicker data transfer rate, a single DVD disk can hold 133 minutes of video, with Dolby surround sound.

It is probable that DVD drives will be an increasingly important removable storage device, particularly with the increasing use of video in multimedia products.

✐Self-test questions

1. What main factors determine the type of backing storage device to use for a particular IT application?
2. List as many types of backing-storage devices as you can.
3. How is data organised on a magnetic disk?
4. How is data organised on magnetic tape?
5. Give a major use of magnetic tape.
6. What is a tape streamer?
7. What is the main difference between CD ROM and magnetic disks for data storage?

Chapter 18

Setting up a computer system

This chapter deals with the following aspects of setting up a computer system:

❑ Connecting the hardware.

❑ Powering up the system.

❑ Installing device drivers, such as printer drivers.

❑ Tailoring a GUI 'desktop'.

❑ Installing and configuring applications software.

Connecting the hardware

Although some additional devices, such as a scanner and camera may be included in a system, the guidelines which follow deal with a typical minimum configuration. The connections to be made are:

❑ system unit;

❑ monitor;

❑ keyboard;

❑ mouse;

❑ printer;

❑ power supplies for the printer, monitor and system unit.

Figure 18.1 illustrates the connection of these devices. Obviously, safety requires that the entire task must be carried out without connection to the power supply.

Monitor connection

The system unit communicates with the monitor through a *data cable*. The data cable is permanently attached to the monitor as shown. The other end usually has a 15 pin, male, D-type plug to connect it to the 15 pin, female, D-type socket on the system unit. This is labelled 'Display port' in the figure.

The 'D' shape of the plug and socket mean
that the connection can only be made in one
way. The screws on the side of the plug are
used to secure the connection.

Keyboard connection

Keyboard to system unit; this is sometimes a
coil stretch cable as shown in Figure 18.1.
The cable is fixed to the keyboard. The other
end has a 5 pin, male, round connector which
connects to the 5 pin, female socket on the
system unit. The plug simply pushes into the
socket.

Mouse connection

A serial mouse (see Serial port in Chapter 1)
connects to the serial port, commonly
known by its MS-DOS name of COM1. The
mouse has a fixed cable. The other end has a
9 pin, female, D-type plug which connects to
the 9 pin male socket on the system unit.

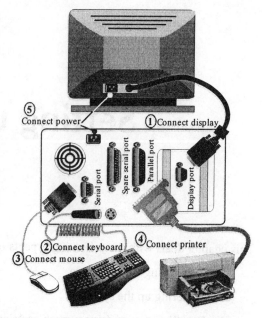

Figure 18.1. *Connecting the computer hardware*

Screws are used to secure the connection. If the mouse is to be connected to the other serial
port (labelled 'Spare serial port' in the figure), which has 25 pins, an adapter must be used.
This port is known as COM2 and can be used to attach other serial devices, such as an external *modem*.

Parallel printer connection

Although some printers allow either serial or parallel connection, the parallel port is the usual
connection point. Data can be transferred to a printer more quickly in parallel than it can serially. The parallel port is often known as a Centronics interface. The printer cable is not fixed
to the printer and is usually bought separately. The printer end of the cable is a 25 way, (not
pins) male plug which attaches to the 25 way, female socket on the printer. The system unit
end of the cable has a 25 pin male plug which attaches to the 25 pin female socket on the system unit. Spring clips secure the cable to the printer. Screws are used to secure the cable to the
system unit.

Power connections

The system unit, monitor and printer each have a separate power supply and these should be
the final connections.

Powering up the system

Having checked that all components are properly connected, the power supply and switches
on the printer, monitor and system unit should be switched on.

Power on self-test

The system goes through a self-checking procedure and if properly set up will load the operating system (Chapter 15). If errors or faults are detected, a suitable error message may be displayed. Although you would need to check the computer manufacturer's user manual, the following table shows some example errors, possible causes and solutions.

Error	Possible cause	Possible solution
Keyboard error	Not properly connected	Push home connection
Non-system disk or disk error	Floppy disk left in drive on power up	Remove floppy disk
C: drive failure	Corruption of software on hard disk	Run ScanDisk
C: drive failure	Damaged hard disk	Call manufacturer
HDD controller failure	Hard disk ribbon cable or power supply not properly connected	Open system unit and check cables properly connected
FDD controller failure	Floppy drive ribbon cable or power supply not properly connected	Open system unit and check cables properly connected

Installing device drivers

Device drivers are programs which control the way a device works. All attached devices, including for example, the graphics card (to control the display), sound card, disk drive controller and printer need device drivers. For example, without the appropriate driver, the computer system will be unable to take advantage of all the printer's features. So, a particular make of printer, with facilities to print text and graphics at a resolution of 600 dpi, will only provide all those facilities with the correct driver. The incorrect driver may prevent printing of graphics or even print gobbledygook. A printer driver can be installed with the installation program provided by the printer manufacturer, or with the appropriate operating system utility.

Printer install program

A new printer will include its associated software on disk, and the driver is installed through the use of this software. The following notes illustrate a typical printer install process.

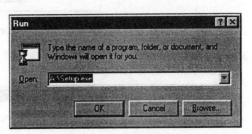

Figure 18.2

1. The operating system is instructed to 'Run Setup.exe'. In this case the setup program is on the first floppy disk supplied with the printer (Figure 18.2).

2. The setup program prompts for the parallel port to be used by the printer. In this case, the system only has one such port, LPT1, so this is the only option (Figure 18.3).

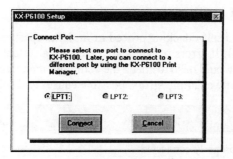

Figure 18.3

3. The user is asked to confirm the hard disk directory into which the programs will be installed. Generally, the default is chosen, unless there is a particular reason for changing it.(Figure 18.4)

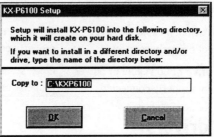

Figure 18.4

4. The setup continues with the copying of files from the floppy to the named directory on hard disk (Figure 18.5).

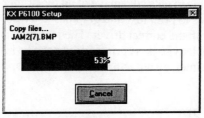

Figure 18.5

5. If the setup programs occupy more than one floppy disk, the user is prompted when the next one is needed.(Figure 18.6)

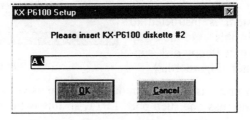

Figure 18.6

6. When the setup is complete, various configuration files may be altered and the process is completed.

7. For the changes to take effect, the operating system has to be restarted. This is because the changes to the configuration files are detected when the operating system is first loaded. Figure 18.7 shows the prompt to restart.

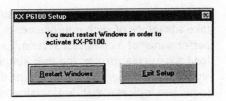

Figure 18.7

Printer install utility

In the case of Windows 95, a new printer can be installed with printer Install Wizard. Figure 18.8 shows the Printers window with two installed printers and the 'Add Printer' utility. Running the 'Add Printer' utility, calls up the Wizard. This provides the options of selecting a driver already available on the hard drive, or one held on another disk (such as that provided by the manufacturer). Figure 18.9 shows a list of drivers already available on the hard drive.

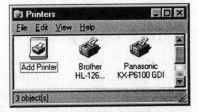

Figure 18.8. *Printer install utility*

Downloading drivers from the Internet

Figure 18.10 shows the download page on the Brother.com Web Site. Manufacturers often modify their device drivers to improve the features or performance of the devices they control.

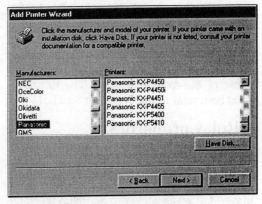

Figure 18.9. *List of available printer drivers*

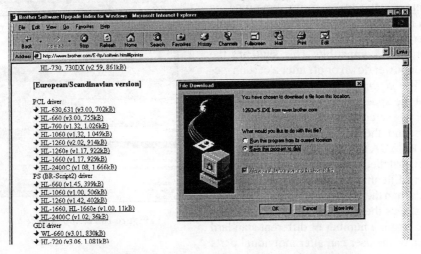

Figure 18.10. *Downloading drivers from the a Web site*

It is often worth downloading the latest device driver from the manufacturer's Web site, to take advantage of such improvements. Obtaining the latest graphics driver can improve the performance of a computer system, for example, by speeding up screen redraws. To download a particular driver, the user simply clicks on the appropriate driver name. The figure shows that the user has requested the download of the Brother 1260 printer driver. The dialogue box indicates that the downloaded file can be copied straight to memory or to the hard disk. The downloaded file will normally include a program to automate the installation process.

Setting GUI preferences

A major benefit of a GUI is that its appearance can be altered to suit an individual user or a group of users. If the settings are made for a group, then a generally accepted appearance has to be agreed. If one user in the group decides to change settings, without proper agreement, this can be annoying or even confusing for the other members of the group. There are too many different settings to deal with them all here, so we will concentrate on some of the most important. The examples used here refer to the Windows 9x GUI.

Display properties

The Windows 95 Display Properties window is shown in Figure 18.11. Each tab deals with a different aspect of the display. The displayed tab gives access to *Screen Saver* and energy saving controls. Setting a screen saver prevents a static image from remaining on screen and burning a permanent shadow into it. Energy saving features can only be used if the screen is compatible. This switches the monitor power down or off after a certain period. The *Settings* tab allows the user to control the appearance of the screen display, including screen resolution, number of colours and the font size. The figure also shows an MGA settings tab, which is specific to the installed graphics card, an MGA Matrox Millennium. It provides more varied controls than the standard Settings tab. Figure 18.12 shows the *Appearance* settings can be selected from a number of different standard models, or the user can alter individual parts of the screen, such as the colour of the desktop or spacing of icons.

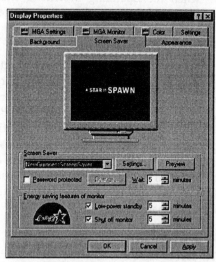

Figure 18.11. *Display properties window*

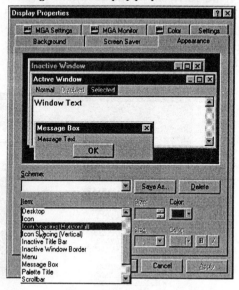

Figure 18.12. *Appearance tab*

Date and time

Figure 18.13 shows the date and time window in Control Panel. Figure 18.14 shows the MS-DOS prompt and the alteration of the date and time through typed commands.

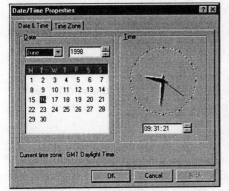

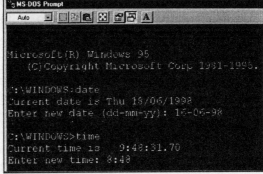

Figure 18.13. *Setting the date and time*   **Figure 18.14.** *Using DOS prompt to set date and time*

Software installation

Much of this process is automated through an *install program.* An example is shown in Figure 18.15.

Figure 18.15. *A software install program*

Install settings

Some installations are quite straightforward and the only major decision to be made concerns the drive and directory in which the programs are to be stored. The above example, shows that the directory is \qbooksw, on the E: drive. The default is usually C:, but E: was chosen because of limited space on the C: drive. Although the drive and directory can be changed from that suggested by the install program, it is usually sensible to accept the default. The C:\ drive is normally the preferred location for applications programs, but another hard drive, or partition of the hard drive can be used. If an alternative is chosen, the operating system will still require some files on its own drive, usually the C: drive.

Other entries include:

❑   acceptance of licence arrangements. This restricts the number of machines on which the software can be installed at the same time.

❑   user name and company; these details are required for technical support from the software supplier.

❑   key code. This is supplied to the licensee and is designed to discourage pirate copies. The key code must be entered before the installation can continue.

Type of installation

The *typical* installation is useful if you wish to be certain that the facilities required by most users are provided. However, if you are knowledgeable about the facilities, a custom installation is usually better. Custom installation ensures that all the facilities you require are installed (your needs may not be typical) and that facilities you do not need are not installed. This can save considerable disk space.

Testing the installation

Completion on installation involves:

❑   copying of program files to the named directory;

❑   alteration of configuration files which 'tell' the operating system that the program is installed and where it is located.

Sometimes, the system needs to be restarted for the settings to be detected by the operating system. Once the above tasks are completed, the program can be run and tested with sample tasks or data. Whether the installation meets all of the user's requirements cannot be thoroughly checked until the full range of tasks has been attempted. Obviously, if the range of tasks is wide, this may take a considerable time. If a required option has not been installed, the install program may:

❑   require the full installation to be repeated;

❑   allow the additional option to be installed without full installation.

Removing programs

Most commercial programs provide an *uninstall* program. The uninstall program should be used wherever possible. It is generally a bad idea to simply delete the program files. The configuration files will still contain details and the operating system will still 'think' that the program is installed. At best, only space will be wasted. At worst, the operating system may display error messages on startup, which although not damaging are a great nuisance.

Figure 18.16 shows the Windows 95 utility for starting the removal of programs from the system, with a list of the installed software.

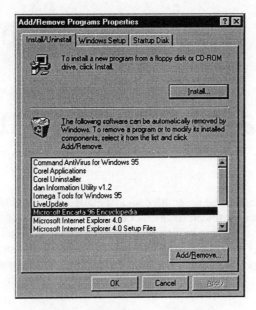

Figure 18.16. *Removing programs*

System security

Loss of important data can be disastrous for an organisation. For example, if a business loses its sales accounting records, it may prevent collection of sales debts (amounts owed by customers for goods bought on credit). The loss of income may then prevent it from paying its suppliers, resulting in bankruptcy or liquidation. The causes of data loss are varied, but the computer *virus* is one important threat. An important part of the protection system is the virus protection program (Chapter 5).

Data loss can also result when unauthorised persons gain access to a computer system. Protection systems include physical methods, such as the use of security staff and locked doors, and software methods, including passwords (Chapter 5).

Self-test questions

1. When setting up a typical PC what connections need to be made?
2. What are device drivers?
3. What is the main purpose of a screen saver program?
4. How are most modern commercial programs removed from computer systems?
5. What do you understand by the term computer virus?
6. What methods can be used to protect PCs from viruses?
7. Why are passwords often used in computer systems?

Chapter 19

PC assembly and upgrade

Modern PCs are designed to be assembled and upgraded quickly and easily. System cases, whether standard desktop or tower, have brackets, screw holes and connector slots that allow all essential, basic components to be fitted easily and without the need for special tools or extensive experience and training. In this chapter we describe the steps required to fit and connect basic PC components. Diagrams and photographs will help to identify standard PC components and show how they are fitted and connected. We describe fitting and connecting the

- ❏ motherboard
- ❏ memory modules
- ❏ processor chip
- ❏ expansion boards
- ❏ hard drive, floppy drive and CD ROM drive

It is assumed that the system case already has a suitable power supply and fan fitted since PC cases are usually sold this way.

Before you start

Precautions

There are three very important precautions that you must take before starting to work on assembling or modifying a computer:

1. **Make sure that you have made backups of any essential files held on your system.** Things can go wrong when upgrading a computer so assume the worst and make backups of important files if you have not already done so.

2. **Make sure that the power cable to the computer is physically disconnected.** Do not just switch off the power supply at the power socket - physically pull out the power supply lead from the power socket at the rear of the computer case. Always put the cover back on the case before re-connecting the power supply.

   These precautions are essential to remove the risk of getting an electric shock when working on components installed inside the case.

3. **Draw a diagram of the back panel leads and connectors before you disconnect anything.** It is easy to forget which lead goes where. A good idea is to attach numbered labels to leads and use a marker pen to write corresponding numbers near to the appropriate back panel sockets.

4. **Make sure that you have neutralised any electrostatic charge that might have built**

up in your body. Without knowing it you can easily build up thousands of volts of static electricity on your body and if you have done so, and you touch an electronic component such as a memory module, you could easily damage it. You can easily discharge yourself by touching a metal object that is plugged into a wall socket. For example, you could touch a metal part of a lamp or a power tool. The object does not need to be turned on for this purpose.

Tools

The only tools that you are likely to need are a Phillips screwdriver, a flat blade (ordinary) screwdriver and a pair of long-nosed pliers

The Motherboard components and connectors

Figure 19.1 shows the structure of a typical motherboard for a Pentium processor.

Features of importance to the placement and connection of components are described below.

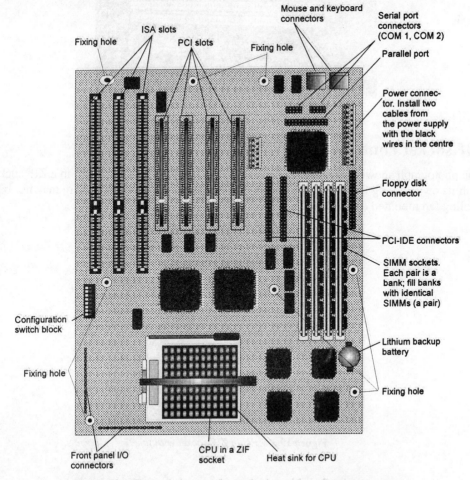

Figure 19.1. *Example layout of a motherboard for a Pentium processor*

This information is important when assembling a PC as described in a later section (see **Assembling a PC**)

Expansion board slots

The motherboard illustration shows three ISA and four PCI slots for expansion boards. The photograph in Figure 19.2 shows two empty PCI expansion board slots on a motherboard.

Figure 19.2. *PCI slots*

ZIF socket containing the CPU

The photograph shown in Figure 19.3 shows a Pentium processor package in a ZIF socket with its own cooling fan on top. Depending on the particular processor, there may not be a cooling fan mounted on the unit.

Figure 19.3. *CPU in ZIF socket with fan*

SIMM sockets

SIMMs (or DIMMs for more recent motherboards) are plugged into the four sockets. This motherboard requires SIMMs to be installed in identical pairs. These pairs can be FPM or EDO SIMMs and either parity checking or non-parity checking. (parity-checking SIMMs have eight chips on a single module, eight of them being memory chips and the ninth a parity checking chip; non-parity checking SIMMs have eight memory chips). For example the SIMM banks could contain two 16MB EDO SIMMs and two 8MB FPM SIMMs. Motherboard documentation will usually specify SIMM requirements. Figure 19.4 shows a bank of four SIMMs.

Figure 19.4. *SIMM banks*

Primary and secondary IDE connectors

These are connectors for connecting hard drives, CDROM drives and backup drives such as ZIP drives. These connectors are shown in Figure 19.5.

Ribbon cables are used to connect devices to the motherboard connectors. See the section on installing drives for more information about connecting and configuring hard drives and other types of drive.

The secondary connector can be used for a CDROM or ZIP drive or both if they are daisy chained together.

Figure 19.5. *Primary and secondary IDE connectors*

Floppy disk connector

In addition to the Primary and Secondary IDE connectors, Figure 19.5 also shows the smaller connector for the floppy disk drive.

Power supply connectors

There are two main forms of power supply plugs. The photograph in Figure 19.6 shows the old type of connector type that uses twin power supply plugs.

These plugs can be fitted incorrectly - when plugged in correctly, the four black wires are in the centre.

The other type of plug, which is for an ATX power supply, is a single unit that can only be fitted one way.

Port connectors

Figure 19.6. *Power supply connectors*

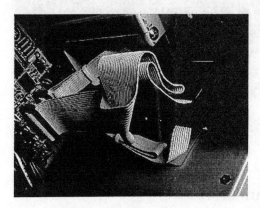

Figure 19.7. *Port connectors*

There are three port connectors shown in Figure 19.7. There are two serial port connectors, COM 1 and COM 2, and a single parallel port connector. These connectors are linked to sockets on the back of the PC chassis by means of ribbon cables as shown in Figure 19.7.

Some motherboards have the port sockets mounted on them so that no ribbon cables are required.

Front panel connectors

These are connected to the various switches and indicators on the front of the PC case by means of small connectors. For instance there are connectors for the hard disk drive activity light, for the reset switch and for the internal speaker. There is also a connector for the internal fan. The uses of the pins are labelled on the motherboard or described in the documentation. Figure 19.8 shows a photograph of some of the front panel connectors on a typical motherboard.

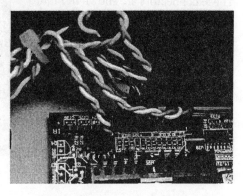

Figure 19.8. *Front panel connectors*

Configuration switch block

This is a bank of tiny switches that change various motherboard and processor parameters. For instance some of the switches are used to specify processor speed for motherboards that can take processor upgrades. The function of each switch is dependent on the type of motherboard and will be described in documentation. You may need to use a small screw driver or a ballpoint pen cap to flip the switches if they need altering.

Installing and removing SIMMS

SIMM connectors pivot forward to allow memory modules to be installed and removed more easily.

When installing SIMMs, angle the connector at about 45° and push the module in, as shown in Figure 19.9 , until it snaps into position and is held by the two metal clamps at the two ends of the connector.

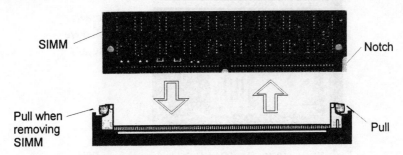

SIMM

Notch

Pull when removing SIMM

Pull

Figure 19.9. *A SIMM and connector*

To remove a memory module, first gently release the metal clamps at the ends of the socket. Then tilt the module forward and lift it out. The metal clamps **must** be released first to avoid damage to the module.

Installing and removing a processor

Inserting the processor

ZIF sockets have an integral handle to facilitate seating and removing the processor chip. Before installing the processor, unlatch and raise the handle.

Align the processor over the socket making sure that all the pins match the pin holes in the socket. Then push the processor into place being very careful not to bend any of the pins. Then lower and lock the handle. A heat sink and fan for the processor may also need to be locked in place over the processor once it is inserted in the socket.

Removing the processor

If there is a fan over the processor, release the sprung wire retaining brackets and lift the fan away. Then if necessary remove the heat sink from the top of the processor. The ZIF socket handle must then be unlatched and lifted to release the processor.

Installing and removing drives

PCs can accommodate a number of different types of drives, including hard disk drives, floppy disk drives, CDROM drives and ZIP drives. All of these drives are installed and re-moved in much the same way. The main difference is that since hard drives do not use removable media such as floppy disks or CD ROMs they do not have a face plate in the front panel of the computer; all of the other types of drives need to be accessed from the front of the computer so that disks or cartridges can be inserted or removed.

Installing a hard disk drive

Hard disk drives are usually located behind the front panel of the computer or in a bay above the power supply unit as illustrated in Figure 19.10. Before fixing the drive in place, make sure that the jumper settings are correct.

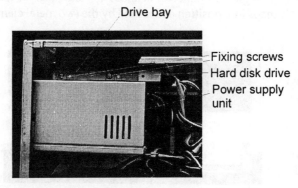

Figure 19.10. *Hard Disk Drive mounted above PSU*

Usually the main hard drive (the one that is used to boot the system on startup) is connected to the Primary IDE connector on the motherboard and a second hard drive can be daisy-chained to it using the same ribbon cable. Hard drive ribbon cables usually have two connectors at one end for this purpose. If two hard drives are being connected in this way, the main drive must be configured as the Master drive and the other as the Slave drive. These settings are made using *jumpers* which are tiny two-pin plugs that join pairs of connections on the hard drive jumper pins. The illustration of a hard drive in Figure 19.11shows the connections for the jumpers, the ribbon data cable and the power supply.

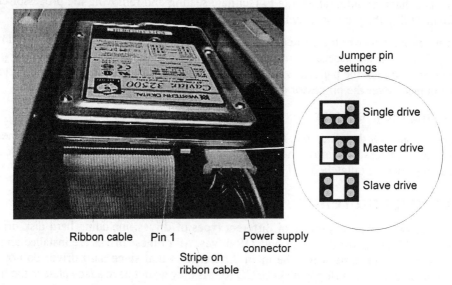

Figure 19.11. *Hard drive connections and jumper settings*

The jumper settings in the illustration will probably be different for other makes of hard drive. The settings are usually written on the casing of the hard drive or included in documentation for the device.

When plugging in the ribbon cables, make sure that they are the right way round; some connectors are constructed so that it is impossible to get them the wrong way round, but this is not always the case. In Figure 19.11 the right hand side of the ribbon cable connector, closest to the jumper pins, is Pin 1 and it corresponds to a stripe on the ribbon cable. The motherboard IDE connectors have the pins labelled from 1 to 40. (See Figure 19.5). Getting the connector orientation wrong won't damage the hard drive, but of course it won't work. (When you try to start the system, the hard drive light usually stays on permanently if the connector is the wrong way round).

Before installing the hard drive check the location of Pin 1 on the 40 pin socket so that the stripe on the ribbon cable can be aligned with it later.

Four small screws (two on each side) secure the drive unit to the drive bay as illustrated in Figure 19.10. The ribbon data cable and power supply connectors need to be plugged in once the drive is fixed in place.

Installing a CDROM drive

Before installing the CDROM drive, set any jumpers or switches. Details of jumper and switch settings should be included in the documentation for the device. Remember that if more than one CDROM drive or an IDE hard drive are to be installed on the same cable, they must be configured as master and slave.

The CDROM drive occupies one of the front panel bays. If necessary, remove a blank panel to allow the drive to be slid in from the front as shown in Figure 19.12. Once positioned flush with the front of the case, use the fixing screws to fix the unit in place and attach the 40 pin data ribbon cable and the power cable. As with hard drives, ensure that the ribbon cable stripe is positioned at pin 1 of the CDROM drive connector.

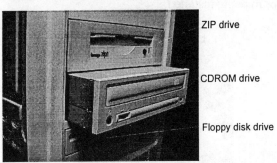

ZIP drive

CDROM drive

Floppy disk drive

Figure 19.12. *CDROM drive being installed*

The secondary IDE connector on the motherboard is usually used for drives other than hard drives or floppy disk drives. In addition, so that the CDROM drive can output sound, an audio cable must be connected to the sound card, if there is one, or to the motherboard if it includes sound circuitry. Figure 19.13 shows an audio cable connected to a sound card from the CDROM drive..

Figure 19.13. *Audio cable from CDROM drive*

Installing a floppy disk drive

The procedure for installing a floppy disk drive is essentially the same as that for a CDROM drive, the main difference being that the ribbon cable has a split in it at the end that connects to the floppy drive A: and the other end goes into the floppy disk connector on the motherboard (see Figure 19.5) or to a floppy disk controller expansion board . The ribbon cable will usually have a connector in the middle for a possible second floppy disk drive B:. Check that any jumper settings are correct (usually the factory settings are appropriate) as detailed in the drive's documentation. Also note the position of pin 1 which is probably labelled on the case or circuit board of the floppy disk drive; the coloured wire of the ribbon cable goes to this pin.

For old-style cases it may be necessary to use an expansion frame for a 3.5 inch drive if the drive bay is too wide. Some older cases also require plastic or metal slide rails on each side of the bracket assembly. Four screws are used to secure the drive in position.

Attach the end of the ribbon cable with the twist to the floppy disk connector and plug in the power cable.

Installing Expansion boards

Expansion boards plug into the ISA or PCI slots on the motherboard. Figure 19.14 shows an expansion board prior to being installed.

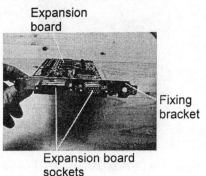

Figure 19.14. *Expansion board prior to installation*

Expansion boards are positioned such that the metal bracket at the end of the board (where there are usually connectors for peripheral devices) can be held in position by a single screw (see Figure 19.15).

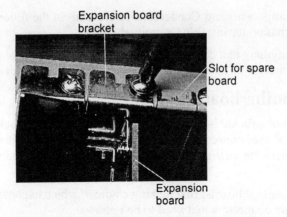

Figure 19.15. *Securing an expansion board*

If the position for the bracket on the rear of the chassis is covered by a plate, prise it off with a small flat-blade screwdriver (or unscrew it if this is possible). Then align the board over the appropriate expansion socket and gently push the connector strip of the board into the socket. Make sure that the connector strip is fully inserted into the expansion socket before securing the board with a screw.

Installing a new motherboard

Precautions

If you intend to upgrade a PC by installing a new motherboard in the old system case, before buying the motherboard it is a good idea to check the following details:

❑ CPU compatibility - if you are not changing the processor, make sure that it is compatible with the new motherboard. This includes the type of socket required as well as the type of processor.

❑ Power supply requirements - new motherboards (for Pentium IIs and above) generally require an ATX power supply which provides different voltages and motherboard connector from the older type power supply units. In addition ATX motherboards may not fit an older type system casing. If the new motherboard does require the ATX power supply, it is probably advisable to buy a new ATX system case with the power supply unit already installed.

❑ CMOS settings - modern hard disk drives auto-configure on startup. In other words they are able to provide the CPU with the drive type and the number of cylinders and tracks they have automatically; this information is essential to accessing data on the drive. For many older drives this information needs to be provided manually to the CMOS setup program (see Chapter 18). Just to be sure that there is no risk of losing essential setup information, make a copy the current CMOS settings on paper before replacing the motherboard.

Read through **both** of the following two sections before removing and/or installing a motherboard; this is so that you know in advance what needs to be done in both cases. The section on the Motherboard Components and Connectors, referenced in the following sections, contains essential information for installing a motherboard.

If you assume that anything that can go wrong, will go wrong, and take all possible precautions, you are more likely to be able to install a new motherboard without any major hitches.

Removing a motherboard

If there is already a motherboard installed in the system casing, first attach labels to all cables and draw a diagram of the connectors to which they were attached. This will be of great help when trying to connect the new motherboard. Then disconnect all cables attached to the motherboard.

Next, remove all expansion boards, first making a note of which expansion slots they occupied and labelling any connectors that need to be removed.

The motherboard is usually secured to the PC chassis by a combination of several plastic standoffs (see Figure 19.16) that fix into slots and two or more screws that go through the motherboard and screw into hexagonal metal standoffs attached to the chassis. Figure 19.17 is a sectional view of a PC chassis showing a plastic and metal standoff.

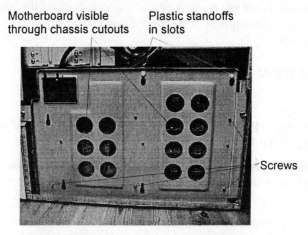

Figure 19.16. *Installing and removing a motherboard*

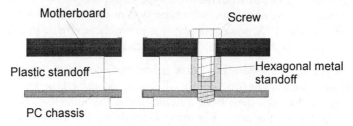

Figure 19.17. *Motherboard standoffs*

Remove the screws and slide the motherboard sideways to free the plastic standoffs. The motherboard can then be lifted out.

Installing a motherboard

This is more or less the reverse of the process of removing a motherboard described in the previous section.

First set any switches or jumpers that are needed to configure the system; these settings should be explained in the documentation that came with the new motherboard.

Fit memory modules if not already installed. (See **Installing and removing SIMMs**).

If there are no standoffs already on the motherboard, push three or four of them into the motherboard fixing holes that align with appropriate chassis slots. Again if necessary, screw in and tighten two or three hexagonal metal standoffs into chassis screw holes. The metal and plastic standoffs should be evenly distributed over the motherboard, the intention being to keep the printed circuits on the underside of the motherboard from touching the metal casing, and also to prevent the motherboard from flexing too much when components such as expansion boards and memory modules are being fitted later.

Now align the motherboard with the plastic standoff holes and metal standoffs. Lower the motherboard so that the wide bases of the plastic standoffs go through the wide parts of the chassis slots and then slide the motherboard sideways so that the plastic standoffs are firmly engaged in the slots. Now fix the motherboard in position with metal screws that screw into the hexagonal metal standoffs attached to the chassis.

Connect the front panel LED wires and the internal speaker wires. The motherboard should have some markings to indicate where each of the small connectors is located.

Next connect the power supply cable or cables (see **Power supply connectors** earlier) making sure that where two connectors are required the black wires of both are together in the middle.

If IDE controllers are on the motherboard, connect ribbon cables from the appropriate drives to these. (See **Primary and secondary IDE connectors**). Also attach the cable from the floppy disk drive to the motherboard connector if appropriate.

If there are pins on the motherboard for serial and parallel ports, attach the ribbon cables to these. (See **Port connectors**).

Now re-install all expansion boards and connect any cables that were disconnected when the old motherboard was removed.

Before replacing the cover, check that all cables are connected and that all connectors are seated properly. Finally, replace the cover and reconnect cables to peripheral devices.

When you switch the machine on, you may get error messages regarding unrecognised disk drives. This has two most probable causes:

1. IDE and floppy drive connectors have not been replaced properly. You will need to open the case and check that connectors are seated properly and that drives are configured correctly. Also check that the ribbon cables are connected to the drives the right way round, with the striped wire to pin 1 of the drive connectors.

2. The CMOS memory requires drive information if drives do not autoconfigure. Before removing the old motherboard you should have made a note of the required CMOS settings for just this eventuality.

✍️Self-test questions

1. Explain safety precautions that should be taken before adding or removing components from the inside of a PC?

2. What connectors are usually provided on a motherboard?

3. What two main types of expansion board slots are usually provided on motherboards?

4. What is a ZIF socket?

5. What restriction often applies to installing SIMMs of different memory sizes on a motherboard?

6. What is usually connected to the Primary IDE connector?

7. When the motherboard's power supply socket requires two connectors, how should they be plugged in?

8. What is the purpose of the *Configuration Switch Block* on a motherboard?

9. What is the significance of Master and Slave disk drives? How is a hard disk drive set to be a single drive, a Master drive or a Slave drive.

10. What is the guideline for fitting a hard drive ribbon cable?

11. What precautions should be taken before installing a new motherboard?

Developmental Exercises

Computer Installation

Activity 1

Demonstrate the connection of stand alone computer system components. You can use the the checklist a guide.

Hardware Connection	Tick
1. Power cable to system unit.	
2. Keyboard to system unit.	
3. Mouse to system unit.	
4. Display to system unit.	
5. Power cable to display	
6. Printer to port in system unit.	
7. Power cable to printer.	
8. Connect power supply and power up.	

Activity 2

Set up and **configure** a computer system to a specification, detailing the system's:

a. *purpose* (for example, a drawing program);

b. *inputs* (for example, parameters for shapes and colours, etc);

c. *processing* activity (calculation of vector co-ordinates and drawing of images);

d. *output* (screen and printer); required performance (for example, speed of screen re-draws, image resolution, colour definition, precision drawing).

Activity 3

The hardware or software components of the system will be deficient for the required specification in one or more respects. You will have to identify the deficiencies and suggest how the system can be improved. The activity has two main parts: *configuration* of hardware use by the operating system; *installation* and *testing* of software. Note that most software is automatically installed as you respond to a series of screen prompts, but this activity requires that you create the necessary directories/folders and copy the program files into them.

a. **Configure** the system, **install** the software and **test** the system. The precise steps will depend on the specification and the equipment you are using, but you can use the following table as a checklist. **Keep notes** of **each step** you take and any *problems* which occur.

	Activity	Tick
	Configure operating system to use hardware	
1	Install specified screen driver and check operation.	
2	Memory settings (e.g. files and buffers, HIMEM in config.sys, or virtual memory in Windows 3.1). Copy initial settings.	
3	Install mouse device drivers (possibly included in *autoexec.bat*).	
4	Set date and time (MS-DOS prompt or in Windows Control Panel).	
	Install application and test	
1	Create directory to hold executable and other files for application.	
2	Copy application files from floppy disk into the new directory.	
3	If necessary, use Windows Setup to install application for Windows use.	
4	Run application and set defaults (e.g. work file locations, tools displayed).	
5	Enter test data, save and print.	
6	Assess performance, identify deficiencies and suggest how to improve (for example, faster processor, more memory, higher resolution screen).	

b. **Produce** a short *report* on the procedures carried out in Activity 2, identifying any difficulties experienced, methods used to solve them and recommendations for improvement of the system.

Unit 5

Systems analysis

Chapters

Assessment Evidence

You need to produce

☐ a feasibility report
☐ a system specification to meet the requirements.

(You must also show evidence of data modelling with an entity-relationship diagram (erd) that has at least three related entities.)

To achieve a grade E your work must show:

☐ a clear statement of purpose and user requirement for the system including a scope definition and a high-level (contextual view) dfd
☐ appropriate low-level dfds to describe the main system events
☐ an erd and a data dictionary that clearly lists and describes the entities, their attributes and the relationships
☐ accurate input and output specifications and details of resource implications
☐ suitable process specifications using an appropriate method
☐ a conclusion that makes recommendations for development.

To achieve a grade C your work must show:

☐ good understanding and effective use of structured analysis tools in the development of your dfds, the identification of events and the production of process specifications
☐ good understanding and method in the development of your erd and data dictionary to resolve problems and ensure first normal form
☐ that you can work independently to produce your work to agreed deadlines.

To achieve a grade A your work must show:

☐ show a systematic approach to your analysis of the existing system, investigation of potential improvements and selection of priorities fordevelopment
☐ define clearly in your input specification appropriate sources of data, methods of data capture, layout of screen data input forms and validation and verification techniques
☐ define clearly in your output specification the information to be output in screen or printed reports and appropriate ways of organising and presenting it
☐ specify clearly in your conclusion the possible alternatives, constraints, risks and potential benefits, and include a cost-benefit analysis to support your recommendations.

Chapter 20

Overview of systems analysis

System life cycle

In business, *systems analysis and design* is the process of investigating a business, existing or new, with a view to determining how best to manage the various procedures and information processing tasks that it involves. Though it frequently means considering the use of a computer system to replace some manual operations, this need not always be the case. The *systems analyst,* whose job it is to perform the investigation, might recommend the use of a computer to improve the efficiency of the information system under consideration, but he/she might equally well decide that a manual system is adequate, or even preferable. Thus, the intention in systems analysis is to determine how well a business copes with its current information processing needs, and whether it is possible to improve the procedures involved in order to make it more efficient, or more profitable, or both. Systems design involves planning the structure of the information system to be implemented. In other words, analysis determines what the system should do, and design determines how it should be done.

The job of the systems analyst starts with studying the current, or proposed, system; this involves collecting facts which will help the analyst to determine whether a computer would improve the information system, and if so, in what areas it would be most beneficial. Once the decision has been made to go ahead with a new or improved system, the analyst must develop a plan for putting the proposed system into practice. This includes specifying all the procedures involved, computerised or otherwise, how data is to be captured, what software will be required to process the data, what equipment will be necessary, what staff will be needed and how they will be trained, and so on. In other words, the analyst must provide a complete plan of every detail of the proposed system. A key feature of this complex task is communicating with staff, whether they are ordinary employees or managers. The people who work in the business are most likely to know what works and what does not, what causes problems and how they can be avoided, and where improvements to the current system are most necessary.

This Chapter describes the *system development life cycle* (Figure 20.1) the sequence of activities involved in analysing, designing and implementing an information system. As well as systems analysts, who play key roles in the process, other personnel such as computer programmers and computer managers are also involved to a large degree.

Though the steps are described separately, in practice they may be performed in a different order, or even be difficult to distinguish one from another; sometimes one part of the system will be in the process of being implemented while another is still being analysed. The cyclic nature of system development is illustrated in Figure 20.1. The system development stages illustrated in the diagram may be repeated a number of times during the life of a system. Each time a significant change or improvement is required, the cycle is repeated.

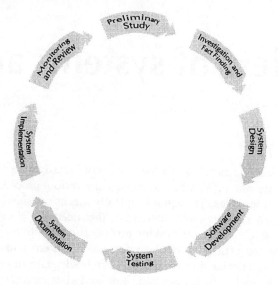

Figure 20.1. *System life cycle*

Preliminary study

Before an organisation embarks on a costly project involving the development of a new information system, it is necessary to determine whether the system is possible to achieve and, if so, whether there will be sufficient benefits in doing so. The main part of this investigation is called a *feasibility study*. However, even before the feasibility study commences, it will be necessary to fully clarify what is being proposed. The systems analyst dealing with the proposal will talk with the people who have suggested the project in order to determine exactly what they have in mind and their reasons.

Once the proposal has been fully clarified, the feasibility study can be undertaken. The feasibility study is usually carried out by a team of people with experience in information systems techniques, with a knowledge of the type of system being proposed and who are skilled in systems analysis and design. The team will be responsible for determining whether the potential benefits of the proposed system can justify the costs involved in developing it. It may be that the consequences of not adopting the new system make the change essential. For example, if a company is unable, through volume of work, to deal with customers effectively, the latter may take their business to more efficient competitors. It then becomes essential to the company's survival to improve its information system.

The feasibility study must also establish whether the new system can operate with available technology, software and personnel. In most instances, for example where a currently manual system is to be replaced or improved by using a computer system, the existing technology will most probably exist, but a new, innovative idea might require hardware or software that don't exist. If this is the case, the feasibility study team will attempt to determine whether the new items can be developed within a reasonable time.

Finally, the team will consider how well the system will be received by the people who will have to use it. This must have been a prime concern, for instance, of the first analysts who considered the use of cash points such as those now commonly provided by banks and building societies: would customers trust them and would they be sufficiently easy to use?

Investigation and analysis

If the feasibility study produces a favourable report, the next stage, that of making a detailed analysis of the current system, will commence. The systems analyst will investigate all aspects of the current system:

❏   what services are being offered;

❏   what tasks are being performed;

❏   how they are being performed;

❏   how frequently they are done;

❏   how well they are done;

❏   what staff are involved and the nature of their involvement

❏   what is lacking in the system;

❏   any faults with the system;

❏   how the system can be improved.

Finding the answers to these questions requires the analyst to talk to all the people involved in operating the current system, from ordinary employees to managers and directors. This will frequently involve the use of questionnaires as well as personal interviews with employees, the study of manuals and reports, the observation of current working practices, and the collection and study of forms and other documents currently used. As this process is going on, the analyst will be starting to form views on how the new system should work in order to overcome the problems with the current system. At the end of this stage, the systems analyst will thoroughly understand how the current system works and be in a position to begin to design and produce a *Requirements Specification* for the new system.

The Requirements Specification should clearly present what the system is meant to do and achieve, but design considerations should be left until the Design stage. Of course, some design aspects, such as the need for bar code scanning for an EPOS (electronic point of sale) system, may be obvious and can be taken for granted. Some parts of the design may be constrained by the need for compatibility with existing hardware and software. Otherwise, creating a precise design at this stage is unwise because as the development proceeds new design possibilities or unforeseen 'glitches' are almost certain to arise.

Although the systems analyst is responsible for drawing up the Requirements Specification, he or she needs to ensure that users are closely involved in its development. The systems analyst should listen carefully to users and ensure that their comments and suggestions have been properly interpreted before incorporating the information into the specification.

System design

This stage produces the details of how the system will meet the requirements identified in the previous analysis stage. A major part of this stage involves identifying the inputs to the system (what they are and how they are to be captured), and the outputs from the system, such as reports, invoices, bills and statements. The designers will also specify in detail what files will be needed, their structures and what devices and media will be used to store them. All this information will be written down in the form of reports, tables and diagrams. Such diagrams as system flow charts and data flow diagrams (Chapter 26) will be used to show how the overall system is integrated. The system designers will also provide detailed specifications on what the software is required to do so that programmers in the next stage will have a clear idea of what they are expected to produce.

Software development

Depending on the system requirements, existing software may be purchased or it may be necessary to have software written specially. Software that is already available will usually be much cheaper than software that has to be custom-designed, but in many instances suitable software will not be available. Large organisations frequently employ their own systems analysts and programmers, but smaller firms may have to resort to using a software house for the necessary programs.

System testing

Before the system is put fully into operation, all aspects of it must be tested, not just the software that has been developed, but also the manual procedures involved. Personnel who have not been directly involved in developing the system will often be used to test the system after they have been given some appropriate training; such people may do things that were not anticipated by the system designers. In fact, the people testing the system will often deliberately attempt to make it fail in some way. It is vitally important to discover any serious shortcomings in the new information system before it is fully operational.

System documentation

System documentation serves much the same purposes as program documentation described briefly in the earlier section on software development. All aspects of the system's operation will need to be described in detail. The documentation will include:

❑   user manuals describing the operation of the system;

❑   technical manuals for the computer hardware;

❑   program documentation.

This documentation serves a number of purposes:

❑   To provide reference material for training purposes. This will be of value to all employees using the new system. Each task and procedure will be clearly detailed and explained in terms appropriate to the staff involved.

❑   To explain in detail how the system is intended to work so that the people using the system can cope with problems and unfamiliar situations. This will be of particular value to managers and supervisors responsible for organising the work.

❑ To specify how to test the system to ensure that it is working correctly.

❑ To make it easier to modify or improve the system in future.

Implementing the system

In this stage the system designers will actually install the new system, putting new equipment into operation, installing and setting up software, creating data files and training people to use the system. A common practice is to run the new system in parallel with the old one to ensure that if anything does go wrong, the business will not come to a grinding halt.

When the system has become fully operational, there will still be the possibility of unforeseen events causing problems. The system developers will therefore need to be available to deal with any problems that do arise, as well as making modifications as circumstances change. If an outside firm has developed the system, this system maintenance, normally will be subject to a separate financial arrangement such as an annual charge.

Monitoring and review

The final phase of the system development process is the assessment of the completed system. In this review, or evaluation, a number of factors are examined, including:

❑ How well the system is performing with reference to the needs that were initially identified.

❑ The final cost of the system compared to how much was originally budgeted.

❑ The time taken to complete the work.

Even after the system is fully operational its performance will of course be continually *monitored* throughout its life. At some stage, monitoring will identify needs that are no longer satisfied by the current system, and the system development process will begin once more with a preliminary study.

✍️**Self-test questions**

See end of Chapter 21.

Chapter 21

The Feasibility Study

The traditional purpose of a feasibility study is to determine whether or not the purchase of a computer system can be justified. The study has to answer two fundamental questions: "Can the envisaged applications be carried out by a computer system more efficiently than with existing facilities?"; "Will a computer system be economically viable?". Since the early 1970s, prices of all types of computer system have fallen dramatically and their power has increased to such a degree that, for example, microcomputers challenge the minicomputer in their range of applications. This may be part of the reason why many organisations find it difficult to justify undertaking a detailed feasibility study and argue that no matter how limited their needs there is a computer system to satisfy them at a cost-effective price; it is only necessary to decide on its best application(s). Although this is an understandable view, it should be remembered that any item of equipment should be justified in terms of its costs and benefits to the business and that a computer system should be no exception. Although there are few businesses which cannot benefit from computerisation at all, the process of carrying out a feasibility study disciplines the purchaser to think carefully about how it is to be used.

In modifying the purpose of a feasibility study, the previous questions can be replaced by the following: "Which applications can be computerised to give most benefit to the organisation?"; "What type of computer will be required?"; "What are the likely acquisition and running costs?"; "What are the likely implications, especially those concerning personnel and organisational procedures?".

Pressures for computerisation

There are many and various pressures which can 'trigger' the thought of using a computer, either for the first time or, where a computer is already installed, for other applications still operated manually. Some examples are as follow:

(i)   A business is expanding and to cope with the increased workload it appears that the only the alternative to computerisation is increased staffing.

(ii)   A business is growing at such a rate that more information is needed to manage it properly. To obtain the information manually is too time-consuming and by the time it has been gathered is probably out-of-date.

(iii)   Staff are being asked to work regular and increasing amounts of overtime and backlogs of work are building up.

(iv)   Customers are complaining about the speed and quality of the service provided.

(v)   Where stock is involved, it is difficult to keep track of stock levels and while some customer orders cannot be filled because of stock shortages, other stock is 'gathering dust' on the shelves.

(vi) A great deal of advertising literature is constantly reminding business management that they are out-of-date and at a disadvantage with their competitors.

(vii) Other businesses providing a similar service use a computer.

Examples (i), (ii) and (iii) suggest that the business is operating successfully and needs to take on extra staff or streamline its systems. Examples (iv) and (v) may be symptomatic of generally poor business management and in such cases, computerisation alone may not solve the problems. Examples (vi) and (vii) may tempt the management to computerise simply 'to keep up with the Jones's'. Although a computerisation programme resulting directly from one or more such pressures may be completely successful and worthwhile, the pressure itself should not be the reason for computerisation. Instead, management should establish the organisational objectives they wish to achieve through computerisation.

Establishing objectives for computerisation

It is important for management to establish what they are trying to achieve in terms of the overall objectives of the business and in the light of this, the objectives of the systems which contribute to their achievement. For example, two major business objectives may be to improve the delivery of customers' orders and to minimise the stock levels which tie up valuable cash resources. The achievement of these objectives may involve contributions from several different information processing systems and the list may include the following.

❑ Stock Control - records stock movements and controls stock levels.

❑ Purchasing - responsible for the ordering of new supplies from suppliers.

❑ Sales Order Processing - receives customers' orders and initiates the process of order fulfilment.

❑ Purchase Ledger - the accounting record of amounts owed and paid to suppliers of stock.

❑ Invoicing - the production of invoices requesting payment from customers for goods supplied.

❑ Sales Ledger - the accounting record of amounts owing by and received from customers for goods supplied.

These and other applications within a business are interconnected by the information which flows between them. Such connections can be illustrated with the use of data flow diagrams (DFD), which are described in Chapter 26.

Establishing priorities for computerisation

It is not generally advisable or even practicable to attempt the computerisation of more than one or two applications at the same time, even if they are closely linked. In any case, it is likely that some applications make a greater contribution to the achievement of the required business objectives than do others. Thus, the applications which are going to bring greatest benefit to the business should be computerised first.

Establishing individual system objectives

Before any single application can be computerised, it is necessary to establish its objectives clearly because users may have become so used to its procedures that they no longer question their purpose. It is self-evident that before any informed judgements can be made on the design of a computerised system, the objectives of the relevant application must first be clearly understood.

The following list for stock control serves to illustrate the definition of such objectives.

❑   To maintain levels of stock which will be sufficient to meet customer orders promptly.

❑   To provide a mechanism which removes the need for excessive safety margins of stock to cover customer orders. This is usually effected by setting minimum stock levels which the computer can use to report variations below these levels.

❑   To provide automatic re-ordering of stock items which fall below minimum levels.

❑   To provide management with up-to-date information on stock levels and values of stocks held.

The Feasibility Report

The Feasibility Report should contain the following sections:

Terms of reference

These are statements of the purpose of the proposed system, as agreed by management and detail the business objectives to be achieved, for example:

❑   the improvement of customer service, such that orders are delivered within 24 hours of order receipt;

❑   the provision of more up-to-date management information on current stock levels and projected customer demand;

❑   a tighter control of the business's cash resources, primarily through better stock management.

Applications considered for computerisation

The applications which may assist the achievement of the business objectives set out in the Terms of Reference are listed, for example:

❑   stock control;

❑   purchasing;

❑   sales order processing;

❑   invoicing;

❑   accounts.

The scope of the system should be clearly stated so that the boundaries of the investigation are clearly marked.

System investigations

For each application under consideration there should be:

- ❑ a description of the existing system;

- ❑ an assessment of its good and bad points. For example, the sales order processing system may be slow to process customer orders and this results in poor delivery times, which in turn causes customers to take away their business;

- ❑ an estimate of the costs of the existing system. For example, apart from the cost of staffing, an estimate has to be made of the cost of lost business, which could be avoided with an improved system.

Statement of user requirements

This section should detail, in general terms, those aspects of each application which need to be improved and a broad outline of how each system may operate following computerisation. Of course, it is still possible that not all applications will benefit from computerisation but can be improved by other methods.

Costs of development and implementation

These will include both capital costs and revenue or running costs. Capital costs are likely to be incurred for the following:

- ❑ computer hardware;

- ❑ systems software and software packages (either 'off-the-shelf' or 'tailor-made');

- ❑ installation charges for hardware and software;

- ❑ staff training.

Revenue costs include those for the maintenance and insurance of the system. In addition, unless there are existing computer specialists in the organisation, additional suitable staff may need to be recruited.

Timescale for implementation

This will depend on the scale of the operation, the type of application and whether or not packaged software is to be used.

Expected benefits

These are more difficult to quantify than the costs but may include, for example:

- ❑ estimated savings in capital expenditure on photocopiers or office space.

- ❑ more efficient stock management allows customer service to be maintained whilst keeping stock levels lower. This releases valuable cash resources and reduces possible interest charges on borrowed capital;

❑   expansion in business turnover, without the need for extra staff and reduced overtime requirements.

Other considerations

The staff have to support any development for it to be properly successful and this usually means consultation at an early stage in the feasibility study and the provision of a proper staff training programme. Customers must also be considered. For example, when a customer receives a computer-produced invoice it should be at least as easy to understand as the type it replaced. Assuming that the feasibility study concludes that the proposed computerisation is worthwhile, according to the criteria set out in the report, then more detailed investigation and design can follow.

✍️Self-test questions

These questions also relate to Chapter 20.

1. Briefly describe each of the following stages in the System Life Cycle:
    ☐ Preliminary study
    ☐ Initial investigation and analysis
    ☐ System design
    ☐ Software development
    ☐ System development
    ☐ System documentation
    ☐ Implementing the system
    ☐ Monitoring and review
    What name is given to the main activities of the first stage of the System Life Cycle?

2. Suggest four possible reasons for a company undertaking computerisation of one or more of their systems.

3. Using stock control as an example, list possible objectives for computerisation.

4. List the main sections that might be included in a feasibility report.

Chapter 22

System Investigation and Design

Introduction

If the feasibility report gives the go-ahead to the computerisation project, then a more detailed investigation of each candidate system begins. The facts gathered about each system will be analysed in terms of their bearing on the design and implementation of a computerised version. The objectives of the analysis are to gain a thorough knowledge of the operational characteristics of the current system and to settle, in a fair amount of detail, the way in which a computerised system will operate. It is extremely important that the new system does not simply computerise existing procedures. The design should, as far as possible, ignore existing departmental structures which may inhibit the introduction of different and improved procedures. For example, it may be that customer credit limits are fixed by the Accounts Department and that Sales staff have to refer to the Accounts Department before accepting a customer order. A computerised system may allow Sales staff to access credit limits directly without reference to the Accounts Department. This method could be used in most cases and the computer could indicate any customer accounts which needed to be specially referred to the Accounts staff. The aim of the investigation and design process is to produce a specification of users' requirements in documented form. This is referred to as the Statement of User Requirements and will be used to tender for supply of hardware and software.

Fact-finding methods

There are several methods which can be used to gather facts about a system: (i) interviewing; (ii) questionnaires; (iii) examination of records and procedure manuals; (iv) examination of documents; (v) observation. Each method has its own particular advantages and disadvantages and the method or methods chosen will depend on the specific circumstances surrounding the investigation, for example, the size of the business, the number of staff employed and their location and distribution.

Interviewing

This method has much to recommend it, in that the facts can be gathered directly from the person or persons who have experience of the system under investigation. On the other hand, a business with a number of geographically distributed branches makes the process of extensive interviewing expensive and time-consuming. Further, interviewing skills need to be acquired if the process is to be effective. The interviewer needs to know how to gain the confidence of the interviewee and ensure that the information which is given will be of value in the design of the new system. Questions need to be phrased unambiguously in order that the interviewee supplies the information actually required and a checklist of points will help to ensure that all relevant questions are asked. Of course, the interview may need to stray from the points in the checklist, if it becomes apparent that the interviewee is able to provide relevant information not previously considered. For example, clerical procedures may be designed quite satisfactorily but may be made less effective because of personality conflicts between staff. Such tensions may only be revealed through personal interview.

The interviewer also needs to detect any unsatisfactory responses to questions and possibly use alternative methods to glean the required information. Unsatisfactory responses include:

- ❑ Refusal to answer. Such refusal may indicate, for example, that set procedures are not being followed and that the member of staff does not wish to be 'incriminated'.

- ❑ Answer with irrelevant information. It may be that the question is ambiguous and has to be re-phrased in order to elicit the required information.

- ❑ Answer with insufficient information. If a system is to be designed which covers all foreseeable user requirements and operational circumstances, it is important that the analyst has all relevant information.

- ❑ Inaccurate answer. The interviewer may or may not be aware that an inaccurate answer has been given but it is important that other sources of information are used to cross-check answers.

Questionnaires

Questionnaires are useful when only a small amount of information is required from a large number of people, but to provide accurate responses, questions need to be unambiguous and precise. The questionnaire has a number of advantages over the interview:

- ❑ each respondent is asked exactly the same questions, so responses can be analysed according to the pre-defined categories of information;

- ❑ the lack of personal contact allows the respondent to feel completely at ease when providing information, particularly if responses are to be anonymous;

- ❑ questionnaires are particularly suited to the gathering of factual information, for example, the number of customer orders received in one week;

- ❑ it is cheap, particularly if users are scattered over a wide geographical area.

A number of disadvantages attach to the use of questionnaires:

- ❑ questions have to be simple and their meaning completely unambiguous to the respondents;

- ❑ if the responses indicate that the wrong questions were asked, or that they were phrased badly, it may be difficult to clarify the information, particularly if the respondents were anonymous;

❑ without direct observation it is difficult to obtain a realistic view of a system's operation. The questionnaire often provides only statistical information on, for example, volumes of sales transactions or customer enquiries.

Examination of records and procedure manuals

If existing procedures are already well documented, then the procedure manuals can provide a ready-made source of information on the way procedures should be carried out. It is less likely, however, that procedures will be documented in the smaller organisation. In any event, it is important to realise that procedures detailed in manuals may not accord entirely with what actually happens. The examination of current records and the tracing of particular transactions can be a useful method of discovering what procedures are carried out.

Special purpose records which may involve, for example, the ticking of a box when an activity has been completed, can be used to analyse procedures which are causing delays or are not functioning efficiently. The use of special purpose records imposes extra burdens on staff who have to record procedures as they happen and the technique should only be used when strictly necessary.

Examination of documents

It is important that the analyst examines all documents used in a system, to ensure that each:

❑ fulfils some purpose, that is, it records or transmits information which is actually used at some stage. Systems are subject to some inertia, for example, there may have been a 'one-off' requirement to record and analyse the geographical distribution of customers over a single month and yet the summary document is still completed because no-one told the staff it was no longer necessary;

❑ is clear and satisfies its purpose, for example, a form may not indicate clearly the type of data to be entered under each heading. In any case, it may well require re-designing for any new system which is introduced.

The documents, which should include, for example, source documents, report summaries, customer invoices and delivery notes, help to build a picture of the information flows which take place from input to output.

Observation

It is most important to observe a procedure in action, so that irregularities and exceptional procedures are noticed. Observation should always be carried out with tact and staff under observation should be made fully aware of its purpose, to avoid suspicions of 'snooping'.

The following list details some of the features of office procedures and conditions which may usefully be observed during the investigation:

❑ office layout - this may determine whether the positioning of desks, filing cabinets and other office equipment is convenient for staff and conducive to efficient working;

❑ work load - this should indicate whether the volume of documents awaiting processing is fairly constant or if there are peak periods of activity;

❑ delays - these could show that there are some procedures which are constantly behind schedule;

❑ methods of working - a trained observer can, through experience, recognise a slow, reasonable or quick pace of working and decide whether or not the method of working is efficient. It is important that such observations should be followed up by an interview to obtain the co-operation of the person under observation;

❑ office conditions - these should be examined, as poor ventilation, inadequate or excessive temperatures, or poor lighting can adversely affect staff efficiency.

Often the observation will be carried out in an informal way but it may be useful on occasion to, for example, work at a user's desk, so as to observe directly the way that customer orders are dealt with. It is important to realise that a user may 'put on a performance' whilst under observation and that this reduces the value of the information gathered.

Documenting the results of analysis

A number of standard approaches, apart from narrative description, can be used to document the result of the system analysis, including: *data flow diagrams* (DFDs); *organisation charts*; *system flowcharts*. Their applications are illustrated in the following section, which examines the categories of information which need to be gathered and recorded during a system investigation; data flow diagrams are further examined in Chapter 26.

Categories of system information

The major categories of information which need to be gathered involve:

❑ functional relationships and data flows;

❑ personnel and jobs;

❑ inputs;

❑ processes;

❑ outputs;

❑ storage.

Functional relationships and data flows

A business has a number of functional areas, such as Sales, Accounts, Stock Control and Purchasing, each having its own information system. However, the computerisation of a system in one functional area cannot be carried out without considering its effects on the rest of the business. Information systems within a business interact with and affect one another. The business, as an entity, also interacts with and is influenced by individuals and organisations in the surrounding environment and the business's individual information systems should be co-ordinated to allow the achievement of overall business objectives. The data flows between individual functional areas can be illustrated with the use of a *data flow diagram*.

Personnel and jobs

It is possible to design a computerised system without involving staff, but it is likely to be less successful, partly because users can provide valuable insights into the practical aspects of system operation and partly because they will feel less motivated if they have had little or no influence on the final design.

A formal organisation chart can be used to gain an overall picture of staff relationships and responsibilities but it should be borne in mind that designated and actual job responsibilities can differ radically. For example, it may turn out that a junior sales clerk is carrying out the checking of orders, which should be the responsibility of the sales supervisor. Thus, it may be necessary for the analyst to draw an alternative informal organisation chart to show the actual working relationships of staff. An example is given in Figure 20.1.

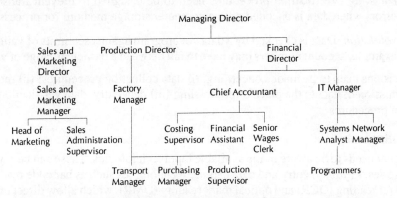

Figure 20.1. *Organisation chart*

Apart from identifying working relationships between staff, it is useful to draw up brief job descriptions so that consultation on individual system procedures can take place with the appropriate staff. For example, a job description for a sales clerk may include the following activities: completion of standard order forms; checking stock availability; notification of orders to accounts. Therefore, although the sales departmental manager may have knowledge of such procedures, the sales clerk will have practical experience of their operation and should be consulted.

System inputs

A number of details concerning the data inputs to a system need to be established:

❏ *source*. It may, for example, originate from a customer, a supplier, or another department in the business;

❏ *form*. The data may arrive, for example, by telephone, letter, or a standard form such as an order form or supplier's invoice;

❏ *volume* and *frequency*. For example, the number of orders received daily or weekly;

❏ *contents*. For example, the individual items of data which appear on a supplier's invoice.

Such information will allow the analyst to make recommendations on the most appropriate methods of computer input. The design of appropriate input methods also has to take account of several tasks involved with the collection and entry of data to a system:

❑   *recording*. For example, the completion of a customer order form following receipt of a customer order by telephone;

❑   *transmission*. For example, the order details may need to be transferred to another department or branch of the business for encoding and computer processing or they may be keyed in directly at the point of collection;

❑   *visual checking*. It may be, for example, that a customer order has no quantities entered;

❑   *encoding*. Verification procedures need to be designed to prevent transcription errors when data is encoded onto a computer storage medium for processing;

❑   *validation*. Data is checked by a data vet program against set limits of validity, for example, account numbers may have to fall between a particular range of values.

Thus, decisions need to be made concerning: (i) data collection procedures; (ii) methods for the transmission of data to the place of processing; (iii) data entry, data verification and data validation procedures.

Data collection

The designer needs to be aware of the available input technologies. These can be divided into two categories, keyboard entry and data capture technologies such as bar code reading, optical character reading (OCR) and optical mark reading (OMR), which allow direct input to the computer from specially designed input forms.

Keyboard entry

This is the most common method of input and requires the transcription of data from source documents. These can be designed to minimise the possibility of transcription errors at the data collection stage.

Direct input

Bar codes are pre-encoded and are thus immune from errors of transcription (assuming that the bar code is correct in the first place). Optical mark reading requires that pencil marks are used to indicate particular values from a limited set on a pre-designed form. Although no keyboard entry is required, mistakes may be made by the originator of the document and good design is therefore important.

Data transmission

It may be that no data transmission is necessary because the data is processed at the point of collection. For example, customer orders may be recorded on order forms at the sales desk and then taken into the next room for keying into the computer. Alternatively, the data may have to be transmitted some distance, perhaps to another floor of the building or to another building some miles away. A fundamental decision has to be made, whether to localise processing at the points of collection, or to use a central facility with data communications links from each location.

Data entry

The data entry method chosen will depend on the data collection methods used and may involve keyboard transcription from source documents or data may be captured directly from bar codes, OCR or OMR type documents. Where keyboard transcription is used, verification and validation procedures are likely to be interactive, in that the data entry operator has to respond to prompts on screen and make corrections as and when the system indicates

Most small business computer systems will be used for on-line processing, where transactions are processed immediately with master files at the data entry stage. Consequently, validation and verification have to be carried out immediately prior to the processing of each transaction.

On-screen verification

At the end of each transaction entry, the operator is given the opportunity to scan the data on the screen and to re-enter any incorrect entries detected. This usually takes the form of a message at the bottom of the screen which is phrased in a way such as Verify (yes or no).

On-screen validation

Character, data item and record checks, such as range and mode checks, can be made each time the RETURN key is pressed during data entry. For example, the screen may prompt for the entry of an account number, which must be 6 digits long and be within the range 000001 to 500000. Any entry which does not conform with these parameters is erased and the prompt re-displayed for another attempt.

Appropriate screen dialogue to allow the data entry operator to enter into a 'conversation' with the computer is a crucial part of the input design process and is dealt with as a separate topic in Chapter .

Batch data entry

The type of keyboard transcription used will be affected by the type of input data. Where, for example, files only need to be updated weekly, transaction data may be batched and entered onto magnetic disk for processing at a later stage in one update program run.

System processes

All the clerical and machine-assisted processes, which are necessary to achieve the desired output from the given inputs, need to be identified. This will allow the systems analyst to determine the role of the computer in the new system, the programs necessary to take over the processing stages and the changes needed to clerical procedures, before and after computer processing.

There are many instances when the processing requires not only the input data but also data retrieved from files. For example, to generate a customer invoice requires:

(i)   input data concerning commodity codes and quantities ordered;

(ii)   data from the stock master file concerning prices of items ordered by reference to the input commodity codes;

(iii)   customer details from the customer master file.

The above processes can be completely computerised but other processes may require human intervention. For example, before a customer order is processed, the customer's credit status may need to be checked and referred to a supervisor before authorisation.

Non-standard procedures

Most processes will follow standards suitable for their particular circumstances. For example, before an order is processed, stock items ordered are checked for availability. It is important, however, that the investigation identifies and notes any non-standard procedures. For example, what procedure is followed when there is an insufficient quantity of an ordered item to completely fulfil a customer order? It may be that some customers will take part-orders, whilst others require the full quantity of an item or none at all. If non-standard procedures are needed, it is important to know their complexity, how often they are used and what extra information is required. Ideally, a system should be designed to cope with all possible circumstances, but cost sometimes forces a compromise. If cost prohibits the inclusion of certain system features, for example, the ability to deal with part-orders, then it is important that the business is aware of such limitations so that it can modify its business objectives.

Document flow

System flowcharts can be used to model the movement and interaction of documents and the data they record, as well as the processes involved, as they pass from one functional area or department of the business to another. In order that the involvement of each section, department or personnel grouping in the processes can be identified, the system flowchart is divided into columns representing these divisions of responsibility.

A system flowchart may use a range of standard symbols which are illustrated in Figure 20.2. A number of standards exist for the drawing of system flowcharts and the range of symbols used depends on which stage of the investigation and design process has been reached. For example, in the early stages of investigation of an existing manual system, there will be no representation of computer methods of input, processing, output or storage. At a later stage, when computer methods are being considered, it will be necessary to use suitable symbols in the flowchart.

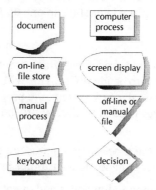

Figure 20.2. *Flowchart symbols*

Figures 20.3 to 20.5 show example system flowcharts. Figure 20.3 illustrates a manually operated order processing and invoicing system.

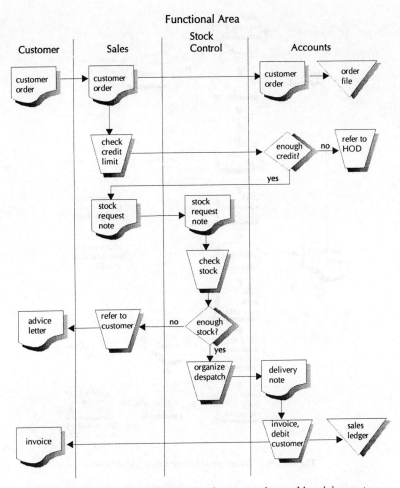

Figure 20.3. *Flowchart of manual order processing and invoicing system*

Figure 20.4 represents a batch processing update of a stock master file. Notice the sorting and validation stages, which are essential to batch processing (transactions are accumulated and processed periodically, rather than as they occur) systems.

Most business systems require alternative actions to be taken dependent upon some variable condition or circumstance. For example, 15 per cent customer discount may be allowed if the invoiced amount is paid within, say, 14 days of the invoice date, after which time all discount is lost.

In order that computerised and non-computerised processes can be properly designed, the investigation must identify all:

❑ decisions made during system operation;

❑ conditions and circumstances which lead to alternative decisions;

❑ actions to be taken following a decision.

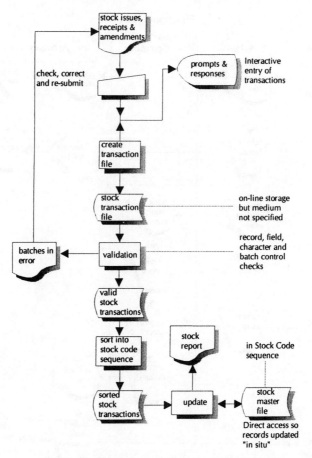

Figure 20.4. *Batch processing stock file update*

Figure 20.5 represents the computerised aspects of a similar system, but does not detail procedures needed to prepare, for example, the data for input or the distribution of output. A computerised system must have the necessary clerical procedures to support it. Some decisions and consequent actions will need to be documented for clerical procedure guidelines, whilst others which involve computer processing will form part of program specifications used in program writing or as bases for choice of packaged software.

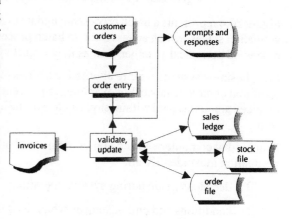

Figure 20.5. *On-line order processing*

System outputs

Output design first requires identification of the following:

❑ data items required as output. Some may be revealed in the existing system, whilst others may be requested by users as being desirable in any new system;

❑ form of the output, for example, whether or not printed copy is required;

❑ volume of data with each output and the frequency of the output. This information assists decisions on the type and number of output devices required.

Based on the above information, the following tasks can be carried out: (i) selection of an appropriate output device to display or communicate the outputs. Available technologies are described in Chapter ; (ii) designing output screen and document layouts. This topic is examined in more detail in Chapter .

System storage (files)

The storage of historic and current information is a vital part of any business system. For example, to produce a payslip not only requires transient input data concerning hours worked and sickness days but also data on rate of pay, tax code, deductions of tax and superannuation to date etc., which are held in the payroll master file stored on magnetic disk. Information on the contents of files will be gathered from existing manual files, together with responses from users regarding the output requirements of any new system. If packaged software is to be used then the contents of files will be dictated by the package, in which case some data item types may be surplus to requirements, whilst others which are required may not be available.

File contents

Each file consists of a number of logical records, each of which has a number of associated data items. For example, each stock record in a stock master file may include: Stock Code; Description; Unit Price; Minimum Stock Level; Re-order Quantity; Quantity in Stock.

File organisation and access

This concerns the logical ordering of records within a file. The available file organisation and access methods are described in Chapter 27.

Database management systems (DBMS)

An increasingly popular alternative to traditional file processing systems is to construct databases controlled by a DBMS. The design process requires that data is analysed according to subject area, for example, raw materials or staffing, rather than by department or functional area. The tools and techniques for database design are examined in Chapter ; the structured analysis and design techniques examined in Chapter 26 are relevant to both database and non-database systems.

Choice of storage device

Choice is concerned with storage capacity, mode and speed of access.

✍ Self-test questions

1. List and briefly describe five fact-finding methods.
2. Briefly describe the following methods of documenting systems:
   - ☐ Data flow diagrams
   - ☐ Organisation charts
   - ☐ System flowcharts
3. Name and briefly describe six categories of information that need to be collected during the fact-finding process.
4. What are the two main technologies used for data collection?
5. Why does the systems analyst need to identify the clerical and machine-assisted processes during fact-finding?
6. What is the purpose of a systems flowchart?
7. What types of information need to be gathered regarding system storage, that is, files?

Chapter 23
Processing Methods

Data processing systems make use of one or more processing methods, depending on the requirements of the application. The methods can be categorised according to the ways in which data is controlled, stored and passed through the system; the major categories are: *batch* processing; *on-line* processing, which includes *real-time* and *time-share* processing; *distributed* processing and *centralised* processing; *database* systems. To allow particular methods of processing a computer must have the necessary *operating system* software; thus any particular computer system is equipped with, for example, a batch processing or real-time operating system, or even a combination of types, depending on the needs of the user organisation.

Batch processing

Such systems process *batches* of data at regular intervals. The data is usually in large volumes and of identical type. Examples of such data are customer orders, current weekly payroll details and stock issues or receipts. The procedure can be illustrated with the example of payroll, which is a typical application for batch processing. Each pay date, whether it is every week or every month, the payroll details, such as hours worked, overtime earned or sickness days claimed, are gathered for each employee (these details are referred to as *transactions*) and processed in batches against the payroll *master file*. The computer then produces payslips for all employees in the company. A major feature of this and similar applications is that a large percentage of the payroll records in the master file are processed during the payroll 'run'. This percentage is known as the *hit rate*. Generally, high hit rate processing is suitable for batch processing and if, as is usual, the master file is organised sequentially, then the *transaction file* will be sorted into the same sequence as the master file. In the case of magnetic tape, transactions must be sorted because the medium only allows *serial* (one record after another in their physical order) access.

The batch processing method closely resembles manual methods of data processing, in that transactions are collected together into batches, sent to the computer centre, sorted into the order of the master file and processed. Such systems are known as traditional data processing systems. There is normally an intermediate stage in the process when the data must be encoded using a *key-to-tape* or *key-to-disk* system. A disadvantage of batch processing is the delay, often of hours or days, between collecting the transactions and receiving the results of processing and this has to be remembered when an organisation is considering whether batch processing is suitable for a particular application. Conversely, batch processing has the advantage of providing many opportunities for controlling the accuracy of data (Chapter 24) and thus is commonly used when the immediate updating of files is not crucial.

On-line processing systems

If a peripheral, such as a Visual Display Unit or keyboard, is *on-line*, it is under the control of the computer's processor or Central Processing Unit (CPU). On-line processing systems therefore, are those where all peripherals in use are connected to the CPU of the main computer. Transactions can be keyed in directly. The main advantage of an on-line system is the reduction in time between the collection and processing of data. There are two main methods of on-line processing: *real-time* processing; *time-share* processing.

Real-time processing

Process control in real-time

Real-time processing originally referred only to process control systems where, for example, the temperature of a gas furnace is monitored and controlled by a computer. The computer, through an appropriate sensing device, responds immediately to the boiler's variations outside pre-set temperature limits, by switching the boiler on and off to keep the temperature within those limits. Real-time processing is now used in everyday consumer goods, such as video cameras, because of the development of the 'computer on a chip', more properly called the *microprocessor*. An important example of the use of the microprocessor is the engine management system, which is now standard on an increasing range of cars. A car's engine performance can be monitored and controlled, by sensing and immediately responding to, changes in such factors as air temperature, ignition timing or engine load. Microprocessors dedicated to particular functions are referred to as *embedded systems*. Further examples of the use of microprocessors can be found on the automated production lines of engineering works and car plants, where operations requiring fine engineering control can be carried out by *computer numerical controlled* (CNC) machines. The important feature common to all real-time applications is that the speed of the computer allows almost immediate response to external changes.

Information processing in real-time

To be acceptable as a real-time information processing system, the *response-time* (that is the time between the entry of a transaction or enquiry at a VDU terminal, the processing of the data and the computer's response) must meet the needs of the user. The delay or response time may vary from a fraction of a second to 2-3 seconds depending on the nature of the transaction and the size of the computer. Any delay beyond these times would generally be unacceptable and would indicate the need for the system to be updated. There are two types of information processing systems which can be operated in real-time: *transaction processing*; *information storage and retrieval*.

Transaction processing

This type of system handles clearly defined transactions singly, each transaction being processed completely, including the updating of files, before the next one is dealt with. The amount of data input for each transaction is small and is usually entered on an *interactive* basis through a VDU. The user can enter queries through the keyboard and receive a response, or the computer can display a prompt on the screen to which the user responds. Such 'conversations' are usually heavily structured and in a fixed format and so do not allow users to ask any question they wish. A typical example of transaction processing is provided by an *airline booking system* and the following may describe a client's enquiry for a seat reservation.

(i)   A prospective passenger provides the booking clerk with information regarding his/her flight requirements.

(ii)   Following prompts on a screen, the clerk keys the details into the system, so that a check can be made on the availability of seats.

(iii)   Vacancies appear on the screen and the·client can confirm the booking.

(iv)   Confirmation of the reservation is keyed into the system, usually by a single key stroke and the flight seating records are immediately updated.

(v)   Passenger details (such as name, address, etc.) can now be entered.

Such a system needs to be real-time to enable reservations to be made at once, while the client is there (or on the telephone) and so that the seating records accurately reflect availability at all times.

Information storage and retrieval

This type of system differs from transaction processing in that, although the information is updated in real-time, the number of updates and the number of sources of updating is relatively small. Consider, for example, the medical records system in a hospital. A record is maintained for each patient currently undergoing treatment in the hospital. Medical staff require the patient's medical history to be available at any time and the system must also have a facility for entering new information as the patient undergoes treatment in hospital. Sources of information are likely to include a doctor, nurses and perhaps a surgeon, and new entries probably do not number more than one or two per day. This is an entirely different situation from an airline booking system where the number of entries for one flight record may be 200-300 and they could be made from many different booking offices throughout the world.

Time-share processing

The term *time sharing* refers to the activity of the computer's processor in allocating *time-slices* to a number of users who are given access through terminals to centralised computer resources. The aim of the system is to give each user a good *response time*. These systems are commonly used where a number of users require computer time for different information processing tasks. The processor time-slices are allocated and controlled by a time-share operating system. The CPU is able to operate at such speed that, provided the system is not overloaded by too many users, each user has the impression that he or she is the sole user of the system. A particular computer system will be designed to support a maximum number of user terminals. If the number is exceeded or the applications being run on the system are 'heavy' on CPU time the response time will become lengthy and unacceptable. Time-share systems are possible because of the extreme speed of the CPU in comparison with peripheral devices such as keyboards, VDU screens and printers. Most information processing tasks consist largely of input and output operations which do not occupy the CPU, leaving it free to do any processing required on other users tasks.

Distributed processing

As the term suggests, a distributed processing system is one which spreads the processing tasks of an organisation across several computer systems; frequently, these systems are connected and *share resources* (this may relate to common access to files or programs, or even the processing of a single complex task) through a data communications system. Each computer system in the network must be able to process independently, so a central computer with a number of remote intelligent terminals cannot be classified as distributed, even though some limited validation of data may be carried out separately from the main computer. Examples of distributed systems include mini or mainframe computers interconnected by way of *wide area networks*, or a number of *local area networks* similarly linked. Distributed systems provide a number of benefits:

Economy. The transmission of data over telecommunications systems can be costly and local database storage and processing facilities can reduce costs. The radical reduction in computer hardware costs has favoured the expansion of distributed systems against centralised systems.

Minicomputers and microcomputers. The availability of minicomputer and microcomputer systems with data transmission facilities has made distributed processing economically viable. An increasingly popular option, in large multi-sited organisations, is to set up local area networks of microcomputers at each site and connect them through communications networks to each other and/or to a central mainframe computer at the Head Office. This provides each site with the advantages of local processing power, local and inter-site communications through *electronic mail* (Chapters and) and access to a central mainframe for the main filing and database systems.

Local management control. It is not always convenient, particularly where an organisation controls diverse activities, to have all information processing centralised. Local management control means that the information systems will be developed by people with direct knowledge of their own information needs. Responsibility for the success or otherwise of their division of the organisation may be placed with local management, so it is desirable that they have control over the accuracy and reliability of the data they use.

Centralised systems

With this type of system, all processing is carried out centrally, generally by a mainframe computer. The continuing reduction in hardware costs and the increase in computer power has led the move towards distributed processing systems. This is achieved through computer networks.

Self-test questions

See end of Chapter 24.

Chapter 24
Data Control

ICT systems present particular problems for the control of data entering the system, because for much of the time this data is not in human-readable form and even when it is stored, the information remains invisible unless it is printed out or displayed on a VDU screen. If proper system controls are not used, users cannot rely on the quality of the information it provides; the phrase 'garbage in garbage out' holds true for any ICT system.

This chapter describes fundamental principles and techniques for controlling the accuracy and validity of data in an ICT system.

Data collection and input procedures

Before describing the controls it is necessary to outline the activities which may be involved in the collection and input of data. Depending on the application these may include one or more of the following:

❏ Source document preparation. To ensure standardisation of practice and to facilitate checking, data collected for input, for example, customer orders, are clerically transcribed onto source documents specially designed for the purpose.

❏ Data transmission. If the computer centre is geographically remote from the data collection point, the source documents may be physically transported there, or be keyed and transmitted through a terminal and telecommunications link to the computer.

❏ Data encoding and verification. This involves the transcription, usually through a keyboard device, of the data onto a storage medium such as magnetic tape or disk; a process of machine verification accompanied by a repeated keying operation assists the checking of keying accuracy. *Key-to-disk* and *key-to-tape* systems are used for encoding, commonly making use of diskette and cassette tape storage, from which media the data is then merged onto a large reel of magnetic tape or a disk pack for subsequent rapid input.

❏ Data input and validation. Data validation is a computer controlled process which checks the data for its validity according to certain pre-defined parameters, so it must be input to the computer first. The topic of validation is examined in more detail later.

❏ Sorting. In order to improve the efficiency of processing, input data is sorted into a sequence determined by the *primary key* of each record in the relevant master file; this is always necessary for efficient sequential file processing, but direct access files allow records to be processed by transactions in the same order that they are received.

Collection and input controls

Transcription of data from one medium to another, for example, from telephone notepad to customer order form, or from source document to magnetic disk, provides the greatest opportunity for error. A number of strategies can be adopted to help limit data collection and input errors, including:

- ❑ minimising transcription. This may involve the use of automated input methods such as bar code reading. Another solution is to use *turnaround documents*, which are originally produced by the computer and later become input documents, for example, remittance advices which, having been sent to customers, are then returned with their payments. Because these remittance advices already show customers' details, including account numbers, only the amounts remitted need to be entered for them to become complete input documents;

- ❑ designing data collection and input documents in ways which encourage accurate completion;

- ❑ using clerical checking procedures such as the re-calculation of totals or the visual comparison of document entries with the original sources of information;

- ❑ using codes with a restricted format, for example, customer account numbers consisting of two alphabetic characters, followed by six digits, permits easy validation;

- ❑ employing *batch* methods of input which allow the accumulation and checking of batch control totals, both by clerical and computerised methods;

- ❑ using screen verification before input data is processed and applied to computer files. Screen dialogue (the form of conversation between the computer and the user) techniques, which allow data verification and correction at the time of entry, can be used to provide this facility;

- ❑ checking input data with the use of *batch* or *interactive* screen validation techniques;

- ❑ ensuring that staff are well trained and that clerical procedure manuals are available for newly trained staff;

- ❑ controlling access to input documents. This is important where documents are used for sensitive applications such as payroll. For example, input documents for changing pay rates should only be available to, say, the Personnel Manager.

File processing controls

Once validated data has entered the computer system, checks have to be made to ensure that it is; (i) applied to the correct files; (ii) consistent with the filed data.

Header records

Files can have header records which detail the function, for example, Sales Ledger, *version number* and *purge date*. The purge date indicates the date after which the file is no longer required and can be overwritten. Thus, a file with a purge date after the current date should not be overwritten. Such details can be checked by the application program to ensure that the correct file is used and that a current file is not accidentally destroyed.

File validation checks

Some validation checks can only be made after data input when reference can be made to the relevant master file data. These are described in the later section on data control in batch processing systems.

Data integrity

The printing of all master file changes allows the user department and auditors to check that all such changes are *authorised* and *consistent* with transaction documents. All data used by applications for reference purposes should be printed periodically; price lists, for example, may be held as permanent data on master files or in table form within computer programs.

Output controls

It might reasonably be supposed that input and file processing controls are sufficient to ensure accurate output. Nevertheless, a number of simple controls at the output stage can help to ensure that it is complete and is distributed to the relevant users on time. They include:

❏ the comparison of *filed* control totals with *run* control totals. For example, when an entire sequential file is processed, the computer counts all processed records and compares the total with a stored record total held in a *trailer record* at the end of the file;

❏ the *conciliation* of control totals specific to the application, with totals obtained from a related application. For example, the sales transactions total posted to the Sales Ledger for one day should agree with the total sales transactions recorded in the Sales Day Book or Journal;

❏ the following of set procedures for the treatment of error reports;

❏ the proper checking and re-submission of rejected transactions.

Data control in batch processing

It is extremely important that all relevant data is processed and that accuracy is maintained throughout the data processing cycle. The controls which are used will depend on the type of processing method in operation, but batch processing provides the greatest opportunity for exerting control over the data, from the input stage through to the output stage. Amongst the control methods outlined above, there are two which are particularly important - *verification* and *validation*. These control methods can be used to maximum advantage in a batch processing system and typical procedures are described in the following section. The stages involved in a batch processing *system cycle* are illustrated in Figure 24.1 with a systems flowchart for a payroll run.

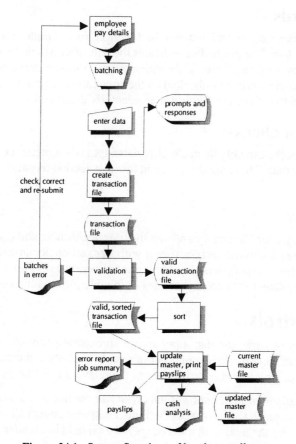

Figure 24.1. *System flowchart of batch payroll system*

The following controls can be used at certain stages within the cycle.

Clerical controls

These can be used at any stage in the cycle when the data is in a human-readable form. The types of check include:

- ❑ visual checking of source documents to detect missing, illegible or unlikely data values, an example of the latter being a total of 100 in the weekly overtime hours entry for an individual worker;

- ❑ the verification of entries by checking them against another source, for example, the price catalogue for the price of a stock item on an invoice;

- ❑ the re-working of calculations on a source document, for example, the checking of additions which make up the total quantity for an item on an order form.

Verification

Before processing, data has to be transcribed from the source documents onto a computer in-put medium, usually involving a keying operation to encode the data onto magnetic tape or magnetic disk. This stage can be prone to error, particularly if large volumes of data are involved and verification, which is usually a machine-assisted process, can ensure that data is encoded accurately. Magnetic tape encoders (*key-to-tape* systems), for example, can operate in two modes, *record* and *verify*. The operation involves one person keying the data in the record mode, after which a second person re-keys the data with the machine in verify mode. In effect the machine reads the data from the first keying operation and then checks it against the second keying as it occurs. The machine signals if characters do not agree, thus indicating a possible transcription error. *Key-to-disk* systems operate on a similar principle, either with stand-alone workstations or through terminals linked to a minicomputer and usually incorporate some facility for *validation* of data.

Validation

This process is carried out after the data has been encoded onto the input medium and involves a program called the *data vet* or *validation program*. Its purpose is to check that the data falls within certain parameters defined by the systems analyst. A judgement as to whether or not data is valid is made possible by the validation program, but it cannot ensure absolute accuracy. That can only be achieved by the use of all the clerical and computer controls built into the system at the design stage. The difference between *validity* and *accuracy* can be illustrated by the following example.

Example of validation

A company has established a Personnel file. Each record in the file may contain a field for the Job Grade. The permitted values of job grade are A, B, C or D. An entry in an individual's record may be *valid* and accepted by the system if it is recorded as A, B, C or D, but of course this may not be the *correct* grade for the individual worker concerned. Whether or not the grade is correct can only be established by the clerical checks discussed earlier.

Types of validation check

Character, field and record checks

❑ *Size*. The number of characters in a field is checked. For example, an account number may require 6 characters and if there are more or less than this, then the item is rejected.

❑ *Mode*. It may be that particular fields must contain particular types of character, for example alphabetic or numeric. If the system is programmed to accept only numbers then letters would be rejected.

❑ *Format*. This refers to the way characters within a field are organised. For example, an Item Code may consist of 2 alphabetic characters followed by 6 numeric characters, so the system would reject any entry which did not correspond to this format.

❑ *Reasonableness*. Quantities can be checked for unusually high or low values. For example, a gas consumer with one small appliance may have a meter reading appropriate to a consumer with a large central heating system and a reasonableness test could be used to reject or highlight it.

❑ *Presence*. If a field must always have a value then it can be checked for existence.

For example, the field 'Sex' in a Personnel record would always have to have an M(ale) or F(emale) entry.

❏ *Range*. Values are checked for certain upper and lower limits, for example, account numbers may have to be between 00001 and 10000.

❏ *Check digit*. An extra digit calculated on an account number can be used as a self checking device. When the number is input to the computer, the validation program carries out a calculation similar to that used to generate the check digit originally and thus checks its validity. This kind of check will highlight transposition errors caused by, for instance, keying digits in the wrong order.

The following example serves to illustrate the operation of one such check digit method.

Modulus 11 check digit example

Consider a stock code consisting of six digits, for example 462137. The check digit is calculated as follows:

(i)   Each digit of the stock code is multiplied by its own weight. Each digit has a weight relative to its position, assuming the presence of a check digit in the rightmost position. Beginning from the check digit position (x) the digits are weighted 1, 2, 3, 4, 5, 6 and 7 respectively, as shown in Table 24.1

Stock Code	4	6	2	1	3	7	(x)
multiplied by weight	7	6	5	4	3	2	(1)
product	28	36	10	4	9	14	

Table 24.1.

(ii)   The products are totalled. In this example, the sum produces 101.

(iii)   Divide the sum by modulus 11. This produces 9, remainder 2.

(iv)   The check digit is produced by subtracting the remainder 2 from 11, giving 9.

Whenever a code is entered with the relevant check digit, the validation software carries out the same algorithm, including the check digit in the calculation. Provided that the fourth stage produces a remainder of zero the code is accepted as valid. This is proved in Table 24.2, using the example in Table 24.1.

Stock Code	4	6	2	1	3	7	9
multiplied by weight	7	6	5	4	3	2	1
product	28	36	10	4	9	14	9

Table 24.2.

The sum of the products in Table 24.2 is 110, which when divided by 11, gives 10, with a remainder of 0. Therefore the number is valid.

If some of the digits are *transposed* (swap positions) the check digit is no longer applicable to the code and is rejected by the validation program because the results of the algorithm will not leave a remainder of zero. This is shown in Table 24.3.

Stock Code	6	4	1	2	3	7	9
multiplied by weight	7	6	5	4	3	2	1
product	42	24	5	8	9	14	9

Table 24.3.

The sum of the products equals 111, which when divided by 11, gives 10 with a remainder of 1. The number is, therefore, invalid.

All the above checks can be carried out prior to the master file updating stage. Further checks on data can be made through the use of a validation program at the *update* stage, by comparison with the master file. They are as follow:

❑ *new records*. When a new record is to be added to the master file, a check can be made to ensure that a record does not already use the entered record key .

❑ *deleted records*. It may be that a transaction is entered for which there is no longer a matching master record.

❑ *consistency*. A check is made that the transaction values are consistent with the values held on the master record which is to be updated. For instance a deduction for pension contributions by an employee who is not old enough to be in a pension scheme would obviously be inconsistent.

Validation using batch controls

Batch totals

The purpose of batch totals is to allow a conciliation of manually produced totals for a batch with comparable computer-produced totals. Differences are signalled and the batch is rejected for checking and re-submission. Following the arrangement of source documents into batches of say 30 in each batch, totals are calculated on add-listing machines for each value it is required to control. On an order form, for example, quantities and prices may be separately totalled to provide two control totals. Totals may also be produced for each account number or item code simply for purposes of control although they are otherwise meaningless. For this reason such totals are called hash or nonsense totals.

The totals are recorded on a *batch control slip* (Figure 24.2), attached to the batch, together with a value for the number of documents in the batch and a batch number. The batch number is kept in a register held by the originating department so that missing or delayed batches can be traced. It should be noted that *hash totals* may produce a figure which has a large number of digits, so extra digits over and above the original length of the data item are truncated.

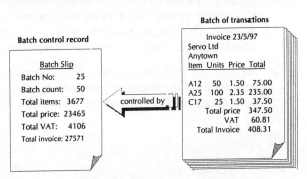

Figure 24.2. *Batch control slip*

Reconciliation of batch totals

The details from each batch control slip are entered with each batch of transactions at the encoding stage. The serial transaction file is processed from beginning to end by the validation program. The sum of the transaction records relating to each batch should match the batch total. If any validation error is detected, either by differences in batch totals or through the character of field checks described earlier, the offending batch is rejected to be checked and re-submitted. Rejected batches are reported on a computer printout.

Validation during updating

Checks can be made in the manner described earlier, on transactions for deleted or new records, or on data which is inconsistent with the relevant record on the master file. These controls can be used in conjunction with proper clerical procedures to ensure that as far as possible, the information stored on the master files is accurate.

File controls

In addition to controlling the accuracy of data entering the system it is essential to check both that the data is complete and that all relevant data is processed. This can be done through the use of file controls on the transaction file.

Following the validation of the batches of transactions, correct batches are written to another file to be sorted and used for updating the relevant master file. During validation, the validation program accumulates totals for all the correct batches. These can be used during the update run to ensure that the whole transaction file is processed.

Validation in on-line systems

On-line systems tend to be interactive and transactions are processed immediately against the master files at the data entry stage. The main controls which can be introduced to such systems include:

❏   the character, field and record validation checks described earlier. Error messages are displayed on the screen at the time data is entered and require immediate correction at that time;

❏   visual verification. At the end of each transaction entry, the operator is given the opportunity to scan the data on the screen and to re-enter any incorrect entries detected. This usually takes the form of a message at the bottom of the screen which is phrased in a way such as "Verify (yes or no)";

❏   the use of well-trained data entry operators. They should have sufficient knowledge of the data being entered and the application it serves, to respond to error messages and make corrections to data accordingly.

Self-test questions

These questions also relate to Chapter 23.

1. Define the term *hit rate* and explain its significance in file processing.
2. Distinguish between batch and transaction processing, using example applications to illustrate your answer.
3. With the aid of an example, describe the main features of an information storage and retrieval system.
4. Differentiate between *batch* and *transaction* processing. Why is batch processing unsuitable for a cinema booking system?
5. Briefly describe the operation of a *time-sharing* system
6. Briefly describe the main characteristics of *distributed processing*.
7. The Acme Group has three subsidiary companies, each involved in different market areas: car production; supermarket chain; transport and distribution. Write a list of brief arguments favouring the use of distributed processing over centralised processing. Why would the Acme Group need to use wide area network facilities?
8. Outline the activities which may be involved in the collection and input of data.
9. What strategies can be adopted to help limit data collection and input errors?
10. A data entry operator is keying in a batch of customer orders. Order Numbers are 4 digits and range from 0001 to 5000. Old order numbers are re-used after completion. One of the Order Numbers is keyed as 3126, instead of 3216.The order entry system uses verification through a key-to-disk system. Once the orders are stored on disk, they are processed by a validation program.
    (i) What type of error has the operator made with the Order Number?
    (ii) Explain how the verification would work and how it may correct the mistake.
    (iii) Describe how a check digit for the Order Number would be calculated and show how it would detect the keying error.
    (iv) Apart from a check digit, suggest one character and one field validation check that could be made on the Order Number.
    (v) Would either of the validation checks you suggested in (iv) pick up this particular error?
11. The same order entry system uses batch controls. What type of batch control is created if the Order Numbers in each batch are totalled?
12. A company holds its payroll files on magnetic tape. Name the file types used in the process.
13. Approximately 300 transactions update (in-situ) a stock master file every hour and a master file backup is taken every 3 hours. The last backup was taken at 1.30 pm. The current master file is corrupted at 4 pm. Describe what needs to be done.

Chapter 25

System implementation, maintenance and review

There are several clearly identifiable areas which require attention in the implementation of a new system, including: file conversion; system testing; staff training; changeover plan - going live.

File conversion

All records to which the computer requires access must be transferred to the appropriate backing storage medium. Records may include those concerning, for example, customer accounting and stock control. The encoding of large files is a time-consuming process and because live transaction data will be continually changing the values in the master files, they may need to be phased into the computer system in stages. In a stock control system, for example, records for certain categories of stock item may be encoded and computer processed, leaving the remainder to be processed by existing methods and encoded at a later stage. If a business has inadequate staffing to cope with the encoding exercise, a computer bureau may be used. Where possible, the bureau's staff should carry out the work on site because the records will be needed for the continued operation of the business. In favourable circumstances, a large scale encoding exercise may be undertaken to initially create the file and then, through an application program, transactions which have occurred since the encoding began can be used to update the file to reflect the correct values. Users will have to be made aware of which records have already been encoded into the system, so that they can properly update them as transactions occur. An additional problem is that records in their existing state may not conform with the file layouts designed for the new system and the data may have to be copied onto special-purpose input forms to assist with accurate encoding.

System testing

Before a system is made fully operational it should be thoroughly tested, generally in stages. If reputable and popular packaged software is being used, then provided it is being used with a wholly compatible hardware configuration, its reliability can probably be assumed. It is essential, however, that the user tests the system with real data from the business. With tailor-made systems, the testing needs to be more complex and lengthy. Once the reliability of the system has been tested, the user should run it with historical data, for which the results of processing are already known. The computerised results can then be checked for accuracy and consistency against the known manual results; software testing is examined in respect of spreadsheet applications in Chapter 11.

Staff training

The education and training of the users of a system is vital if it is to be operated correctly and the full benefits are to be obtained. Generally, although managerial staff will not carry out routine data entry, except in the event of staff sickness, they should possess skills in the operation of a terminal, desk-top or notebook microcomputer, to allow them, for example, to make database enquiries. The supplier should provide training for everyone connected with the computer system, so that they are aware of its functions and are confident in its use. In the main, this will consist of computer operating skills for data entry staff, but those receiving computer output need to know what to expect and to be able to interpret it readily. Deciding when to carry out the training can be difficult. If too early, some staff will have forgotten what they have been taught by the time the system is introduced. If too late, staff may feel panicked because they have not been properly prepared.

System changeover

Switching from the old to the new system can be carried out in stages or all at once. There are three generally recognised approaches to going live: parallel running; pilot running; direct changeover.

Parallel running

With this approach, the old and new systems are run concurrently and the results of each are compared with the other for accuracy and consistency. The old system is not abandoned until the user has complete confidence in the reliability and accuracy of the new one. Obviously, parallel running places a great administrative strain on the business, in that staff are effectively doing many of the jobs twice. Any inconsistencies in results have to be cross-checked and the source of errors located (they may result from the old or the new system). The major advantage of parallel running is that the old system can be used whenever the computer system crashes or fails to function as it should. However, the two systems cannot operate together indefinitely and "Murphy's Law" will probably ensure that some errors only become apparent after the old system has been abandoned. In conclusion, it can be said that parallel running provides a safe, but expensive and time consuming, method of switching systems. It is unlikely that many businesses will use it for any extended period, except where system failure would be completely catastrophic.

Pilot running

This strategy requires that only a portion of live transactions go through the new computerised system, the rest being processed by the old method. Thus, for example, the transactions for one section of the business, or a sample of transactions from the whole business, could be used to test the system. This is a reasonably safe strategy but again, the transactions which cause errors may be amongst those which do not pass through the computer system.

Direct changeover

This is the riskiest option in that the new system completely replaces the old, without any interim parallel or pilot running. Its major benefit is the lack of administrative costs experienced with the other two methods. The potential costs can be severe, in that system failure could mean complete loss of data access and business failure. To minimise these risks, changeover should be preceded by careful system testing and thorough staff training. It is also helpful if the changeover is carried out during a slack period so that staff are not under pressure. The considerable cost of parallel and pilot running mean that this, the riskiest strategy, is often used in small businesses.

System maintenance

Following its initial introduction, a system will not remain static and dealing with the necessary changes is termed *system maintenance*. Problems will probably become apparent as the system is operated but even if they do not, the information needs of the business will probably change after a time. Some changes will come from within the business, as staff and management identify new possibilities for the system, whilst others may be forced upon the organisation because of changes in the strategies of competitors or government legislation. The most important catalyst for change is probably the desire for better and more timely information by management, to assist their decision-making and planning. Maintenance may concern updating of hardware or amendment of software. The hardware purchased should be expansible and the software should, ideally, be flexible enough to allow amendments to be made. Often, where packaged software is used the manufacturer provides, either free or more usually for an additional payment, upgraded versions of the software with extra features (this can be a supplier-led method of system maintenance).

System review

The final phase of the system development process is the assessment of the completed system. In this *review*, or *evaluation*, a number of factors are examined, including:

❑   How well the system is performing with reference to the needs that were initially identified.

❑   The final cost of the system compared to its original budget.

❑   The time taken to complete the work.

Even after the system is fully operational its performance is continually *monitored* throughout its life. At some stage, monitoring will identify needs that are no longer satisfied by the current system, and the system development process will begin once more with a preliminary study.

Self-test questions

1. Why is thorough testing of tailor-made software more important than testing reputable, popular packaged software.
2. Using a sales order processing system as an example,
3. Identify two difficulties for system users at the file conversion stage.
4. Suggest two alternatives an organisation may choose from when considering staff training for a new system. Identify one advantage and one drawback of each alternative.
5. Acme plc is introducing a new customer invoicing system. It is vital that there is continuity between the old and the new systems. Short-term failure of the system would cause extreme difficulty, but any extended failure would be catastrophic. Identify the changeover alternatives and select the most appropriate for Acme plc.

Chapter 26
Structured analysis tools

Data analysis - entity relationship models

Data analysis is a technique primarily concerned with determining the *logical structure* of the data, its *properties* and the *processes* needed to make use of it. Its objective is to produce a model which represents the information needs of a particular information system or sub-system and it should be understandable by users as well as analysts, in order to provide a basis for discussion and agreement. The main tool used within data analysis is the *Entity-Relationship Modelling (ERM)*, which classifies information into:

❑ entities;

❑ attributes;

❑ relationships.

Entities are objects which are of interest or relevance to the organisation, for example, Supplier, Customer, Stock. An entity will normally equate with a database table; an *entity occurrence* is normally synonymous with a *record* within that table.

Attributes comprise those properties of an entity which are identified as being of interest to users. It may be helpful to equate attributes with fields in a conventional record, but it is important to note that in database systems (where the term data item type is sometimes used), it is not always necessary to have all the attributes for an entity stored in the relevant record in the database; it is necessary, however, to ensure that all attributes relevant to a particular entity can be associated with it.

Relationships exist between entities. For example, an Employee works for a particular Department and a Purchase Order is sent to one particular Supplier. The degree of the relationship may be one-to-one, one-to-many (or the reverse, many-to-one), or many-to-many.

The practical application of this analysis is that the entities, attributes and relationships are used to determine the tables, fields and foreign keys (Chapter 29) which will define the database.

One-to-one relationship

Figure 26.1 provides an example of a one-to-one relationship. Each hospital patient develops a unique medical history and each medical history can only relate to one hospital patient.

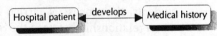

Figure 26.1. *One-to-one relationship*

One-to-many relationship

Figure 26.2 illustrates that an order may comprise one or many order lines, but each order line will be unique to a particular order. Note the double arrow head to indicate the *many* side of the relationship. By many, we mean one or more, whereas one means one only.

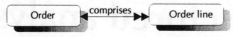

Figure 26.2. *One-to-many relationship*

Many-to-many relationship

A stock item may be ordered in a number of purchase orders and a single purchase order may
include a number of stock items. This is symbolised in Figure 26.3.

Figure 26.3. *Many-to-many relationship*

Some of the practical implications of these relationship types are explained in the *Stock Control* case study in Chapter 30 (Editing Tables through Query Dynasets).

An ERM for a given information system or sub-system may consist of a number of entities, the attributes associated with each and the relationships between those entities. The modelling process requires that any given model is continually refined until its efficiency in satisfying users' needs is optimised and its structure is in a form dictated by the requirements of the RDBMS in use.

An ERM for an Academic database

Figure 26.4 shows a normalised (Chapter 29 entity relationship diagram (representing the ERM) for the *Academic* database outlined in Chapter 29.

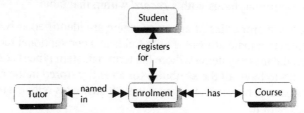

Figure 26.4. *Normalised ERM for Academic database*

The diagram can be interpreted as follows.

❏   Each student registers for one or more enrolments, but each enrolment relates to only one student. This is a one-to-many relationship, the enrolments being the many side. The single arrow head indicates the one side and the double headed arrow, the many side.

❏   Each tutor is named in many enrolments, but each enrolment only names one tutor; this is also a one-to-many relationship. Although tutors are assigned students, the process is carried out through the enrolment entity, so there is no direct relationship between the Student and Tutor entities; instead the connection is through the Enrolment entity. This structure is arrived at through the normalisation process.

❏   Each course has many enrolments, but each enrolment only concerns one course. Therefore, there is a one-to-many relationship between the Course and Enrolment entities.

An ERM for a Personnel database

Figure 26.5 is an entity relationship diagram for the *Personnel* database, used as a tutorial case study in Chapter 31.

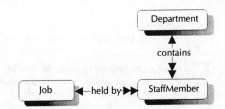

Figure 26.5. *Normalised ERM for Personnel database*

The diagram shows the following relationships between the three entities.

❏   Each department contains many staff, but each member of staff is based in a single department - a one-to-many relationship between Department and StaffMember.

❏   Each job (job title or grade) is held by one or more members of staff, but each member of staff has only one job title. The relationship between Job and StaffMember is also one-to-many.

The ERMs shown in Figures 26.4 and 26.5 illustrate database structures after data normalisation. They can be drawn at various stages of the modelling process, to help clarify the entities which are needed and the relationships which arise between them. Thus, an ERM drawn for the Academic database after the first stage of normalisation (1NF), would only show the Student and Enrolment entities (see Chapter 29). The second and third stages of normalisation are fine-tuning the structure, but it must be in first normal form (no repeating groups) before you can attempt to construct a database. Entity relationship modelling can be a complex process, which requires much training and experience, so at this stage, you are likely to be constructing databases from fully normalised ERMs.

Data flow diagrams (DFDs)

Figure 26.6 shows some typical, standard symbols for the drawing of data flow diagrams. DFDs are used to illustrate, in a diagrammatic form, the logical data flows between entities, accompanying processes and any file storage or data stores.

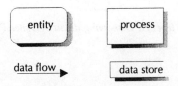

Figure 26.6. *DFD symbols*

DFDs can be used at various stages in the analysis and design process. In the early stages, they will be at a high level and may, for example, show little detail except for a department's general function, such as sales accounting or stock control; later, DFDs may be drawn at a lower, more detailed level, to show for example, the checking of a customer's account before sending an invoice reminder or statement of account.

Figure 26.7 shows a *high level* DFD for a typical trading organisation. More details on the data flows in its Sales Order Processing system are shown in the low level DFD in Figure 26.8.

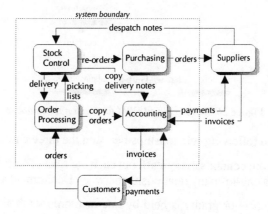

Figure 26.7. *High level DFD for trading business*

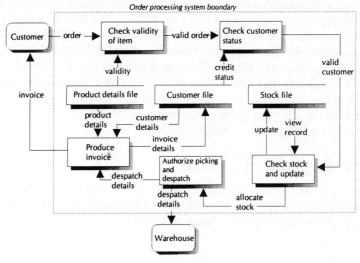

Figure 26.8. *Low level DFD showing detail of Order Processing System*

Normalisation

Normalisation (see Chapter 29) is a technique which is particularly useful in the design of relational database models. It is used to determine the validity of the logical data model produced in the data analysis stage and is particularly concerned with:

❏ minimising data redundancy or duplication;

❏ establishing dependencies between data items and grouping them in the most efficient way;

❏ obtaining a measure of data independence, such that a database can be supplemented with new data without changing the existing logical structure and thus the applications programs.

CASE (computer-aided software engineering) tools

Software engineering is a concept which recognises the fact that the principles of engineering normally applied to other disciplines, can be highly relevant to the 'engineering' of information systems; the parameters for the effectiveness and quality of an information system have to be set at the design stage, if users' needs are to be properly met.

A CASE tool can loosely refer to any software tool used in the development of information systems, for example:

❏ language processors (compilers and interpreters);

❏ fourth generation languages (4GLs);

❏ graphics programs to allow analysts to draw DFDs or ERMs.

A more precise definition of the term requires reference to the typical features of CASE proprietary software; complete CASE packages or toolkits are commercially available to aid the systems analyst and/or programmer in system development.

A CASE toolkit would normally contain components for:

❏ diagram construction;

❏ data dictionary development and control;

❏ interface generation;

❏ source code generation;

❏ project management.

Diagram construction

This tool is essential for the support of a structured systems methodology. The graphical facilities allow the drawing, storage and modification of diagrams and charts, such as data flow diagrams (DFDs), entity-relationship models (ERMs) and data structure diagrams (for program development).

Data dictionary

Being particularly important in the development of database systems for the control and consistency of data, the function of data dictionaries is described in Chapter 26 and illustrated in Chapter 31.

Interface generation

Interface generators support the preparation of prototypes of user interfaces, such as screen dialogues, menus and reports.

Source code generation

These tools allow the automated preparation of computer software, in other words, the conversion of a system specification into the source code of a chosen programming language, which can then be compiled into executable object or machine code. CASE tools for code generation are general purpose and are, as a consequence less efficient in the production of source code than specialised applications generators; most code generators will only produce, say, 75% of the code automatically, leaving the rest to be hand-coded by a programmer.

Project management

Such tools support the scheduling of analysis and design activities and the allocation of resources to the various project activities.

Integrated CASE tools

CASE tools can be used as separate, discrete elements or as a complete system. The integrated use of CASE tools can best be managed through windowing software, which allows, for example, the simultaneous viewing of data flow diagrams and data dictionary entries on screen. Integration also has the benefit of allowing data from one component of the toolkit to be transferred to another, for example, data dictionary entries to entity-relationship diagrams.

Process models

Process models describe tasks that can be broken down into logical sequences of activities. Such models can be used to describe computer processing tasks that require computer programs, purely manual systems or combinations of both. There are many forms of process models; here we describe four of them:

- ❏   Structured English
- ❏   Structure charts
- ❏   Flowcharts
- ❏   Decision tables.

Structured English

Structured English, and a similar form of notation (not discussed here) called pseudocode, uses a technique called top-down, stepwise refinement to analyse and describe processes. Structured English involves first describing a task in terms of a sequence of simpler tasks each of which, in turn, is further broken down into simpler tasks. This process of successive refinement of tasks continues until there is sufficient detail for the resulting description to be of practical use. In the case of describing a solution method for a computer programming task, that is defining an *algorithm*, the task refinement process halts when there is sufficient detail to allow the algorithm to be easily converted into a computer program; this is usually when a task is one simple action that cannot easily be refined further. Keywords such as `if`, `while` and `do`, are used to specify standard programming constructs. Line indentation and delimiters such as `endif` and `endwhile` are used to designate the extent of blocks of instructions governed by keywords..

To illustrate the syntax of Structured English and its use in defining a computer programming problem, we will analyse the following example:

The sales details for a number of company sales representatives are held as a set of records in a computer file. Each record in the file contains the following data:

- ❏ name (of rep)
- ❏ item-code (a six-digit numeric code)
- ❏ units-sold (number of units of this item sold)
- ❏ value (value of this sale)

There may be several such records in the file for each sales representative. The records in the file are ordered according to sales representative, ie all the records for a particular salesperson are grouped together, and they are in alphabetical order of sales representative name. Sales representatives receive commission on their total sales value. This commission depends on code of the item sold. For codes of 100000 - 199999 commission is calculated at 10%, for codes of 200000 - 299999 the commission is 15% and for codes of 300000 - 399999 the commission is 20%.

A report is to be produced giving the total sales value and commission due to each salesperson, and the grand totals of sales values and commissions for all the salespersons. The report is to have the following structure:

ACME COMPUTER SERVICES

SALES REPORT March 2000

Salesperson	Total sales value	Commission
Moray, R	1334.90	133.49
Scott, P Y	2452.76	245.28
Smith, J	1213.55	121.36
Williams, I	1668.22	166.82
Winns, J R	1167.23	116.72
Tyson, M	932.34	93.23
GRAND TOTALS	8769.00	876.90

The file to be processed has the form illustrated below:

Name	Item	Sold	Value
Moray, R	100232	5	725.00
Moray, R	301567	3	609.90
Scott, P Y	200234	2	1204.40
Scott, P Y	223045	1	605.00
Scott, P Y	301067	4	652.20
Smith, J	122077	5	1213.55
Winns, J R	356099	8	400.00
Winns, J R	367234	4	334.00
Winns, J R	100034	2	433.23
Tyson, M	301023	8	932.34

Adopting a top-down approach, that is first identifying the main processes involved in producing the report, the report program can be described as a sequence of three tasks:

```
report program
        1. print headings
        2. process report body
        3. print grand totals
END report program
```

Each of these three steps needs to be further refined, particularly the second step which involves processing a file of records.

```
report program
1. print headings
        1.1. print page headings
        1.2. print column headings
2. process report-body
        while more sales reps to process do
        2.1. process salesrep records
        2.2. print detail line
        2.3. Accumulate sales value and commission grand totals
        endwhile
3. print grand totals
        3.1. print sales value
        3.2. print commission
end report program
```

This second level of refinement introduces a processing loop which is defined by while..endwhile. Because there are a number of sales reps, step 2 involves repeatedly processing the records for each rep and printing the details for that rep. All of the steps between while and endwhile are repeated until there are no more reps to process..

After this second level of refinement, the first and the third tasks are sufficiently detailed. However, the second step still requires more detail. Firstly, we need to define step 2.1., how to process a sales rep's records.

```
2.1 process salesrep records
        while more sales records do
        2.1.1. read sale value
        2.1.2. add sale value to sales total
```

```
        2.1.3. calculate commission
        2.1.4. add commission to commission total
endwhile
```

This step involves another loop in which each record in turn for the current rep being is read. The record is processed by accumulating the reps sales value for the item just read and calculating and accumulating the commission due for that sale. This process repeats until there are no more records for that rep. Steps 2.2.and 2.3, shown below, are then completed.

```
2.2. print detail line
        2.2.1. print sales rep name
        2.2.2. print total sales value
        2.2.3. print total commission
2.3. Accumulate sales value and commission grand totals
        2.3.1. add total sales value to sales value grand total
        2.3.2. add total commission to commission grand total
```

The final level of refinement is to specify precisely how commission is calculated. We refine step 2.1.3 calculate commission as follows:

```
2.1.3 calculate commission
        2.1.3.1 case item-code
                100000 to 199999: calculate commission @ 10%
                200000 to 299999: calculate commission @ 15%
                300000 to 399999: calculate commission @ 20%
        endcase
```

The value of item-code determines which one of the three possibilities is selected so that the appropriate commission will be calculated.

We are now in a position to define the complete algorithm for the report program:

```
report program
1. print headings
    1.1. print page headings
    1.2. print column headings
2. process report-body
    while more salesreps to process do
        2.1. process salesrep records
        while more sales records to process do
            2.1.1. read sale value
            2.1.2. add sale value to sales total
            2.1.3. calculate commission
                2.1.3.1 case item-code of
                    100000 to 199999: calculate commission @ 10%
                    200000 to 299999: calculate commission @ 15%
                    300000 to 399999: calculate commission @ 20%
                endcase
            2.1.4. add commission to commission total
        endwhile
        2.2. print detail line
            2.2.1. print sales rep name
            2.2.2. print total sales value
            2.2.3. print total commission
        2.3. accumulate sales value and commission grand totals
            2.3.1. add total sales value to sales value grand total
            2.3.2 add total commission to commission grand total
    endwhile
```

```
3. print grand totals
   3.1. print sales value
   3.2. print commission
end report program
```

Note that the only actions that are performed are those that are not further refined. For instance, in step 3 above, 3.1 and 3.2 define precisely how to `print grand totals`, and step 3 itself is simply a description of the two refined steps, not an action to be performed.

Structured English constructs

Our example illustrates the three Structured English constructs of:

❑   Sequence - a set of instructions performed in order of appearance

❑   Selection - the `case` statement used for calculating commission

❑   Iteration - the `while` statements that defined instructions to be repeated

In the following amplifications of these three terms, the word *statement* refers to a single instruction which can either be a single action, a selection or an iteration. As you will see, this means that any one of the above three constructs can contain, nested within the block of instructions that it governs, any of the other constructs. Thus these three simple constructs are capable of being used to define algorithms of almost any degree of complexity.

Sequence

This is simply one or more actions performed in the order in which they appear. For instance, the following four actions constitute a sequence:

```
2.1.1. read sale value
2.1.2. add sale value to sales total
2.1.3. calculate commission
2.1.4. add commission to commission total
```

Selection

This involves selecting one course of action from two or more when a decision needs to be made. In our example, the commission rate for a sales item was determined by the item's code number. The `case` statement used specified that the commission was to be selected from three alternatives which depended on the value of `item-code`:

```
2.1.3 calculate commission
    2.1.3.1 case item-code of
        100000 to 199999: calculate commission @ 10%
        200000 to 299999: calculate commission @ 15%
        300000 to 399999: calculate commission @ 20%
    endcase
```

Each case in a `case` statement can comprise a number of statements, not just one.

An alternative form of selection statement is the `if` statement which is more convenient when there are only one or two possible courses of action. The `if` statement has the form:

```
if <conditional expression> then
    <statements>
else
    <alternative statements>
endif
```

If the <conditional expression> is true, then the first statement or block of statements is performed, otherwise the alternative statement or statements are performed.

For example, we could write

```
if tax-code = 4 then
        VAT=17.5%
else
        VAT=0%
endif
```

Iteration

This is another name for performing a loop in which a block of statements are repeated until a specified condition is true. In our example, this took the form of a while statement that de- fined a loop for processing each sales rep in turn. The condition that specified when to exit the loop and continue with the next statement following endwhile was

(*while*) more sales reps to process *(do)*

Another example of a while loop is shown below.

```
set count = 0
while count is less than 10 do
    .........
    add 1 to count
endwhile
```

This is a loop which repeats exactly ten times before exiting. The count is called a *variable* whose value can be modified within the algorithm. In this case, count is incremented every time the loop instructions are repeated and it is used within the while condition to determine when the loop is to be exited.

Note that if the while condition is already true before the while statement is encountered, the loop exits without obeying any of the instructions within the loop.

Alternative forms of loops, such as repeat..until and for..next are sometimes used as alternatives to the while loop; however, they are really just variations of while that are use- ful when the target computer language contains similar constructs.

Structure charts

A Structure Chart is a diagrammatic form of a Structured English algorithm. Rectangles or- ganised into a tree structure are used to represent the problem solution. Again, sequence, selection and iteration constructs are nested within one another to enable complex problem solutions to be illustrated. Figure 26.9 shows the sales rep problem that was discussed in the previous section as a Structure chart. Note the symbols '*' and 'o' placed in top right-hand corners of some of the rectangles to indicate iterations and selections respectively. In the case of a selection, only one of the circle boxes is chosen, depending on the condition indicated above the boxes. The asterisk indicates that all boxes connected to it are to be repeated while the specified condition is true. Structure charts are also developed using top-down, stepwise refinement as discussed earlier.

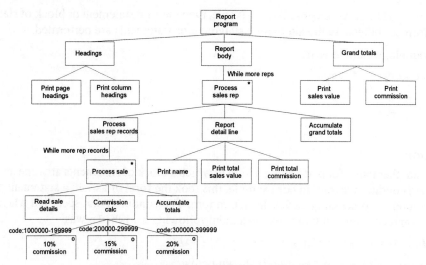

Figure 26.9. *Structure chart of sales rep problem*

The structure chart is read from top to bottom and left to right, the rectangles that are not further refined being actions to perform. Thus the order of execution of the actions shown in the chart is:

1. Print page headings

2. Print column headings

3. Read sale details 1 for sales rep 1

4. Calculate 10% or 15% or 20% commission depending on item code 1

5. Accumulate value and commission totals

6. Read sale details 2 for sales rep 1

7. Calculate 10% or 15% or 20% commission depending on item code 2

8. Accumulate value and commission totals

        (repeat steps 3-8 for rest of records for sales rep 1)

9. Print summary line for sales rep 1

10. Accumulate grand totals for sales value and commission

11. Read sale details 1 for sales rep 2

12. Calculate 10% or 15% or 20% commission depending on item code 1

13 Accumulate value and commission totals

14. Read sale details 2 for sales rep 2

15. Calculate 10% or 15% or 20% commission depending on item code 2

16. Accumulate value and commission totals

        repeat steps 11-16 for rest of records for sales rep 2

17. Print summary line for sales rep2

18. Accumulate grand totals for sales value and commission

      repeat for rest of sales reps

19. Print sales value grand total

20. Print commission grand total

Being a graphical interpretation of a problem, Structure Charts can provide a more convenient and easily understood interpretation of a problem than that obtained using Structured English.

The Flowchart, discussed in the next section, is also a visual problem solving tool.

Flowcharts

A flowchart can be used to represent any well-defined sequence of activities. In the context of computer programming, a flowchart is used to convey in diagrammatic form, the logic, processing operations and flow of control required of a computer program.

Flowcharts are used by programmers in two main ways:

❑   to plan the structure of a program before it is written;

❑   to describe the structure of a program after it has been written.

The first use is primarily for the benefit of the programmer to aid program design; the second use is to document program structure in a form that anyone with an understanding of the symbols used will be able to understand.

However, a flowchart can be used to convey a sequence of events unconnected to computer programming. The next example illustrates such a use. Though rather frivolous, Figure 26.10 (see next page) illustrates how a flowchart can show the logical order in which the actions involved in "Questioning a Suspicious Person" are to be performed by a police constable.

To read the flowchart you follow the direction indicated by the arrows. A diamond shaped box indicates a point where a decision, leading to one of two different routes, has to made. The question to be asked at a decision point is written inside the box, and the only possible answers are indicated on the two lines leading from the decision symbol. The question inside the box needs to be phrased in such a way that there can be only two possible answers such as Yes (Y) and No (N) or Male (M) and Female (F), as illustrated in the figure.

Loops, that is, repeated sections of the flowchart, are indicated by lines leading back to a previously encountered section. For example, the policemen is required to say "Hello" three times, so this is shown by a loop in which the question, "Said Hello 3 times?" is asked inside a decision box. After going around the loop three times, the answer to the question is "Yes" and you can continue to the next box. If a flowchart is too big to be shown as a single diagram, it can be split into a number of sections using connectors shown by circles containing numbers or letters. When you come to a connector you simply continue at the next section starting with the same number or letter.

When a flowchart is being used to represent the operation of a computer program, it is usual to use one further symbol for input or output operations, that is, where information has to be read in to the computer or is to be produced by the computer so that it can be read by us.

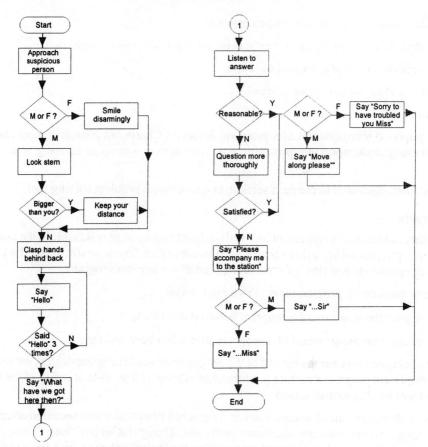

Figure 26.10. *Questioning a suspicious person*

The minimum set of symbols used in flowcharts is shown in Figure 26.11.

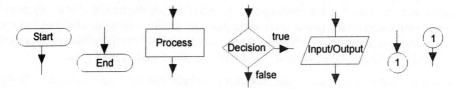

Figure 26.11. *Basic flowcharting symbols*

The oval symbols are used to indicate the start or end of a process. The rectangle represents a calculation or other processing operation, the nature of which is written inside the box. The diamond shape shows that a decision is to be made between two alternatives, and the criteria for making the decision is shown inside the symbol. Any input or output operations are shown by the parallelogram. Finally, a small circle containing a number or letter is used to split a large flowchart into smaller parts.

Now suppose that the requirement is to write a computer program to read and calculate the average of one thousand numbers.

Figure 26.12 illustrates how a flowchart can summarise a lengthy process by using a loop.

Notice that the arrows on the lines joining the symbols show the direction to follow when reading the flowchart, and that the decision box provides the means by which a loop can be introduced. This example introduces the idea of using a variable, namely Count, as a counter which starts at a value of zero and increases by one every time a number (Num) is read. The expression, Count = Count + 1, is a form that is used very frequently in computer programming, and it simply means that the value of Count is to be replaced by its current value plus one. That is, Count is to be incremented by 1. A third variable, Total, also initially set to zero, accumulates the numbers as they are read in: Total = Total + Num simply means "replace the value of Total by its current value plus Num.

For example, if the first five numbers to be read in were 3, 2, 4, 6 and 9, then the following table shows the values three variables Count, Num and Total change:

When 1000 numbers have been read, Count will be equal to 1000 and Total will be the sum of all the numbers. The average value is found by dividing the sum of the numbers by the number of numbers, that is, Total H Count.

Decision boxes can also show how to cope with different situations that might occur during some processing activity. For instance, suppose that a program is required to calculate the selling price for some item which may or may not be VAT rated. The flowchart fragment in Figure 26.13 shows how this situation could be represented.

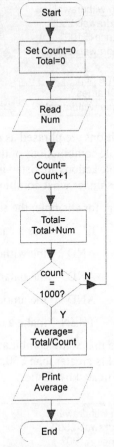

Figure 26.12. *A flowchart to find the average of 1000 numbers*

Decision tables

As an alternative, or even supplement, to a flowchart, a program designer might use a decision table to define the logical requirements of a program. A decision table identifies possible combinations of conditions that might arise, and defines what action must be taken in each case.

Suppose that a bank uses the following procedure for determining charges on transactions for its deposit account customers:

There is a charge of 50p for each cash withdrawal unless the account is in credit by at least £100, in which case there is no charge. If the customer would become overdrawn as a result of the cash withdrawal, the transaction is not allowed and no charge is made. The maximum cash withdrawal allowed at any one time is £50. If the transaction is a deposit, no charge is made.

A decision table for the logic might look like this:

Cash withdrawal?	y	y	y	y	y	y	y	y	n	n	n	n	n	n	n	n
Withdrawal>£50?	y	y	y	y	n	n	n	n	y	y	y	y	n	n	n	n
Balance<£100?	y	y	n	n	y	y	n	n	y	y	n	n	y	y	n	n
Withdrawal>Balance?	y	n	y	n	y	n	y	n	y	n	y	n	y	n	y	n
Charge 50p						x										
No Charges							x	x	x	x	x	x	x	x	x	x
Refuse withdrawal	x	x	x	x	x											

Conditions are phrased as questions and appear in the top left-hand quarter of the table. All possible combinations of the answers (Yes or No) are listed in the top right-hand quarter. All possible actions are listed in the bottom left-hand quarter. An x in the bottom right quarter indicates under what combinations of conditions the action is to be performed.

Taking, for example, the sixth column of y/n combinations, it shows that

IF   it is a cash withdrawal

AND   the withdrawal is not greater than £50

AND   the balance is less than £100

AND   the amount of the withdrawal is not greater than the current balance

THEN   make a charge of 50p

Notice that some combinations of conditions are not relevant. For example, if a cash withdrawal is greater than £50, then the final two conditions are irrelevant. Irrelevant conditions are indicated by dashes:

Cash withdrawal?	y	y	y	y	y	y	y	y	n	n	n	n	n	n	n	n
Withdrawal>£50?	y	y	y	y	n	n	n	n	-	-	-	-	-	-	-	-
Balance<£100?	-	-	-	-	y	y	n	n	-	-	-	-	-	-	-	-
Withdrawal>Balance?	-	-	-	-	y	n	-	-	-	-	-	-	-	-	-	-
Charge 50p						x										
No Charges							x	x	x	x	x	x	x	x	x	x
Refuse withdrawal	x	x	x	x	x											

Notice also that several combinations are now repeated so that the table could be summarised as

Cash withdrawal?	y	y	y	y	n
Withdrawal>£50?	y	n	n	n	-
Balance<£100?	-	y	y	n	-
Withdrawal>Balance?	-	y	n	-	-
Charge 50p			x		
No Charges				x	x
Refuse withdrawal	x	x			

When drawing decision tables it is important to ensure that all combinations of conditions have been included. The maximum number of combinations is calculated as follows:

Number of conditions	Combinations
2	2x2=4
3	2x2x2=8
4	2x2x2x2=16
5	2x2x2x2x2=32
etc	

There is also a certain way of writing these combinations so that all of them are covered:

1. Determine the maximum number of combinations;

2. Halve this number;

3. Along the first condition line write this number of y's followed by the same number of n's until the line is complete;

4. Halve this number;

5. Repeat steps (3) and (4) until the final condition line consisting of alternate y's and n's has been completed.

For example, suppose there are 3 conditions, then the number of combinations is $2x2x2 = 8$. Half of this is 4. Therefore the first line is

     y y y y n n n n

The second line will consist of two y's followed by two n's alternating to the end of the line:

     y y n n y y n n

The last line has one y and one y alternating:

     y n y n y n y n

Thus the decision table will have the form

Condition 1	y	y	y	y	n	n	n	n
Condition 2	y	y	n	n	y	y	n	n
Condition 3	y	n	y	n	y	n	y	n
Actions								

✎ Self-test questions

1. Give an example of each of the relationships: one-to-one, one-to-many, many-to-one and many-to-many.

2. Identify the *entities*, *attributes* and *relationships* in each of the applications:
   (i) patient records in a General Medical Practice;
   (ii) a library lending system;
   (iii) an estate agency's 'houses for sale' monitoring system.

3. Draw an *entity-relationship model* (ERM) for each application.

4. Define the terms: *normalisation*; *data dictionary*.

5. What is the purpose of a data flow diagram?

6. In top-down design, what is the name given to the process of replacing program components by sequences of smaller components?

7. Name and briefly describe four different forms of process model.

8. What are the three control structures used in structured English?

9. Try drawing a flowchart for a common task such as making a cup of tea or cooking a soft boiled egg.

10. Produce a flowchart and decision table for the following problem:

A company bills its customers on the last day of each month. If the bill is paid before the start of the second week of the next month, the customer is given a discount of 5%. If the account is settled after the second week but before the last week, the customer is charged the amount of the bill. Payment after the beginning of the last week of the month results in an interest charge of 5%.

11. Give three examples of CASE tools.

Developmental Exercises

Practical Systems Analysis

These activities are based on the Barford Properties Case Study given at the end of this Developmental Exercise section. To extend them you may carry out some additional research into the operation of an estate agency in your area. The Property Sales system is to be computerised.

Activity 1

Produce a plan of the *systems analysis stages*, which you will need to follow. Explain the purpose of each stage and the general activities it involves.

Activity 2

Identify the user categories who would be expected to have access to the records and analyse their requirements.

Activity 3

Undertake a *feasibility study* of the proposal. Define the *purpose* of the Property Sales System and establish its *objectives*. Other systems within the estate agency, which may interact with it, also need to be identified. Produce a word processed *feasibility report*.

Activity 4

Briefly describe the standard techniques for gathering users' system requirements, select the technique(s) you consider most appropriate for the estate agency proposal and explain your choice. Design and use appropriate software to produce, a *questionnaire* for gathering information from buyers. It should identify Barford Properties and establish a corporate style. The aim of the questionnaire is to establish which types of information on houses they most need in the initial stage of an enquiry and the form(s) in which they would like the information to be presented to them. You also want to know which types of house and price ranges are most in demand and the number of houses each respondent has bought. Most people have bought at least one house, so you should obtain around 20 *responses*. You should make use of any software you consider appropriate to produce the questionnaire.

Activity 5

Use a *spreadsheet* to analyse your findings and produce useful statistics. Produce two types of *chart* from these statistics, using *spreadsheet graphics* facilities.

Activity 6

Use a suitable *graphics package*, to draw an *organisation chart* to represent the divisions of responsibility in the agency; it is likely to be a fairly 'flat' structure.

Activity 7

Draw an *information flow* diagram (using vector drawing tools), showing the *functional* areas of the agency and the information flows between them. These should cover all information systems in the agency, including property for sale records, viewing appointments, accounts, buyer and vendor records, and connections with outside bodies, such as solicitors, banks and building societies and the Land Registry.

Activity 8

Analyse the Property Sales system, and word process a *system analysis report* (using the same corporate style, established in Activity 4). It must include a *data flow diagram* (computer produced and embedded in the document) in respect of the existing manual system. Your analysis should detail the current: *data collection methods* and *inputs*; *documents used*; *operations* and *decisions*; *storage*; system *outputs*. Also, include in your report, *recommendations* for a computerised system. These should:

- ❑ **describe** the different types of system (for example, batch processing, transaction processing, information storage and retrieval) and make an argued recommendation for a particular type;

- ❑ **detail** *input* (including form, source and collection method), *processing* (form of processing activity), *storage* and *reporting* requirements of the system; you should also detail expected *volumes* of data and *frequency* of input and outputs;

- ❑ **identify** *expectations* of the system.

- ❑ *costs* and *savings* of a new system, identifying resources needed and any constraints on its development or use.

Activity 9

Obtain user comments on your analysis and **make modifications**, as necessary.

System Specification

These activities are based on the Barford Properties Case Study at the end of this Developmental Exercise section and builds on the feasibility and systems analysis reports produced in Practical Systems Analysis. These activities lead to the production of a system specification for the Property Sales system. To begin with, Activities 10 and 11 require you to demonstrate your knowledge of the terminology associated with this subject.

Activity 10

Word process (using table facilities) a *glossary*, listing and briefly describing the following elements of a system specification: *input specification; output specification; process specification; resources; constraints; first normal form (1NF) data model.*

Activity 11

Word process a similar *glossary*, explaining, with examples, the following types of processing activity: *sorting; selecting; merging; calculation; interrogation; repetition.*

Activity 12

Produce a system specification (word processed in the corporate style established in Activity) in the following stages. At each stage, include an explanation of its purpose and the specification element(s) it comprises.

a. **Refine** and re-**draw** the *data flow diagram* produced in Study Component 7, Activity 8, and **identify** the *entities* which form the Property Sales system. **Produce** *data definitions* for each entity, and if necessary *normalise* to first normal for (1NF). **Establish** a *data dictionary* and **record** the details.

b. **Produce** an *input specification*, detailing data source(s), capture methods; screen layouts, verification, validation parameters.

c. **Produce** an *output specification*, with designs for screen and printed reports.

d. **Produce** a *process specification* (if appropriate, use decision tables to refine the efficiency of processes). Use at least one of the following methods to define the process(es): *structured English; structure diagram, flow chart.*

e. **Identify** and **describe** resource implications of the specification, including hardware, software, people, time scale for implementation and costs.

Activity 13

Describe the *alternative information technology methods*, which may be used to implement the specification and **suggest** for *which aspect of development* each may be appropriate (with reasons; otherwise indicate as inappropriate).

Case Study

This case study is the basis for the Activities in this section.Barford Properties is a small firm of estate agents, with three partners, each one specialising in a particular aspect of the business. The specialisms are:

❑   property valuation;

❑   mortgage, insurance and conveyancing;

❑   marketing.

There are five sales negotiators and a potential buyer or vendor is assigned to one sales negotiator. The partner responsible for marketing has an assistant. These staff are directly responsible to the partners. An office manager is responsible for two accounts staff and one administrative clerk. Two secretaries are also employed, with a range of duties including general correspondence, and the production of property descriptions (including photographs).The agency operates a number of functions, as follows:

❑   Property valuations. When a client first approaches the agency with a request to handle the sale of their property, the responsible partner visits the property to assess its market value. The establishment of a selling price is usually a matter for negotiation. The client has a minimum figure in mind, which may coincide with the valuation assessment by the agency. If the valuation is less than the minimum figure put forward by the client, they are advised to lower the asking price accordingly. However, the final decision is made by the client. The asking price may be reviewed, depending on the response or otherwise of potential buyers. In making the assessment, the agency draws on its local experience, but also on data concerning regional and national trends in the housing market.

❑   Property sales. Once an asking price is agreed, fees are settled. Charges vary according to the value of the property, as the agency takes a percentage of the ultimate selling price, plus costs of advertising. Other charges for conveyancing work are also made. The sales negotiator assigned to a vendor handles their routine enquiries and correspondence to keep them informed of progress. If a client is not satisfied with progress and wants a different asking price, for example, he or she is referred to one of the partners.

❑   Marketing. This section deals with the placing of advertisements in local and national newspapers and property journals. It also organises the window displays and property details leaflets which are given out to interested buyers.

❑   Mortgage, conveyancing and insurance services (the agency acts as a broker). Buyers of properties handled by the agency are offered these services, and many clients make use of them, particularly if they are first-time buyers. The agency does not have Independent Financial Adviser status and mortgages are arranged with the Barford and Bamford Building Society. Property, mortgage protection and endowment insurances are obtained from the Buzzard Life Insurance Company.

❑   Financial accounting. This section handles all the customer accounts and deals with receipts and payments flowing between the agency, building societies, solicitors and insurance companies.

A brief outline of the procedures involved in a property sale is given below.

1. The initial request from a client wishing to sell a property is dealt with by the responsible partner, who makes an appointment to visit the property. Details of location, type, agreed asking price, number of rooms and so on are recorded. Photographs are also taken.

2. The property details are transcribed onto one of two standard forms, depending on whether the property is residential or business. This process is carried out in the Property Sales section.

3. The staff categorise the property according to basic criteria, including property location, type, size, quality, number of rooms and price range. These basic details are transcribed onto record cards, which are the initial point of reference when a potential buyer makes an enquiry.

4. To match prospective buyers with properties for sale, a Buyer Clients file is maintained. Details of suitable properties are sent (using a mailing list) to potential buyers.

5. When a buyer expresses an interest in a property, a viewing appointment is arranged between the buyer and the vendor (if the property is empty, one of the partners will accompany the buyer).

6. If a buyer expresses interest, they are asked to make an offer, which is then put to the vendor for consideration. Apart from the offer price, other factors are considered; for example, whether, the buyer has a property to sell.

7. Once a sale is agreed, solicitors take over the process of carrying out the various conveyancing operations and agreeing a completion date, when payment is made and the property ownership changes hands. When this is completed, the agency requests payment of the fees by the vendor. Buyers are not charged by the agency, although they do incur conveyancing costs.

Process models

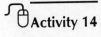

Activity 14

For each of the following problems, produce a flowchart, structure chart, structured English or a decision table, as indicated in brackets.

Decisions

1. Read a number and display a message which states whether the number is positive, negative or zero. (Flowchart)

2. Read a number and print it only if it is between 10 and 20. (Flowchart)

3. Read a number followed by a single letter code. The number represents the price of an item and the code indicates whether tax is to be added to the price. If the code is 'V' then the tax is 20% of the item's cost. If the code is 'X' then the item is not taxed. Print out the total cost of the item. (Structured English)

4. Read three positive, non-zero integers which may represent the sides of a triangle. The numbers are in ascending order of size. Determine whether or not the numbers do represent the sides of a triangle. (Decision table)

5. Extend the previous question to determine the type of triangle if one is possible with the values provided. Assume that the only types of triangles to consider are: *scalene* - no equal sides; *isosceles* - two equal sides; *equilateral* - three equal sides. (Decision table)

6. Read in a single character and print a message indicating whether or not it is a vowel. (Structure chart)

Loops

7. To produce conversion tables for:
   (i)   Inches to centimetres (1 to 20 inches, 1 inch = 2·54 centimetres);
   (ii)   Pounds to kilograms (1 to 10 pounds, 2.2 pounds per kilogram);
   (iii) Square yards to square metres: 10, 20 , 30,..., 100 sq yds (1yd = ·91 m)
          (Structured English)

10. A program reads an integer representing the number of gas bills to be processed, followed by that number of customer details. Each set of customer details consists of a customer number, a single character code representing the type of customer and the number of units used. Customers are of type 'D' (domestic) or 'B' (business). Domestic customers are charged 8p per unit and business customers are charged 10p per unit. For each customer print the customer number, the number of units used and the cost of the gas used. Print the total number of units used for this batch of customers and the total amount charged.
    (Structured English)

11. Repeat the previous question assuming that all the domestic users are first and that separate totals are required for domestic and business users. (Structure chart)

Unit 6

Database design

Chapters

Assessment Evidence

You need to produce

☐ a relational database to a given specification requiring at least three related tables
☐ design and analysis notes for the database
☐ annotated printed copy and test results for the database
☐ a user guide and technical documentation.

To achieve a grade E your work must show:

☐ the initial draft design and final data model correctly normalised to at least first normal form
☐ clearly the entities, attributes, keys, relationships, and internally generated or processed data in your design notes
☐ a working relational database that allows users to append, delete and edit data, initiate queries and print reports
☐ suitable and correct data input forms
☐ a user guide that enables novice users to make efficient use of the database
☐ clear and accurate definition, in the technical documentation, of:
   - the database structure and data relationships
   - a data dictionary
   - the range of acceptable data
   - example output from queries and reports
   - test procedures
☐ printed reports and screen prints that clearly demonstrate the operation of the database, annotated to explain their purpose.

To achieve a grade C your work must show:

☐ reports that make correct and effective use of queries, grouping, arithmetic formulae and related tables
☐ fluent use of technical language, good use of graphic images and use of annotated screen prints to create effective user instructions and technical documentation
☐ that you can work independently and meet agreed deadlines by carrying out your work plans effectively.

To achieve a grade A your work must show:

☐ detailed design and analysis notes that include graphic images to define the data model clearly and demonstrate that it is correctly normalised to third normal form
☐ effective use of validation and of automatic counter, date or time fields in data input forms
☐ test procedures, designed and implemented, that check reliable operation including rejection of data outside the acceptable range
☐ user-friendly, well laid out screen data input forms with title labels, field names, set widths, pull-down lists and instructions as appropriate to enable data entry into multiple tables.

Chapter 27

Computer Files

Files, records and fields

In data processing, it is necessary to store information on particular subjects, for example, customers, suppliers or personnel and such information needs to be structured so that it is readily controllable and accessible to the user. In traditional data processing systems, each of these 'topics' of information is allocated a file. Figure 27.1 shows the structure of a book file. The *file* is a collection of *records*, one for each book. Each record

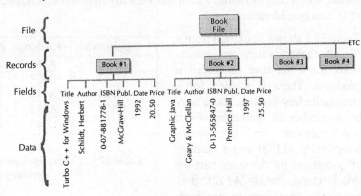

Figure 27.1. *Data file structure*

contains details of the book's title, its author(s), ISBN number, publisher, date of publication and cost; each of these *data items* is allocated physical space, known as a *field*, within the record.

Types of file

Master files. They are used for the storage of *permanent*, or *semi-permanent*, data which is used in applications such as stock, sales or payroll. Some of the fields tend to contain data which is fairly static, for example, customer name and address, whilst data in some fields is continually changing, for example, customer balance, as transactions are applied to the file. Such *updating* is carried out, either through the direct entry (on-line) of individual transactions, or from an accumulated set of entries stored on a *transaction* file.

Transaction files. These are transient and only exist to update master files. Each transaction record contains the *key field value* of the master record it is to update (to allow correct matching with its relevant master record), together with data gathered from source documents, for example, invoice amounts which update the balance field in customer accounts.

Reference files. These contain data used for reference or look-up purposes, such as price catalogue and customer name and address files.

Archival or **historical files**. These contain data which, for legal or organisational reasons, must be kept and tend to be used on an ad hoc basis and may be referred to only occasionally.

Record identification - primary and secondary keys

In most organisations, when an information system is operational it will be necessary to identify each record uniquely. In a Personnel File, for example, it might be thought that it is possible to identify each individual record simply by the employee's Surname and this would be satisfactory as long as no two employees had the same surname. In reality, many organisations will have several employees with the same surnames, so to ensure uniqueness, each employee is assigned a unique Works Number. The works number field is then used as the primary key in the filing system, each individual having his or her own unique Works Number and so a unique primary key. There are certain circumstances when the primary key may be a *composite key*, that is, one made up of more than one field and the following example shows how a pair of fields, which individually may not be unique, can be combined to provide a unique identifier.

Table 27.1 shows an extract from a file which details suppliers' quotations for a number of different products. There is a need for a composite key because there may be a number of quotations from one supplier (in this case, SupplierNo 41192) and a number of quotations for the same part (in this instance, PartNo A112). It is

SupplierNo	PartNo	Price	DeliveryDate
23783	A361	2.59	31/01/96
37463	B452	1.50	29/01/96
40923	A112	3.29	30/01/96
41192	A112	3.29	28/01/96
41192	C345	2.15	30/01/96

Table 27.1. *Extract from quotation file with composite primary key*

necessary, therefore, to use both SupplierNo and PartNo to identify one quotation record uniquely. Uniqueness is not always necessary. For example, if it is required to retrieve records which fulfil a criterion, or several criteria, *secondary keys* may be used. Thus, for example, in an information retrieval system on Personnel, the secondary key Department may be used to retrieve the records of all employees who work in, say, the Sales Department.

Self-test questions

1. Using a stock control system as an example, distinguish between *master* and *transaction* files.
2. Using the example of a criminal records system, illustrate the functions of *reference* and *archive* files.
3. Using the example of a personnel system, illustrate the meaning of the terms: *field*, *record* and *file*.

Chapter 28

Overview of databases

This chapter explains the function of databases, introduces some important concepts concerning their construction and operation and also looks at some of the ways organisations develop and use them. We begin by comparing the structure of a database to that of the traditional file and its components of *record* and *field*. The traditional file has a flat, or two-dimensional, structure, as illustrated by the Customer Order file extract in Table 28.1. Each *record* contains the same categories of information, held in *fields* identified by the column headings. <u>OrderNo</u> is the primary key which uniquely identifies each customer order.

OrderNo	AcctID	Name	Address1	Address2	Order Total
0001	11003	The Red Lion	33 May Be	Nowhere	£1500.35
0002	11005	The Black Horse	45 Round About	Somewhere	£315.77
0003	11008	The Fat Ox	28 Just About	Anywhere	£425.66
etc	etc	etc	etc	etc	etc

Table 28.1. *Flat file structure*

Of course, not all information occurs in two-dimensional form. Figure 28.1 shows the three-dimensional structure which is created when there are repeated details for each order.

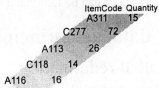

```
                                      ItemCode  Quantity
                                      A311      15
                              C277       72
                      A113       26
                 C118      14
            A116      16
  0001 11003  The Red Lion  33 May Be Nowhere    £1500.35
```

Figure 28.1. *Three-dimensional data structure*

For an order of 5 items this would add 10 fields to the record length. Table 28.2 shows the addition of some of these repeated fields.

OrderNo		Order Total	ItemCode1	Quantity1	ItemCode2	Quantity2	etc
0001	....	£1500.35	A116	16	C118	14	
0002	....	£315.77					
0003	....	£425.66					
etc		etc					

Table 28.2. *Accommodating repeated fields in a single flat file*

The additional fields could be handled by extending the length of the record, but if customers could order any number of items, this would make for a very unwieldy structure. Alternatively, the details of each order could be held in an entirely separate file. To link orders with order details, the programmer would have to explicitly link them by including the OrderNo field in both files. However, the information is essentially three-dimensional and would be better accommodated in a database structure which is designed to handle it effectively. Some complex database structures are designed to accommodate information of the three-dimensional form shown in Figure 28.1. Databases of this type are based on *network* structures (see later). However, these more complicated file structures can still be broken down into groups of flat files and accommodated in simpler database structures, such as the tables used in *relational* databases (Chapter 29).

General definition of a database

A database can be defined as - *a collection of structured data, generally related to some subject or topic area and serving the needs of a number of different applications, but with a minimum of duplicated data items.*

From this definition it is possible to identify specific features of a database:

❑ A database contains data of use in a *variety* of applications.

❑ The data is *structured* to allow separate data items to be connected, to form different *logical* records according to the requirements of users and hence, to applications programs.

A database will normally be used for different applications, but those applications should have some *common interests* concerning the data items they use. For example, sales, purchasing, stock control and production control applications are likely to use common data in respect of raw materials or finished goods. On the other hand, a database containing data on both materials and personnel may be difficult to justify; even then connections between the separate databases can be facilitated if the information requirements so justify.

Basic database principles

Controlled redundancy

'Controlled redundancy' means reducing to a minimum the number of data items which are duplicated in a database. In traditional computerised filing systems, each department in an organisation may keep its own files, which results in a massive amount of duplication in the stored data. Although the removal of duplicated items is a desirable aim in terms of keeping database volume to a minimum, there are occasions when duplication is necessary to provide efficient access to the database.

Data independence

Periodically, the *physical* database needs to be changed to accommodate changes in user requirements. However, there is no need to alter all applications programs, because the way the data is *physically* stored on the storage medium is independent of the *logical* record structures required by applications programs. Figure 28.2 illustrates the use of a database by two separate applications with some common data requirements. Programmers need have no knowledge of the way data is actually organised and each is given the 'data view' he or she needs for the particular application. If the database contents are rearranged or supplemented to accommodate the needs of a new application, existing applications will continue to operate correctly.

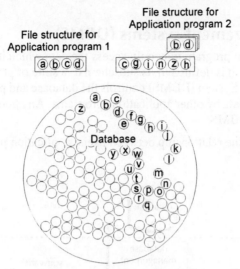

Figure 28.2. *Applications with some common data requirements*

In a database, records can be stored essentially in two different ways.

❑ Independently - the primary key is used to decide the physical location of a record; frequently this is effected through a *randomising* process to distribute records efficiently on the storage medium.

❑ In association - records are stored according to their relationship with other records and connections may be made between them with the use of *pointers*. A *physical pointer* gives the address where a record is stored and can be used to relate records anywhere in the database; a *logical pointer* is a value from which the physical address can be calculated.

The physical and logical database

A database has to satisfy the differing information needs of many users, generally through specially written applications programs. Therefore, it is often necessary to add further data items to satisfy changes in users needs. The software which controls the database must relate to the data at data item, rather than at record level, because one programmer's logical record requirements may contain some data items which are also required for another programmer's logical record description. The physical database must allow for both. It must be possible for data items to be connected into a variety of logical record forms.

Creating and manipulating the database

A special language called a *data description language* (DDL) allows the database to be created and changed and the logical data structures to be defined.

A *data manipulation language* (DML) enables the contents of the database to be altered by adding, updating or deleting records. The language is used by programmers to develop applications programs for users of the database. The functions of both these languages are combined, together with a query language facility in *Structured Query Language* (SQL) - Chapter .

Database management systems (DBMS)

So that each application program may only access the data which it needs for processing or retrieval (that data which is defined in its subschema), a suite of programs referred to as the Database Management System (DBMS) controls the database and prevents accidental or deliberate corruption of data by other applications programs. An application cannot access the database without the DBMS.

Figure 28.3 illustrates the relationship between users, application programs, the DBMS and the database.

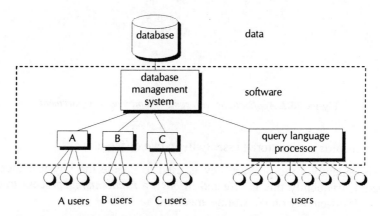

Figure 28.3. *Relationship between DBMS, applications and users*

A DBMS has the following functions.

❑   It is the common link between all applications programs and the database.

❑   It facilitates the use and organisation of a database and protects the database from accidental or deliberate corruption.

It restricts a programmer's logical view of the database to those items of data which are to be used in the applications program being written.

Types of database

The logical structure of a database can be based upon one of a number of natural data structures which the Database Management System (DBMS) uses to establish links between separate data items. Physical pointers inform the DBMS where the next logical record is to be found. In certain types of database the logical organisation of the database is constrained by whatever data structure is used and can therefore be described as *formatted*. Two main categories of data structure are used in such databases:

❑   *hierarchical* or *tree* structure;

❑   *complex* and *simple plex* structure (often called *network* structures).

These types of database are primarily for use on mainframe systems and are not of concern here. To avoid some of the restrictions inherent in formatted databases, a popular method of database management is to use a *relational* approach (Chapters 29 to 31).

Schemas and sub-schemas

Because the database must allow for various user applications programs accessing it at the same time, direct access storage must be used. There are many ways of physically organising the data, but whatever method is used it must allow for the variety of logical record forms needed by applications programs. The applications programmer does not need to know how the data is physically stored. The programmer's knowledge of the data held in the database is restricted to the *logical view* required for the program. The complete or global logical data-base is termed the *schema*. The restricted or local logical views provided for different applications programs are termed *subschemas*. An example logical schema is shown in Figure 28.4.

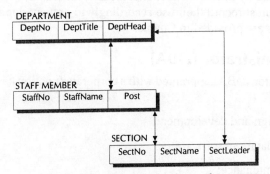

Figure 28.4. *Example database schema*

Although logical schemas can be used to represent the structure of any type of database, we can explain Figure 28.4 in the context of a relational database structure (Chapter 29). There are 3 entities: Department; StaffMember; Section. Each entity would occupy a table in the database and be defined as follows. The attributes are in brackets and each attribute would become a field in the table definition.

```
Department    (DeptNo, DeptTitle, DeptHead)
Section       (SectNo, SectName, SectLeader)
StaffMember   (StaffNo, StaffName, Post)
```

The underlined fields identify the *primary key* (unique identifier for each record) for each table. The single and double headed arrows linking the entities express the degree of the relationship (one-to-many) between the entities they connect. Thus, for example, each Department may have many staff but each StaffMember can only belong to one Department.

This Unit is concerned with the development and use of relational databases and you will be using entity-relationship diagrams (ERD - Chapter 26) to model their structure. Their appearance is similar to the schema diagram shown above.

Database administration

Data dictionary

A data dictionary system is a ICT department's own information system, with the database administrator, systems analysts and programmers as the main users.

An essential part of the database design process is to maintain a data dictionary. Its main function is to store details of all the data items in a database. Such details can be wide ranging, but should include, as a minimum:

(i)   field names and the table(s) in which they occur;

(ii)   field definitions, including field types and lengths;

(iii)   additional properties, concerning, for example, data formats and validation controls;

(iv)   synonyms. Sometimes, the same field occurs in more than one table, but using different names. Generally it is better not to use synonyms.

The dictionary's main role is to ensure consistent data usage; if synonyms are used (different data names may be used by different functional areas of an organisation to refer to the same field), the dictionary must record their use accordingly to prevent duplication. Examples of data dictionary entries are provided in Chapter 31.

Database administrator (DBA)

A database administrator (DBA) appointed with a corporate function has special responsibility for:

❑   database design and development;

❑   selection of database software;

❑   database maintenance;

❑   database accuracy and security.

A DBA should have a working knowledge of both the DBMS and the organisation. A DBA will supervise the addition of new data items to the database (changes to the schema). Supervision of the data dictionary is also the DBA's responsibility. The DBA has to ensure the consistent use of data across the whole database. For example, a functional area may request new data to be added to a database, when it already exists. This can happen when different departments in an organisation refer to a field by different names. For example, a Sales department may refer to the name Product Code, whilst the Warehouse staff may use the term Stock Code, when referring to the same field. During database development, it is easy to forget the precise definitions given to a field and when adding the field to another table, introduce inconsistencies.

Benefits and drawbacks of databases

The following list details some of the generally accepted advantages and disadvantages.

❑   Apart from controlled redundancy, there is no unnecessary duplication of data as occurs in traditional filing systems. Apart from the economic advantage, this means that transactions can update all affected areas of the database through a single input.

❏ Because of the single input principle, there is less chance of inconsistency as may occur if the same transaction is keyed in several times to different files. Equally, of course, an incorrect entry will mean that all applications programs using the data will be working with the wrong data value.

❏ The opportunities for obtaining comprehensive information are greatly improved with a central pool of data.

❏ On-demand or ad hoc enquiries are possible through the use of a query language.

❏ Security opportunities are enhanced because access to a single database can be more readily controlled than is possible with a system based on numerous separate files. On the other hand, database design and creation is a complex process and the failure of a database affects all applications which make use of it.

Database development

Although database systems provide considerable benefits (see above) in reducing data dupli-cation and ensuring consistency of information values across an organisation, they are more complex to develop and require much greater planning than traditional file processing sys-tems. The traditional file system allows for a much more piecemeal approach, because each application area creates and maintains its own information system.

Database systems, even if they are only dealing with the information needs of one functional area (Chapter 7), should take account of the information requirements of other functions. If this is done, then extending the database to include other applications will be simplified. Schema, subschema and entity relationship models (Chapter 26) all provide methods of de-fining the logical structure of information systems which is so important to the planning of database systems. High and low level data flow diagrams (Chapter 26) take the design pro-cess further by defining the way information moves between the functions which appear in the schema or entity relationship models.

Hierarchical and network structured data-bases, which are mentioned earlier in this chapter, use pointers to link data items into the various logical record structures required by the applications programs. Figure 28.5 show an example of a hierarchical (or tree) structure. The tree structure only allows one-to-many relationships, as does a rela-tional database, but the use of pointers to link data into various logical structures can make

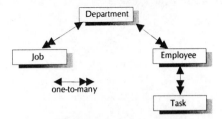

Figure 28.5. Tree structure

modification of the database complex. Altering the pointers to take account of a new applica-tion's requirements can cause difficulties for other applications. As the database grows, so does its complexity and the risks of some application failures. Relational databases do not use these complex structures, but instead use flat files called *tables* (or relations), with *for-eign keys* to establish the required relationships between them.

Database applications

A major application of database technology is the Management Information System (MIS), described in Chapter 9, but such applications are designed for medium to large organisations. As explained earlier, the planning and design requirements for such corporate projects are considerable and beyond what you will be expected to achieve in this Unit. However, the tabular structure used by a relational database mean that you should be able to visualise logical structure of numerous, smaller applications. Useful subjects for relational database development include: medical practice; estate agent; car sales company, library; criminal records; video rental; personnel system; sports club.

Self-test questions

1. Suppose that the following data items are amongst those held in the personnel database of a multi-national organisation.

   Surname; Forename; DateOf Birth, Salary; Qualifications; JobTitle; Department; DepartmentAddress; HeadOfDepartment; Country.

   a. Suggest two, separate *logical record* structures (list the fields in each) which may be useful.

   b. Suggest a *primary key* for each of the logical record structures you described in (i).

   c. If the database is relational, how would connections be made between the two logical record structures you defined in a.?

   d. What is the role of the database management system (DBMS) in relating the physical database to the logical record structures used by applications?

2. Distinguish between the terms *schema* and a *sub-schema*.

3. A database provides *data independence*. What does data independence mean and how is it beneficial for maintaining applications programs.

4. A particular company has separate departments to handle payroll and personnel information. The company operates a traditional file processing system, with each department maintaining its own files.

   a. Give examples of data in these systems which may be duplicated

   b. Briefly explain how the feature of *controlled redundancy*, provided by a database system, would help reduce such duplication.

5. An academic database maintains the following information concerning students, departments, courses and tutors. Each student is assigned to a particular course and has one personal tutor. A tutor will be responsible for a number of student tutees. Each course operates in one of the five departments within the college and each department runs many courses. The system also records previous qualifications obtained by students.

   Using the example in Figure 28.2 as a guide, draw a *schema* to reflect the information held in the academic database.

6. A company maintains copies of customer records in two separate departments, sales and marketing.

   a. In this context, give an example of *data inconsistency* and suggest how it might arise.

   b. If the customer information were held in a database and both departments used the database, how would this avoid data inconsistency?

Chapter 29

Relational database design and development

This chapter examines the principles of database design and definition, as well as the role of a *relational database management system* (RDBMS) package. RDBMS software packages are designed for the construction and control of *databases*. Packages, such as dBase, Paradox and Access, are often loosely referred to as databases. Strictly and to avoid confusion, they are database management systems (DBMS).

A fair amount of jargon is associated with database theory but the ideas represented are straightforward and simple to understand. A relational DBMS is designed to handle data in two-dimensional, *table* form and a single database is likely to contain a number of separate, but related, tables. This tabular view of data is easy to understand; everyday examples include telephone directories, train timetables and product price lists. An example of tabular data is given in Table 29.1. For information and clarity, when referring to other texts on relational databases, some of the jargon is defined below, by reference to Table 29.1. The underlined terms are not used further in this text.

❑ A table is sometimes referred to as a *relation* and each entry in the table is a single data item value. For example, PartCode 012 is a data item value consisting of 3 characters.

PART_SUPPLIER		
PartCode	Price	SupplierNo
012	3.25	14
015	0.76	07
016	1.26	14
018	7.84	05

Table 29.1. *Tabular data*

❑ Each column in the relation contains values for a given *data item type*. We will use the word *field*. The set of values for a given data item type is called its *domain*. A domain is identified by its description, that is, the name for the data item type. For example, in Table 29.1 the set of values in the second column is called the Price domain.

❑ Each row in a relation is a record occurrence and is called a *tuple*; we use the more usual word, *record*.

Database design

Design is an important pre-requisite for database construction. For example, a common mistake is to create one table, containing all the data items required by the applications programs.

Consider the Product table in Figure 29.1. Additional fields could be included for suppliers' names and addresses, but, on the assumption that many products come from one supplier, much data would be needlessly duplicated. It is more useful to create a separate table for the suppliers' names and addresses, as shown in Figure 29.2. Note that the Supplier table also contains a Supplier Code field; this allows a *relationship* to be established with the Product table. Similarly, a database for the maintenance of student records, may contain a single table consisting of twenty or thirty data items ranging from student name, address, and date of entry, to all assignment and exam grades for all subjects studied within a given course. Clearly, such a database is unwieldy when, for example, a list of student names and addresses is all that is required by a particular user. The following sections describe some of the more important concepts and techniques relating to proper database design.

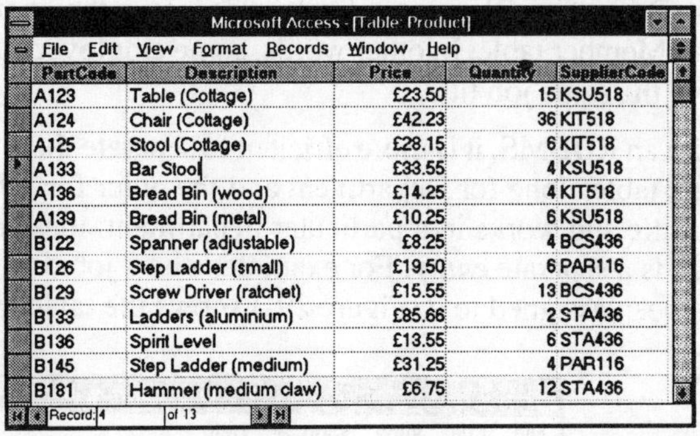

PartCode	Description	Price	Quantity	SupplierCode
A123	Table (Cottage)	£23.50	15	KSU518
A124	Chair (Cottage)	£42.23	36	KIT518
A125	Stool (Cottage)	£28.15	6	KIT518
A133	Bar Stool	£33.55	4	KSU518
A136	Bread Bin (wood)	£14.25	4	KIT518
A139	Bread Bin (metal)	£10.25	6	KSU518
B122	Spanner (adjustable)	£8.25	4	BCS436
B126	Step Ladder (small)	£19.50	6	PAR116
B129	Screw Driver (ratchet)	£15.55	13	BCS436
B133	Ladders (aluminium)	£85.66	2	STA436
B136	Spirit Level	£13.55	6	STA436
B145	Step Ladder (medium)	£31.25	4	PAR116
B181	Hammer (medium claw)	£6.75	12	STA436

Figure 29.1. *Product table*

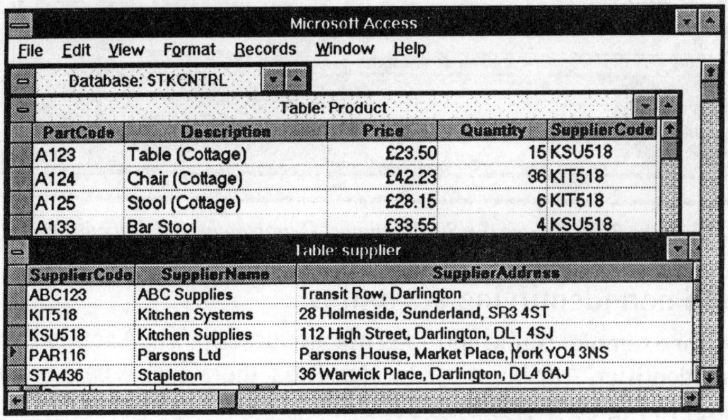

PartCode	Description	Price	Quantity	SupplierCode
A123	Table (Cottage)	£23.50	15	KSU518
A124	Chair (Cottage)	£42.23	36	KIT518
A125	Stool (Cottage)	£28.15	6	KIT518
A133	Bar Stool	£33.55	4	KSU518

SupplierCode	SupplierName	SupplierAddress
ABC123	ABC Supplies	Transit Row, Darlington
KIT518	Kitchen Systems	28 Holmeside, Sunderland, SR3 4ST
KSU518	Kitchen Supplies	112 High Street, Darlington, DL1 4SJ
PAR116	Parsons Ltd	Parsons House, Market Place, York YO4 3NS
STA436	Stapleton	36 Warwick Place, Darlington, DL4 6AJ

Figure 29.2. *Product and Supplier tables*

Entities

A database should contain a number of logically separate tables, each corresponding to a given subject or part-subject (an *entity*). In the example of the product database (Figure 29.2), two logically separate tables (one for the Product entity and the other for the Supplier entity) are constructed. *Entities* are the objects of the real world, which are relevant to a particular information system.

Attributes

An entity has a number of related *attributes*, which are of interest to users. Consider, as an example, a Personnel database (see also *Personnel* case study in Chapter 31). An entity, StaffMember, may have the attributes of StaffCode, Name, JobCode, JobTitle, DeptCode, DepartmentName. These attributes determine the *fields* which are associated with the StaffMember *table*. Some attributes may be kept in a separate table. For example, JobTitle and DepartmentName are likely to contain the same values in numerous records in the StaffMember table. In other words, some employees work in the same department and some have the same job title.

With an RDBMS, it is more efficient to separate these attributes, through the creation of separate tables (one for Department and the other for Job). Although an employee has a given job title and works in a particular department, these attributes are also of separate interest; each is a separate *entity*. For example, a new job title may be identified before an employee has been assigned to it. Figure 29.3 shows the tables which represent these entities.

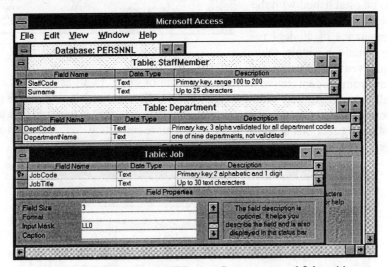

Figure 29.3. *Tables for StaffMember, Department and Job entities*

Identifying and non-identifying attributes

Some attributes, for example, Name and JobTitle, are descriptive. Another (StaffCode) may serve as a unique identifier. Attributes can be classified, therefore, as being either *identifying* or *non-identifying*. In Figure 29.11, StaffCode acts as the unique identifier (or *primary key field*) for a StaffMember record; Department and Job records use DeptCode and JobCode, respectively. These entity and attribute structures can be expressed in the form shown in Figure 29.4. Unique identifiers are underlined.

```
StaffMember (StaffCode, Name, JobCode, DeptCode)
Job(JobCode, JobTitle)
Department(DeptCode, DepartmentName)
```

Figure 29.4. *Entity structures*

Sometimes, more than one attribute is needed to uniquely identify an individual record; such attributes form a *composite identifier* or *key*. An example of such a key is shown in Figure 29.5.

```
Order Line (OrderNo, ItemNo, Description, Price, Quantity)
```

Figure 29.5. *Entity structure using composite primary key*

An order form usually has several lines, each relating to a separate item which a customer wants. The same item may be ordered by other customers, so the OrderNo and ItemNo are needed to identify a particular order line, relating to a particular customer order.

Relationships, link fields and foreign keys

Notice that, in Figure 29.4, the JobCode and DeptCode fields also remain in the StaffMember table. This is necessary to allow relationships, or links, to be established between the tables. Suppose, for example, that a user wishes to view a list of employee details, which includes Name, DepartmentName and JobTitle. The list is obtained by *querying* (see Chapter 29) the database.

To process the query, the RDBMS needs to extract information from more than one table. An examination of the entity structures in Figure 29.4 reveals that all three are needed (StaffMember, Job and Department). The user must specify which fields are used to link the tables to one another. Figure 29.6 illustrates these links.

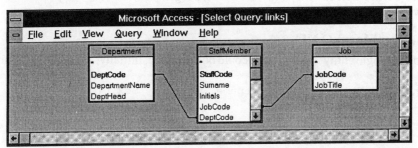

Figure 29.6. *Link fields to establish relationships between tables*

DeptCode is the primary key for the Department table, but the same attribute also appears in the StaffMember table. When the two are linked, DeptCode in the StaffMember table is acting as a *foreign key*. JobCode in the StaffMember table also serves as a foreign key when it is used to link with the Job table.

Data analysis

This process is concerned with establishing what the entities, attributes and links (*relationships*), for any given database, should be. To make such an analysis, it is obviously necessary to have knowledge of the organisation to which the information relates, because there will be certain items of information which only have significance to that particular organisation. For example, in an Academic database, the following entities may be identified and a table established for each.

```
Student; Course; Tutor; EducationHistory; ExamGrade
```

Normalisation

Normalisation is a technique established by E.F. Codd to simplify the structure of data as it is *logically viewed* by the programmer or user. The data requirements for a database are systematically analysed to establish whether a particular attribute should be an entity in its own right, or simply an attribute of some other entity. When an attribute is identified as a separate entity, the link or relationship must be maintained with the original entity. Normalisation is a step-by-step process for analysing data into its constituent entities and attributes. Its main aim is to improve database efficiency. There are three stages of normalisation described here, though there are others which are beyond the scope of this text. To illustrate the process of normalisation, the example of an *Academic* database is used. When a student enrols for one or more courses, a registration form is completed. An example is shown in Figure 29.7.

Malverley College Wareham Dorset DO5 3DD		Principal: Peter Ansell, BA, PhD		
Student Registration Form				
Student Number		G234563		
Surname		Harrison		
Forename		Pauline		
Address		123 Newcastle Road, Sunderland, SR3 2RJ		
Sex		Female		
Course Code	Course Title		Tutor Code	Tutor
4PDCS1	Computing		124	Watkin
4PDNE1	Electronics		133	Parks
4PDFR1	French		118	Teneur
4PDGE1	German		166	Roberts

Figure 29.7. *Extract from student registration form*

First normal form (1NF)

Treated as a single entity, the structure could be described, initially, as shown in Figure 29.8.

```
Student (StudNo, Surname, Forename, Address, Sex, [CrseCode,
CrseTitle, TutNo, TutName])
```

Figure 29.8. *Structure of Student entity*

The unique identifier (primary key), StudNo, is underlined. Each student registration form (see Figure 29.7) may show enrolments on several courses. Thus, the attributes [CrseCode, CrseTitle, TutNo and TutName] can be identified as a *repeating group*.

The first stage of normalisation demands the removal of any repeating groups. This is achieved by creating a new entity. The attributes in question relate to the activity of enrolment, which is of separate interest and an entity in its own right. The new entity is called Enrolment-1 and is used to store details of individual enrolments; each enrolment will be a separate record in the Enrolment table. Neither StudNo nor CrseCode, on its own, uniquely identifies an individual enrolment. A *composite key*, using both attributes, is used to uniquely identify a single enrolment. The two entity descriptions are shown in Figure 29.9.

```
Student-1 (StudNo, Surname, Forename, Address, Sex)
Enrolment-1 (StudNo, CrseCode, CrseTitle, TutNo, TutName)
```

Figure 29.9. *Entity structures after conversion to first normal form (1NF)*

The entities are now in first normal form (1NF) and this is indicated by suffixing each entity name with a 1. The unique identifier is underlined in each entity description. Note the *composite key* in the Enrolment entity.

To relate the Enrolment records to the relevant Student records requires that StudNo (as the link field) appears in both the Student and Enrolment tables in the Academic database. Thus, to ensure that entities and attributes are in first normal form requires the removal of repeating groups of attributes, rewriting them as new entities. The identifier of the original entity is always included as an attribute of any such new entity, although it is not essential for it to form part of the identifier of the new entity (it could be a non-identifying attribute). Some necessary *data redundancy* is created by including StudNo in both entities, to allow a given student to be connected with a particular enrolment. Such duplication of data does not necessarily mean an increased use of storage because normalisation is concerned with the *logical structure* of the data and not with the ways in which the data is physically organised.

Second normal form (2NF)

The second stage of normalisation ensures that all non-identifying attributes are *functionally dependent* on the unique identifier (the primary key); if the identifier is composite (comprising more that one attribute), then non-identifying attributes must be functionally dependent on the whole of the identifier. This rule is best explained by example. Consider the 1NF entity descriptions, produced from the first stage of normalisation (Figure 29.9). Referring to the Enrolment entity, it can be seen that TutNo and TutName each depend on both parts of the composite identifier. For example, if a student enrols on more than one course, he or she has a different tutor for each course. To identify a tutor in an enrolment record, requires specification of both values (StudNo and CrseCode). However, CrseTitle is not functionally dependent on the whole of the composite identifier, only on CrseCode; the title of a course could be found through entry of the CrseCode value alone. Figure 29.10 illustrates both these points with a diagram. An arrowed line connects the box, which surrounds the composite identifier, to TutNo and TutName. CrseTitle is connected only to CrseCode. The second stage of normalisation is

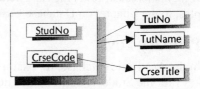

Figure 29.10. *Functional dependency*

achieved by the creation of a new entity, Course-2, with the attributes CrseCode (the identifier) and CrseTitle. The entity descriptions now appear as in Figure 29.11. The suffix 2 indicates that all entities and attributes are now in second normal form.

```
Student-2(StudNo, Surname, Forename, Address, Sex)
Enrolment-2(StudNo, CrseCode, TutNo, TutName)
Course-2(CrseCode, CrseTitle)
```

Figure 29.11. *Entity structures in second normal form (2NF)*

Benefits of 2NF

Conversion of entities and attributes to second normal form brings advantages apart from the avoidance of some data duplication. The entry of new data into the database is also facilitated. Suppose, for example, that a new course is to be added to the database and that the data is stored as arranged after the first stage of normalisation. The new course entry could not be made until the first enrolment for that particular course. Also, if a particular course has no enrolments, then information concerning the course is not held in the database.

Third normal form (3NF)

At this stage we are concerned with finding any *func-tional dependencies* between non-identifying attrib-utes. These can be identified from Figure 29.11 as TutNo and TutName and are illustrated in Figure 29.12. Again, the problem is solved by the creation of a new entity, Tutor-3. The entity contains TutNo as the identifier and TutName as a non-identifying attribute. The entities are in third normal form (indicated by the suffix, 3), as shown in Figure 29.13.

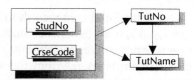

Figure 29.12. *Functional dependencies*

```
Student-3(StudNo, Surname, Forename, Address, Sex)
Enrolment-3(StudNo, CrseCode, TutNo)
Course-3(CrseCode, CrseTitle)
Tutor-3(TutNo, TutName)
```

Figure 29.13. *Entity structures in third normal form (3NF)*

Defining a database structure

Each entity structure, shown in Figure 29.13, must be defined as a table in the *Academic* data-base. In the case of Student-3, it would be beneficial to sub-divide Address into separate attributes of, say, Street, Town and PostCode. Each definition includes reference to *primary keys*, *field names*, *data types* and *field lengths*. All these terms are explained, through exam-ples, in the Chapter on Database Case Studies, but are briefly defined below.

Primary keys

In the Academic database, for example, StudentNo, CrseCode and TutorNo, act as primary keys for the Student, Course and Tutor tables, respectively. Although an Enrolment record can be identified through the combined use of StudNo and CrseCode, you could add an addi-tional field, such as EnrolmentNo, to act as the primary key.

Data types

A typical RDBMS provides the following data types.

Character, text or alphanumeric

This is for a field which may contain text, or a mixture of text, symbols and numbers. Some-times a field may only contain numeric digits, perhaps an account number or telephone number. If it is not treated numerically, but as text, character type is normally used.

Numeric

This type must be used for fields containing numerical values (such as money amounts or quantities) to be used in calculations.

Logical (yes/no)

This type allows the entry of two possible values, indicated by *true* or *false*. Sometimes, *yes* and *no*, respectively, may be used instead. For example, the Student table in the academic database contains a field to record the sex of a student. Use of the field name Male means that Yes is entered for a male student and No for a female. If the field name Female is used, No is entered for a male and Yes for a female student. The name of the field determines whether an affirmative or a negative (Yes or No) is entered.

Date

Although character type may be used for the storage of dates, the *date* type allows the correct sorting of dates. Also, in defining queries, date type fields enable the database to compare dates held in records, with a specified date. This is not practical with a character type field.

Field lengths

Logical and *date* type fields invariably have a pre-determined length, typically, 1 and 8 respectively. For a character field, a maximum length must be specified (allowing for the number of digits, letters or symbols to be accommodated within it). Numeric fields are defined according to the number range which needs to be accommodated and the number of decimal places.

Abbreviating and coding data

There are a number of benefits to be gained if data can be abbreviated or coded, without obscuring its meaning. Some are described below.

❑ *Saving space*. Codes and abbreviations take up less space, but must be of sufficient length to allow the entry of unique values. The minimum length of such a field is determined by the number of different values which need to be represented.

❑ *Query expressions* can be shorter. As long as users are aware of what the codes mean and are happy with using them, much time and keying effort can be saved.

❑ *Data entry*. If there are a large number of records to be keyed in, the procedure is extremely time-consuming and tedious. Coding and abbreviating data may reduce the time and labour requirements considerably.

Querying a database

A query is a request for information from a database. Queries can include *criteria* for the selection of information. For example, the Academic database could be queried for details of all male students, or students on a particular course. If the query requires that the RDBMS takes data from more than one table, appropriate link fields must be indicated.

Suppose, for example, that a report is required listing the names of all students, together with the name(s) of the course(s) on which they are enrolled. It is assumed that no criteria are specified. Student names are held in the Student table, the course code is in the Enrolment table, and the name of the course is in the Course table. Therefore, to process the query requires that these three tables are used. The QBE form of the query is shown in Figure 29.14.

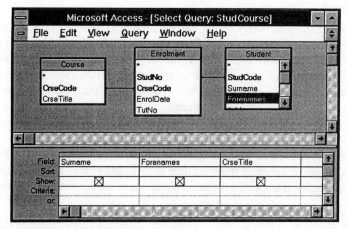

Figure 29.14. *Query (QBE form) using three tables from Academic database*

The query can also be expressed in *Structured Query Language* (SQL), as in Figure 29.15.

```
SELECT DISTINCTROW Student.Surname, Student.Forenames,
Course.CrseTitle
FROM Student INNER JOIN (Course INNER JOIN Enrolment ON
Course.CrseCode = Enrolment.CrseCode) ON Student.StudCode =
Enrolment.StudNo;
```

Figure 29.15. *Structured Query Language (SQL) form of query in Figure 29.14*

The query produces more than one record per student, but this is because a student may be enrolled on more than one course. The output appears in Figure 29.16.

Surname	Forenames	CrseTitle
Pallister	Robert	Electronics - Foundation
Atkinson	Fiona	French - Foundation
Wilson	John	German - Foundation
Cancello	Carla	German - Foundation
Williamson	Peter	Art - Foundation
Adamson	Rachel	Art - Foundation
Erikson	Karl	Art - Foundation
Pallister	Robert	German - Intermediate
Laing	Alan	Electronics - Advanced
Pompelmo	Paolo	Electronics - Advanced

Record: 6 of 10

Figure 29.16. *Output from query in Figure 29.22*

Secondary keys

Apart from the primary keys, which are used to identify records uniquely, an important function of an RDBMS is to allow the querying of the database, by reference to *secondary key* values. Thus, in the Academic database, useful secondary keys could be CrseTitle, and

TutName (if neither code was available). Secondary keys can also be used as *foreign keys* (see Relationships and Link Fields), when joining tables in a query.

Sorting

Although a table or query output may have a particular sequence, perhaps in the order of the primary key, there will be occasions when you want to change the sequence. If for example, you are viewing a list of personnel, you may wish the list to be in alphabetical order by surname. Alternatively, you may prefer to see them first grouped into departments (which you also want in alphabetical order) and then, within each department, ordered alphabetically by surname. Before executing a sort, you need to indicate which column or field is to dictate the sequence; apart from this, you can choose ascending or descending order. Indexing (see below) can be used to speed the sorting process.

Indexing

Indexes are used to speed the sorting and retrieval of records. If you index a field, this speeds the sorting and retrieval of records, using that field as a key. The effect will only be noticeable with databases containing hundreds of records. Table 29.2 illustrates an index for the job Grade field in a Personnel table. To find the records of Grade C staff, for example, without an index would require that all records are examined, a lengthy process if there are thousands of records. Using the index allows the immediate identification of all the relevant records for a particular Grade.

Grade	Primary keys or pointers to records				
A	301011	301019	301023	301067	etc
B	301014	301015	301027	301033	etc
C	301012	301013	301065	301077	etc
D	301088	301090	301122	301133	etc
E	301001	301005	301186	301111	etc

Table 29.2. *Field index*

The principle is the same as that used for a book index which lists the page numbers on which a particular topic can be found. In this example, it is assumed that there are 5 job Grades, A, B, C, D and E. Each Grade letter in the table has a list of pointers to the records which contain that letter in the Grade field. In this example the pointer is the WorksNo, which is the primary key for each record. Suppose that you indexed the SupplierCode field in a Product table in Figure 29.1, each value in that column would be in the index file. Each value would then have a pointer which indicated the physical location of the record containing that value. Referring to Figure 29.1, you can see that some supplier code values are duplicated; this is necessary because numerous products may be supplied by a single supplier. You can choose that the index allows for duplicates. The primary key in the Product table in Figure 29.1 is indexed and duplicates are not permitted; this is obvious, because the purpose of the primary key is to uniquely identify a record. The RDBMS creates an index file for each field you index and has to update it every time you modify the contents of the table to which it relates. Indexes take up space and because of the need for their updating, may have the effect of slowing data entry and editing. For this reason, you should avoid using them indiscriminately.

Structured query language (SQL)

Many new RDBMS packages provide a Structured Query Language (SQL). Practical examples of SQL are given earlier in this chapter and in Chapter 30. Developed by IBM, SQL is a *non-procedural* language and as such belongs to the group of programming languages known as 4th Generation Languages (4GLs); this means that programmers and trained users can specify what they want from a database without having to specify how to do it. Procedural languages such as COBOL, Pascal and C, require the programmer to detail, explicitly, how a program must navigate through a file or database to obtain the necessary output. The programmer must, for example, code procedures such as read the first master record, process it, read the next, process it and so on until the end of the file is reached. As explained below, SQL is an attempt to provide a language which includes the facilities normally provided separately by a *data description language*, a *data manipulation language* and a *query language* (to allow on-demand queries by users).

Features of SQL

The example database extract in Figure 29.17 is used here to illustrate some of the main features of SQL by showing how a programmer or trained user could use SQL to access a database without specifying procedures.

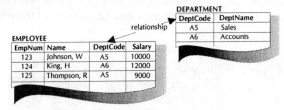

Figure 29.17. *Extract from company database*

Selection by criteria

Referring to Figure 29.17 if the Name and Salary of EMPLOYEE 124 is required, the SQL statements may take a form similar to the example in Figure 29.18.

```
SELECT Name, Salary
FROM EMPLOYEE
WHERE EmpNum = 124
```

Figure 29.18. *SQL statement to extract details of Employee 124*

The output would be as in Figure 29.19.

Name	Salary
King, H	12000

Figure 29.19. *Output from query in Figure 29.18*

SQL supports all the functions expected of a *relational* language including, for example, the operators, JOIN and PROJECT.

Updating the database

SQL can also change values in a database; for example, to give all employees in the A5 (Sales) department a 6 per cent pay increase, the statements shown in Figure 29.19 may be used:

```
UPDATE EMPLOYEE
SET Salary = Salary * 1.06
WHERE DeptCode = A5
```

Figure 29.19. *SQL update query*

SQL has built-in functions and arithmetic operators to allow the grouping or sorting of data and the calculation of, for example, average, minimum and maximum values in a particular field.

Defining the database

As a multi-purpose database language, SQL can be used to define, as well as manipulate and retrieve data. This definition function is traditionally carried out using a separate data description language (DDL) but SQL incorporates this facility for implementing the logical structure (*schema*) for a database. For example, to create a new table called QUALIFICATIONS the statements in Figure 29.20 may be entered:

```
CREATE TABLE QUALIFICATION
(EmpNum CHAR (3)
Qual VARCHAR (20));
```

Figure 29.20. *SQL statement to create a table*

The table would contain two fields, namely, EmpNum with a fixed length of three characters and Qual with a variable number of characters up to twenty. Following creation of the table, data can be entered immediately if required.

Modifying the database definition

Tables can be modified to allow for the removal or addition of fields, according to changes in user requirements. Existing data does not have to be re-organised and applications programs unaffected by data changes do not have to be re-written. The independence of the logical database from the applications programs is known as *logical data independence* and constitutes one of the main features of a relational database.

Two major aims are inherent in the design of SQL:

❏ As a non-procedural language it is expected to increase programmer productivity and reduce the time and costs involved in application development.

❏ SQL allows easier access to data for the purposes of on-demand or ad hoc queries.

Self-test questions

1. Pair those database terms which have the same meaning:

   tuple; *domain*; *record*; *table*; *field*; *relation*.

2. With the use of examples, define the terms:

   entity; *attribute*; *relationship*; *foreign key*.

3. When is it necessary to use a composite primary key? Illustrate your answer with an example.

4. What is the general purpose of data normalisation?

5. Convert the following structure to First Normal Form. NB [] indicates repeated items.

   Book(AccessCode, Title, Author, Synopsis [Copy No, Location])

6. List the field types typically provided by a database package, giving an example of data which would be stored in each.

7. What is the main benefit and main drawback of using field indexing?

8. What is the function of SQL?

Chapter 30

Relational database case studies

This chapter contains two database case studies to provide varied illustrations of RDBMS usage. They are: *EuroTent*, holding information on European campsites and *Stock Control*, which records details of products and suppliers. In Chapter 29, another case study, *Academic*, is used to illustrate the design process for a relational database. Chapter 31 is a complete database tutorial based on a personnel case study, *Pilcon Electronics*.

The *EuroTent* database has only one table, which holds all the information on the European campsites it has in its brochure. *Stock Control* is a database comprising two tables, one for product and the other for supplier details.

EuroTent database case study

EuroTent is a small holiday agency, specialising in a range of French campsites, details of which are published in its brochure. It also provides a ferry and site reservation service. Some clients have no clear idea about the sites they wish to use and sometimes are not even sure which region they want to visit. For these clients, the main criteria for selection are price and campsite rating. Campsites charge on a nightly basis, but the price varies according to the season. There are two charging periods: Low Season (March to May and September to October) and High Season (from June to August). Most campsites are closed outside those periods.

A computer database would allow flexible retrieval of information, using criteria, such as price range or region. Also, amendments, perhaps to site ratings or prices, could be recorded. This would allow checks to be made on the current situation, where the printed brochure may be out of date. EuroTent decide to create a single table database to manage the campsite information. A database named EuroTent is created and the task for defining the campsite table begins.

Defining the Campsite table

Figure 30.1 shows the table definition, including field names, data types and field descriptions. The lower half of the figure, shows the field properties chosen for the Pitches field.

Note that:

(i)   you can see that the selected data type is number and that the field size is *integer* (whole number only). Other optional field sizes allow for the storage of *real* numbers (they can have a fractional element) at different levels of precision (more or fewer significant digits);

(ii)   a validation rule has been set, using the expression '>=30 And <=500'. This ensures that only values between 30 and 500 are accepted; the validation text is the message which appears when an attempt is made to enter a value outside this range.

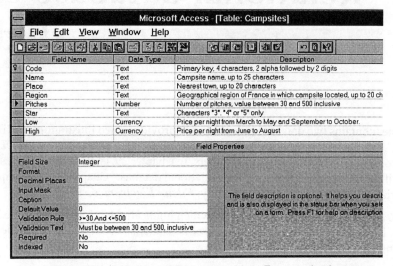

Figure 30.1. *Definition of Campsites table in Eurotent database*

The properties for three of the other fields are shown in Figure 30.2 and the entries are explained below. The Name, Place and Region fields are all text fields of varying lengths, with no other properties specified.

	Code	Star	Low
Field size	4	1	Currency
Format			
Input mask	LL00	0	
Validation rule		='3' Or '4' Or '5'	>=7 And <=25
Validation text		Characters 3, 4 or 5	Must be £7 to £25
Required	Yes	No	No
Indexed	Yes (no duplicates)	No	No

Figure 30.2. *Field properties for Code, Star and Low fields*

(i)   Code field. As you can see from Figure 30.1, this is a text field. Figure 30.2 shows that the size has been set to 4. If no other controls are exerted, any four characters can be entered. However, an *input mask* ensures that the data must have a particular pattern of entry. 'LL00', in the Access RDBMS, ensures that the first two characters are letters (A-Z) and that the last characters are digits (0-9). You can only use an input mask to set patterns for a *text*, *date* or *time* field. The field is indexed, but as the primary key for the table, it allows no duplicates (each campsite has a unique code).

(ii)　Star field. This stores a 'star' rating for a site. You can see from Figure 30.1 that this is a text field, even though the input is apparently numeric (sites are rated as '3', '4' or '5' Star). This enables an input mask to be used (0) which ensures entry of a single digit between 0 and 9. You cannot do this with a numeric field. A byte field, for example, which allows storage of values between 0 and 255 (an integer field allows –32,768 to 32,767) will not prevent the entry of real numbers, but will simply round them to the nearest whole number. The validation control for the Star field is completed by the expression ='3' Or '4' Or '5'. A suitable error message is set to display if any other characters are entered.

(iii)　Low field. This stores the price of a pitch (per night) during the less popular seasons. The High field stores the high season price. It will hold prices in sterling and the currency format ensures that if values are entered without a £ sign or without 2 decimal places, it is altered to this format. A validation rule is included to restrict values to the range 7 to 25 (you do not enter the £ sign in the expression, but it is shown in the validation text message). The High season price field has similar settings except that the prices are from £10 to £28.

Form data entry

Figure 30.3 shows some sample records in the Campsite table. You can use a *form* to enter, view and edit records. You can do the same in the table's 'data sheet' view, but you have no control over the layout or the fields which are displayed.

Code	Name	Place	Region	Pitches	Star	Low	High
DR13	Camping De Roffy	Sarlat	Dordogne	200	3	£10.00	£14.00
DR14	La Palombiere	Sarlat	Dordogne	150	4	£15.00	£19.00
DR19	St. Avit Loisirs	Le Bugue	Dordogne	180	4	£10.00	£14.50
DR22	Les Hauts De Ratebout	St. Foy	Dordogne	180	5	£17.00	£24.50
DR23	Camping Limeuil	Limieul	Dordogne	80	3	£9.00	£14.50
HP11	Camp Du Verdon	Castellane	Haute Provence	300	5	£16.50	£19.50
HP12	Les Lacs Du Verdon	Regusse	Haute Provence	150	3	£16.00	£22.00
MC11	Camping L'Ardechois	Vallon	Massif Central	120	4	£11.00	£14.50
MC16	Val De Cantobre	Cantobre	Massif Central	200	3	£9.50	£12.00
MC19	Les Tours	St Amans	Massif Central	130	3	£7.00	£10.50
MC21	Camping L'Europe	Murol	Massif Central	175	4	£13.00	£17.50
RV13	Camping De La Baie	Cavalaire	French Riveria	350	4	£14.00	£19.00
RV14	Domaine Des Naiades	Port Grimaud	French Riviera	200	4	£13.00	£16.00
RV15	Camping Des Pecheurs	Roquebrune	French Riviera	100	3	£10.00	£14.50
RV16	L'Etoile D'Argens	St. Aygulf	French Riviera	300	5	£16.50	£22.00
RV17	Residence Du Campeur	St. Aygulf	French Riviera	300	4	£13.00	£18.50
RV19	Camping De La Baume	Frejus	French Riviera	400	4	£13.50	£17.00
RV22	Les Pins Parasols	Frejus	French Riviera	80	4	£10.00	£14.50

Record: 1　of 18

Figure 30.3. *Sample records of Campsite table*

Figure 30.4 shows a form generated with a form wizard.

The form has then been modified, in design view, to include different entry labels. Unless you specify otherwise, the field names from the table definition are used.

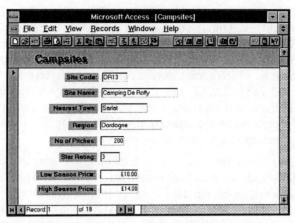

Figure 30.4. *Form with modified entry labels*

Database queries

EuroTent query 1 - Low Season Prices

The design of the first query, 'Low Season Prices', is shown in Figure 30.5.

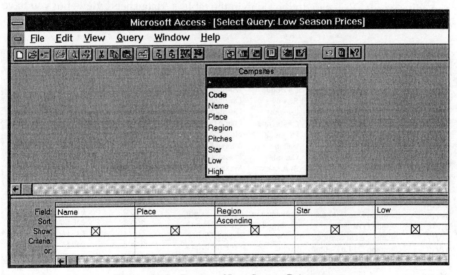

Figure 30.5. *Design of Low Season Prices query*

A customer is visiting France during March, which is part of the low season and is willing to consider any area at the moment. Therefore, a list of all sites is appropriate, but only showing the prices for the relevant season. As the figure shows, the Campsites table is selected for the query (as it happens, the database only has one table at present). Then the fields to be included in the query (Name, Place, Region, Star and Low) are placed in the relevant row in the QBE grid. If the query is to be used in a report, you can alter the order of the fields through the report design.

This query does not filter records with criteria, because a list is required of all sites in the database. However, not all details are needed and as Figure 30.5 reveals, only five field names have been placed in the QBE grid. The query is also sorting the records into ascending alphabetical order, by region.

The query, expressed in SQL, is shown in Figure 30.6.

```
SELECT DISTINCTROW Campsites.Name, Campsites.Place, Campsites.Region,
Campsites.Star, Campsites.Low
FROM Campsites
ORDER BY Campsites.Region;
```

Figure 30.6. *SQL form of Query 1 to display low season prices of sites*

The SQL reserved words 'SELECT', 'DISTINCTROW' and 'FROM' have already been used and defined in the Overview. The phrase 'ORDER BY' means sequence, or sort, using the named field; in this case it is 'Region' and is prefixed by the name of the table. Every time you use a field name in an SQL statement, you need to prefix it with its table name. This is despite the fact that the EuroTent database has only one. Note from Figure 30.5 that the table used in the QBE query has to be selected first. The table must always be named, because you can use the same field name repeatedly, provided each occurrence is in a different table. The output from the Low Season Prices query is shown in Figure 30.7.

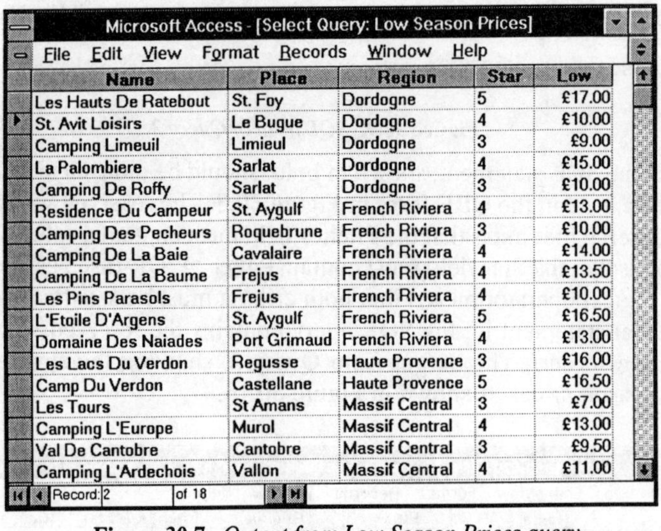

Name	Place	Region	Star	Low
Les Hauts De Ratebout	St. Foy	Dordogne	5	£17.00
St. Avit Loisirs	Le Bugue	Dordogne	4	£10.00
Camping Limeuil	Limieul	Dordogne	3	£9.00
La Palombiere	Sarlat	Dordogne	4	£15.00
Camping De Roffy	Sarlat	Dordogne	3	£10.00
Residence Du Campeur	St. Aygulf	French Riviera	4	£13.00
Camping Des Pecheurs	Roquebrune	French Riviera	3	£10.00
Camping De La Baie	Cavalaire	French Riviera	4	£14.00
Camping De La Baume	Frejus	French Riviera	4	£13.50
Les Pins Parasols	Frejus	French Riviera	4	£10.00
L'Etoile D'Argens	St. Aygulf	French Riviera	5	£16.50
Domaine Des Naiades	Port Grimaud	French Riviera	4	£13.00
Les Lacs Du Verdon	Regusse	Haute Provence	3	£16.00
Camp Du Verdon	Castellane	Haute Provence	5	£16.50
Les Tours	St Amans	Massif Central	3	£7.00
Camping L'Europe	Murol	Massif Central	4	£13.00
Val De Cantobre	Cantobre	Massif Central	3	£9.50
Camping L'Ardechois	Vallon	Massif Central	4	£11.00

Record: 2 of 18

Figure 30.7. *Output from Low Season Prices query*

EuroTent query 2 - Pitches 150 or less, Low Season, 4 to 5 Star

Customers visiting France when campsite prices are lower can afford to be more selective and frequently choose small, but good quality sites. This query (Figure 30.8) is designed to produce the kind of information they require.

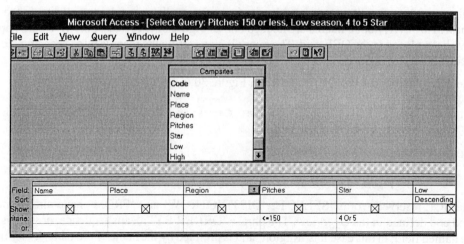

Figure 30.8. *Design of Query 2*

The SQL form of Query 2 is shown in Figure 30.9.

```
SELECT DISTINCTROW Campsites.Name, Campsites.Place, Campsites.Region,
Campsites.Pitches, Campsites.Star, Campsites.Low
FROM Campsites
WHERE ((Campsites.Pitches<=150) AND (Campsites.Star="4" OR
Campsites.Star="5"))
ORDER BY Campsites.Low DESC;
```

Figure 30.9. *SQL form of Query 2*

The meaning of the SQL statement, shown in bold, should be quite clear when you compare it with the criteria used in the QBE form in Figure 30.8. The reserved word WHERE is followed by two criteria; the first is that the Pitches field must contain a value of 150 or less; the second criterion is that the Star field must contain either '4' OR (used as a *logical operator*) '5'. The AND logical operator means that both criteria must be satisfied, before a record is selected. The final statement in this SQL query contains the reserved word DESC, which means *descending* (order). The output from Query 2, showing the smaller, better quality sites, with low season prices, is shown in Figure 30.10.

Name	Place	Region	Pitches	Star	Low
La Palombiere	Sarlat	Dordogne	150	4	£15.00
Camping L'Ardechois	Vallon	Massif Central	120	4	£11.00
Les Pins Parasols	Frejus	French Riviera	80	4	£10.00

Record: 1 of 3

Figure 30.10. *Output from Query 2*

EuroTent query 3 - French Riviera £14 to £19

This query is in response to a more precise request for information. A family wish to stay in the Riviera region during the High season and are willing to pay between £14 and £19 a night. The query design is displayed in Figure 30.11.

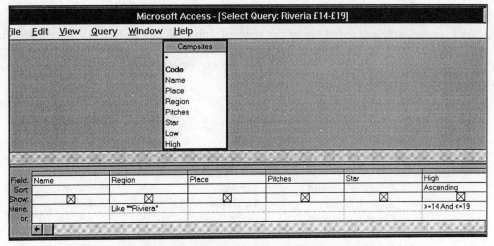

Figure 30.11. *Design of query for Riviera sites between £14 and £19*

The main point to note is that there are two criteria, one concerning the Region and the other, the High season price. The latter is similar to the criterion used in Query 2. The criterion that the Region should be the French Riviera could have been expressed fully, in the form ='French Riviera'. QBE does not require the use of an '=' sign, so you could simply type 'French Riviera' as the criterion. In Figure 30.11, a wild card (*) is used, thus: *Riviera. The RDBMS takes this as being a request for any string of characters which ends with 'Riviera' and prefixes it with 'Like', which is the proper form of the expression.

If there were other occurrences of the string 'Riviera' in the Region column, such as 'Italian Riviera', you would have to be more specific.

The SQL form of Query 3 is displayed in Figure 30.12.

```
SELECT DISTINCTROW Campsites.Name, Campsites.Region, Campsites.Place,
Campsites.Pitches, Campsites.Star, Campsites.High
FROM Campsites
WHERE ((Campsites.Region Like "*Riviera") AND (Campsites.High>=14 And
Campsites.High<=19))
ORDER BY Campsites.High;
```

Figure 30.12. *SQL form of Query 3*

The results of running Query 2 are displayed in Figure 30.13.

Name	Region	Place	Pitches	Star	High
Les Pins Parasols	French Riviera	Frejus	80	4	£14.50
Camping Des Pecheurs	French Riviera	Roquebrune	100	3	£14.50
Domaine Des Naiades	French Riviera	Port Grimaud	200	4	£16.00
Camping De La Baume	French Riviera	Frejus	400	4	£17.00
Residence Du Campeur	French Riviera	St. Aygulf	300	4	£18.50
Camping De La Baie	French Riviera	Cavalaire	350	4	£19.00

Record: 1 of 6

Figure 30.13. *Output from query for Riviera sites at £14 to £19 per night*

A grouped column report

Query 1 produces the full list of campsites, ordered alphabetically by Region. Since there are several sites in each region, each region's name is repeated. A grouped column report only displays each group name once. Figure 30.14 shows an extract from a grouped report on the output from EuroTent's Query 1.

EuroTent		*14-May-95*	Low Season Prices	
Region	**Name**	**Place**	**Rating**	**Price**
Dordogne				
	Camping Limeuil	Limieul	3	£9.00
	St. Avit Loisirs	Le Bugue	4	£10.00
	Camping De Roffy	Sarlat	3	£10.00
	La Palombiere	Sarlat	4	£15.00
	Les Hauts De Ratebout	St. Foy	5	£17.00
French Riviera				
	Camping Des Pecheurs	Roquebrune	3	£10.00
	Les Pins Parasols	Frejus	4	£10.00
	Residence Du Campeur	St.Aygulf	4	£13.00
	Domaine Des Naiades	Port Grimaud	4	£13.00
	Camping De La Baume	Frejus	4	£13.50
	Camping De La Baie	Cavalaire	4	£14.00
	L'Etoile D'Argens	St. Aygulf	5	£16.50
Haute Provence				
	Les Lacs Du Verdon	Regusse	3	£16.00

Figure 30.14. *Extract from grouped report on output for Query 1*

Stock Control database case study

This example makes use of the Product table, used for illustration in the Overview, plus a Supplier table. The full definitions of the database are not given here. The main purpose of the Stock Control case study is to illustrate editing tables through a query *dynaset* (the data extracted by a query) and further aspects of *forms*.

Editing tables through query dynasets

The contents of the Product and Supplier tables are shown in Figures 30.15 and 30.16, respectively. Suppose, for example, that you wish to view and edit the combined information from both tables. You could join the tables in a query, the design of which is shown in Figure 30.17. The simple datasheet view of the resulting dynaset is shown in Figure 30.18.

You should notice that each supplier name and address is repeated several times. The relationship between the Supplier and Product tables is one-to-many, which means that many products are bought from a single supplier, but each product is ordered from a single supplier. Although the information from both tables can be viewed, only certain fields can be edited to update the tables, upon which the query is based. In the case of a one-to-many relationship, changes can only be made to dynaset fields which come from the *many* side of the relationship.

Microsoft Access - [Table: Product]

File   Edit   View   Format   Records   Window   Help

PartCode	Description	Price	Quantity	SupplierCode
A123	Table (Cottage)	£23.50	15	KSU518
A124	Chair (Cottage)	£42.23	36	KIT518
A125	Stool (Cottage)	£28.15	6	KIT518
A133	Bar Stool	£33.55	4	KSU518
A136	Bread Bin (wood)	£14.25	4	KIT518
A139	Bread Bin (metal)	£10.25	6	KSU518
B122	Spanner (adjustable)	£8.25	4	BCS436
B126	Step Ladder (small)	£19.50	6	PAR116
B129	Screw Driver (ratchet)	£15.55	13	BCS436
B133	Ladders (aluminium)	£85.66	2	STA436
B136	Spirit Level	£13.55	6	STA436
B145	Step Ladder (medium)	£31.25	4	PAR116
B181	Hammer (medium claw)	£6.75	12	STA436

Record 6   of 13

Figure 30.15. *Sample contents of Product table*

Microsoft Access - [Table: supplier]

File   Edit   View   Format   Records   Window   Help

SupplierCode	SupplierName	SupplierAddress
BCS436	BCS Supplies	Imperial Buildings, Darlington DL3 4ST
KIT518	Kitchen Systems	28 Holmeside, Sunderland, SR3 4ST
KSU518	Kitchen Supplies	112 High Street, Darlington, DL1 4SJ
PAR116	Parsons Ltd	Parsons House, Market Place, York YO4 3NS
STA436	Stapleton Bros	36 Warwick Place, Darlington, DL4 6AJ

Record 1   of 5

Figure 30.16. *Sample contents of Supplier table*

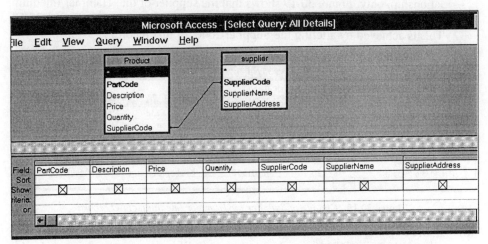

Figure 30.17. *Query to join information from Product and Supplier tables*

PartCode	Description	Price	Quantity	SupplierCode	SupplierName	Su
B181	Hammer (medium claw)	£6.75	12	STA436	Stapleton Bros	36 Warwick Place, Dai
B133	Ladders (aluminium)	£85.66	2	STA436	Stapleton Bros	36 Warwick Place, Dai
B136	Spirit Level	£13.55	6	STA436	Stapleton Bros	36 Warwick Place, Dai
A124	Chair (Cottage)	£42.23	36	KIT518	Kitchen Systems	28 Holmeside, Sunder
A125	Stool (Cottage)	£28.15	6	KIT518	Kitchen Systems	28 Holmeside, Sunder
A136	Bread Bin (wood)	£14.25	4	KIT518	Kitchen Systems	28 Holmeside, Sunder
B126	Step Ladder (small)	£19.50	6	PAR116	Parsons Ltd	Parsons House, Marke
B145	Step Ladder (medium)	£31.25	4	PAR116	Parsons Ltd	Parsons House, Marke
A123	Table (Cottage)	£23.50	15	KSU518	Kitchen Supplies	112 High Street, Darlir
A133	Bar Stool	£33.55	4	KSU518	Kitchen Supplies	112 High Street, Darlir
A139	Bread Bin (metal)	£10.25	6	KSU518	Kitchen Supplies	112 High Street, Darlir
B129	Screw Driver (ratchet)	£15.55	13	BCS436	BCS Supplies	Imperial Buildings, Dai
B145	Spanner (adjustable)	£8.25	4	BCS436	BCS Supplies	Imperial Buildings, Dai

Record: 2   of 13

Figure 30.18. *Dynaset from query joining Product and Supplier tables*

Two important points need to be understood.

(i)   Referring to Figure 30.17, if the query uses the SupplierCode from the Product table, you will be able to alter the Supplier codes in the dynaset shown in Figure 30.18. The name and address will then change accordingly (by using the relationship established with the Supplier table). The changes to the supplier details will be applied to the underlying Product table. Changes affect the many side of the relationship, only. Figure 30.19 shows that the supplier of the 'Hammer (medium, claw)' is now 'Parsons Ltd', instead of 'Stapleton', as shown in Figure 30.18. This is achieved by altering the SupplierCode for that record.

Description	Price	Quantity	SupplierCode	SupplierName	Su
Hammer (medium claw)	£6.75	12	PAR116	Parsons Ltd	Parsons House, Marke
Ladders (aluminium)	£85.66	2	STA436	Stapleton	36 Warwick Place, Dai
Spirit Level	£13.55	6	STA436	Stapleton	36 Warwick Place, Dai
Chair (Cottage)	£42.23	36	KIT518	Kitchen Systems	28 Holmeside, Sunder
Stool (Cottage)	£28.15	6	KIT518	Kitchen Systems	28 Holmeside, Sunder
Bread Bin (wood)	£14.25	4	KIT518	Kitchen Systems	28 Holmeside, Sunder

1   of 13

Figure 30.19. *Change of Supplier for Hammer (medium, claw) record*

(ii)   If, in designing the query in Figure 30.17, you use the SupplierCode from the Supplier table, the RDBMS would not let you edit it through the dynaset. In this example, this means that you can edit the Product table (the *many* side), but not the Supplier table (the *one* side), through the query dynaset.

If the underlying tables have a one-to-one relationship there are no editing restrictions through the dynaset. If you want to prevent any editing through a dynaset, the RDBMS provides an option to disable the facility. There are other circumstances when dynaset editing is restricted, but they are beyond the scope of this text.

Viewing and editing with main/sub forms

Figure 30.18 shows a dynaset which provides a view of all the information in both the Product and Supplier tables. The main drawback is that the suppliers' names and addresses are repeated several times. In addition, as a dynaset, the Supplier table (the *one* side of the one-to-many relationship) cannot be edited through it. Editing could be carried out using a separate form for each table, or more effectively, with the main/sub form shown in Figure 30.20.

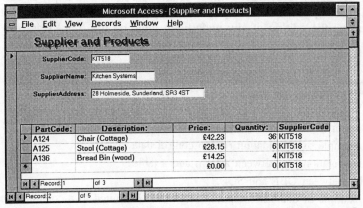

Figure 30.20. *Main/sub Form showing one Supplier record and the associated Products*

The form can be created using a form wizard, but you can start with separate forms and then combine them, making the Product form the sub. As you scroll through each Supplier record (you can see that there is a scroll bar for each part of the form), all the associated (through the SupplierCode relationship) Product records appear in the lower, sub form. You can edit or add new Supplier Records, by using the upper, main form.

Figure 30.21 shows a new supplier record entered within the main form, but before entry of any product records for that supplier.

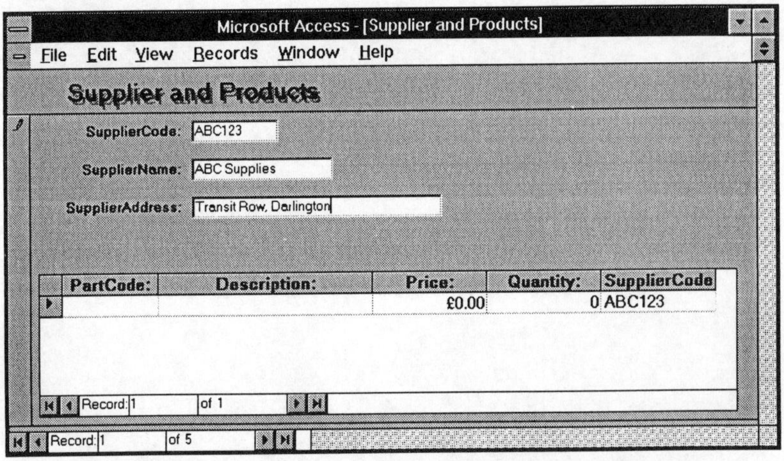

Figure 30.21. *Entry of new Supplier, but before entry of Products*

Entry of a new supplier code would mean that there would be no Product records in the sub form; you could then enter any details of products supplied by the new supplier. Similarly, you can edit or add new Product records in the sub form, for an existing supplier. Remember, changing a SupplierCode in the Product section of the form (the *many* side) will not affect records in the Supplier table (the *one* side).

Forms for dynasets

The rules which apply to dynaset editing, detailed already, also apply to editing through a form. Thus, creating a form for the dynaset shown in Figure 30.18, does not alter the restrictions concerning the editing of any underlying table on the 'one' side of a one-to-many relationship.

Self-test questions

1. What is an input mask?
2. Give an example of a validation rule to control data entry.
3. What is the relationship between a form and a table?
4. Distinguish between QBE and SQL.
5. Give an example of database output which would be suited to a column report.
6. Use an example to illustrate the use of a main/sub form.

Chapter 31

Relational database tutorial

This Tutorial guides you through the process of designing, creating and using a Personnel database with Microsoft Access, a relational database management system. The chapter concludes with an illustration of how the database might be documented. The aim of this Tutorial is to show you the main practical steps that you need to follow and use them to explain some important relational database concepts. With a proper understanding of these concepts you will be better able to design, create and use databases for other applications. Pilcon Electronics is a manufacturer with a traditional hierarchical staffing structure. The Personnel department is setting up a database to hold personal staff details which are currently stored manually. Each staff member's details are held on a single sheet as shown in Figure 31.1.

Pilcon Electronics Staff Record						
Staff Code	Surname	Initials	Job Title	Salary	Start Date	Pension Scheme
108	Winkle	R.V.	Supervisor	£18,000	1 Sep 85	Yes

Dept Head	Dept Name
I. Lostem	Warehousing

Course Date	Course Title	Duration	Certificated
8 Jul 99	Excel SS 2	4	No
8 Dec 99	Excel SS 3	4	No
5 Mar 00	Access 1	3	No

Figure 31.1. *Manual staff record in Pilcon Electronics*

Data normalisation

Converting this information into a suitable form for entry to a relational database requires the application of data normalisation rules. Normalisation is a technique established by E.F. Codd to simplify the structure of data as it is *logically viewed* by the programmer or user. With the relatively simple structure shown in Figure 31.1, it is not difficult to identify the separate subjects or *entities* which exist within it. There are the personal details of Mr. Winkle, the name of his Department, his Job title and the Courses he has attended. So, without any consideration of normalisation rules, we could suggest that four tables (one for each entity) should be created, as follows:

STAFFMEMBER   DEPARTMENT   JOB   TRAINING

However, when the information is split into these separate tables, the relationship between each staff member and the associated department, job title and training record must be maintained. The application of three normalisation rules will help us to do this and for more complex structures, the process is essential. We begin by considering the first rule of normalisation - the removal of repeating groups.

First Normal Form (1NF)

Notice that Mr. Winkle has attended three training courses; using standard computer file terminology, Course Date, Course Title, Duration and Certificated are *repeating groups*. Table 31.1 shows that a relational database table cannot accommodate repeating groups because it results in repetition of the same primary key value for multiple records, when the primary key for each record must remain unique.

Staff Code	Surname	etc	Course Date	Course Title	Duration	Certificated
108	Winkle	......	8 Jul 99	Excel SS 2	4	No
108	Winkle	....	8 Dec 99	Excel SS 3	4	No
108	Winkle	....	5 Mar 00	Access 1	3	No

Table 31.1. *Illegal duplicated primary key value*

The first stage of normalisation demands

❑   removal of any repeating groups.

This is the only normalisation rule that <u>must</u> be satisfied for data to be stored in a relational database. It <u>may</u> be desirable to apply the second and third stages but it is not essential. The original data structure can be expressed formally as follows.

```
StaffMember(Staff Code, Surname, Initials, Job Title, Salary, Start
Date, Pension, Dept Name, DeptHead [Course Date, Course Title,
Duration, Certificated])
```

Figure 31.2. *Personnel data structure before normalisation*

The fields bounded by square [brackets] identify the repeating groups which are to be placed in a separate entity called TRAINING, as follows. The entity names have the suffix 1 for 1NF.

```
STAFFMEMBER-1(StaffCode, Surname, Initials, JobCode, JobTitle, Salary,
StartDate, Pension, DeptCode, DeptName, DeptHead)

TRAINING-1(CourseDate, StaffCode, CourseTitle, Duration, Certificated)
```

Figure 31.3. *Personnel entity structures in First Normal Form (1NF)*

Note the addition of two attributes, JobCode to associate with JobTitle and DeptCode, to associate with DeptName and DeptHead. They are not needed in the manual system, but we will need them when defining the relational database structure.

Relationships and foreign keys

Figure 31.3 shows that to retain the link between a staff member and his or her training details, `StaffCode` (primary key for STAFFMEMBER-1) is included in TRAINING-1 as a *foreign key*. Some necessary *data redundancy* is created by including `StaffCode` in both entities. However, such duplication of data does not necessarily mean an increased use of storage because normalisation is concerned with the *logical structure* of the data and not with the ways in which the data is physically organised.

Composite primary keys

To ensure the uniqueness of each TRAINING-1 record, the `CourseDate` and `StaffCode` form a composite primary key. `CourseDate` on its own cannot ensure a unique value because there may be several members of staff attending the same course or other courses which start on the same day. Equally, StaffCode could not guarantee uniqueness because a member of staff may attend several courses (but not on the same day).

Second Normal Form (2NF)

The second rule of normalisation requires that

❏ all non-identifying attributes are *functionally dependent* on the unique identifier (the primary key).

If the identifier is composite (comprising more that one attribute), then non-identifying attributes must be functionally dependent on the whole of the identifier. Referring back to Figure 31.3 showing the 1-NF entities, it can be seen that in the TRAINING-1 entity the non-identifying attributes of `CourseTitle`, `Duration` and `Certificated` do depend on the entire composite key. Put simply, to obtain details of a particular course you would need to specify a date an a staff code value, for example, 3/4/99 and 103. Entering 3/4/99 on its own may bring up several records for courses which started on the same day. If the staff member 103 had attended several courses, this value would also result in the retrieval of multiple records. In this case, the 1-NF structures also satisfy the 2-NF rules and can be given the suffix-2 as shown in Figure 31.4.

```
STAFFMEMBER-2(StaffCode, Surname, Initials, JobCode, JobTitle, Salary,
StartDate, Pension, DeptCode, DeptName, DeptHead)

TRAINING-2(CourseDate, StaffCode, CourseTitle, Duration, Certificated)
```

Figure 31.4. *Unmodified Personnel entity structures in Second Normal Form (2NF)*

An alternative structure

To show what would happen if the 2NF rules did require the modification of a structure, consider the slightly modified Personnel 1NF entities in Figure 31.5.

```
STAFFMEMBER-1(StaffCode, Surname, Initials, JobCode, JobTitle, Salary,
StartDate, Pension, DeptCode, DeptName, DeptHead)

TRAINING-1(CourseCode, StaffCode, CourseTitle, Duration, Certificated)
```

Figure 31.5. *Modified structure which does not meet the Second Normal Form rule*

Figure 31.5 shows that `CourseDate` has been replaced by a `CourseCode`, which identifies a particular course which is not dependent on a date, but exists in its own right. In this case, `CourseTitle`, `Duration` and `Certificated` are only dependent on `CourseCode`.

To convert the structure to 2NF requires that the Course details are made a separate entity, as shown in Figure 31.6.

```
STAFFMEMBER-2(StaffCode, Surname, Initials, JobCode, JobTitle, Salary,
StartDate, Pension, DeptCode, DeptName, DeptHead)

TRAINING-2(CourseCode, StaffCode)

COURSE-2(CourseCode, CourseTitle, Duration, Certificated)
```

Figure 31.6 *Application of 2NF rules to create separate COURSE entity*

The relationship between the Training record and Course record is maintained through `CourseCode`. The potential benefit of having a separate entity `COURSE-2` is that new Course records could be created before any staff had attended the courses that they detail. This would be appropriate, if for example, an organisation (such as a college) ran numerous internal courses. This is not the case in Pilcon where Course details are only associated with staff attendance, that is, particular course details do not appear in the database unless a staff member attends it. However, it has to be recognised that the arrangement does lead to some duplication of course details. Our original structure could be modified to allow the use of a separate Course entity, but this does not suit the requirements of Pilcon.

Third Normal Form (3NF)

For convenience, the 2NF structures are repeated below.

```
STAFFMEMBER-2(StaffCode, Surname, Initials, JobCode, JobTitle, Salary,
StartDate, Pension, DeptCode, DeptName, DeptHead)

TRAINING-2(CourseDate, StaffCode, CourseTitle, Duration, Certificated)
```

The third stage of normalisation requires:

❑   the removal of any *functional dependencies* between non-identifying attributes.

A simple test is to ask "Are there any non-identifying attributes which would act as the unique identifier in a separate table?" `STAFFMEMBER-2` contains two such attributes, namely, `JobCode` and `DeptCode`. Clearly, `JobTitle` is dependent on `JobCode` and `DeptName` is dependent on `DeptCode` and in their present form the entities do not satisfy the 3NF rule. We can satisfy the rule by creating an entity for each. Figure 31.7 shows the structure in 3NF.

```
STAFFMEMBER-3(StaffCode, Surname, Initials, JobCode, Salary,
StartDate, Pension, DeptCode)
TRAINING-3(CourseDate, StaffCode, CourseTitle, Duration, Certificated)
JOB-3 (JobCode, JobTitle)
DEPARTMENT-3 (DeptCode, DeptName, DeptHead)
```

Figure 31.7. *Personnel structure in Third Normal Form (3NF)*

In STAFFMEMBER-3, JobCode and DeptCode are foreign keys to maintain the relationships with the JOB-3 and DEPARTMENT-3 entities respectively.

Defining the database dictionary

A data dictionary (Chapter 26) system is a data processing department's own information system, with the database administrator, systems analysts and programmers as the main users.

A dictionary for the Personnel database is shown in Tables 31.2, 31.3, 31.4 and 31.5. It is good practice to prepare it before setting up the database.

STAFFMEMBER				
Field name	StaffCode	Surname	Initials	JobCode
Data type	text	text	text	text
Field size	3	25	4	3
Input mask	000			LL0
Validation rule	>=100 and <=200			
Validation text	Range 100 to 200			
Required	Yes	No	No	No
Indexed	Yes (no duplicates)	No	No	No
Field name	DeptCode	Salary	StartDate	Pension
Data type	text	currency	date	yes/no
Field size	3	0 decimal places		
Input mask	LLL			
Validation rule	ACC or GOS or MIS or PER or PRO or PUR or RAD or SAL or WAR	>=8000 and <=45000	<=now()	
Validation text	Invalid Code	Range 8000 to 45000	Invalid date	
Required	No	No	No	No
Indexed	Yes (duplicates OK)	No	No	No

Table 31.2. *STAFFMEMBER data dictionary definition*

TRAINING		
Field name	CourseDate	StaffCode	CourseTitle
Data type	date	text	text
Field size		3	30
Input mask		000	
Validation rule		>=100 and <=200	
Validation text		Range 100 to 200	
Required	Yes	Yes	No
Indexed	Yes (Duplicates OK)	Yes (Duplicates OK)	No

Field name	Duration	Certificated	
Data type	number	yes/no	
Field size	integer 0 decimal places		
Input mask			
Validation rule	>=1 and <=10	>=8000 and <=45000	
Validation text	Range 1 to 10	Range 8000 to 45000	
Required	No	No	No
Indexed	No	No	No

Table 31.3. *TRAINING data dictionary definition*

JOB		
Field name	JobCode	JobTitle
Data type	text	text
Field size	3	35
Input mask	LL0	
Validation rule		
Validation text		
Required	Yes	No
Indexed	Yes (No duplicates)	No

Table 31.4. *JOB data dictionary definition*

DEPARTMENT			
Field name	DeptCode	DeptTitle	DeptHead
Data type	text	text	Synonym for
Field size	3	35	StaffCode
Input mask	LLL		
Validation rule	same as in STAFFMEMBER		
Validation text	Invalid code		
Required	Yes	No	
Indexed	Yes (No duplicates)	No	

Table 31.5. *DEPARTMENT data dictionary definition*

Setting up the Personnel database

Having set up a new blank database in Access, you need to define a table for each entity. Refer to the data dictionary definitions shown on the previous two pages. The four completed table definitions are shown in Figures 31.8, 31.9, 31.10 and 31.11. Note the use of the Description column to further clarify the nature of each field.

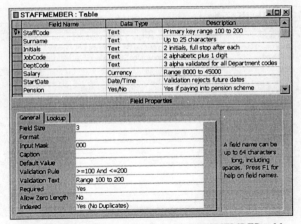

Figure 31.8. *Access definition of STAFFMEMBER table*

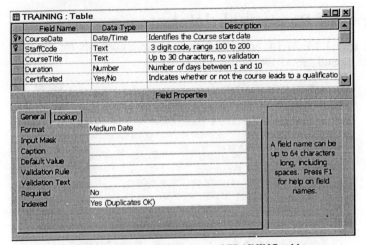

Figure 31.9. *Access definition of TRAINING table*

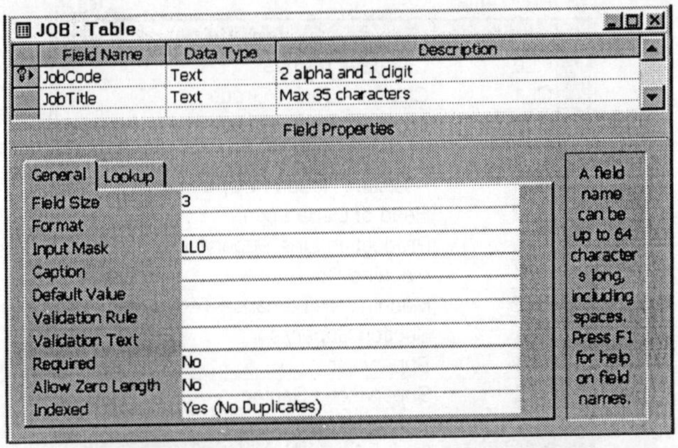

Figure 31.10. *Access definition of JOB table*

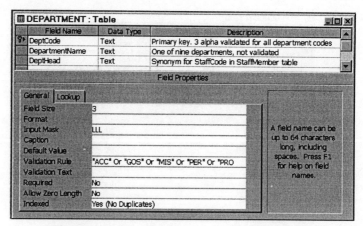

Figure 31.11. *Access definition of DEPARTMENT table*

Contents of Personnel database

Figures 31.12, 31.13, 31.14, and 31.15 show sample contents for the DEPARTMENT, JOB, STAFFMEMBER and TRAINING tables, respectively.

DeptCode	DeptName	DeptHead
ACC	Accounting and Finance	128
GOS	General Office Services	155
MIS	Management Information Services	160
PER	Personnel	168
PRO	Production	149
PUR	Purchasing	136
RAD	Research and Development	172
SAL	Sales and Marketing	180
WAR	Warehousing	187

Record: 1 of 9

Figure 31.12. *Sample contents for DEPARTMENT table*

JobCode	JobTitle
CL0	Clerical - Trainee
CL1	Clerical - Junior Grade
CL2	Clerical - Middle Grade
CL3	Clerical - Senior
HD1	Assistant Head of Department
HD2	Head of Department
LS1	Production Line Supervisor
OP1	Machine Operator
OP2	Machine Maintenance Technician
SS1	Section Supervisor
SU1	Supervisor
SU2	Supervisor - Senior

Record: 1 of 12

Figure 31.13. *Sample contents for JOB table*

StaffCode	Surname	Initials	JobCode	DeptCode	Salary	StartDate	Pension
100	Picket	W.	CL2	ACC	£15,000	23-Jan-77	☑
101	Ringwood	K.	HD1	PRO	£33,000	14-May-95	☑
103	Clacket	D.	CL0	GOS	£13,500	01-Jan-85	☐
106	Boreham	L.	SS1	ACC	£23,000	23-Sep-72	☑
108	Winkle	R.V.	SU1	WAR	£18,000	01-Sep-85	☑
110	Dickens	C.	OP1	PRO	£8,000	14-May-95	☐
115	Cratchit	B.	CL2	ACC	£8,500	01-May-94	☐
118	Boffin	C.	HD1	RAD	£38,000	01-Sep-66	☑
123	Heap	U.	HD1	SAL	£37,500	31-Oct-93	☑
124	Miggins	M.	SU1	GOS	£14,500	31-Oct-93	☑
126	Squeers	W.	SS1	PER	£37,500	13-Jun-88	☑
128	Chiseller	M.	HD2	ACC	£43,000	01-Apr-83	☑
131	Marley	J.	OP1	PRO	£8,600	16-Jun-91	☐
133	Server	I.	HD1	WAR	£32,000	01-Sep-60	☑
136	Grabbit	U.	HD2	PUR	£45,000	12-Apr-66	☑
138	Stackit	I.	OP1	WAR	£9,200	03-Apr-68	☐
139	Broaket	H.E.	OP2	PRO	£13,000	17-Apr-85	☑
145	Ramidos	Z.	SU1	MIS	£17,900	12-Jun-88	☑
149	Machem	I.	HD2	PRO	£40,000	01-Apr-90	☑
155	Pusher	P.	HD2	GOS	£44,000	01-Feb-60	☑
159	Nervey	M.	OP1	WAR	£10,000	01-Apr-95	☐
160	Surcoat	I.	HD2	MIS	£40,000	02-May-66	☑
168	Sached	U.R.	HD2	PER	£37,000	02-Mar-66	☑
172	Tefal	B.	HD2	RAD	£37,000	02-Mar-85	☑
180	Leavmey	B.	HD2	SAL	£42,000	01-Oct-72	☑
187	Lostem	I.	HD2	WAR	£32,500	31-Oct-88	☑
190	Fezziwig	M.	CL1	SAL	£9,000	14-Jun-85	☑
195	Swidger	F.	CL1	SAL	£10,000	10-May-74	☑
197	Dilber	C.	CL2	MIS	£11,400	09-Sep-82	☐

Record: 1 of 29

Figure 31.14. *Sample contents for STAFFMEMBER table*

CourseDate	StaffCode	CourseTitle	Duration	Certificat
02-Mar-99	103	Pegasus Accounts 1	5	☑
09-Mar-99	110	CAD 3 Circuit Design	3	☑
09-Mar-99	118	Neural Networks Advanced	10	☐
16-Mar-99	145	Oracle Server Concepts 1	1	☑
04-Apr-99	103	Pegasus Accounts 2	5	☑
07-Jun-99	115	Pegasus Advanced	4	☑
07-Jun-99	168	Access Database 1	3	☐
08-Jul-99	108	Excel Spreadsheet 2	4	☐
14-Jul-99	106	Pegasus Advanced	4	☑
18-Jul-99	131	CAD 2 Circuit Design	3	☑
15-Sep-99	197	Oracle Server Concepts 1	1	☑
20-Oct-99	197	Oracle Server Concepts 2	3	☐
13-Nov-99	139	CAD 1 Circuit Design	4	☐
08-Dec-99	108	Excel Spreadsheet 3	4	☐
08-Jan-00	145	Oracle Server Concepts 2	3	☐
05-Mar-00	108	Access Database 1	3	☐

Record: 1 of 16

Figure 31.15. *Sample contents for TRAINING table*

Forms

You can use a form to tailor your view of information held in a table. A form is always associated with a particular table (or query - see later) and allows you to enter, edit and view the data held within it. A form is not a separate store of data, but simply an alternative view of its associated table. A benefit of a form is that it allows you to view or edit one record at a time; the standard *datasheet* view (see previous screen shots of sample table contents) in Access displays as many records as can be accommodated within its window. Figure 31.16 shows a form associated with the STAFFMEMBER. It has a column layout and was created with Form Wizard.

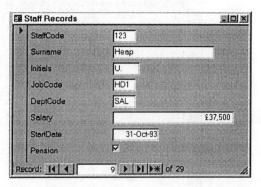

Figure 31.16. *Form view of STAFFMEMBER table*

You can begin with a blank form and design your layout, or more easily, you can produce one with a wizard and then modify it to your requirements. Figure 31.17 shows the Staff Records Form in design mode, with the StaffCode field label selected and the Toolbox used for, amongst other things, inserting *command buttons* and *list boxes*. You can see from the Figure that a form consists of a number of objects, including *field labels* and *data entry* points. Each data entry point uses the field name defined in the table definition and ensures that each entry point on the form is associated with the correct field in a record. As a consequence, field names should not be altered on the form (unless

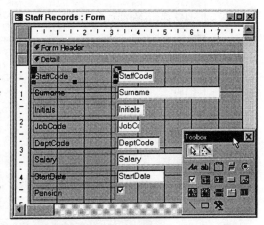

Figure 31.17. *Form design view and toolbox*

they are also altered in the table definition). Field labels, on the other hand can be altered; the field names are used by default, unless you specify otherwise. The form design is divided into sections: *header* (for titles); *detail* (for the field names and data entry points); *footer* (for additional comments, perhaps to guide the data entry process).

Reports

Report facilities allow you to decide what information from a table (or query) is visible when you view it or print it. Reports are usually categorised as:

❑ *Single column*. Records are displayed in full down the side of the page or screen, rather than across the page in columns.

❑ *Multiple column*. A column is provided for each field you specify and records are placed one after another. You can allow the field names to be used as column headings, or design your own.

- ❑ *Grouped*. If the information can be grouped into different levels, then the report can be presented in this way, with sub-totals or other calculations on numeric or currency fields, at the end of each group or subgroup.

Figure 31.18 shows a report on screen, generated with a 'report wizard', using the `TRAINING` table . The sequence is by StaffCode and this was specified as part of the report construction process. As with *forms*, you can design a report from scratch or use a wizard and then switch to Design view and modify the design as necessary. The headings in the report have been changed using design view.

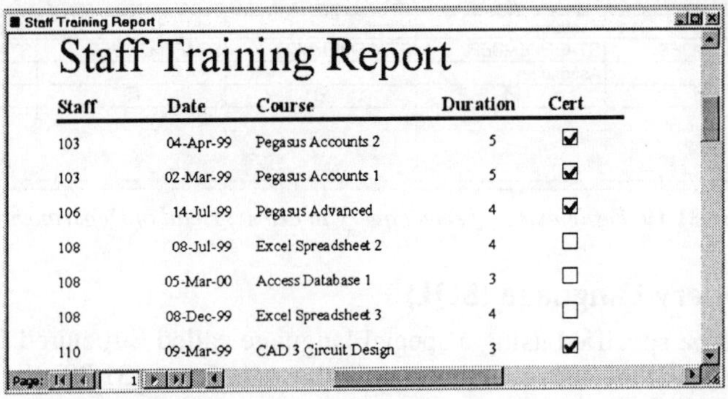
Staff Training Report

Staff Training Report

Staff	Date	Course	Duration	Cert
103	04-Apr-99	Pegasus Accounts 2	5	☑
103	02-Mar-99	Pegasus Accounts 1	5	☑
106	14-Jul-99	Pegasus Advanced	4	☑
108	08-Jul-99	Excel Spreadsheet 2	4	☐
108	05-Mar-00	Access Database 1	3	☐
108	08-Dec-99	Excel Spreadsheet 3	4	☐
110	09-Mar-99	CAD 3 Circuit Design	3	☑

Page: 1

Figure 31.18. *Column report on contents of TRAINING table with modified headings*

To include, for example, staff names in the Report would require that it be based on a query which used the STAFFMEMBER and TRAINING tables. We will look at such a query next.

Queries

A query is a request for information from a database. You can use a query to:

(i) display information from several tables by *joining* them (see later);

(ii) display limited information by specifying that only certain fields are displayed;

(iii) use *criteria* to *filter* records from one table or from several joined together.

Select query

To illustrate (iii), we will specify that records are to be filtered from the `STAFFMEMBER` table if the `JobCode` field contains "HD2", which according to the Pilcon coding system means Heads of Department. Although the JobCode field must be used in the query, we can choose not to display its contents, which would simply be a repetition of "HD2". Also we will specify that the records are listed in ascending `StaffCode` order. Figure 31.19 shows the *select* query designed to meet these requirements.

The Figure shows the query design grid with the criterion ="HD2" in the `JobCode` column, the 'Show' box deselected and 'Ascending' in the `StaffCode` column to dictate the sequence. `DeptCode` has been left out of the query.
This form of specifying queries is often referred to as a query by example (QBE).

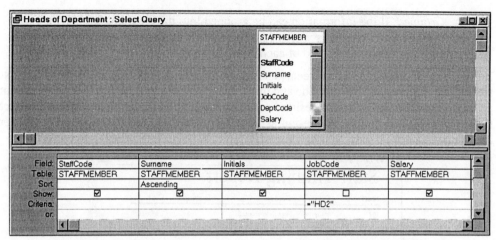

Figure 31.19. *Design view of select query to extract Head of Department records*

Structured Query Language (SQL)

Queries can also be specified using a special language called Structured Query Language. The SQL equivalent of the above select query is shown in Figure 31.20. Access allows you to view the SQL equivalent of any query you create.

```
SELECT STAFFMEMBER.StaffCode, STAFFMEMBER.Surname,
STAFFMEMBER.Initials, STAFFMEMBER.JobCode, STAFFMEMBER.Salary
FROM STAFFMEMBER
WHERE (((STAFFMEMBER.JobCode)="HD2"))
ORDER BY STAFFMEMBER.Surname;
```

Figure 31.20. *An example of Structured Query Language*

We are not concerned with the details of this language in this chapter (see Chapter 30 for more examples), but you should be able to see that it is a rather stilted form of natural language. Many new RDBMS packages provide SQL. Developed by IBM, SQL is a *non-procedural* language and as such belongs to the group of programming languages known as 4th Generation Languages (4GLs); this means that programmers and trained users can specify what they want from a database without having to specify how to do it. Procedural languages such as COBOL, Pascal and C, require the programmer to detail, explicitly, how a program must navigate through a file or database to obtain the necessary output. The programmer must, for example, code procedures such as read the first master record, process it, read the next, process it and so on until the end of the file is reached.

Relationships

For a query to extract information from more than one table requires that relationships exist between them, through the use of primary and foreign keys. If the keys which relate two tables use the same name, for example, JobCode, the primary key in JOB and JobCode, the foreign key in STAFFMEMBER, then Access will detect and establish the relationship when you first use the tables in a query. Otherwise, if one key is a *synonym* for the other, for example, DeptHead in DEPARTMENT is a synonym for StaffCode in STAFFMEMBER, the relationship will not be automatically detected. Figure 31.21 shows a query design with the four Personnel database tables, with all relationships detected save for the one between `DeptHead` and `StaffCode`.

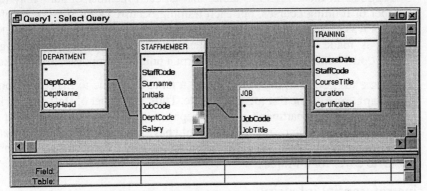

Figure 31.21. *Relationships can be automatically detected, except for synonyms*

Establishing relationships explicitly

Relationships can be established explicitly as shown in Figure 31.22, by dragging the foreign key from its table to the relevant primary key field in the related table.

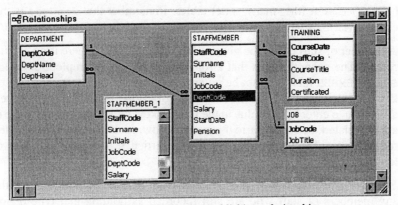

Figure 31.22. *Explicitly establishing relationships*

The lines between the tables in Figure 31.22 indicate the one-to-many degree of the relationship between each pair, as follows (the extra copy of the STAFFMEMBER_1 table in the Figure because `StaffCode` is connected in two relationships).

❏ `DeptCode` in DEPARTMENT (the *primary* table) has a one-to-many relationship with `DeptCode` in STAFFMEMBER (the *related* table); that is, each department can have many staff, but each member of staff can only belong to one department. For the database, this means that each record in the DEPARTMENT table has a unique value for `DeptCode` (the primary key), but a `DeptCode` value in the STAFFMEMBER table may occur many times.

❏ `JobCode` in the JOB table has a one-to-many relationship with `JobCode` in the STAFFMEMBER table, which fits with the fact that each job title may be held by many staff, but each member of staff only has one job title.

❑   StaffCode in the STAFFMEMBER table has a one-to-many relationship with StaffCode in the TRAINING table; that is, each member of staff may take a number of training courses, but each training occurrence (it may be helpful to think of it as a qualification) relates to only one member of staff. Each TRAINING record is made unique to a particular member of staff by combining the StaffCode with the CourseDate to form a unique, composite, primary key.

❑   Finally, StaffCode in the STAFFMEMBER table has a one-to-many relationship with DeptHead in the DEPARTMENT table. Thus, a member of staff may be Head of more than one department, but each department has only one member of staff as its Head. A one-to-one relationship could have been specified, but if a Head of Department leaves or is absent through illness, it may be necessary for another Head to cover for a while.

Enforcing referential integrity

Figure 31.22 identifies the one and the many side of relationships with the symbols '1' and '00', respectively. In Access this indicates that *referential integrity* has been enforced when the relationship was set. If you choose to apply referential integrity to a relationship, you need to be aware of a number of restrictions this places on the operation of the database.

These restrictions are described using the example relationship between the JOB (the 'one' side) and STAFFMEMBER (the 'many' side) tables. Remember that JobCode is the foreign key in the STAFFMEMBER table which links records to the relevant record in the JOB table.

❑   A member of staff cannot be given a Job Code for which there is no existing JOB record. The general rule is that a foreign key (in this example, JobCode in the STAFFMEMBER table) cannot be given a value which does not exist as a primary key in the primary table (in this example, JobCode in the JOB table). Access does allow you to enter a Null value in the foreign key, which indicates that the records are not related. In our scenario this would allow, for example, entry of a new staff record before they had been assigned to a particular job (the JobCode would be left blank).

❑   You cannot delete a JOB record, or change the value of its primary key, if there are any members of staff who are still recorded as holding that type of job. The general rule is that you are not allowed to delete a record from a primary table, or change the value of its primary key, if matching records exist in a related table.

Query using multiple tables

This multiple table example uses the STAFFMEMBER and JOB tables to list the Surname, Salary, JobTitle and StartDate of each employee who is a member of the pension scheme. Heads of Department are excluded from the list. Figure 31.23 show the design of this select query. JobCode is needed in the query to allow use of the criterion <>"HD2" and <> "HD1" which filters out any non-Heads of Department and Pension is needed to filter out non-pension scheme members. To exclude both fields from the query results, their 'Show' boxes are deselected. The results of the query are shown in Figure 31.24.

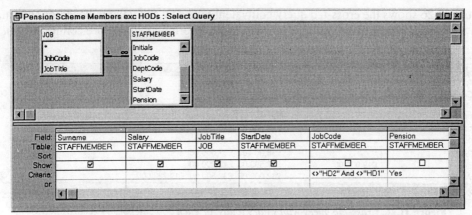

Figure 31.23. *Query to list pension scheme members, excluding Heads of Department*

Surname	Salary	JobTitle	StartDate
Picket	£15,000	Clerical - Middle Grade	23-Jan-77
Boreham	£23,000	Section Supervisor	23-Sep-72
Winkle	£18,000	Supervisor	01-Sep-85
Miggins	£14,500	Supervisor	31-Oct-93
Squeers	£37,500	Section Supervisor	13-Jun-88
Broaket	£13,000	Machine Maintenance Technician	17-Apr-85
Ramidos	£17,900	Supervisor	12-Jun-88
Fezziwig	£9,000	Clerical - Junior Grade	14-Jun-85
Swidger	£10,000	Clerical - Junior Grade	10-May-74

Figure 31.24. *List of pension scheme members, excluding Heads of Department*

Cross tab query

A cross-tab query uses row and column headings to display results in a more compact form. Figure 31.25 is a conventional select query which displays the salaries received by staff in each department, according to `JobCode`.

DeptCode	JobCode	Salary
ACC	CL2	£8,500
ACC	CL2	£15,000
ACC	HD2	£43,000
ACC	SS1	£23,000
GOS	CL0	£13,500
GOS	HD2	£44,000
GOS	SU1	£14,500
MIS	CL2	£11,400
MIS	HD2	£40,000
MIS	SU1	£17,900
PER	HD2	£37,000
PER	SS1	£37,500
PRO	HD1	£33,000
PRO	HD2	£40,000
PRO	OP1	£8,000
PRO	OP1	£8,600

Figure 31.25. *Extract of select query results (29 records in all)*

Figure 31.26 shows the cross-tab query equivalent with row and column headings and salaries summed according to JobCode, to present the information in a more compact form.

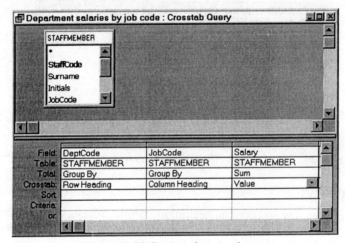

DeptCode	CL0	CL1	CL2	HD1	HD2	OP1	OP2	SS1	SU1
ACC			£23,500.00		£43,000.00			£23,000.00	
GOS	£13,500.00				£44,000.00				£14,500.00
MIS			£11,400.00		£40,000.00				£17,900.00
PER					£37,000.00			£37,500.00	
PRO				£33,000.00	£40,000.00	£16,600.00	£13,000.00		
PUR					£45,000.00				
RAD				£38,000.00	£37,000.00				
SAL		£19,000.00		£37,500.00	£42,000.00				
WAR				£32,000.00	£32,500.00	£19,200.00			£18,000.00

Record: |◄| ◄ | 1 | ► | ►| |►ᴾ| of 9

Figure 31.26. *Cross-tab query with salary totals for each Job category (9 records in all)*

The design of the cross-tab query is shown in Figure 31.27.

Figure 31.27. *Design of cross-tab query*

The design has three elements, which must be included in a cross-tab query:

❑ one field selected as a Row heading;

❑ one field selected as a Column heading;

❑ one field with a Value option. The Total row for this field must have an aggregate function, such as Sum, Avg with which to summarise this numeric field. In the example, the Sum function is used to calculate sub totals for each Job category within each Department.

Parameter query

A parameter query requests entry of information before it is executed, such as criteria for filtering records or a value to be entered into a field. It is not a separate type of query but rather an extension of the facilities provided by select and cross-tab queries.

Figure 31.28 shows an example for a simple select query which uses a parameter.

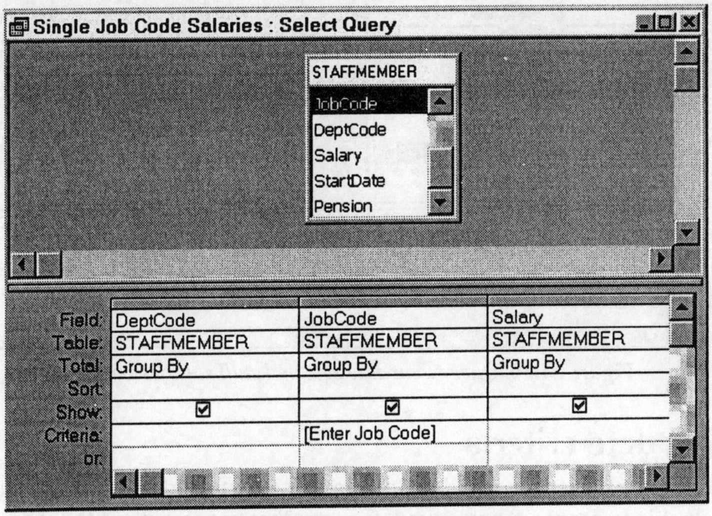

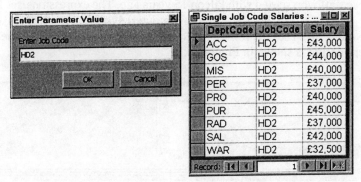

Figure 31.28. *Parameter query design*

The prompt [Enter JobCode] is used in the parameter query dialogue box when the query is executed. The dialogue box and the query results are shown in Figure 31.29.

Figure 31.29. *Parameter dialogue box and results of query*

Update query

An update query is an example of an action query and as the name suggests updates all or selected records in a table. The example applies a 3% increase to staff salaries, except for Heads and Assistant Heads of Department. The query design in shown in Figure 31.30.

The criteria for excluding Heads and Assistant Heads of Departments from the update uses the logical operator 'and'. The expression to update the `Salary` field is placed in the Update To row. Other action queries can be used to append new records, or delete existing records in a similar fashion to the update query. The results of action queries can not be reversed by any undo feature.

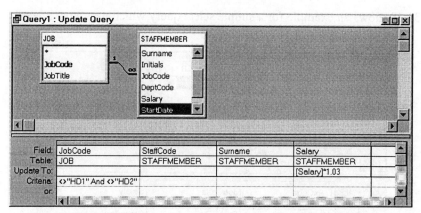

Figure 31.30. *Query to update selected staff salaries by 3%*

Query using date criteria

When a database is defined you could choose to use a text field to store dates or times, but you would be unable to carry out any calculation or other processing of those values. For this reason it is always sensible to use the proper date/time data type.

This query example, selects STAFFMEMBER records according to whether the StartDate field contains a date which is within the year 15 years before the current year. In other words, the query lists those staff who started with Pilcon 15 years ago. The expression uses the function Year(Now())-15. Now() takes the current (computer) system date and Year extracts the year part. The query also uses the DEPARTMENT table to allow the display of the DeptName field. The query design is shown in Figure 31.31.

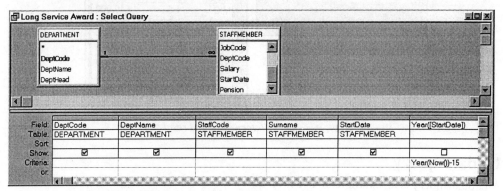

Figure 31.31. *Query to list staff who joined Pilcon 15 years ago*

The results of the query are shown in Figure 31.32.

If we wished to list staff who joined Pilcon within the last 15 years, we would use the expression >Year(Now())-16 and to list staff who joined between 5 and 10 years ago, the expression >Year(Now())-11 And <Year(Now())-4 would yield the required results.

Long Service Award : Select Query					‑□×
DeptCode	**DeptName**	**StaffCode**	**Surname**	**StartDate**	
▶ GOS	General Office Services	103	Clacket	01-Jan-85	
WAR	Warehousing	108	Winkle	01-Sep-85	
PRO	Production	139	Broaket	17-Apr-85	
RAD	Research and Development	172	Tefal	02-Mar-85	
SAL	Sales and Marketing	190	Fezziwig	14-Jun-85	
*					

Record: |◀ ◀   1   ▶ ▶| ▶※ of 5

Figure 31.32. *Staff who started with Pilcon 15 years ago*

Simplifying and controlling data entry

You will have noticed that adding records to, for example, the STAFFMEMBER table would require the entry of values (JobCode and DeptCode) which already exist in the JOB and DEPARTMENT tables, respectively. To avoid the need for users to type in these codes for each STAFFMEMBER record and to restrict the values which can be entered, we can use *pull down lists* or *list boxes* containing the required range of values. The explanation which follows relates to the JobCode field and the use of the Lookup Wizard which automates the creation of pull down lists.

Creating a list box

You need to view the STAFFMEMBER table in design view and select Lookup Wizard as the data type for the JobCode field shown in Figure 31.33.

STAFFMEMBER : Table			
Field Name	**Data Type**	**Description**	
⑨ StaffCode	Text	Primary key range 100 to 200	
Surname	Text	Up to 25 characters	
Initials	Text	2 initials, full stop after each	
▶ JobCode	Text ▾	2 alphabetic plus 1 digit	
DeptCode	Text	3 alpha validated for all Department codes	
Salary	Memo	Range 8000 to 45000	
StartDate	Number	Validation rejects future dates	
Pension	Date/Time	Yes if paying into pension scheme	
	Currency		
	AutoNumber	erties	
	Yes/No		
General Lookup	OLE Object		
Field Size 3	Hyperlink		
Format	Lookup Wizard...		
Input Mask LLO		The data type	
Caption		determines the kind of	
Default Value		values that users can	
Validation Rule		store in the field. Press	
Validation Text		F1 for help on data types.	
Required No			
Allow Zero Length No			
Indexed Yes (Duplicates OK)			

Figure 31.33. *Selecting Lookup Wizard as the data type*

The opening screen for the Lookup Wizard appears, as shown in Figure 31.34.

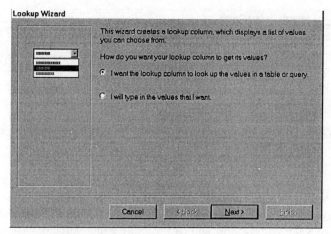

Figure 31.34. *Lookup Wizard opening screen*

Notice that you can choose to type in the values that you want to appear in the list box, or use values already held in another table. The JobCode values already exist in the JOB table, so we can choose the default option. The next Wizard screens ask for the name of the table and then the field from which values are to be taken. Finally, you are given the opportunity to adjust the width of the list box and alter the field label. If you have already created a form for data entry, this will have to be re-generated with the Form Wizard for the list box to take effect, although it will already operate in the STAFFMEMBER table's datasheet view. The Staff form, with JobCode list box added, is shown in Figure 31.35.

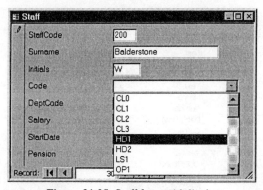

Figure 31.35. *Staff form with list box*

The list box provides an effective control over data input and avoids the need for separate validation controls. This is particularly important when the number of values to be controlled is extensive and the writing of a validation expression rather laborious. The validation of the DeptCode field in the STAFFMEMBER table would be redundant after the addition of a list box for that field.

Testing the database

General principles

Any ICT system your develop needs to be tested to determine that it meets the client's specification and that it performs as expected. There are general principles for the testing of all ICT systems and all are based on the design of appropriate test data.

In the context of a relational database project, your test data should ensure

- ❑ that every operation and facility within the database is executed at least once;
- ❑ the effectiveness of every control devoted to detecting invalid input is verified;
- ❑ every possible sequence of database operation is tested at least once.
- ❑ the accuracy of any processing carried out by the database is verified;
- ❑ the database operates according to its original design specification.

In order to achieve these aims, the you must be inventive in the design of the test data. Each test case must check something not tested by previous checks; there is no point in proving that a database which can print one selection of records from a table can also print the another selection of records from the same table. The goal is to strain the database to its limit, and this is particularly important when the database is to be used frequently by a number of different people. There are three general categories of test data:

1. *Normal data*. This includes the most general data for which the database was designed to handle.

2. *Extreme values*. These test the behaviour of the database when valid data at the upper and lower limits of acceptability are used. The process of using extreme values is called 'boundary testing' and is often a fruitful place to look for errors. For numeric data this could be the use of very large or very small values. Text could be the shortest or longest sequence of characters permitted.

3. *Exceptional data*. A database can be designed to accept a certain range or class of inputs. If invalid data is used, that is data which the database is not designed to handle, the database should be capable of rejecting it rather than attempting to process it. This is particularly important when the database is to be used by people other than the developer, since they may be unaware of what constitutes invalid data. A developer should from the outset assume that incorrect data will be used with the database.

Examples of database testing

Here we suggest ways in which you can develop a suitable test plan for a database.

Validation controls

Some validation is achieved by the setting of data types. For example, numeric, date and logical fields will prevent the user from entering data which does not conform to the relevant data type. Text or character fields are open and will accept any type of data and are more likely to need additional field controls to be put in place. For example, you may wish to prevent the entry of numeric characters, or in the case of a telephone number only allow digits and spaces. Whatever controls you put in place, you need to design test data which will test them to the limits. Range controls are a common requirement. For example, you may wish to limit a quantity in a stock record from 0 to 300 and restrict them to whole numbers, so your test data must include the entry of the values 0 and 300, a value between those figures, negative values and values greater than 300, as well as fractional values. The use of relational operators, such as >, = and < in validation expressions are a common source of error and need to be carefully tested.

Where the range of data inputs is small, for example, a set of codes to identify job types, list boxes are a useful way of restricting input and remove the need for separate validation controls. Of course, the operation of a list box should also be tested for correct operation and to ensure that values are assigned to the correct field.

Forms

Although a form can be created with a wizard, it is important to check that it displays the required fields and field labels and that values entered are assigned to the correct fields. This is especially important if you have modified the design and perhaps altered the field controls which determine the table and field to which each field is linked.

Queries

Every query must be tested to ensure that the record set it produces is consistent with the criteria for selection. As with validation values for criteria need to be tested to the limit. This is particularly important for parameter queries where the values are not pre-determined by the developer.

Reports

A number of aspects of a report can be checked, including the results in calculated fields, the labelling of columns, the correct sequencing or grouping of records and column headings and layout which conform to specification. You need to check that values are displayed in the required format, for example, money amounts with a £ sign, dates in 'dd mmm yy' format and that column headings and data do not 'wrap around' or obscure the data in adjacent columns.

Documenting the database

Your documentation could usefully include the following:

Technical documentation

Agreed user specification

The level of detail may vary depending on the degree to which the user wishes to control the appearance and operation of the system. If the user is knowledgeable about the facilities which a database provides, then he or she will be able to agree a specification with considerable detail. The skill and competence of those who will use the database will also be important in deciding the stringency of security, input controls and the user-friendliness of the interface.

Hardware and software resources

These include minimum and recommended requirements for hardware, such as processor speed, disk space, screen size and resolution and printer facilities. If the database is not converted to an independent application, then it is Access or whatever database package is being used that will be the primary determinant of hardware and software needs. Databases require frequent disk access and disk performance is vitally important if the database is large and makes extensive use of indexed fields (Chapter 29).

Database design and definition

This section should include entity relationship diagram(s), data dictionary, validation and verification controls (these can be obtained from the table definitions held within Access), details of all input and output screens, printed reports and a test specification (Chapter 11).

User documentation

This section should provide a detailed description of the operation of the database, including how to add, modify and delete records, use queries and reports and respond to error messages. These error messages should be those which you have produced to deal with attempts to enter invalid data into fields, although the testing procedure may have highlighted an error for which you have not catered. In all software development work it is inevitable that problems and difficulties will occur, because the effects of a particular user requirement can not always be anticipated. Although this is not desirable, it may be that the user has requested a facility which would only function properly and reliably after extensive programming, which was not part of the brief. You would then have to modify the specification, or if the error occurred under specific and uncommon circumstances, advise the user on how to avoid it.

Self-test questions

1. An extract from a video shop's records is shown below. The data is not normalised for use in a relational database. A member can rent several videos at one time. Members' names and addresses are recorded separately.

VideoCode	Title	CopyNo	Class	Rental	Issued	MemberNo	Date issued
0110	The Dark	1	Horror	£3.00	No		
0110	The Dark	2	Horror	£3.00	Yes	300	3-Oct-00
0110	The Dark	3	Horror	£3.00	No		
0111	The Light	1	Family	£2.00	Yes	501	4-Oct-00
0111	The Light	2	Family	£2.00	Yes	300	4-Oct-00
etc							

   (i)   Examine the data in the table and explain what aspects of the data are not normalised.
   (ii) Convert the table into third normal form, showing the first and second stages in the process.
   (iii) Draw an entity-relationship model (ERM) for the video shop database.
   (iv) Create a data dictionary for the database.

2. Using the above or other suitable examples, define the terms:

(i)   select query;

(ii)   cross tab query;

(iii) update query;

(iv)   parameter query;

(v)   referential integrity.

Developmental Exercises

Database Design and Use

Activity 1

This activity is based on the Barford Properties Case Study in the Developmental Exercise section of the Systems Analysis Unit and the system specification produced for Property Sales in Activity 3 of that Unit. Keep notes as evidence that you have completed the various requirements of this activity.

a. Apply the *second* and *third normalisation* rules (1NF and 2NF) to the data model from the Barford Properties specification, creating new entities as necessary. Ensure that the data definitions for each entity are as required for the specification.

b. Draw the *normalised entity relationship model* (ERM), using suitable graphics software.

c. Produce a *table definition* for *each entity*, identifying field names, lengths, types (for example, time, date, logical, character, number) and formats. Also identify primary (single or composite), and secondary keys (which may be used in queries, or to establish a relationship with another table).

d. Update the *data dictionary* to include, for each table: field names; synonyms; lengths; types; formats; and descriptions.

e. Use your notes to append the details of this data model to the system specification produced in the Development Activities for the Systems Analysis Unit..

Activity 2

This activity concerns creation and use of the database. Keep and file all the evidence produced in this activity.

a. Create a *database*, defining the tables with an RDBMS package and setting key fields and field properties, as specified in 1D. The properties should include *validation* settings and field *patterns* to help control data entered into the database. The validation settings should work in combination with the other controls, such as field types and field lengths.

b. Ensure that all table definitions comply with the data dictionary and modify as necessary).

c. Create a screen *input form* for *each* table in the database, using the design screen to modify them to *suit the specification*. Save the forms and use them to enter sample data (you need to produce this for testing purposes) into each table.

d. Create four suitable queries to service the report requirements *defined in the system specification*. Two should be created using *QBE* and two with *SQL statements* or *xBase commands*. Save the queries and test them.

e. Design and save the screen and printed report layouts as specified in the Property Sales system specification. This should detail: field order and position, spacing and layout. The layouts should define: pagination; footers; headers; data grouping (where appropriate); totals and calculated fields (where applicable).

f. Use the appropriate *report* to display or print the results of each *query*.

Activity 3

This activity uses the database you have developed in Activities 1 and 2.

The work you do on this needs to be continued over a relatively long period of, perhaps, several weeks, to satisfy the performance criteria. During that period you need to gather evidence that you have used a number of file maintenance activities, data handling processes, report types, verification and validation checks. You will have used many of these during Activities 1 and 2, but you should use the following checklist to ensure that you use all those listed (make sure that you show contents of a table before and after any such changes, unless your work is observed).

a. Maintain a log, over an extended period of the *file saving* and *back-up* procedures completed, detailing operation, file names, date, location (directory or disk number). Also record details of any relevant *security measures* you have used (for example, passwords).

b. Write notes *evaluating* the *effectiveness* of the data handling system, in terms of its *speed*, *reliability*, *cost*, *benefits* to the organisation (Barford Properties) and the *volume* of data it can handle.

Activity	Tick
File maintenance activities	
1. data entry	
2. amending records	
3. deleting records	
4. appending new records	
Data handling processes	
1. calculating (numeric total fields)	
2. character conversion (amendment of field type)	
3. sorting (one field, multiple field)	
4. searching (using comparison and logical operators)	
5. merging (query joining tables)	
6. grouping	
Report production	
1. operational (this is any routine report for regular use)	
2. summary	
3. grouped	
4. exception	
Accuracy checks	
1. verification (checking screen input against source document before entry)	
2. validation (you should have set validation parameters on several fields)	

Microsoft Office Tutorials

Chapters

Chapter 32

Word Processing 1

The purpose of a word processor such as Microsoft's Word for Windows is to make the creation and modification of text-based documents as easy as possible for computer users.

In this tutorial we will concentrate on the basic operations required to create a short document. The tutorial assumes no previous experience of using Word. By carefully working through the tutorial you will gain a sound basis for using more advanced features of Word. More advanced features are described in the chapter, Word Processing 2.

Objectives

In this tutorial we introduce the basic features of a word processor necessary to produce a simple document, save it to disk and print it. On completion of this tutorial you will be able to:

❏ Identify the features of the word processor necessary to create a simple document.

❏ Use a standard keyboard to create and modify text.

❏ Use a mouse to utilise features of the word processor.

❏ Save a document to disk.

❏ Print a document.

❏ Retrieve a document from disk.

❏ Make a back-up copy of a document.

Any point at which you are required to carry out a procedure in the word processor is indicated by the following action bullet.

☞ This means do what the text says.

The explanation of what you are required to do is normally accompanied by annotated pictures of the relevant screen area. Use these to help you understand the written instructions.

The Microsoft Word screen

Before investigating the use of Microsoft Word we need to look briefly at some components of the Word screen, shown on the next page.

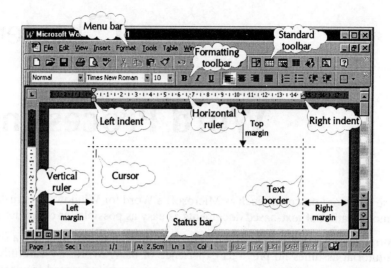

- [ ] The **main text area** is indicated by the grey **text border** on the white 'paper'. This shows the area that the text will occupy when it is printed.

  The text area is surrounded by four adjustable margins called the Left Margin, Right Margin, Top Margin and Bottom Margin (not shown).

- [ ] The **text cursor,** shown in the top left-hand corner of the text area, will appear as a small flashing vertical line. Its current position is called the *insertion point*, that is the position where text will appear when you start typing.

- [ ] The **left indent** shows the leftmost position of text on the current line. You can use the mouse to drag this indent left or right within the text area.

- [ ] The **right indent** shows the rightmost position of text on the current line, and you can use the mouse to move this indent too.

- [ ] The **menu bar** provides access to a number of drop-down menus which are activated when the menu name is clicked.

  For example, clicking on the File menu will provide a list of options which include facilities to save, load and print documents.

  We refer to a menu option by specifying the name of the menu followed by the name of the option separated by a vertical bar. Thus File|Save As means selecting the Save As option from the File menu.

- [ ] The **formatting toolbar** provides the means to alter the appearance of text in a number of ways.

  For example you can use it to:

  ○ Change the text font (that is the style of the text characters) and size

  ○ Make sections of text bold, italicised or underlined

  ○ Left align, centre, right align or justify paragraphs

- ❏ The **standard toolbar** provides icons which you can click to perform a range of useful functions, including:
  - O Creating new documents
  - O Retrieving documents from disk
  - O Saving documents to disk
  - O Printing documents
- ❏ The **status bar** provides information about your current document, including
  - O Current page
  - O Number of pages
  - O Line and column of the text cursor
- ❏ The **horizontal ruler** and the **vertical ruler** allow you to plan the layout of your documents accurately.

The Target Document

Your aim is to produce the **Target Document** entitled 'THE BATTLE OF NEVILLE'S CROSS', which follows on the next page.

To make best use of the tutorial do not try to produce the Target Document directly. Instead follow the instructions carefully, only doing what is asked. This way, you will gain a sound knowledge of the most efficient ways to use Word. Step-by-step instructions are given in the sections which follow the document. You will start by creating a blank document and then continue by typing in a small amount of text which will form the basis of the rest of the exercise.

1 Creating a new document

Click on the New icon with the left mouse button.

This creates a blank document ready for you to begin entering text. You will be presented with a blank page and a cursor in the top left-hand corner of the page indicating where text will appear once you start typing.

2 Changing the view

Microsoft Word allows you to view a document in several different ways. There are two main views for text entry:

- ❏ Normal
- ❏ Page Layout

You change the view by selecting the relevant option from the View menu, as shown on the next page.

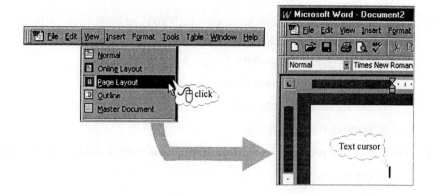

☞ Now choose Page Layout view.

Target Document

THE BATTLE OF NEVILLE'S CROSS

Why Neville's Cross?

The battle of Neville's Cross was fought on October 17th 1346, in the reign of Edward III. The battlefield is within the boundaries and to the north of, Durham City. The battle is named after Ralph, Lord Neville, one of the leaders of the victorious English forces. A stone cross was erected on the Brancepeth road, but it was defaced and broken up in 1589. In its place, although some distance from the supposed site of the battle, is a stone shaft. It is, in fact, an old milestone.

While King Edward was away in France fighting the Battle of Crecy, King David led his Scottish forces over the English border and laid waste to towns and villages as far as Durham. Although King Edward was not there to resist them, Queen Philippa and her nobles managed to raise an army of 16,000 men.

How did the armies come to Neville's Cross?

The English army marched north towards Durham as quickly as it could and halted at the village of Merrington. From the top of a tower, they could see the Scots assembled at Beaurepaire (now known as Bearpark). From there, they went along an old Roman road to Ferryhill Village and then through Hett to the Redhills. These hills overlooked the eventual Battle site.

Who were the leaders?

The Scots were led by

      King David   William Douglas   Robert Steward.

The leaders on the English side, were

      Thomas Rokeby   Henry Percy   Ralph Neville.

What was the outcome?

It is estimated that out of an army of 30,000 Scots and French auxiliaries, 15,000 were killed. There are many theories as to why the Scots were so badly beaten. One theory suggests that the Scots were unable to keep to their usual chevron (arrow) formation because of a narrowing of the valley through which they came. It is also likely that the English army's archers made an important contribution.

Did the battle take place around the Redhills?

There is some doubt concerning the actual site. It is certain that many bodies would have been left or buried where they lay, but excavations for building in that area have not revealed such evidence.

In Page Layout view you see the document as it will appear when it is printed, and we will use this view throughout the exercise. The top left-hand corner of your screen should appear as shown above with the text cursor blinking to show where text appears when you start typing.

3 Entering text

The boxed text below is part of the target document entitled 'THE BATTLE OF NEVILLE'S CROSS'.

THE BATTLE OF NEEVILLE'S CROSS¶
Why Neeville's Cross?¶
The battle of Neeville's Cross was fought on October 17th 1346, in the reign of Edward III. The battlefield is within the boundaries and to the north of, Durham City. The battle is named after Ralph, Lord Neeville, one of the leaders of the victorious English forces. A stone cross was erected on the Brancepeth road, but it was defaced and broken up in 1589. In its place, although some distance from the site of the battle, is a stone shaft. It is, in fact, an old milestone.¶
While King Edward was away in France fighting the Battle of Crecy, King David led his Scottish forces over the English border and laid waste to towns and villages as far as Durham. Although King Edward was not there to resist them, Queen Philippa and her nobles managed to raise an army of 16,000 men.¶
What was the outcome?¶
It is estimated that out of an army of 30,000 Scots and French auxiliaries, 15,000 were killed. There are many theories as to why the Scots were so badly beaten. One theory suggests that the Scots were unable to keep to their usual chevron (arrow) formation because of a narrowing of the valley through which they came. It is also likely that the English army's archers made an important contribution.¶
Did the battle take place around the Redhills?¶
There is some doubt concerning the actual site. It is certain that many bodies would have been left or buried where they lay, but excavations for building in that area have not revealed such evidence.

You may notice some mistakes in the text. Just for the time being <u>don't worry about correcting them</u>, or any additional ones that you accidentally make – how to correct errors will be explained in due course.

To type a block of text completely in capitals, press the Caps Lock key once. To return the keyboard to its normal mode of operation, after you have typed the title, press the Caps Lock key again.

Caps Lock Key

☞ Press the Caps Lock key.

☞ Type the title, 'THE BATTLE OF NEEVILLE'S CROSS' in capital letters on the first line.

☞ Press the Caps Lock Key.

☞ Move the cursor to the beginning of the next line by pressing the Enter key.

Only use the Enter key when you want to start a new paragraph, or when you want to leave a blank line. It is not necessary to press Enter when you reach the right-hand side of the page, in the middle of a sentence, because Word will automatically move the text cursor to a new line for you. In the practice text, the symbol ¶ has been inserted to remind you when to press Enter.

Note also that to produce a single capital letter for the beginning of a sentence you need to hold down one of the two shift keys while you type the letter. For example, to produce the capital letter 'W', hold down the right shift key, press and release 'W' and then release the shift key.

The space bar should only be used to separate words; there are better ways to indent paragraphs or centre text as we will see later.

☞ Now, referring to the boxed text on the previous page, start typing in the text following the heading.

4 Saving your work

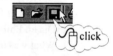

It is advisable to save your document to disk regularly as you work.

☞ Click the disk icon on the tool bar, which then displays the Save As dialogue box, shown below.

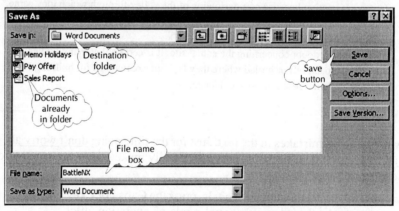

The first time you save a document, you will need to specify where it is to be saved and give it a *filename*.

☞ Set the destination of the document (by selecting from the Save in drop down list). This may require selection of a *drive letter* as shown on the next page and then a *folder* (in the previous figure, called 'Word Documents').

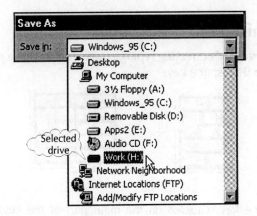

☞ Enter the document name ('BattleNX' in the figure) by editing the File name box and click on the Save button.

When you re-save a previously saved document, clicking the disk icon will cause Word to save your work without the need to supply any more information.

❑ Note, however, that when you do this you will be <u>replacing</u> the previous version of your document with the current version.

If you want to keep the old version as well as the latest one, you will need to save the latest version under a different name or in a different location.

5 Moving around the document

If you are reasonably proficient in the use of the mouse, the easiest way to move the text cursor to a particular part of your document is to simply position the mouse pointer there and then click the left button.

If your document is more than a single page in length, and the text required is not visible, you will need to use the *vertical scroll bar* (see adjacent figure) controls to bring the text into view.

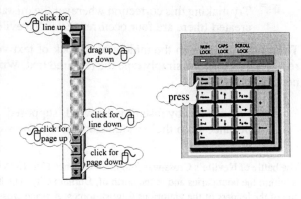

If you are happier using the keyboard, then there are four keys on the numeric keypad (shown above) which will allow you to move the text cursor up(↑), down(↓), left(←) and right(→). You can also use the page up (Pg Up) and page down (Pg Dn) keys to move from page to page in your document.

6 Correcting mistakes

There are a number of ways of correcting typing errors. Two keys are particularly important: the Delete key and the Backspace key.

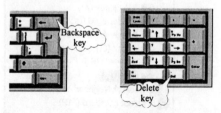

❑   The Backspace key, situated on the main part of the keyboard, removes the character immediately to the <u>left</u> of the text cursor.

❑   The Delete key is found on the numeric keypad as shown, though it may be duplicated on some keyboards. It will delete the character immediately to the <u>right</u> of the text cursor.

So, for example, to correct the misspelling of Neeville's in the second line of the text:

> Why Neeville's Cross?

you could move the cursor to this position, between the two 'e's.

> Why Neeville's Cross?

and either press the Backspace key or the Delete key. The extra 'e' will be removed.

☞   Try making this correction wherever the mistake occurs in the text that you have created (there are four occurrences of 'Neeville' to be corrected).

To insert characters in the middle of a block of text you again move the text cursor to the required position and simply type the required text. Word automatically makes space for the new characters.

☞   Practise this by inserting the word 'supposed' after the phrase '..although some distance from the' as indicated below. The word is missing from your practice text.

The battle of Neville's Cross was fought on October 17th 1346, in the reign of Edward III. The battlefield is within the boundaries and to the north of, Durham City. The battle is named after Ralph, Lord Neville, one of the leaders of the victorious English forces. A stone cross was erected on the Brancepeth road, but it was defaced and broken up in 1589. In its place, although some distance from the site of the battle, is a stone shaft. It is, in fact, an old milestone.

Insert 'supposed' here

7 Improving the appearance of your work

If you glance back at Target Document, you will notice that the appearance of the document has been improved by:

❑   Centring the title.

- ❏ Underlining the headings.
- ❏ Making text bold.
- ❏ Italicising words and phrases.
- ❏ Tabulating the lists of battle leaders in the paragraph headed 'Who were the leaders?'.
- ❏ Indenting the lists of leaders.
- ❏ Justifying paragraph text so that the left and right margins are straight.

You will now be shown how to apply these improvements to your text.

Centring lines of text

You should be able to see these symbols at the top of your screen. They are part of the Formatting tool bar. If it is not visible then you will need to make it visible by accessing the View menu as shown on the right.

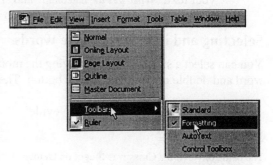

The four rightmost symbols in the adjacent figure show how the lines within a paragraph of text will appear when the symbol is clicked with the mouse button.

☞ Centre the title of your text by moving the text cursor to the title line and clicking the icon shown alongside.

The title should become centred between the left and right margins of your page.

Underlining the headings and making them bold

To underline (or otherwise format) a block of text you must first select it (that is, highlight it). There are several methods of achieving this, but in the case of a heading simply

☞ move the mouse pointer left of the heading line and when you see a right sloping arrow (as shown below), click.

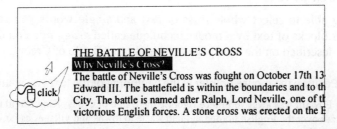

THE BATTLE OF NEVILLE'S CROSS
Why Neville's Cross?
The battle of Neville's Cross was fought on October 17th 13
Edward III. The battlefield is within the boundaries and to th
City. The battle is named after Ralph, Lord Neville, one of th
victorious English forces. A stone cross was erected on the E

The heading should then appear as shown above, that is as white text on a black background.

☞ Now underline the heading by clicking the <u>U</u> (underline) icon.

click

☞ While the heading is selected make it bold by clicking the **B** (bold) icon to the left of the underline icon.

click

☞ Now click the mouse somewhere else in your text to deselect the heading. You should see that the heading is <u>underlined</u> and in **bold** type as required.

☞ Practise using these effects by repeating the steps for the other two headings in your text, 'What was the outcome?' and 'Did the battle take place around Redhills?'. In addition, make the main title at the top bold.

Selecting and italicising single words

You can select a single word by moving the mouse pointer (which looks like this⌶) over the word and double clicking the mouse button. The word becomes highlighted.

☞ Double click on the word 'Neville'.

Why Neville's Cross?

The battle of Neville's Cross was fought on October 17th 1346, in the reign of Edward III. The battlefield is within the boundaries and to the north of, Durham City. The battle is named after Ralph, Lord Neville, one of the leaders of the victorious English forces.

double
click

Why Neville's Cross?

The battle of Neville's Cross was fought on October 17th 1346, in the reign of Edward III. The battlefield is within the boundaries and to the north of, Durham City. The battle is named after Ralph, Lord Neville, one of the leaders of the victorious English forces.

☞ Now click on the *I* (italics) icon to italicise the word.

click

☞ Practise italicising some other words in the body of your text by double clicking them and then clicking on the italics icon.

Selecting a block of text

As well as being able to select whole lines of text and single words you can also select phrases and other blocks of text by a mouse technique called *dragging*. You do this by following the steps described on the next page for the phrase 'Battle of Crecy'.

☞ **Step 1.** Position the mouse pointer at the beginning of the text you want to select.

While King Edward was away in France fighting the⌶Battle of Crecy, King David led his Scottish forces over the English border and laid waste to towns and villages as far as Durham. Although King Edward was not there to resist them, Queen Philippa

Position
cursor here

☞ **Step 2.** Click the mouse button and hold it down.

> While King Edward was away in France fighting the Battle of Crecy, King David led his Scottish forces over the English border and laid waste to towns and villages as far as Durham. Although King Edward was not there to resist them, Queen Philippa

click and hold

☞ **Step 3.** Keeping the button pressed, move the mouse pointer to the end of the text to be selected and release the button.

> While King Edward was away in France fighting the **Battle of Crecy**, King David led his Scottish forces over the English border and laid waste to towns and villages as far as Durham. Although King Edward was not there to resist them, Queen Philippa

Move to end and release

Italicising text

☞ Now change the selected phrase to italics by clicking italics icon as before.

click

Undoing formatting

If you change your mind about formatting text after you have formatted it using bold, italics or underline, then simply select the text that you want to change back and click the same icon that you used before.

For example, if you want to return a block of text to normal after you underlined it, select it again and click the underline icon. The underlining will be removed. The same applies to bold and italicised text.

Combining bold, italics and underline

Sometimes you may want to have text bold and underlined, or bold and italicised or even in bold, italics and underlined. Whatever the combination, you follow the same procedure as before of first selecting the text and click on each of the required formatting icons in turn before deselecting the text being formatted.

You have already practised this when you underlined the headings and made them bold.

Saving your work again

☞ Before proceeding to the next section on tabulating lists, make sure that your document looks like the one shown below.

THE BATTLE OF NEVILLE'S CROSS

Why Neville's Cross?

The battle of Neville's Cross was fought on October 17th 1346, in the reign of Edward III. The battlefield is within the boundaries and to the north of, Durham City. The battle is named after Ralph, Lord *Neville*, one of the leaders of the victorious English forces. A stone cross was erected on the Brancepeth road, but it was defaced and broken up in 1589. In its place, although some distance from the supposed site of the battle, is a stone shaft. It is, in fact, an old milestone.

While King Edward was away in France fighting the *Battle of Crecy*, King David led his Scottish forces over the English border and laid waste to towns and villages as far as Durham. Although King Edward was not there to resist them, Queen Philippa and her nobles managed to raise an army of 16,000 men.

What was the outcome?

It is estimated that out of an army of 30,000 Scots and French auxiliaries, 15,000 were killed. There are many theories as to why the Scots were so badly beaten. One theory suggests that the Scots were unable to keep to their usual chevron (arrow) formation because of a narrowing of the valley through which they came. It is also likely that the English army's archers made an important contribution.

Did the battle take place around the Redhills?

There is some doubt concerning the actual site. It is certain that many bodies would have been left or buried where they lay, but excavations for building in that area have not revealed such evidence.

☞ Make any changes and then save it by clicking on the Save icon.

Remember that this will automatically replace the previously saved version of your document under the same name and in the same location as when you first saved it.

Tabulating a list

The Tab key can be used to align text accurately into neat columns. In our target document it was used to arrange the list of army leaders. Pressing the Tab key moves the text cursor a fixed distance to the right.

You can control the distance the cursor moves but a *default* value is assigned to the Tab key for a new document, and for the moment we will not change it.

The section of the target document with the heading 'Who were the leaders?' is going to be inserted after the first paragraph in your document.

☞ To do this, you need first to move the text cursor to the end of the first paragraph, shown below.

While King Edward was away in France fighting the Battle of Crecy, King David led his Scottish forces over the English border and laid waste to towns and villages as far as Durham. Although King Edward was not there to resist them, Queen Philippa and her nobles managed to raise an army of 16,000 men.

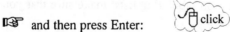

☞ and then press Enter:

While King Edward was away in France fighting the Battle of Crecy, King David led his Scottish forces over the English border and laid waste to towns and villages as far as Durham. Although King Edward was not there to resist them, Queen Philippa and her nobles managed to raise an army of 16,000 men.

Enter

You will notice that a blank line has been inserted, providing space for you to insert the new text shown below.

Tab key

☞ Enter the new text, shown below.

Where you see the symbol → , press the Tab key and remember to press Enter where you see ¶).

Who were the leaders?¶

The Scots were led by¶

King David   →   W illiam Douglas → Robert Steward.¶

The leaders on the English side, were¶

Thomas Rokeby   →Henry Percy →   Ralph Neville.¶

Indenting text

In order to make the list of leaders stand out a little from the surrounding text they can been *indented*. You can indent a paragraph by first positioning the text cursor anywhere in the paragraph and then clicking the Increase Indent icon as shown above.

click

☞ Now move the text cursor to anywhere on the first line of leaders (beginning 'King David') and then click the Increase Indent icon twice.

☞ Repeat this procedure with the line beginning 'Thomas Rokeby' so that the list of leaders eventually looks like this:

Who were the leaders?

The Scots were led by

       King David   William Douglas   Robert Steward.

The leaders on the English side, were

       Thomas Rokeby   Henry Percy   Ralph Neville.

Notice that to the left of the Increase Indent icon there is a Decrease Indent icon which, as you might guess, moves text to the left if it is already indented to the right. In other words, it reverses the effect of the Increase Indent icon.

☞ Before experimenting with Decrease Indent, **Save** your work.

Justifying text

If you look back again to the target document you will see that the text has been aligned so that both the left and the right margins are straight. The text that you are reading now is also formatted in this way.

❑   When both margins are straight, the text is said to be *justified*.

❑   If only the left hand side is straight it is *left aligned*.

❑   If only the right hand side is straight it is *right aligned*.

❑   When neither the left nor the right hand side is straight it has been *centred* (like the heading in our target document).

To change the alignment of a paragraph of text you position the text cursor anywhere in the paragraph and click on the required alignment icon.

☞   To fully justify the first paragraph of our document click in the paragraph and then click the Justify icon, as follows.

Why Neville's Cross?

The battle of Neville's Cross was fought on October 17th 1346, in the reign of Edward III. The battlefield is within the boundaries and to the north of, Durham City. The battle is named after Ralph, Lord Neville, one of the leaders of the victorious English forces. A stone cross was erected on the Brancepeth road, but it was defaced and broken up in 1589. In its place, although some distance from the supposed site of the battle, is a stone shaft. It is, in fact, an old milestone.

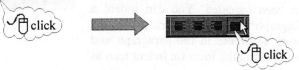

Your fully justified text should now look like that shown below.

Why Neville's Cross?

The battle of Neville's Cross was fought on October 17th 1346, in the reign of Edward III. The battlefield is within the boundaries and to the north of, Durham City. The battle is named after Ralph, Lord Neville, one of the leaders of the victorious English forces. A stone cross was erected on the Brancepeth road, but it was defaced and broken up in 1589. In its place, although some distance from the supposed site of the battle, is a stone shaft. It is, in fact, an old milestone.

Formatting the whole document

The previous formatting exercise enabled you to format a single paragraph using one of the four alignment icons. However, this method would be laborious if you wanted to format every paragraph in the document, or if you wanted to alter the whole document in some other way.

The solution is to use one of the options in the Edit menu on the menu bar. The Edit|Select All option selects all of the text in the current document so that you can then alter it in one operation.

☞   Apply full justification to the complete document by following the procedure illustrated at the top of the next page.

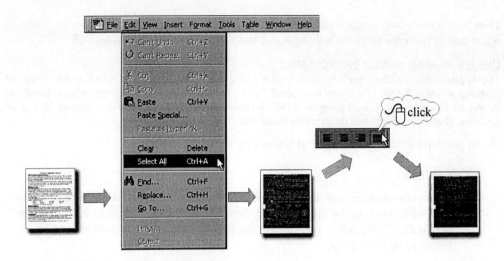

☞ Remove the black highlighting from the text by clicking anywhere in your document.

It should now look very similar to the Target Document, except that we have yet to insert one more heading and paragraph, and this is the purpose of the next exercise.

8 Cut, Copy and Paste

One of the great advantages of a word processor over a traditional typewriter is the ease with which it allows you to modify your document after it has been created. You can, for example:

❏   delete sections of text;

❏   move sections around;

❏   copy sections from one place to another.

These operations are often performed using the Cut (scissors), Copy (two identical documents) and Paste (Clipboard) icons as shown.

When you select a section of text and then click on the Cut icon, the selected text removed from your document and temporarily stored on the Clipboard, a part of computer's memory. You can then copy it to a new location by moving the text cursor to the required position and then clicking on the Paste icon.

We will practise this procedure in a moment, but first

☞ add the new text shown on the next page to the end of your document. It is the missing text from the target document and we will use it to practise cutting and pasting. You can also take this opportunity to practise formatting skills by making the new text look exactly like that on the next page.

There is some doubt concerning the actual site. It is certain that many bodies would have been left or buried where they lay, but excavations for building in that area have not revealed such evidence. ¶

How did the armies come to Neville's Cross?

The English army marched north towards Durham as quickly as it could and halted at the village of Merrington. From the top of a tower, they could see the Scots assembled at Beaurepaire (now known as Bearpark). From there, they went along an old Roman road to Ferryhill Village and then through Hett to the Redhills. These hills overlooked the eventual Battle site.

When you have finished entering and formatting the new section,

☞ highlight it.

> Do this by clicking with the mouse just to the left of the first letter of the heading and, while holding the mouse button down, dragging the mouse to the end of the paragraph. Then, when you release the mouse button, the section should be selected as shown below.

There is some doubt concerning the actual site. It is certain that many bodies would have been left or buried where they lay, but excavations for building in that area have not revealed such evidence.

How did the armies come to Neville's Cross?

The English army marched north towards Durham as quickly as it could and halted at the village of Merrington. From the top of a tower, they could see the Scots assembled at Beaurepaire (now known as Bearpark). From there, they went along an old Roman road to Ferryhill Village and then through Hett to the Redhills. These hills overlooked the eventual Battle site.

☞ Now click the Cut icon and you should find that the highlighted text disappears.

> It has been copied to the Clipboard and is available to be pasted anywhere in the document. We will paste it before the second section of the document.

☞ Click the mouse at the beginning of the title 'Who were the leaders?' and then click on the Paste icon.

> The new section should have been inserted as shown below.

While King Edward was away in France fighting the Battle of Crecy, King David led his Scottish forces over the English border and laid waste to towns and villages as far as Durham. Although King Edward was not there to resist them, Queen Philippa and her nobles managed to raise an army of 16,000 men.

How did the armies come to Neville's Cross?

The English army marched north towards Durham as quickly as it could and halted at the village of Merrington. From the top of a tower, they could see the Scots assembled at Beaurepaire (now known as Bearpark). From there, they went along an old Roman road to Ferryhill Village and then through Hett to the Redhills. These hills overlooked the eventual Battle site.

Who were the leaders?

The Scots were led by

You can use the Copy function in much the same way as Cut, the only difference being that Copy does just that: it copies the selected text to the Clipboard leaving the original intact. But, as with Cut, you can still Paste the copy somewhere else.

Of course, if you only want to delete some text rather than move or copy it, then you simply use Cut without Paste.

[Note that if you Cut or Copy a selection and then later Cut or Copy another selection, you will only be able to Paste the last one: the first selection will have been replaced on the Clipboard by the second one.]

If you have followed all of the preceding instructions accurately your document should look very much like the Target Document. Now is therefore a good time to

☞ Save your work again.

9 Printing your work

If you have a printer attached to your system then printing your document is simply a matter of clicking the Print icon on the Standard toolbar. However, before you do so,

☞ first make sure that the printer is switched on, loaded with paper and, if appropriate, on-line.

☞ If everything is OK, you are ready to print so click on the Print icon and after a few seconds your finished document should appear.

10 Making a backup copy

Making a backup copy of a document, which might have taken you a considerable amount of time and effort to produce, is your insurance against accidental loss or corruption.

A simple way of making a backup is to access File | Save As and select a different location, such as a floppy disk, to which to save your document.

☞ Select File | Save As.

☞ Set the destination of the document (by selecting from the Save in drop down list).

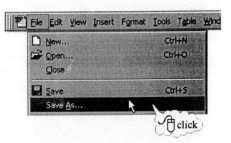

☞ Enter the document name (by editing the File name box).

☞ Click on the Save button. In the example on the next page, the current document is to be saved to a floppy disk using the name 'BattleNX'.

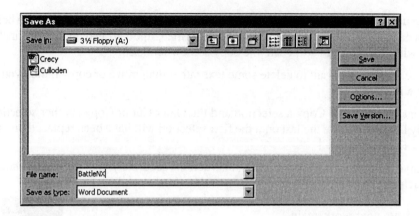

11 Opening documents

After you have finished working on your word processor you will close it down and, perhaps switch off your computer for the day. You will have saved your work previously onto your hard disk or to a floppy disk.

When you resume work on your word processor at some later date, you can either create a new document as you did in this exercise, or you can continue working on a document that you created at a previous session. In the second case you need to *Open* the document, that is, retrieve it from its stored location and load it into your word processor.

There are a number of ways of doing this, but we will start with the way that will always be possible, and then investigate a quicker method that will usually but not always be available.

☞ Using File|Exit, quit the word processor and then re-load it.

The icon which allows you to open documents is shown on the standard toolbar as a folder opening. The process of opening a document is described below and illustrated on the next page.

☞ Click on the Open icon. The Open dialogue box is displayed.

☞ Select the document you want – 'BattleNX' in the example on the next page – and then click on the Open button.

The document will then be loaded into Word. If your document is in another location and is not shown in the window, then you need to change the Look in box to the appropriate folder or disk drive.

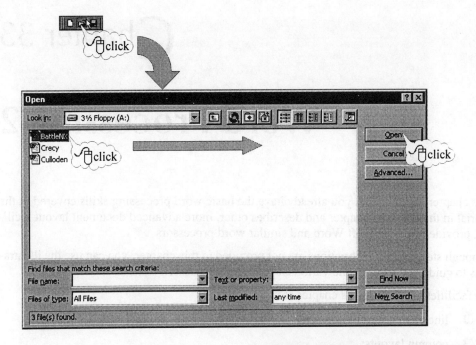

A second and quicker method of opening a document depends on how recently you last used the document in question.

Word keeps a record of the last few documents that you used and installs their names in the File menu. An example is shown on the right. Four files are listed, of which the first one, used most recently, has been selected. It will be loaded into Word and opened automatically without the need to go through the Open dialogue box.

However, if the document to be opened was not one of the last four accessed, it would not appear in this list and the previously described method would need to be used to open it.

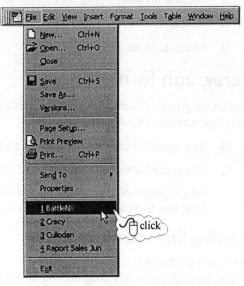

Chapter 33

Word Processing 2

This chapter assumes that you already have the basic word processing skills covered in the tutorial in the previous chapter and describes other, more advanced document layout facilities, provided by Microsoft Word and similar word processors.

Although step-by-step instructions are not provided in this chapter, you can use the illustrations to guide you through the various layout facilities described here.

The facilities covered in this chapter are:

❑ line and paragraph spacing;

❑ column layouts;

❑ tables;

❑ headers, footers and page numbering;

Paragraph formatting

Any line or group of lines, with only one carriage return at the end of the last line is treated by a word processor as a *paragraph*.

❑ The spacing between lines can be altered.

❑ The space between paragraphs can also be changed.

Space between one paragraph and the next can be created by inserting a blank line; this is done be pressing Return twice at the end of a paragraph.

Altering line spacing

The figure on the next page shows how the *line spacing* for a selected block of text can be altered, through Format|Paragraph on the menu bar.

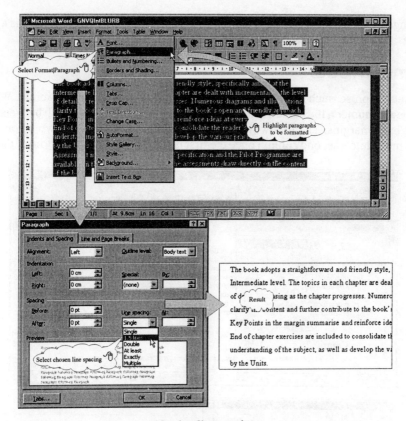

Altering line spacing

Altering paragraph spacing

The same method can be used to alter the paragraph spacing.

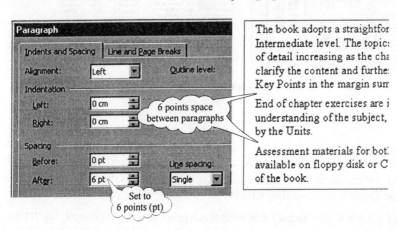

Setting paragraph spacing

The settings for paragraph spacing in the figure are set to '6 points after' (a *point* is a spacing unit). For clarity, the line spacing has been reset to single line.

Column layouts

For continuous prose, such as appears in a newspaper, you need a column facility. When you create a new document, the default setting is one column, spanning the width between the left and right page margins. The following figure shows text formatted into two columns. Text will only move into a second column once the first is filled, that, is at the bottom of the page.

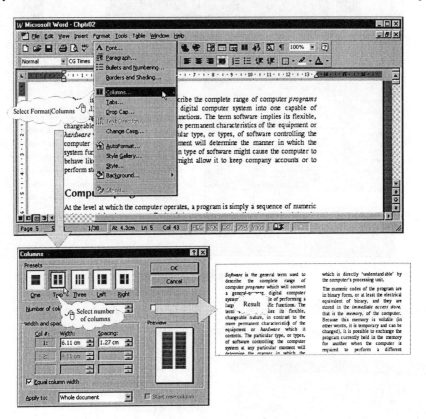

Formatting text into two columns

Tables

If you need to present text in table form, you can use tabulation, but the table tool allows much greater control over layout. Tables can be formatted by shading and borders to enhance their appearance and even allow simple, spreadsheet-type calculations on numeric data. The next figure shows the process for inserting a table.

The selection in the figure will produce a table with three rows and four columns. Each rectangle in the table is known as a *cell*. To enter data into a cell, simply click inside the cell and begin typing. To move to another cell, use the arrow keys or press Return.

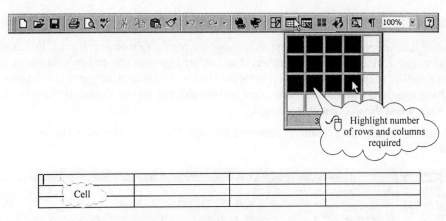

Inserting a table

A quick way to format a table with shading and borders and the correct column widths, is to use Table|Table AutoFormat from the menu bar. The next figure shows an example.

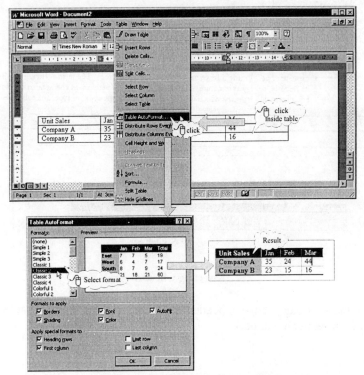

Using AutoFormat to format a table

Having inserted the table, it can be manipulated in a variety of ways, for example, the width of columns can be changed, cells can be merged with another and new rows or columns can be inserted. All these facilities can be accessed through the Table menu.

Headers, footers and page numbering

A *header* is descriptive text which appears above the top margin on every page. For example, a header may include the page number, date, report title and the author's name. A *footer* serves a similar purpose, except that it is located below the bottom margin on each page. You only have to enter a header and footer once and the word processor automatically places it on each page when the document is printed.

In Word, the header and footer is accessed through View|Header and Footer, as shown below.

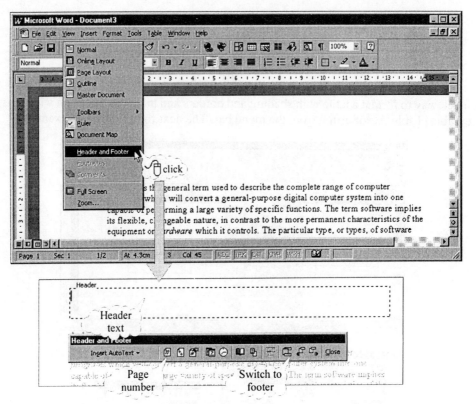

Inserting a header

The figure on the next page shows a header and footer in Print Preview (accessed through File|Print Preview on the menu bar).

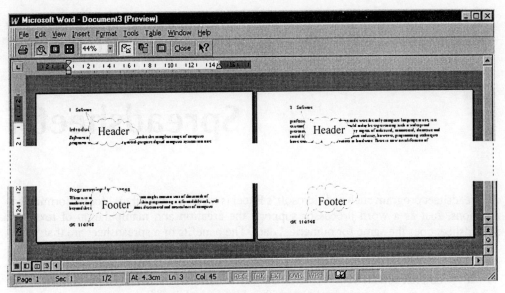

Print preview showing headers and footers

Chapter 34

Spreadsheet 1

A spreadsheet program such as Microsoft's Excel is a very powerful tool for performing calculations. Just as a word processor supports the creation and manipulation of text, so a spreadsheet does the same for numerical data. The benefits of a spreadsheet are that:

❑ Non-programmers can use it effectively;

❑ Complex calculations are automatically recalculated when any data, on which the calculation depends, is changed. This idea is explained by numerous examples in this chapter.

❑ Graphs can be linked to a spreadsheet so that a pictorial representation of the data can be provided alongside numeric information.

This tutorial concentrates on the basic operations required to set up simple calculations which illustrate important spreadsheet ideas. By carefully working through the tutorial you will gain a sound basis for using more advanced features of Excel.

Objectives

The principal objective of this tutorial is to be able to create a simple spreadsheet. On completion of this chapter you will be able to:

❑ Create a new blank spreadsheet.

❑ Recognise and use a number of toolbar functions.

❑ Enter data into spreadsheet cells.

❑ Enter simple formulas into spreadsheet cells.

❑ Modify spreadsheet cells.

❑ Format cells.

❑ Save spreadsheets to disk.

❑ Insert and delete rows and columns.

❑ Print spreadsheets.

❑ Retrieve spreadsheets from disk.

Any point at which you are required to carry out a procedure in the spreadsheet is indicated by the following action bullet.

☞ This means do what the text says.

The explanation of what you are required to do is normally accompanied by annotated pictures of the relevant screen area. Use these to help you understand the written instructions.

The Microsoft Excel Screen

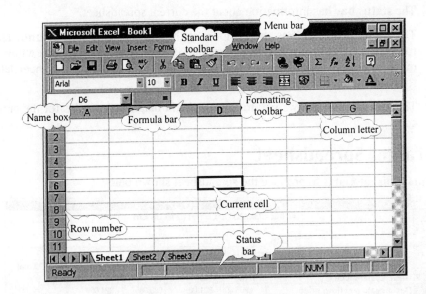

Before we begin to investigate the use of Microsoft Excel we need to look briefly at some of the components of the Excel screen.

❏ The **menu bar** provides access to a number of drop-down menus which are activated when the menu name is clicked. For example, clicking on the File menu will provide a list of options which include facilities to save, load and print documents.

We will refer to a menu option by specifying the name of the menu followed by the name of the option separated by a vertical bar. Thus, File|Save As means selecting the Save As option from the File menu.

❏ The **formatting toolbar** provides the means to alter the appearance of text in a number of ways. For example you can use it to:

○ Change the text font (that is, the style of the text) and size.

○ Make sections of the spreadsheet bold, italicised or underlined.

○ Left align, centre or right align spreadsheet cells.

○ Change the number of decimal places shown in numbers.

❏ The **standard toolbar** provides icons that you can click to perform a range of useful functions including:

        ○ Creating new spreadsheets.

        ○ Retrieving spreadsheets from disk.

        ○ Saving spreadsheets to disk.

        ○ Printing spreadsheets.

        ○ Creating graphs from spreadsheet data.

❏   The **status bar** has information about the current spreadsheet.

❏   The **name box** identifies the position of the **current cell** as a **column letter** followed by a **row number**. A *cell,* which is a small rectangular area within the much larger grid that makes up the spreadsheet, is used to hold spreadsheet data or formulas as we will see shortly.

❏   The **formula bar** allows you to enter and edit data and formulas for the current cell.

The Target Spreadsheet

Your aim in this tutorial is to produce the spreadsheet shown below.

	A	B	C	D	E	F	G	H	I
1			ACME COMPUTER SYSTEMS UK Ltd						
2									
3			Month		Dec	1997			
4			Sales person		H. Simpson				
5									Total
6	Basic system type			P133	P166	P200	P233		
7	Basic system selling price			805.00	821.00	839.00	924.00		
8	Number of systems sold			3	2	5	2		12
9	Extras sold			544.00	335.00	90.00	345.00		1314.00
10									
11	Gross sales value			2959.00	1977.00	4285.00	2193.00		11414.00
12	Commission paid (@12%)			355.08	237.24	514.20	263.16		1369.68
13									
14	Net sales value			2603.92	1739.76	3770.80	1929.84		10044.32
15									

It shows the sales figures for H. Simpson, one of the salesmen working for a computer system retail outlet called Acme Computer Systems UK Ltd.

❏   Acme currently sells four basic types of PC system, the cost of each depending on the speed of the Pentium processor used. The cost of a basic system is given in row 7 - 'Basic system selling price'.

❏   Extra memory, better monitors and higher capacity hard drives can be purchased at an additional cost which is shown as the single figure in row 9 labelled 'Extras sold'.

❏   The gross sales value for each type of basic system is calculated by multiplying the basic cost by the number of units sold, plus the value of the extras sold for that type of system. The answer is displayed in row 11.

❏   Salespersons receive a commission of 12% (12 pence for each £) on their sales, shown in row 12.

❏   The net sales value to Acme, shown in row 14, is the gross value less the commission paid,.

Step-by-step instructions for creating the spreadsheet are given in the following sections.

1 Creating a new Spreadsheet

Click on the New icon with the left mouse button. This creates a blank spreadsheet ready for you to begin entering data. You will be presented with a blank page and the name box will indicate that the current cell is at reference **A1**, the top left-hand corner of the spreadsheet.

2 Changing the current cell

There are two methods of changing the position of the current cell, one method using the mouse and the other using the keyboard. Using the mouse is simply a matter of moving the mouse pointer over the required position and clicking the mouse button. The cell selection is confirmed by the appearance of a heavy black outline around the cell and by the new cell reference appearing in the Name box.

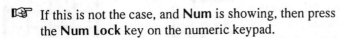

There are four arrow keys on most computer keyboards (on a combined numeric keypad), and these can be used to move the cursor one position up($\uparrow$), down($\downarrow$), left($\leftarrow$) or right($\rightarrow$). However, to use these arrow keys, you must make sure that **Num** is not showing on the status bar.

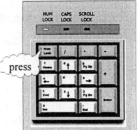

☞   If this is not the case, and **Num** is showing, then press the **Num Lock** key on the numeric keypad.

Num should then disappear from the status bar and the **Num Lock** light on the keyboard (if there is one) should go out. Some keyboards have a separate set of arrow keys, in which case you don't need to worry about the **Num Lock** key.

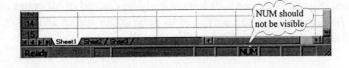

3 Entering the text heading

Now you can begin to create the target spreadsheet. The following figure shows the process for entering the heading.

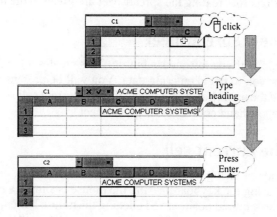

The steps are described below.

☞ Move the cursor to **C1** and enter the heading, 'ACME COMPUTER SYSTEMS'. As you type the text it will appear simultaneously in the formula bar and on the spreadsheet starting at cell **C1**. Press the Enter key after completing the heading. This sequence of actions is illustrated by the diagram on the previous page.

4 Clearing cells

There various ways of completely clearing the contents of cells. Two of these methods use the following keys.

❑ The Backspace key, which is situated on the main section of the keyboard.

❑ The Delete key **(Del)** which is found on the numeric keypad. (Note that on some keyboards, which have a special separate section on the keyboard for cursor navigation, there may be a another delete key that performs an identical function to the one on the numeric keypad).

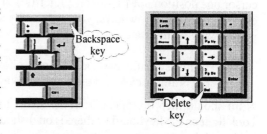

Use of both of these keys requires that you first select the cell or cells to be cleared. You can press Delete and the cell selection will immediately be cleared of all contents. If, however, you press the Backspace key, you will need to press Enter (or an arrow key) immediately afterwards. Otherwise, the cursor stays within the cell.

5 Entering the remainder of the text

☞ Now enter the remaining text so that your spreadsheet looks like the following.

	A	B	C	D	E	F	G	H
	A13							
1			ACME COMPUTER SYSTEMS UK Ltd					
2								
3			Month					
4			Sales person					
5								Total
6	Basic system type			P133	P166	P200	P233	
7	Basic system selling price							
8	Number of systems sold							
9	Extras sold							
10	Gross sales value							
11	Commission paid (@12%)							
12	Net sales value							

Note that the layout of your spreadsheet will not be exactly the same as that shown in the Target Document, but it will be by the end of this tutorial.

6 Saving your work

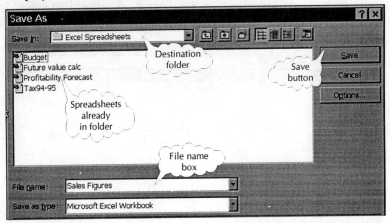

It is advisable to save your document to disk regularly as you work. An easy way to do this is by clicking the disk icon on the tool bar, which then displays the Save As dialogue box, shown below.

The first time you save a spreadsheet, you will need to give it a *filename* and specify where it is to be saved.

☞ Set the destination of the spreadsheet (by selecting from the Save in drop down list). This may require selection of a *drive letter* as shown on the next page and then a *folder*. In the above figure, the folder is called 'Excel Spreadsheets'.

☞ Enter the spreadsheet name (by editing the File name box) and click on the Save button.

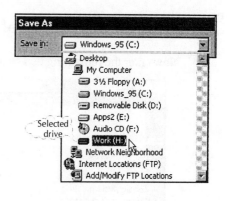

When you re-save a previously saved spreadsheet by clicking the disk icon, Excel saves it without asking for any more information. Note, however, that when you do this you will be <u>replacing</u> the previous version of your spreadsheet with the current version. If you want to keep the old version as well as the latest one, you will need to save the latest version under a different name or in a different location.

7 Entering numeric data

The next task is to enter the numeric data on which the calculations will be performed. These are the figures for:

❑ row 7, labelled 'Basic system selling price';

❑ row 8, labelled 'Number of systems sold';

❑ row 9, labelled 'Extras sold'.

As with text, you select the appropriate cell and then type in the value.

☞ Type in the numeric data shown in the illustration below. Remember to press Enter after every number and select the appropriate cell before entering the next value.

	A	B	C	D	E	F	G	H
1			ACME COMPUTER SYSTEMS					
2								
3			Month		Dec		1997	
4			Sales person		H. Simpson			
5								Total
6	Basic system type		P133	P166	P200	P233		
7	Basic system selling price		805	812	839	924		
8	Number of systems sold		3	2	5	2		
9	Extras sold		544	335	90	354		
10	Gross sales value							
11	Commission paid (@12%)							
12	Net sales value							

Notice that numbers are aligned to the <u>right</u> of the cell, but text it is aligned to the <u>left</u>. We will see later that this alignment can be altered. Although all of the numbers in this example are integers (that is, whole numbers), Excel allows numbers with as many decimal places as you need. The decimal point is the dot on the key shown on the right.

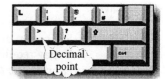

☞ Finally, type in the month, the year and the name of the salesman, also shown in the above figure.

8 Editing the contents of cells

You may have noticed that there are two mistakes in the prices that you have just entered compared with the Target Spreadsheet. Cell **E7** should be '821' and **G9** should be '345'.

The simplest way to correct these two cells is to enter them again.

☞ To change **E7** to the correct value of '821', select cell **E7** and enter the value '821' followed by pressing the Enter key.

☞ Repeat this procedure for **G9** and replace the value '354' by the correct value of '345'.

There is also a mistake in the main heading, which should read 'ACME COMPUTER SYSTEMS UK Ltd'.

Rather than retyping this, we will look at another method of editing a cell. You may have noticed that when you select a cell which already contains some data, its contents are shown in the formula bar. The contents can be edited from there, as illustrated below.

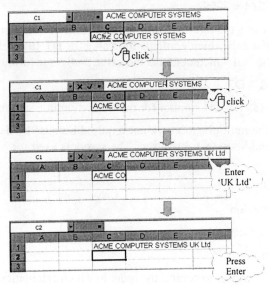

☞ Select cell **C1** and the heading appears in the formula bar.

☞ Click in the formula bar with the mouse.

☞ To add the end of the correct title, click at the end of the title in the formula bar and type 'UK Ltd' followed by Enter.

In general you can click anywhere in the formula bar to edit text, numeric data and formulas. The left and right arrow keys, the delete key and the backspace key all operate as normal when editing in the formula bar.

9 Formulas

The real power of a spreadsheet lies in the use of formulas.

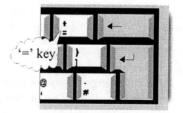

❑ Formulas allow you to perform calculations and other procedures on data that has been entered into spreadsheet cells.

You enter formulas by first selecting a cell and then pressing '='.

A formula will often contain cell references and arithmetic operations, such as addition, subtraction, multiplication or division, to be performed on the contents of these cells.

For example, to calculate the 'Gross sales value' in row 10 for P133s, we need to

❑ multiply the number of systems sold (3) by the basic system selling price (£805) and then add on the extras (£544). In other words we have to calculate

$(3 \times 805) + 544 = 2959$

However, rather than using the figures 3, 805 and 544 in the calculation, we use their cell references, that is **D8** (the cell which contains the value 3), **D7** (the cell which contains the value 805) and **D9** (the cell which contains the value 544). Our formula becomes

= D8 * D7 + D9

Note that you use the asterisk (*) symbol for multiplication in Excel formulas.

The brackets around the multiplication are not required because by default Excel performs multiplication before addition or subtraction. The symbols used for performing arithmetic are

+   (for addition)

−   (for subtraction

*   (for multiplication)

/   (for division)

You can use brackets '(' and ')' to control the order in which calculations are performed. For example:

❑ to add the contents of two cells and then divide the sum by 2 you could use the formula '**= (A1 + A2) /2**'.

This is not the same as using '**= A1 + A2 /2**', which would give a different answer.

After you enter a formula and then press Enter, the result of the calculation is displayed by Excel.

The formula itself can be viewed and edited if required in the formula bar by following the procedure described in section 8 'Editing the contents of cells'. Now enter the formula in cell **D10** by following these steps:

☞ Select cell **D10**.

☞ Type '**=D7*D8 + D9**'.

☞ Press Enter.

These steps are illustrated below.

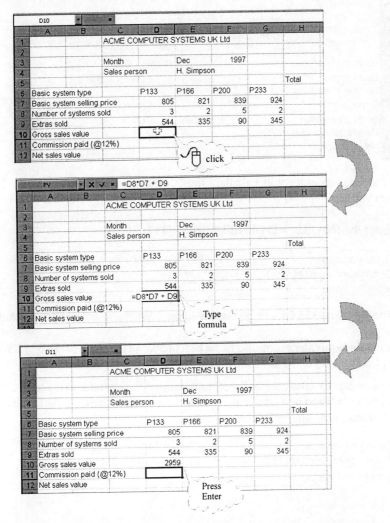

Now repeat this procedure for the columns headed 'P166', 'P200' and 'P233'. The formulas that you need to enter are:

☞ in **E10** enter '=E7*E8 + E9';

☞ in **F10** enter '=F7*F8 + F9';

☞ in **G10** enter '=G7*G8 + G9'.

Your spreadsheet should now look like this:

	G11						
	A	B	C	D	E	F	G	H
1			ACME COMPUTER SYSTEMS UK Ltd					
2								
3			Month		Dec	1997		
4			Sales person		H. Simpson			
5								Total
6	Basic system type			P133	P166	P200	P233	
7	Basic system selling price			805	821	839	924	
8	Number of systems sold			3	2	5	2	
9	Extras sold			544	335	90	345	
10	Gross sales value			2959	1977	4285	2193	
11	Commission paid (@12%)							
12	Net sales value							

The next formulas to enter will calculate the 'Commission paid' by finding 12% of the 'Gross sales value'.

☞ Enter the formula '=D10*12%' in cell **D11**.

10	Gross sales value		2959	1977	4285	2193	
11	Commission paid (@12%)	=D10*12%					
12	Net sales value						

The figure of 355.08 will be displayed once you have entered the formula.

☞ Enter the equivalent formulas of '=E10*12%' in cell **E11**, '=F10*12%' in cell **F11** and '=G10*12%' in cell **G11**.

Remember to select the cell before entering the formula, precede each formula with the '=' sign and finally press Enter to establish the formula in the cell. Row 11 should now appear as shown below.

10	Gross sales value		2959	1977	4285	2193	
11	Commission paid (@12%)		355.08	237.24	514.20	263.16	
12	Net sales value						

10 Copying formulas

The 'Net sale value' is calculated by subtracting the 'Commission paid (@12%)' from the 'Gross sales value' for each of the four columns. The formula that goes in cell **D12** is ' **= D10 – D11**':

10	Gross sales value	2959	1977	4285	2193
11	Commission paid (@12%)	355.08	237.24	514.20	263.16
12	Net sales value	=D10 - D11			

☞ Enter the formula ' **= D10 – D11**' in **D12**. This will give a figure of 2603.92.

At this point you could enter the equivalent formulas in cells **E12**, **F12** and **G12** as before, but there is a much easier method of installing these three formulas.

You probably will have noticed that the formulas which you have been entering along the rows for each of the columns labelled 'P133', 'P166', 'P200' and 'P233' have been identical except for the column letter. This similarity allows us to copy the formula in **D12** for the cells **E12** to **G12** without having to type them in. The procedure is as illustrated below.

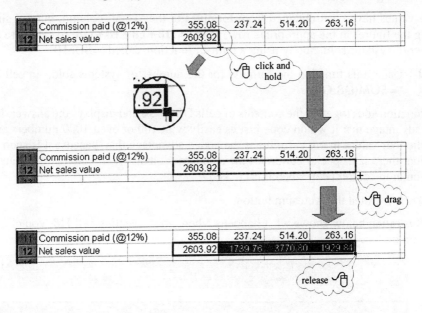

The procedure can be described as follows.

☞ Select cell **D12** and you will notice that there is a tiny rectangle in its bottom right-hand corner and that the mouse pointer changes to a cross-hair cursor if you move the pointer over it.

☞ Click **and hold** the mouse button and drag the mouse horizontally to cell **G12**.

You will notice that cells **D12** to **G12** become enclosed by a grey rectangle. This indicates that when you release the mouse button the formula in **D12** will be copied to this range of cells, while automatically adjusting the formula in **D12** to allow for the increasing row letter.

If, after releasing the mouse button you select, say, cell **F12**, you will see from the formula box that the formula in **F12** is '**= F10 - F11**' as required.

Whenever you need several adjacent formulas which differ only in the row number or the column letter, you can copy the formula in this way.

Remember, though, that you must select the cell containing the formula to be copied <u>before</u> commencing the click and drag operation.

11 Using built-in functions

If you refer back to the Target Spreadsheet shown towards the beginning of this chapter, you will notice that there is a column of figures labelled 'Total'. Thus:

❑   the number of basic systems that have been sold totals 12;

❑   the gross sales value for the month is shown as 11,414.00.

These values have been obtained from formulas in the 'Total' column, but not simply by adding the figures in the appropriate row, as in '**= D8 + E8 + F8 + G8**' to calculate the total number of systems sold, but by using a built-in function, called '**=SUM()**'

❑   Using this function the formula for the number of systems sold, in cell H8, is '**= SUM(D8:G8)**'.

This function adds together the contents of cells **D8** to **G8** and displays the answer. It has the great advantage that it would cope just as easily with 100 or even 1000 numbers as it does with the four values in our case. It has the added advantage that, because it is such a useful function, there is a special button on the standard toolbar which automatically installs the function in the current cell when it is clicked.

❑   It is called the Autosum button.

The illustration below shows what happens when, after selecting cell **H8**, you click on the Autosum button.

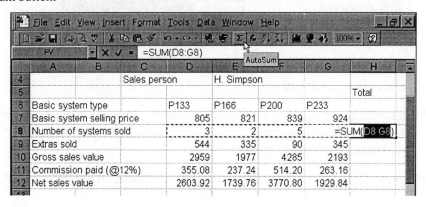

☞ Select **H8**.

☞ Click on the Autosum button.

> All figures to the left of the current cell are enclosed by a dotted line and the **SUM** function appears with the equivalent cell range (**D8:G8**) highlighted.

☞ Press Enter and the function is installed in **H8**.

Since rows 9, 10 and 11 also require a similar function in the 'Total' column:

☞ copy the formula in **H8** using the procedure described in the previous section 'Copying formulas'.

> In this case, because you are copying a formula in a column, you drag the mouse vertically instead of horizontally.

Your spreadsheet should now look like the following illustration.

	A	B	C	D	E	F	G	H
	H15			■				
1			ACME COMPUTER SYSTEMS UK Ltd					
2								
3			Month		Dec	1997		
4			Sales person		H. Simpson			
5								Total
6	Basic system type			P133	P166	P200	P233	
7	Basic system selling price			805	821	839	924	
8	Number of systems sold			3	2	5	2	12
9	Extras sold			544	335	90	345	1314
10	Gross sales value			2959	1977	4285	2193	11414
11	Commission paid (@12%)			355.08	237.24	514.20	263.16	1369.68
12	Net sales value			2603.92	1739.76	3770.80	1929.84	10044.32

Excel provides dozens of functions for many types of calculation, some simple and some complex. The simpler functions include those to calculate, for example:

❑ the average value a set of numbers (=**AVERAGE**);

❑ the number of entries in a range of cells (=**COUNT**);

❑ the minimum value from a range of cells (=**MIN**);

❑ the maximum value from a range of cells (=**MAX**).

Apart from improving its appearance, the spreadsheet is essentially complete, with all the data and formulas established. Now is therefore a good time to

☞ re-save your work.

click

12 Formatting cells

You can improve the appearance of your spreadsheet by formatting cells.

☞ Make the heading bold by selecting **C1** and then clicking on the **B** icon on the formatting toolbar.

☞ Do the same with Month (**C3**), Sales person (**C4**) and Total (**H5**).

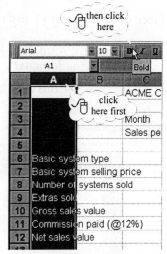

Alternatively, you can select a whole column of cells by clicking the column letter. The column will become highlighted and you can then make the complete column bold by clicking the Bold icon as before. This is shown in the illustration alongside.

Don't highlight the column at present. Instead, you can click a row number to highlight a complete row.

☞ Click on row 6 (on the Row number) to the left of 'Basic system type' and then make the headings in that row bold by clicking the Bold icon.

As well as being able to select a single cell, you can select a rectangular block of cells by clicking and dragging with the mouse.

Experiment as follows.

☞ Make sure that your mouse pointer is in the middle of the top left cell of a block (it doesn't matter which one) and that it looks like this ⊹

☞ Click the mouse button.

☞ Then, holding down the mouse button, drag a rectangular block of cells.

☞ When you release the mouse button the rectangular area will remain highlighted.

☞ Experiment with selecting various rectangular blocks of cells until you can select a block of any size, including a line of cells forming part of a row or column.

You will use this skill in the next section.

Note that any selection of cells can be formatted in a number of different ways, not just by making the selection bold.

For example, you can:

❏   italicise (*I*) or underline (<u>U</u>) text using the two icons to the right of the Bold icon;

❏   align data within cells;

❏   set the number of decimal places that will be displayed.

You will have the opportunity to practise a number of these formatting effects in the following sections.

13 Setting the number of decimal places

A large part of the spreadsheet data involves currency values, and it is customary to display such numbers with two decimal places, even when the value is a whole number.

Thus, for example, we need to format the values in cells **D6** to **G6** so that they have two decimal places rather than none. An easy method of achieving this is by using the Increase Decimal icon on the formatting toolbar.

The following diagram illustrates the procedure.

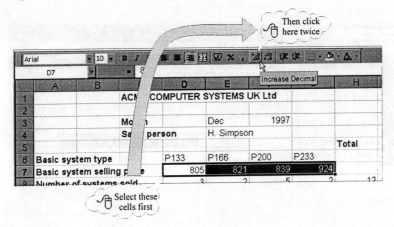

Now format the cells containing currency, as follows.

☞ Select the cells containing the basic prices of each system.

☞ Click on the Increase Decimal button twice to increase the number of decimal places to two, as shown below.

P133	P166	P200	P233
805.00	821.00	839.00	924.00
3	2	5	2

The Decrease Decimal button, situated to the right of the Increase Decimal button on the formatting toolbar, reduces the number of decimal places by one each time it is pressed.

☞ Repeat the procedure for increasing the number of decimal places to two for the block of cells from **D9** to **H12**, thus making sure that all of the currency figures on the spreadsheet show two decimal places.

14 Aligning data within cells

Excel applies default alignment settings as follows: text is aligned <u>left</u> within cells; numbers are aligned <u>right</u> within cells. However, you can change the alignment of any group of cells by using the Alignment buttons on the formatting toolbar.

☞ To centre the headings for the four processor types on row 6, first select the headings, by clicking and dragging the mouse, and then click on the centre button.

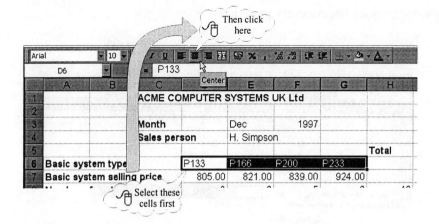

☞ Try doing the same thing for the block **E3** to **F4** which contains the month, year and salesman.

☞ For further practice also centre the five numbers in row 8, representing the number of systems sold.

Before proceeding with the final few refinements to your spreadsheet, first make sure that it now looks like this:

	A	B	C	D	E	F	G	H
1			ACME COMPUTER SYSTEMS UK Ltd					
2								
3			Month		Dec	1997		
4			Sales person		H. Simpson			
5								Total
6	Basic system type			P133	P166	P200	P233	
7	Basic system selling price			805.00	821.00	839.00	924.00	
8	Number of systems sold			3	2	5	2	12
9	Extras sold			544.00	335.00	90.00	345.00	1314.00
10	Gross sales value			2959.00	1977.00	4285.00	2193.00	11414.00
11	Commission paid (@12%)			355.08	237.24	514.20	263.16	1369.68
12	Net sales value			2603.92	1739.76	3770.80	1929.84	10044.32

If your spreadsheet does not look like this, then make the necessary modifications and then

☞ save it.

15 Insert and delete rows and columns

Insert rows and columns

The Target Spreadsheet at the beginning of this tutorial has a number of blank rows and columns which help to make the information presented a little clearer and easier to read. You can insert blank rows and columns by accessing the Insert menu.

☞ To insert an extra row between rows 9 and 10, first click on row number 10 to select that row. (When you insert a row it appears above the currently selected row). Now click on the Insert menu and select Rows. All the rows below row 9 are moved down and a blank row appears where row 10 was located. The diagram below illustrates the procedure.

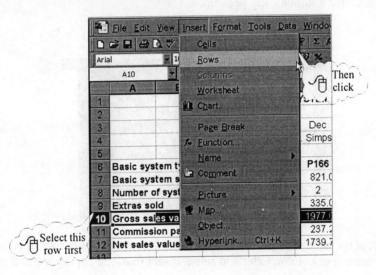

☞ Repeat row insertion so that there is also a blank row between the rows labelled 'Commission paid' and 'Net sales value'.

Note that Excel automatically adjusts any formulas that might be affected by inserting rows and columns, so there is no need to be concerned about having to re-enter all of those formulas. Inserting columns involves an almost identical procedure. Select the column to the left of where the extra column is to appear, by clicking on the column letter, and then select Insert|Columns.

☞ Insert a column between 'P233' and 'Total'. (Click on column letter H first, then select 'Columns' from the Insert menu).

Deleting rows and columns

To delete a row or column, you first select it as previously described, and then select Edit|Delete. This has the effect of removing the row or column entirely.

The illustration on the right shows column D about to be deleted as soon as Edit|Delete has been selected with the mouse.

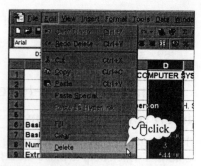

Using the right mouse button to insert and delete columns

An alternative method of inserting rows and columns involves the use of the right mouse button. If you are using Excel on an IBM compatible PC and your mouse has more than one button, you will find that the **right** mouse button can be used very effectively for inserting or deleting rows or columns. For example, to delete column **D** (don't do this) you would click the **right** mouse button when the pointer is over the column letter **D** and then select **Delete** from the menu that automatically pops up.

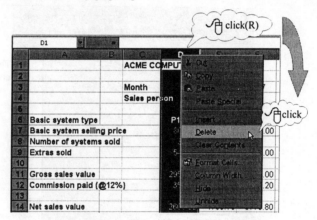

You can adopt the same procedure to insert rows or columns. Simply right click on the appropriate row number or column letter and select **Insert** from the pop-up menu that appears.

16 Adjusting column widths

If you carefully move the mouse pointer to the border between any two column letters, you will see the pointer change shape, as shown on the right.

This indicates that, by clicking and dragging the mouse, you can either:

❑   increase the width of the column to the left of the pointer by moving the mouse to the right;

    or

❑   <u>decrease</u> the width of the column to the left of the pointer by moving the mouse to the <u>left</u>.

Make the following adjustments to the spreadsheet, to match (approximately will do) the column widths in the Target Document.

☞   Increase the width of column **A.** Position the mouse pointer between column letters **A** and **B** and when the pointer changes shape, click and drag the mouse to the right.

☞   You will see column **A** increase in width and all of the other columns move further to the right.

☞   Decrease the width of column **B.** You will need to position the pointer between column letter **B** and **C.**

Your spreadsheet should now look almost identical to the Target Spreadsheet. If it doesn't then make any necessary modifications before

☞   saving it once more.

17 Printing the spreadsheet

If you have a printer attached to your system then printing your document is simply a matter of clicking the Print icon on the Standard toolbar. However, before you do so first make sure that the printer is switched on, loaded with paper and, if appropriate, on-line. If everything is alright, you are ready to print so

☞   click on the Print icon and after a few seconds your finished spreadsheet should appear.

18 Making a backup copy

Making a backup copy of a spreadsheet, which might have taken you a considerable amount of time and effort to produce, is your insurance against accidental loss or corruption.

A simple way of making a backup is to access File|Save As and select a different location, such as a floppy disk, to which to save your document.

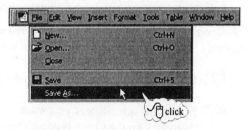

☞   Select File|Save As. The dialogue box appears.

☞   Set the destination of the spreadsheet (by selecting from the Save in drop down list).

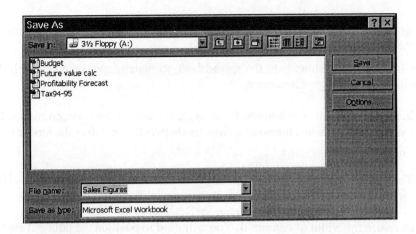

☞ Enter the spreadsheet name (by editing the File name box).

☞ Click on the Save button. In the example above, the current spreadsheet is to be saved to a floppy disk using the name 'Sales Figures'.

19 Opening spreadsheets

After you have finished working on your spreadsheet program you will close it down and, perhaps switch off your computer for the day. You will have saved your work previously onto your hard disk or to a floppy disk. When you resume work on Excel at some later date, you can either create a new spreadsheet as you did in this exercise, or you can continue working on a spreadsheet that you created during a previous session.

In the second case you need to Open the spreadsheet, that is, retrieve it from its stored location and load it into Excel. There are a number of ways of doing this, but we will start with the way that will always be possible, and then investigate a quicker method that will usually, but not always, be available.

☞ Exit from the spreadsheet package and then re-load it.

The icon which allows you to open spreadsheets is shown on the standard toolbar as a folder opening. The process is illustrated on the next page.

☞ Click on the Open icon. The Open dialogue box is displayed.

☞ Select the spreadsheet you want – 'Sales Figures' in the example above – and then click on the Open button. The spreadsheet will then be loaded into Excel. If your spreadsheet is in another location and is not shown in the window, then you need to change the Look in box to the appropriate folder or disk drive.

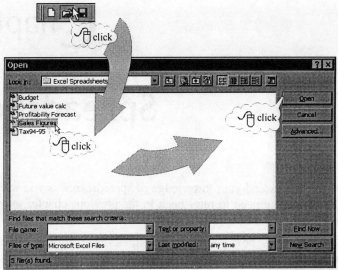

A quicker method of opening a spreadsheet depends on how recently you last used a spreadsheet. Excel keeps a re- cord of the last few spreadsheets that you used and installs their names in the File menu. An example is shown on the right. Four files are listed, of which the first one, used most recently, has been selected. It will be loaded into Excel and opened automatically without the need to go through the Open dialogue box. However, if the spreadsheet to be opened was not one of the last four accessed, it would not appear in this list and the previously described method would need to be used to open it.

Chapter 35

Spreadsheet 2

In this chapter you will extend your knowledge of spreadsheets as you work through two further examples. You may need to refer back to the previous chapter to remind yourself about basic spreadsheet operations.

The first example illustrates how you can use a spreadsheet to investigate the effects of changing certain values. You will use the spreadsheet's automatic calculation feature to investigate *what* happens *if* you change certain key values. In fact spreadsheets are sometimes called *what..if* programs because of this very important capability. This example also illustrates how you can produce a graph automatically from the data in the spreadsheet.

The second example introduces some slightly more advanced calculations. It uses *random numbers* and *if functions* to simulate a local football league.

Objectives

On completion of this chapter you will be able to:

- ❏ Create a spreadsheet to investigate a simple financial model
- ❏ Use the *what..if* capabilities of a spreadsheet
- ❏ Create absolute cell references
- ❏ Use spreadsheet parameters
- ❏ Create a graph from spreadsheet data
- ❏ Create a spreadsheet to simulate football league results
- ❏ Use a range of built-in spreadsheet functions
- ❏ Use shading and different text colours to improve the appearance of a spreadsheet

What if...

Suppose that you have to organise a concert to raise money for a charity. The concert will be held in a community hall. A popular local band will be invited to play and there will also be a buffet for the intermission. Entry to the concert will be by ticket only. The local catering firm that you have contacted have informed you that they can provide food at a cost per person of £1, £2 or £3. It is up to you how much to charge for tickets, but most concerts of this type generally cost between £5 to £10.

You have already found out that the band will charge £100 for the evening, and that the hall hire charge will be £30. In addition, tickets will cost £25 to be printed and there will be a further cost of £20 to get posters printed to advertise the concert. These are fixed expenses over which you don't have much control.

Your problem is how much to charge for tickets and how much to spend on food. If you charge too much for the tickets, you will get fewer people attending. On the other hand, if you charge too little for tickets, you might not even cover the concert expenses. And if you spend too much on the food, you will reduce the amount of money that you will raise for charity.

Parameters

To calculate the amount of profit you can make you need to estimate how many tickets will be sold, decide on how much to spend on food per person and how much to charge for tickets. These three quantities are called *parameters*. Parameters are values that determine the result of a calculation. In this case the three parameters determine how much profit will be made. For example, if you sold 50 tickets at £5 each and spent £2 per person on food, the profit calculation would be as follows:

Expenses	Item	Amount
	Cost of printing tickets	£25·00
	Cost of printing posters	£20·00
	Hall hire	£30·00
	Cost of band	£100·00
	Sub total	**£175·00**
	Cost of meal per person	**£2·00**
	Selling price per ticket	**£5·00**

Income = 50 tickets @ £5 each = £250

Expenditure = £175 + 50 meals @ £2 per person = £275

Profit = Income - Expenditure = £250 − £275 = −£25

This represents a loss of £25 for the figures that we used.

To achieve a profit we must therefore change one or more of the parameters of the calculation. You can probably see that setting up the calculation on a spreadsheet will save a lot of time. You can get the spreadsheet to calculate the profit for different values of parameters. That way you can investigate the effects of choosing different values for food and ticket costs. The screen shot on the top left of next page shows a possible way of designing the spreadsheet.

The table at the head of the spreadsheet shows the fixed costs amounting to £175, and two of the parameters - cost of meal and cost of ticket.

Concert.xls

Charity concert financial analysis

Expenses	Item	Amount
	Cost of printing tickets	£ 25.00
	Cost of printing poster	£ 20.00
	Hall hire	£ 30.00
	Cost of band	£ 100.00
	Sub total	£ 175.00
	Cost of meal per pe	£ 2.00
Income	Selling price of tic	£ 6.00

Tickets sold	Expenses	Income	Profit
10	195.00	60.00	-135.00
20	215.00	120.00	-95.00
30	235.00	180.00	-55.00
40	255.00	240.00	-15.00
50	275.00	300.00	25.00
60	295.00	360.00	65.00
70	315.00	420.00	105.00
80	335.00	480.00	145.00
90	355.00	540.00	185.00
100	375.00	600.00	225.00
110	395.00	660.00	265.00
120	415.00	720.00	305.00
130	435.00	780.00	345.00
140	455.00	840.00	385.00
150	475.00	900.00	425.00

Concert.xls

Charity concert financial analysis

Expenses	Item		Amount
	Cost of printing tickets		25
	Cost of printing posters		20
	Hall hire		30
	Cost of band		100
	Sub total		=SUM(D4:D7)
	Cost of meal per person		2
Income	Selling price of ticket		5

Tickets sold	Expenses	Income	Profit
10	=$A$10+$A$6*A14	=$B$9*A14	=C14-B14
20	=$A$10+$A$6*A15	=$B$9*A15	=C15-B15
30	=$A$10+$A$6*A16	=$B$9*A16	=C16-B16
40	=$A$10+$A$6*A17	=$B$9*A17	=C17-B17
50	=$A$10+$A$6*A18	=$B$9*A18	=C18-B18
60	=$A$10+$A$6*A19	=$B$9*A19	=C19-B19
70	=$A$10+$A$6*A20	=$B$9*A20	=C20-B20
80	=$A$10+$A$6*A21	=$B$9*A21	=C21-B21
90	=$A$10+$A$6*A22	=$B$9*A22	=C22-B22
100	=$A$10+$A$6*A23	=$B$9*A23	=C23-B23
110	=$A$10+$A$6*A24	=$B$9*A24	=C24-B24
120	=$A$10+$A$6*A25	=$B$9*A25	=C25-B25
130	=$A$10+$A$6*A26	=$B$9*A26	=C26-B26
140	=$A$10+$A$6*A27	=$B$9*A27	=C27-B27
150	=$A$10+$A$6*A28	=$B$9*A28	=C28-B28

Because at this stage you won't know exactly how many people will buy tickets, the number of tickets sold is shown as a range of values going from 10 to 150 in the main table. Each row of the main table shows number of tickets sold the expenses, the income and the profit for that number of tickets. The screen shot on the top right of this page shows the formulas used to perform the calculations.

Absolute cell references

Now look at row 17. The calculation for expenses looks like this:

```
=$E$9+$E$10*B18
```

This formula adds the fixed costs in cell E9 to the cost of a meal (given in E10) multiplied by the number of tickets sold (given in A17). Notice the '$' signs in the formula. These make the cell references *absolute references*. This means that if you copy a formula with an absolute cell reference, it stays the same in each copy. For example, all of the formulas in column C were copied from the first one in C17, but the cell references E9 and E10 have not changed in the copies. This is exactly what we want. These two cell references are two of the parameters that are defined in the top table. We want to be able to change these figures only, without having to change all the formulas that depend on them.

The absolute reference for the cost of the ticket is used in the formulas in column D. This is the calculation of the income, that is the number of tickets sold (given in column A) multiplied by the cost of a ticket (given in E12).

You can see for the spreadsheet that there is a profit when between 50 and 60 tickets are sold. If you change the value in cell E12 to £6, the profit increases. If you change the cost of the meal to £3, the profit decreases. In this way you can investigate *what* happens *if* you change any of the parameters. By experimenting with the ticket and meal values you can see how the money you make for charity goes up as you sell an increasing number of tickets.

Creating a break-even chart

It is obviously quite important to make sure that the concert does not make a loss, even if it doesn't make a lot of profit. The point at which the income is exactly the same as the expenditure is called

❑   the *break-even point*.

Because the spreadsheet is in the form of a table showing the figures for a range of tickets sold, it is suitable as the basis of a break-even chart as shown in the next screen shot.

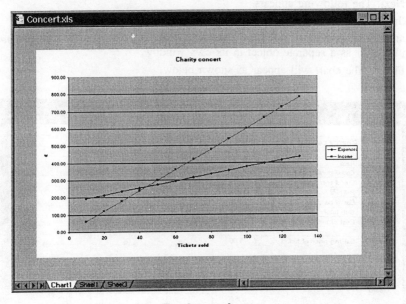

Break even chart

The two lines represent the income (the steeper line) and the expenditure. Where they cross is the break-even point. The chart is easily created using the chart wizard. The chart wizard icon is shown on the right.

To create the graph first select the three leftmost columns in the main table, as shown on the right. Then click on the chart wizard icon on the toolbar. The chart wizard will lead you through the four steps necessary to produce the break-even chart.

1. Click the chart wizard icon. The following appears.

   `Chart Wizard - Step 1 of 4 - Chart type`

2. Select Chart type XY (Scatter).

3. Select Chart sub-type.

4. Click Next. The following appears.

   `Chart Wizard - Step 2 of 4 - Chart Source Data`

   Because you selected the three data columns to be used in the chart before you started the wizard, you can go on to the next step immediately.

5. Click Next. Chart Wizard. The following appears.

   `Step 3 of 4 - Chart Options`

6. Enter the title, 'Charity Concert Finances', in the Chart title box.

7. Enter 'Tickets sold' for Value (X) Axis.

8. Enter '£' in the Value (Y) Axis box.

9. Click Next. The following appears.

   `Chart Wizard - Step 4 of 4 - Chart Location`

   You can choose whether to have the chart embedded in your spreadsheet (the option chosen here) or as a separate object in its own window.

10. Click Finish. The chart will appear as shown below.

By clicking on the border of the chart you can drag it to a different part of your spreadsheet, or you can change its size by dragging one of the small black control points on the border.

The type of chart and its appearance can be edited after it has been created from the Chart menu.

Note that the chart will be redrawn automatically whenever you change any of the data used to create it.

Using a spreadsheet for simulation

The second example in this chapter simulates the scores in a local amateur football league. There are 20 teams in the league. Matches are played once per week and the spreadsheet uses random number functions to simulate the scores for each team.

Points are awarded to the teams as follows

❑   3 points for a win

❑   1 point for a draw

The total points are calculated each week. An example of the spreadsheet for a certain week is shown in the next screen shot.

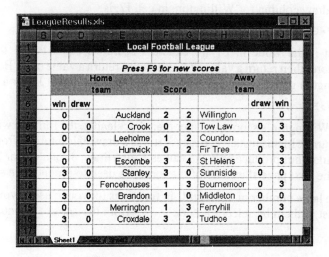

The points awarded for each team is shown in the win and draw columns. The numbers of goals scored can be changed by pressing the function key F9 which makes the spreadsheet recalculate everything. This makes it produce new random numbers for the scores.

Built-in functions

The scores are produced by a formula which uses two built-in functions, RND() and ROUND(). Together they randomly produce the numbers 0, 1, 2, 3 and 4. (For simplicity we assume that it is unlikely for a team to score more than 4 goals). The random number function looks like this when it is used in a formula:

    =RND()

It automatically generates a number between 0 and 1 every time the spreadsheet is recalculated. To produce a random number between 0 and 4 we need to multiply the random number function by 4:

```
=RND()*4
```

However, this will give us numbers such as 2.33 or 0.65 - numbers that do not make sense if they are supposed to represent goals. We need to remove the fractional part of the number so that only whole numbers are produced

The function ROUND() does just this - it converts a value into the nearest whole number. For example, ROUND(3.4) returns a value of 3 and ROUND(2.6) returns 3. So now if we put our random number function inside the ROUND() function we get

```
=ROUND(RND()*4)
```

And as you can see from the previous screen shot, the scores are now whole numbers between 0 and 4. Both of the columns F and G contain this formula in each row of the league table.

Every time the scores change, the spreadsheet also calculates the points awarded to each time. We use another function this time - the IF() function. An example of how the function is used is given below. Look at the first row of the table for Auckland v Willington. The formula for the draw column for Willington, in cell I7, is

```
=IF(F7=G7,1,0)
```

This means that if the value in F7 (Auckland's score) is equal to (=) the value in G7 (Willington's score) then return a value of 1, otherwise return a value of 0). Because the score was 2 - 2, Willington gets 1 point for this result The formula in cell J7 for a win is

```
=IF(G7>F7,3,0)
```

which means if Willington's score is greater than Auckland's, the formula will return 3, otherwise it will return 0. In this instance, because it was a draw, 0 is returned from this function. These two formulas thus produce only the values 1 for a draw, 3 for a win or 0 for a loss. The screen shot on the next page shows all of the formulas used to produce the spreadsheet.

Excel provides a large number of these built-in functions for you to use in your spreadsheets. You can see a list of them by selecting Function.. from the Insert menu.

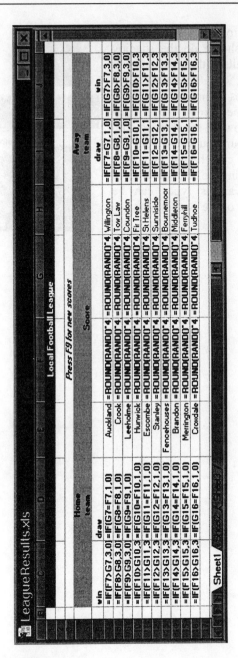

Shading and text colours

Two of the headings in this spreadsheet are shaded grey. This effect can improve the appearance of your spreadsheets. Other ways of making your spreadsheets more attractive are by using different text colours and by putting borders around cells. The three icons that give you access to these facilities are shown on the next page. They are to be found on the formatting tool bar.

If you want to shade a group of cells using the current shading colour shown on the shading icon, simply select the cells with the mouse and then click on the shading icon. The background colour of the cells changes to the current colour. If you want to change the current colour, first click the small down arrow on the shading icon and then select the colour you want from the palette that appears. You can change the colour of text in the same way using the text colour icon. Similarly, borders of various types can be applied to cells by means of the Border icon.

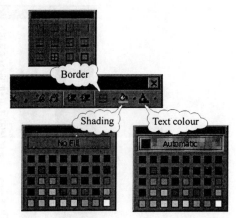

Chapter 36

Database

This tutorial uses the Access database package. Database programs allow you to store and retrieve information related to a particular topic. Employee records, music collections on CDs and hospital records are all examples of databases which can be stored and used with Access. This tutorial provides an introduction to some of the facilities provided by typical database programs.

Objectives

In this tutorial we introduce the basic features necessary to create and use a database. On completion of this tutorial you will be able to:

❑   Design and construct a simple database.

❑   Enter, modify and delete database records.

❑   Sort the database into different orders.

❑   Create and execute queries which can be used repeatedly to sort and filter records from the database.

❑   Create and print reports.

Any point at which you are required to carry out a procedure in the database is indicated by the following action bullet.

☞   This means do what the text says.

The explanation of what you are required to do is normally accompanied by annotated pictures of the relevant screen area. These are to help you understand the written instructions.

The Target Database

The Target Database is for a Sports club. The database holds information on the Sports club's members and the courses available to them. Before you can begin to construct and use this database, you need to understand some basic ideas about its components and the way it organises the information it holds.

Tables, records and fields

The Sports database consists of two *tables*, one holding information on the training courses run by the club (the Course table) and the other containing information on its members (the

Member table). The component parts of a table are described first by reference to the Member table and then by reference to the Course table.

The Member table

The Member table holds basic details about each member, their subscriptions and a code (for example, BA01) to identify their course. For simplicity, it is assumed that each member can only be registered on one course at any one time. The Member table, containing some sample records is shown below.

AutoNumber	Surname	Forename	Sex	Date of Birth	Subs	Charge	Course
1	Williams	Tom	M	17/06/82	☑	£15.00	BA01
2	Crowley	Paula	F	18/02/81	☑	£13.50	SQ01
3	McKenzie	Peter	M	13/02/82	☐	£14.00	VO01
4	Ludwig	Herbert	M	16/09/80	☑	£23.00	SQ03
5	Russo	Mirella	F	15/11/82	☐	£15.00	BA01
6	Hussain	Shahin	M	13/01/81	☑	£13.50	SQ01
7	Hideo	Kato	M	14/02/83	☐	£14.00	VO01
8	Crowley	Paula	F	16/02/82	☑	£15.00	BA01
9	Flannigan	Sara	F	13/04/82	☑	£23.00	SQ03
10	Miller	Peter	M	17/07/80	☐	£23.00	SQ03
11	Alldis	Joan	F	14/05/82	☐	£15.00	BA01
12	Jenkins	Allan	M	16/11/82	☑	£13.50	SQ01
13	Parker	Colin	M	13/02/82	☑	£14.00	VO01
14	McDonald	Lisa	F	14/08/80	☑	£14.00	VO01
15	Al-Fariz	Rashid	M	23/03/81	☐	£15.00	BA01
16	Johnson	Maria	F	28/01/82	☑	£23.00	SQ03
(AutoNumber)					☐	£0.00	

Record: 16 of 16

The following database components can be identified from the figure:

❑ A *record* is held for each member of the Sports club. The figure shows 16 member records.

❑ Each record has a number of *fields*. There are 8 in the example.

❑ Each field contains an item of information about the member.

❑ Each field has a *name* to identify it and suggest its contents. So, for example, the Surname field in each record contains the member's surname.

One field (AutoNumber, in this case) is used as the *primary key* to allow unique identification of a member record. This is necessary because, for example, two or more members could have the same name. The figure shows that two members are called Paula Crowley (records uniquely identified by the primary key as 2 and 8).

❑ The Member *table* holds all the member records.

The Course table

The Course table, containing details of sample training courses, is shown below.

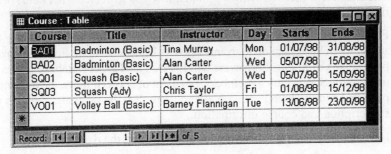

The following database components can be identified:

- ❑ A *record* is held for each course run by the Sports club. The figure shows 5 such courses.

- ❑ Each record has a number of *fields*. There are 6 in the example.

- ❑ Each field contains an item of information about the Course.

- ❑ Each field has a *name* to identify it and suggest its contents. So, for example, the Instructor field contains the instructor's name.

    One field (Course) is used as the *primary key* to allow unique identification of a Course record. This means that, although there are two Badminton (Basic) courses, each can be separately identified by its unique Course code. The Monday class has code BA01 and the Wednesday class has the code BA02.

- ❑ The Course *table* holds all the Course records.

1 Designing the Target Database

Although database design is the subject of entire books, it is possible to use simple common-sense when designing a small database such as this. In this section, you will learn how to:

- ❑ reduce the <u>duplication</u> of information in a database, by splitting it into two or more tables;

- ❑ maintain a <u>relationship</u> between tables, to allow information to be combined as necessary.

There are a number of questions which need to be answered before beginning to construct a database:

- ❑ What is the general subject of the database?

    The answer to this gives you a starting point. For example, once you know a database is to store hospital patient records, you can find out more about the subject. You can't design a database without understanding something about the information to be stored. The Target Database is for a Sports club, so you are likely to be aware of its general purpose.

❑   What is it used for? Has it a single purpose, or several?

The answers to these questions should allow you to decide what kinds of information the database needs to hold.

For example, a library lending system is used to keep records of the books in stock, when books are on loan and who has borrowed them. So, the database must hold details of books, borrowers and loans. The Target Database is used to keep track of the Sports club's members, payment of subscriptions, the training courses provided and the members who attend them. So, the database contains member, subscription and course information.

❑   Is there likely to be duplication of information in the database?

The answer to this question gives guidance on whether more than one table is needed. If the Sports database is constructed with a single table, this would mean that the information on courses would be repeated many times. This is illustrated below.

| Badminton (Basic) | Tina Murray | | Mon | 01/07/98 | 31/08/98 |

er	Surname	Forename	Sex	Date of Birth	Subs	Charge	Course
1	Williams	Tom	M	17/06/82	☑	£15.00	BA01
2	Crowley	Paula	F	18/02/81	☑	£13.50	SQ01
3	McKenzie	Peter	M	13/02/82	☐	£14.00	VO01
4	Ludwig	Herbert	M	16/09/80	☑	£23.00	SQ03
5	Russo	Mirella	F	15/11/82	☐	£15.00	BA01
6	Hussain	Shahin	M	13/01/81	☑	£13.50	SQ01
7	Hideo	Kato	M	14/02/83	☐	£14.00	VO01
8	Crowley	Paula	F	16/02/82	☑	£15.00	BA01
9	Flannigan	Sara	F	13/04/82	☑	£23.00	SQ03
10	Miller	Peter	M	17/07/80	☐	£23.00	SQ03
11	Alldis	Joan	F	14/05/82	☐	£15.00	BA01
12	Jenkins	Allan	M	16/11/82	☑	£13.50	SQ01
13	Parker	Colin	M	13/02/82	☑	£14.00	VO01
14	McDonald	Lisa	F	14/08/80	☑	£14.00	VO01
15	Al-Fariz	Rashid	M	23/03/81	☐	£15.00	BA01
16	Johnson	Maria	F	28/01/82	☑	£23.00	SQ03
er)					☐	£0.00	

16 ▶ ▶I ▶* of 16

The figure shows that the details for the BA01 course, including the course Title, the Instructor's name, the Day and the Start and End dates would be duplicated 5 times in just 16 records. If there are hundreds of members, the duplication would be considerable. The details for other courses would be similarly repeated many times.

To avoid this repetition, the Sports database is designed with two tables, one containing member records and the other containing course records.

❑   If information is split into separate tables, in this case Course and Member, how are they to be related if the need arises?

The process is illustrated and explained on the next page.

Course Title and Instructor's name for SQ01

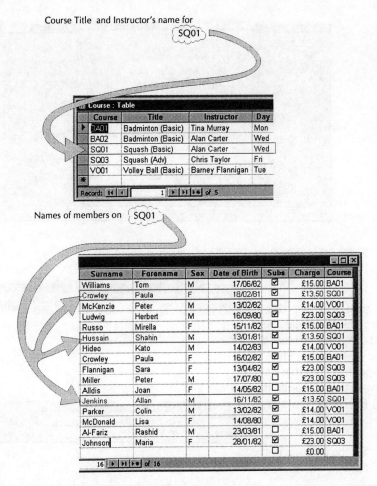

Names of members on SQ01

Suppose, for example, that the Sports club want to list the names of members (held in the Member table) who have signed up for a particular course. The list is to be headed with the course title and the instructor's name (details held in the Course table). This would require:

❑   identification of the course (by its code, for example, SQ01);

❑   using the code to identify the correct record in the Course table and retrieving the Instructor's name and the course Title;

❑   retrieving records which contain the relevant Course code from the Member table.

Although the information is split into two tables,

❑   a *relationship* is maintained through the Course code, which occurs in both tables. This field is a *link field*.

2 Constructing the Target Database

In the design stage, we decided on the tables and their contents. Now we can construct it with Access. The opening screen is shown on the next page.

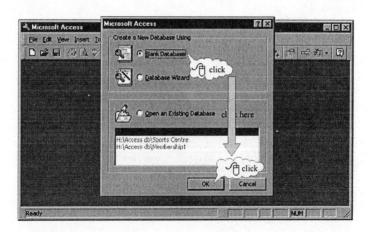

☞ Ensure that the Blank Database option is checked.

☞ Click on OK.

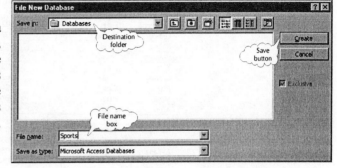

Access then requires that a name is given to the database, so that it can begin to store the database definition. This is done through the familiar Save As dialogue box, although it is labelled File New Database, as shown alongside.

☞ Set the location in the Save in box.

☞ Edit the File name box to enter 'Sports', the name of this database and Click the Save button.

Access then displays the Sports database. At present it is entirely empty, as shown in the next screen shot.

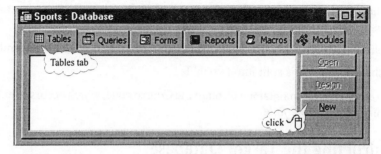

First, Access has to be given a definition for each table. This involves naming each field, stating its type (numeric, text etc.) and in some cases, its length. The default tab is Tables, so:

☞ click the New button, to define the first table.

Access presents the options shown on the right.

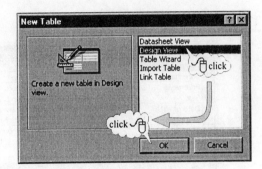

☞ Click on Design View.

☞ Then click the OK button.

3 Defining the Member table

A blank table definition window is displayed as shown below.

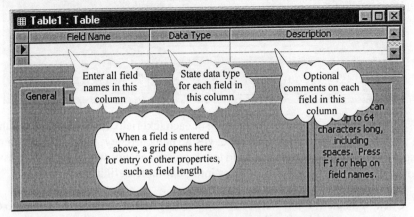

Now you can start to enter the field names and the definition for each.

☞ Enter 'Surname' and the other details as illustrated below.

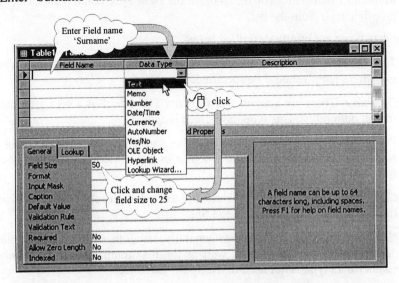

The next figure shows all the fields entered.

The Description column identifies, in the case of each text field, its field size. The other fields include the following data types: date/time, yes/no and currency; they do not need to have a length specified. Use the Description field to tell you the entries which need to be made. You do not need to copy the Description entries into your table definition.

☞ Click in the next Field Name row and, following the same method used to enter the Surname field, enter the rest of the fields, as shown in the above figure. The Field Properties area will clear as soon as you start the next entry.

☞ Remember to use the drop down list in the Data Type column and select the appropriate type from the list.

The main data types are briefly described below.

❑ *Text.* This type of field can accept any character, both letters and numbers. A maximum length should be specified.

❑ *Date/time.* There are a number of formats. The default is a six figure date in the format dd/mm/yy. This type has a fixed length.

❑ *Yes/no.* This is used for a field where there are only two possible values, Yes or No. It is used here to indicate whether or not a member has paid the course subscription.

❑ *Currency.* This is for money values and has a default setting of 2 decimal places (for the pence), for example, £323.55.

❑ *Number.* This is for numeric data generally, rather than currency. The number of decimal places can be set, as well as the maximum size of the number. The *number* data type is not used in the Sports database.

4 Saving the Member table definition

When all the entries are complete and checked, you are ready to save the Member definition (it can be altered later if you have made a mistake). The illustration below shows the save procedure.

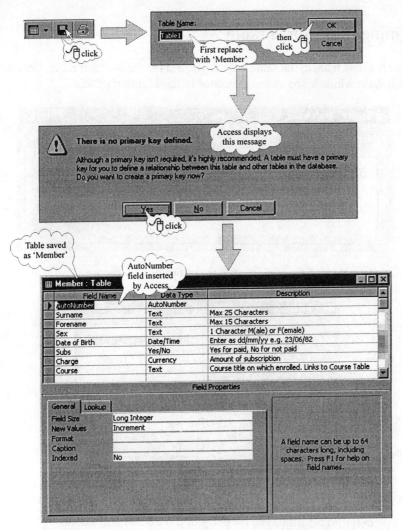

☞ Save the Member table, following the steps in the illustration.

Note that the Access message "There is no Primary Key defined" only appears because we did not include a field for that purpose (a suitable primary key could be Member ID). This was deliberate, to show that Access can provide an AutoNumber field to use as a primary key. Each record is automatically given a number, starting with 1, then 2, 3 and so on.

In the Course table definition we will choose our own primary key.

☞ Close the Member table by clicking as shown below.

5 Defining the Course table

☞ Start a new table in the same way as you did for the Member table. Note that the database window shows the existence of the Member table.

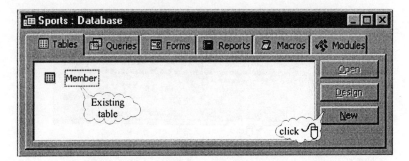

Having clicked on New, Access displays a set of options, as before.

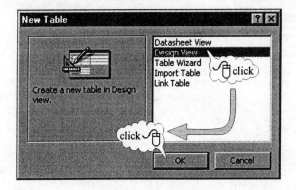

☞ As before, click the Design View option and then click the OK button.

A blank table definition is displayed for entry of the Course definition.

☞ Now enter the field details as shown in the figure on the next page

As before, the Description column details, where appropriate, field sizes for text fields. Remember to use the drop down list to choose a field's data type. Remember also to set the field size in the General tab (default is 50).

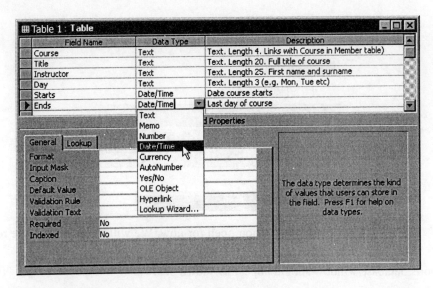

6 Setting the primary key for the Course table

When we defined the Member table, we let Access create its own AutoNumber field as the primary key for that table. However, the Course table includes a field which will have a unique value for each record - it is the Course field. Each course has a unique code, BA01, BA02, SQ01 and so on. To set this field as the primary key:

☞ make sure that the cursor is in the Course field row.

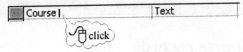

☞ click on the Set Primary Key icon on the Table Design toolbar (this is visible when you are working on table design).

☞ The Course field row should now look like this:

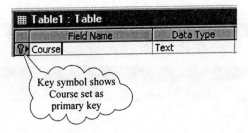

Key symbol shows Course set as primary key

☞ Now save the table as 'Course'.

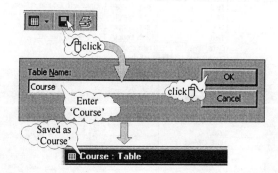

☞ Leave the Course table definition open for now. We will be entering some records into it soon.

The Sports database window should appear as shown below.

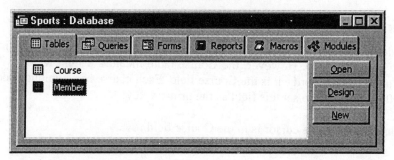

7 Entering the Course records

The Course table should still be open at this stage, in Design View. Before entering records you should

☞ make sure that the Course table is active (click on it, if necessary);

☞ switch to Datasheet View, by clicking on the View button. It 'toggles' between Design and Datasheet View.

The Course table should appear as follows.

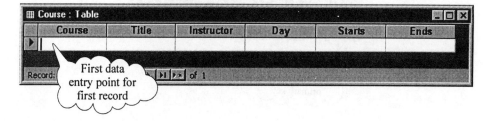

Entering records is simply a matter of typing the relevant values into each field, pressing Enter after each entry. When Enter is pressed after the last field, a new record row is opened and another record can be added.

☞ Enter the sample records shown below. Note that the Course field entries are all 2 letters followed by 2 digits, for example BA01. You do not need to save at intervals because Access automatically saves each record as soon as it is entered.

Course	Title	Instructor	Day	Starts	Ends
BA01	Badminton (Basic)	Tina Murray	Mon	01/07/98	31/08/98
BA02	Badminton (Basic)	Alan Carter	Wed	05/07/98	15/08/98
SQ01	Squash (Basic)	Alan Carter	Wed	05/07/98	15/09/98
SQ03	Squash (Adv)	Chris Taylor	Fri	01/08/98	15/12/98
VO01	Volley Ball (Basic)	Barney Flannigan	Tue	13/06/98	23/09/98

Record: 1 of 5

Notice that the last row is empty and shows an asterisk (*) at the beginning of the row. This indicates the position at which you can enter a new records to the table.

8 Modifying records

If you complete then entry of a record and then discover that you have made a mistake,

☞ click in the relevant field, delete the current entry and type in the new one. As with adding new records, the changes are saved automatically.

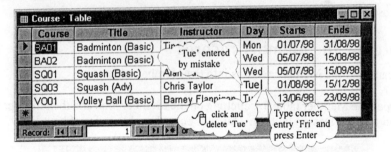

Be careful about editing the Course field, which is the primary key for this table. If you accidentally type in a value which is already taken by another record, Access will not allow you to save changes. To get out of difficulty, press the Escape key (top left on most keyboards) which aborts the operation.

9 Deleting records

Although we do not want to delete records at this stage, you can try the procedure. Access warns that a record is about to be deleted and that the operation cannot be undone. At this point you have the chance to cancel the delete command. Try the Delete Record process (you will cancel it).

☞ Click in the record row you want to delete.

☞ Click on Edit|Delete Record.

☞ Click on the No button to cancel the operation.

The process is illustrated below.

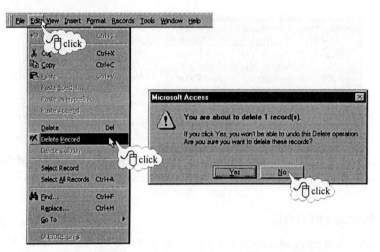

We are finished with the Course table for now, so:

☞ close the Course table.

10 Entering the Member records

Now you can enter the Member records into the Member table.

☞ Open the Member table, by clicking on the Member icon and then the Open button (not the Design button). This will open the table in DataSheet View.

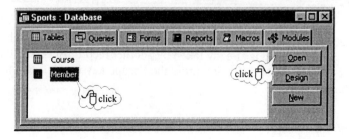

☞ Enter the member records shown on the next page.

Note the following points about the data entry process.

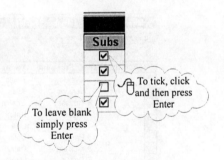

❏ Simply press Enter on the AutoNumber field and Access puts in the value for you.

❏ In the Subs field, press Enter to indicate 'not paid' and the small square in the centre of the field is left blank. To indicate 'paid', click on the small square in the centre of the field and then press Enter.

AutoNumber	Surname	Forename	Sex	Date of Birth	Subs	Charge	Course
1	Williams	Tom	M	17/06/82	☑	£15.00	BA01
2	Crowley	Paula	F	18/02/81	☑	£13.50	SQ01
3	McKenzie	Peter	M	13/02/82	☐	£14.00	VO01
4	Ludwig	Herbert	M	16/09/80	☑	£23.00	SQ03
5	Russo	Mirella	F	15/11/82	☐	£15.00	BA01
6	Hussain	Shahin	M	13/01/81	☑	£13.50	SQ01
7	Hideo	Kato	M	14/02/83	☐	£14.00	VO01
8	Crowley	Paula	F	16/02/82	☑	£15.00	BA01
9	Flannigan	Sara	F	13/04/82	☑	£23.00	SQ03
10	Miller	Peter	M	17/07/80	☐	£23.00	SQ03
11	Alldis	Joan	F	14/05/82	☐	£15.00	BA01
12	Jenkins	Allan	M	16/11/82	☑	£13.50	SQ01
13	Parker	Colin	M	13/02/82	☑	£14.00	VO01
14	McDonald	Lisa	F	14/08/80	☑	£14.00	VO01
15	Al-Fariz	Rashid	M	23/03/81	☐	£15.00	BA01
16	Johnson	Maria	F	28/01/82	☑	£23.00	SQ03
(AutoNumber)					☐	£0.00	

Record: 16 of 16

When you have completed all the entries and checked them, leave the Member table open. The next section uses it to illustrate sorting.

11 Sorting records

The sort ascending icon on the toolbar allows you to order a data table, in this case, the Member table, either in alphabetical order by a Text field, or in ascending numerical order for a Number, Date or Currency field. Now try a sort on the Charge (currency type) field.

☞ Click anywhere in the Charge column

☞ Click the Sort Ascending button. The table will become ordered, as shown on the next page, from the lowest charge to the highest.

The Sort Descending button is next to the Sort Ascending button on the toolbar. The Sort Descending button places records in reverse alphabetical or numerical order.

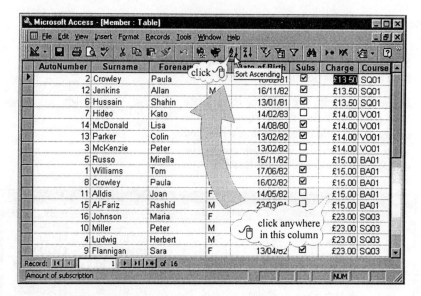

The original order of the records can be restored by clicking the menu options Records|Remove Filter/Sort.

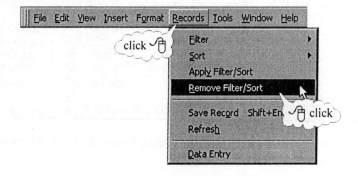

☞   Restore the original order of the Member records.

☞   Now practise ascending and descending sorts on other fields, restoring the order after each one.

In the next section, you will learn how to *filter* records from tables, using *select queries*.

12 Querying the Target Database

This section shows you how to define a select query. Certain records can be extracted from a table or tables, according to specified criteria. Here are some examples.

❏   Find and list those Member records which contain 'BA01' in the Course field. This would, in effect, list details of those members enrolled for the Badminton (Basic) course on a Monday.

❑ Find and list those Member records with a value less than '23/06/82' in the Date of Birth field. This would, in effect, be listing the records of those club members who were born before 23rd June 1982.

❑ Find and list Member records with the Subs field unticked (set to 'no'). This would have the effect of listing details of members who have not yet paid their club subscription.

Select query on the Member table

This query uses the first example and lists the members of the BA01 Badminton (Basic) course held on a Monday. To find the records the query only uses one criterion:

❑ that the Course field should contain the value 'BA01'.

The procedures to create and run the query are as follows.

☞ In the Sports database window click on the Queries tab and then the New button.

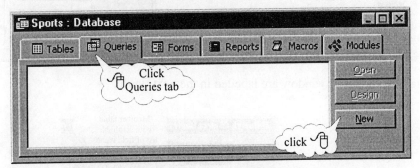

The following options window appears, with Design View as the default.

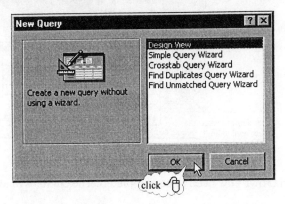

☞ We want Design View, so click on OK.

The Select Query window is displayed with the Add Tables dialogue in front. We wish to search for records in the Member table only and because the table names are in alphabetical order, Course is currently highlighted.

☞   Click on Member and then Add.

The Member table is added to the Query window. We don't need the other table, so now

☞   click on the Close button.

These processes are illustrated below.

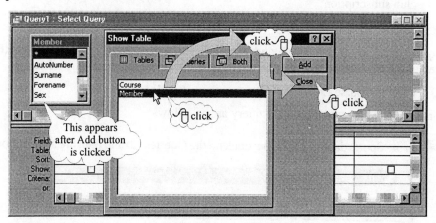

The details of the query window are labelled in the next figure.

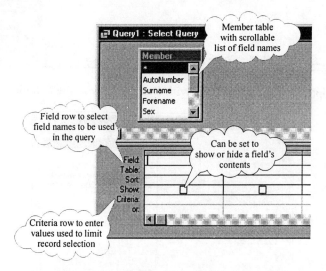

The Field and Criteria rows now need to be completed. The cursor will already be in the first Field entry point, so

☞   open the drop down list and select the Surname field from the list. The Show box is automatically ticked. Leave it that way.

☞   Enter the other two fields, Forename and Course in the next two boxes.

The process is illustrated below.

Field:	Surname	Forename	
Table:	Member	Member	AutoNumber
Sort:			Surname
Show:	☑	☑	Forename
Criteria:			Sex
or:			Date of Birth
			Subs
			Charge
			Course

You can now enter the criterion to select records for Course BA01.

☞ Click in the Criteria row, in the Course column, type BA01 and then press Enter.

As soon as you press Enter (or click the mouse outside the Criteria box), Access puts speech marks around the entry. This indicates that it is being treated as text (the Course field is defined as data type, text. If you try to enter non-numeric data as a criterion for a numeric field, Access will not accept it.

The query is complete and can be 'run'.

☞ Click on the Run icon on the toolbar, as illustrated alongside.

The resulting query should appear as follows with 5 Member records meeting the criterion of 'BA01' in the Course field.

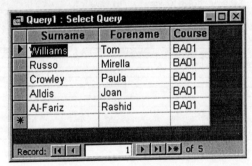

If the query is to be used again, it can be saved, as can the contents of the Select Query table.

☞ Click on the Save icon on the toolbar and save the query as 'BA01 Members'. The process is illustrated on the next page.

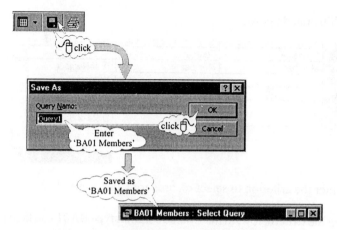

Select query on the Member and Course tables

This query draws information from both tables. To do this, Access uses the link field we created, Course, which exists in both tables. This *link field* allows a *relationship* to be established between the records in both tables. The example query which follows will further explain this idea.

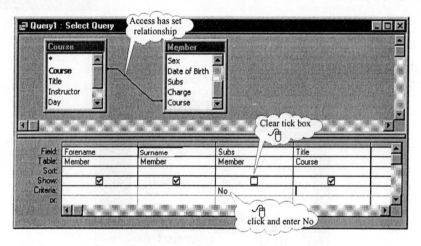

The query is to:

❑   list the full names of those members who have not paid their subscriptions, and for each, the title of their course.

    The names and subscriptions details are held in the Member table, but the title of each course is held in the Course table. The query must therefore use both tables.

The process is the same as for the first query, except for the use of two tables.

☞   As before, create a new query by clicking on the Queries tab in the Sports database window and then click on the New button.

☞ Choose Design View from the new query options.

☞ Add both tables to the query and make the entries shown on the preceding page.

Notice that Access has detected that the Member and Course tables both contain a field named Course, of the same type and length and establishes it as the link field.

The Subs field must be included in the query, because the 'No' criterion relates to that field. The Show box is cleared so that the resulting output will not show that field.

☞ Save the query as 'Unpaid Subs' and Run it.

The output should appear as follows.

Forename	Surname	Title
Peter	McKenzie	Volley Ball (Basic)
Mirella	Russo	Badminton (Basic)
Kato	Hideo	Volley Ball (Basic)
Peter	Miller	Squash (Adv)
Joan	Alldis	Badminton (Basic)
Rashid	Al-Fariz	Badminton (Basic)

Unpaid Subs : Select Query

Record: ◄ ◄ 1 ► ►I ►* of 6

To make the output meaningful a report can be produced with a suitable heading, such as 'Unpaid Subscriptions'. We will show how Access allows you to produce reports later. First, you need to be aware of queries using complex conditions.

Queries using complex conditions

The two example queries already described each use a single criterion for the selection of records. The first required that the Course field in the Member table contained the value 'BA01'. The second query required that the Subs field held the value 'No' (indicated by a blank tick box in the table). Examples of complex conditions are shown below.

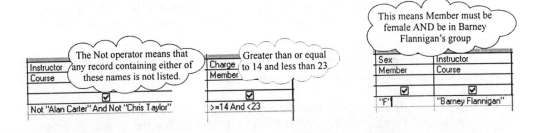

Notice that the 'And' operator can be used in an expression relating to a single field, as in the condition on the left. It is also used (without the word 'And') by entering criteria in more than one field in the criteria row. The condition on the right indicates that the Sex field must contain 'F' (for Female) 'And' the Instructor field must contain 'Barney Flannigan'.

☞ Practise these complex conditions using the Sports database.

13 Reports on the Target Database

Access provides a number of different facilities for producing reports, but one of the simplest to use is the Report Wizard. A report can be made on a table or a query.

The remainder of this chapter guides you through the Report Wizard to produce a report on the Member table.

☞ Select the Reports tab in the Sports database window and then click the New button.

The Reports option window appears as follows.

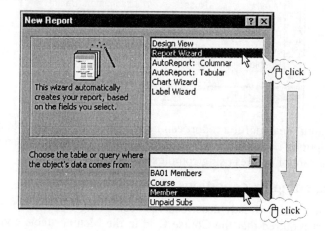

☞ Select Report Wizard and Member from the drop down list and then click the OK button (hidden in the figure). Notice that the two tables and the queries we produced earlier are all in the drop down list. A report can be based on any of these. The Auto Report options produce reports automatically, without giving you any options regarding their content (apart from the table or query on which it is based).

The next window is for the selection of fields to appear in the report. You can determine the order and select fields from more than one table.

☞ Use the single arrow (>) to send the required fields, in the order shown, from the 'Available Fields' (clicking on the relevant field each time) to the 'Selected Fields' panel. Initially, the 'Available Fields' panel contains all the fields in the chosen table. Only transfer those shown in the 'Selected Fields' panel above. Then click on the Next button.

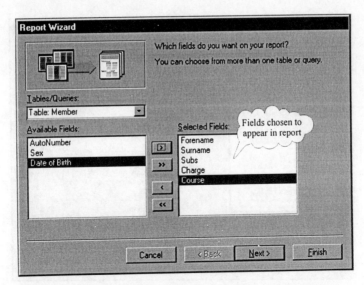

The next option (shown below) allows, where appropriate for the report to be grouped according to a particular field.

Since the various Course codes would be repeated, it is helpful to group according to the Course field.

☞ Select the Course field and click the right arrow (>). The figure shows the result.

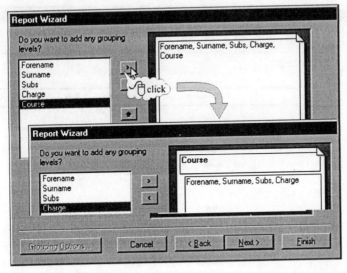

The next window (see next page) allows you to specify a particular order for the records in the report. They are already grouped by Course, but we also want the member records to be in ascending alphabetical order, according to Surname.

☞ Select Surname from the drop down list and then click the Next button.

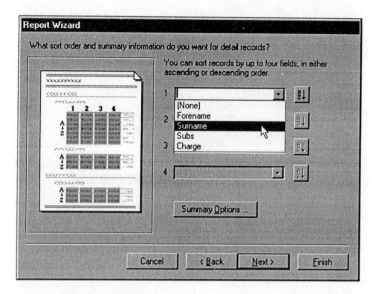

The remaining options allow a choice of various layouts and styles, so you can try these for yourself later. In the meantime

☞ Click the Finish button.

The report is automatically generated and displayed on screen, as shown below.

Member

Course	Surname	Forename	Subs	Charge
BA01				
	Al-Fariz	Rashid	☐	£15.00
	Aldis	Joan	☐	£15.00
	Crowley	Paula	☑	£15.00
	Russo	Mirella	☐	£15.00
	Williams	Tom	☑	£15.00
SQ01				
	Crowley	Paula	☑	£13.50
	Hussain	Shahin	☑	£13.50
	Jenkins	Allan	☑	£13.50
SQ03				
	Flannigan	Sara	☑	£23.00
	Johnson	Maria	☑	£23.00
	Ludwig	Herbert	☑	£23.00
	Miller	Peter	☐	£23.00
VO01				
	Hideo	Kato	☐	£14.00

Page: 1

It can then be printed by clicking on the Print icon on the toolbar.

☞ Print the report.

To quit Access choose File | Exit from the menu bar.

14 Backing up the Target Database

There is no facility within Access for taking a copy of the database. The backing up process must be carried out through Windows Explorer. The figure below shows the process for copying to floppy disk.

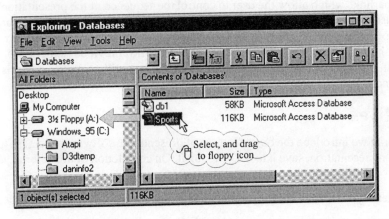

Presentation software

Presentation software packages such as Microsoft's Powerpoint enable the creation and assembly of *slide shows*. Slides may be stand-alone and used, for example, for overhead projector display, or there may be several which follow one another on screen, in a slide show presentation. On-screen displays may include text, graphics, video sequences and sound, as well as hyperlinks which allow the user to control the sequence of the presentation. Package facilities also include *transitions*, such as 'fades' and dissolves', to smooth the transfer from one slide to another. In this tutorial we will concentrate on the basic operations required to create a short presentation. The tutorial assumes no previous experience of using Powerpoint. By carefully working through the tutorial you will gain a sound basis for using more advanced features of Powerpoint.

Objectives

In this tutorial we introduce the basic features of presentation software necessary to produce an on-screen presentation, save it to disk and run it. On completion of this tutorial you will be able to:

❏ Identify the features of the presentation package necessary to create a slide show.

❏ Use text and graphics, transitions and effects within a slide show.

❏ Use hyperlinks to allow the user to control the slide show.

❏ Save a slide show to disk and run a slide show.

Any point at which you are required to carry out a procedure in Powerpoint is indicated by the following action bullet.

☞ This means do what the text says.

The explanation of what you are required to do is normally accompanied by annotated pictures of the relevant screen area. These are to help you understand the written instructions.

The Target presentation

The presentation advertises the services of Holiday World, a package holiday company. Although the full presentation would consist of more slides, this tutorial deals with only three, which is all that is necessary to illustrate the main features of a presentation. Once you have worked through the tutorial, you can practise using Powerpoint by extending the number of slides.

1 Using a standard template and slide layout

When first opened, Powerpoint displays three options for the creation of a new presentation, plus the option to open an existing one. This dialogue box is shown below.

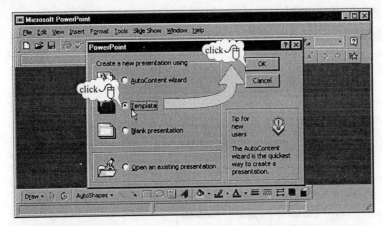

❑ The AutoContent Wizard uses library of standard presentations, each with a suggested content and design. So, for example, one may be aimed at the selling of a product and another might be to explain the workings of a new administrative system.

❑ The blank presentation is just that. You start with a blank slide.

❑ The Template option presents a number of standard backgrounds and layouts for each slide.

☞ Choose the Template option.

The Template options are shown in the next figure.

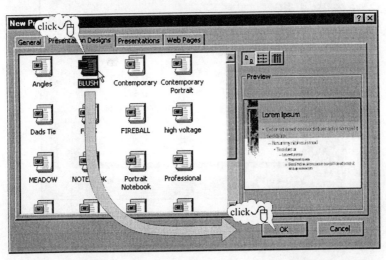

☞ Choose the Blush template and click the OK button.

A number of slide layout options are then displayed. The layout alternatives include, for example:

❏   titles and text bullets;

❏   titles, text bullets and clip art or chart

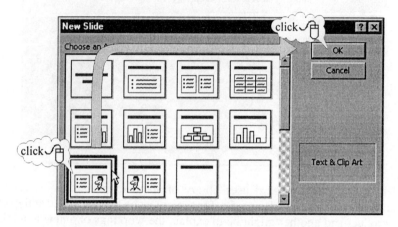

The clip art and charts are inserted objects from related applications.

☞ Choose the option indicated below and click OK.

The first slide, with the chosen template and layout is displayed.

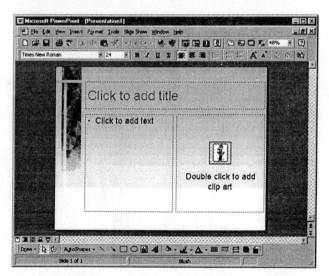

2 Using text boxes and clip art frames

The slide contains two text boxes (to enter text, click inside the box), one for a main title and the other for a series of bulleted text points. There is a clip art frame on the right of the slide (double click to access graphics libraries), to allow the insertion of clipart or other graphical images. We will start with the clip art frame.

☞ Double click on the graphics (clip art) frame. You will need access to either the Microsoft Clip Gallery or another source of clip art images acceptable by Powerpoint.

☞ Click on the chosen image and then click the Insert button, as shown below.

The layout can be altered, for example, by selecting and moving, resizing or deleting the text boxes or graphics frame.

Note that there are tabs for other types of 'clip', including pictures (photographs), video sequences and sounds. These can be inserted in the same way as standard clip 'art'.

☞ Now enter the title and the bullet points as shown below.

☞ Save the presentation before continuing. The procedures are the same as for word processing and spreadsheet, with which it is assumed you are now familiar.

☞ Now insert a new blank slide, that is, one without a standard layout. The process is illustrated in the next figure.

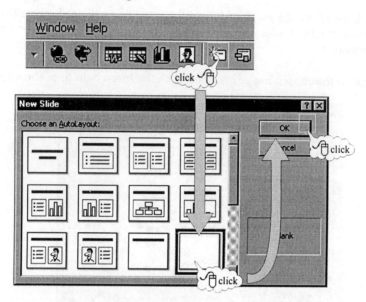

3 Using text tools

☞ Add a text box to the new slide and alter its colour to blue. You will need to use the Drawing toolbar, which is normally located at the bottom of the screen. If it is not visible, use View | Toolbars | Drawing on the menu bar to display it.

The process is illustrated on the next page.

Text tools allow text to be re-formatted in size, font and colour, as well as rotated and animated in a variety of ways. The *Word Art* utility, which is also available in other packages, can be used to insert three-dimensional text. The Word Art icon is shown alongside.

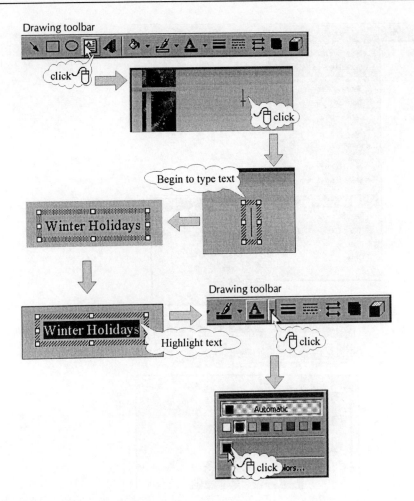

4 Inserting pictures

Pictures and other objects can be inserted through the Insert menu. The figure on the next page shows the Insert | Picture | Clip Art options. The process of inserting a photograph is the same as for a clip art image, through the Microsoft Clip Gallery.

☞ Insert the picture of the skier or other suitable photograph.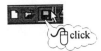

☞ Save the presentation again.

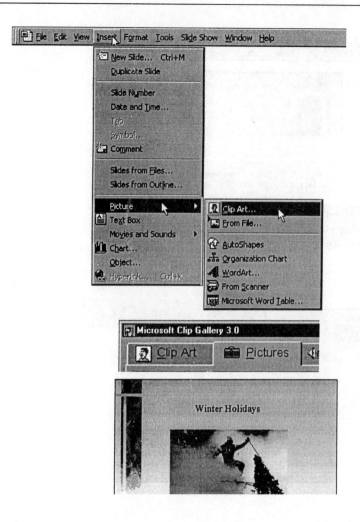

☞ Insert another blank slide. Make the third slide appear as shown below (or use some other suitable photograph). Enter the text 'Beach Holidays' as a heading. Make the text red.

5 Inserting a hyperlink

A hyperlink allows a user to click a particular part of a slide to go to another slide, not necessarily the next one in the sequence. To demonstrate this, we will use a hyperlink on the first slide to go direct to the third. The procedure is illustrated below.

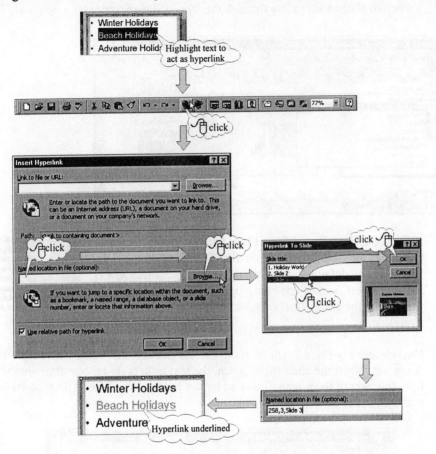

As the illustration shows, to make 'Beach Holidays' a hyperlink to the third slide of that title:

☞ Use the mouse to highlight the bulleted text 'Beach Holidays'.

☞ Click on the Insert Hyperlink icon on the toolbar.

☞ Click in the Named Location in File box and then the adjacent Browse button.

☞ Select Slide 3 form the list in the Hyperlink to Slide dialogue.

☞ This inserts the link into the previous Insert Hyperlink dialogue. Click on OK and the process is complete. The text 'Beach Holidays' in Slide 1 is underlined to indicate it is a hyperlink.

6 Using slide sorter, transitions and effects

Slide sorter view shows a summary of all the slides and is designed to facilitate final sequencing of the presentation, as well as the addition of transitions and effects.

☞ Switch to slider sorter view through the View | Slide Sorter menu options.

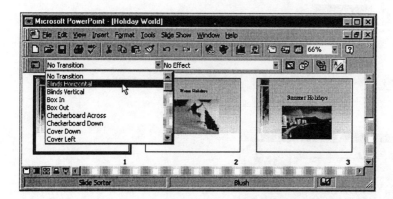

☞ If Slide 1 is not selected (by a black border) click it and then choose Blinds Horizontal from the Transition (set at No Transition by default) drop down list. When the slide show is run, the effect is of blinds being opened before clearing entirely from the slide. The horizontal blinds appear as shown alongside.

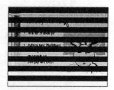

☞ Now choose Fly From Right from the Effects (set at No Effects by default) drop down list. When the slide show is run, the text bullets fly in, one after another, from the right of the screen, followed by the graphic. The Effects drop down list is shown in the next figure.

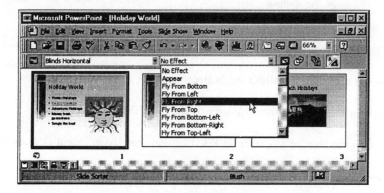

Transitions and effects can be applied separately to each slide, or to groups of slides. To select a group of slides in Slide Sorter view, hold the Shift key down and then click on each slide in turn. The fact that a slide is selected is indicated by a black border. All the slides can be selected using Edit | Select All from the menu bar.

☞ Save the presentation before continuing.

7 Running the show

☞ Choose Slide Show | Set Up Show from the menu bar and then check the two options shown in the next figure.

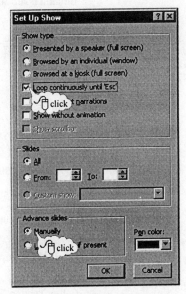

These settings ensure that the show is repeated continuously, until the Escape key is pressed and that slides are advanced manually by clicking the mouse.

☞ Choose Slide Show|View Show from the menu bar and the show will run in full screen.

You should now have the basic skills to extend the show or create your own.

Index